Nietzsche's Therapy

Nietzsche's Therapy

Self-Cultivation in the Middle Works

Michael Ure

LEXINGTON BOOKS

A division of
ROWMAN & LITTLEFIELD PUBLISHERS, INC.
Lanham • Boulder • New York • Toronto • Plymouth, UK

LEXINGTON BOOKS

A division of Rowman & Littlefield Publishers, Inc.
A wholly owned subsidiary of The Rowman & Littlefield Publishing Group, Inc.
4501 Forbes Boulevard, Suite 200
Lanham, MD 20706

Estover Road
Plymouth PL6 7PY
United Kingdom

British Library Cataloguing in Publication Information Available

Library of Congress Cataloging-in-Publication Data

Ure, Michael, 1966–
    Nietzsche's therapy : self-cultivation in the middle works / Michael Ure.
        p. cm.
    Includes bibliographical references and index.
    ISBN-13: 978-0-7391-1996-9 (cloth : alk. paper)
    ISBN-10: 0-7391-1996-6 (cloth : alk. paper)
    1. Nietzsche, Friedrich Wilhelm, 1844–1900. 2. Self (Philosophy) 3. Self-
culture. I. Title.
    B3307.U74 2008
    193—dc22   2008005842

Printed in the United States of America

♾™The paper used in this publication meets the minimum requirements of
American National Standard for Information Sciences—Permanence of Paper for
Printed Library Materials, ANSI/NISO Z39.48-1992.

In memory of my father, David William Ure

Table of Contents

Acknowledgments

This book had its true beginnings in a semester I spent as a graduate student at the University of California (Berkeley). I would like to acknowledge the generous support of the University of Melbourne for funding this research period. I must thank my San Franciscan friends for transforming my *via dolorosa* into a Californian dreaming. I am especially indebted to Camela Bontaites, Jeremy Cantor, Michelle Clay, Rachel Kimerling, Richard O'Connell, and Neil Switz.

I was also fortunate to receive a scholarship to study at the Universität Heidelberg. Without the generous financial assistance of the *Landesstiftung Baden-Württemburg* I could not have completed this book. I would like to thank my gracious hosts, Nicoline and Tara Dorn. I am deeply grateful for the encouragement I received during this period from Christian Stang. Christian and all the TV Schriesheim 1883 athletes proved to be the happy accident of my time in Heidelberg. Melanie Klett, Andreas Rothenhöfer, Barbara Rudat and Tina Tremmel made my research in Heidelberg a memory I shall savour.

During the research and writing of this book I received great support from family, friends, and teachers, especially from my mother, Elizabeth Ure. The following people, each in their own way, enabled me to remain steadfast throughout: Paola Bohorquez, Paul Coombe, Tim Crosbie and Kate Seibold-Crosbie, Richard Devetak and Naomi Smith, Michael Janover, Zil McDonnell, Ruggero Milici, Paul Muldoon and Kate Mazoudier, Francesca Rocca, George and Martha Mildred Short.

I had the good fortune to be supervised by Martin Jay during my time at Berkeley. Martin's breathtaking erudition, masterly pedagogical skills and great humaneness inspired me to see this book to its completion. A special word of appreciation is due to the three noble souls who read and commented on this book's many incarnations: Paul Muldoon, Michael Janover and Anita Harris. They must have felt as cursed as the Danaïds. I owe an enormous debt to Michael Janover, who cast an acute and subtle eye over my haphazard efforts. If this poorest of fishermen perhaps once or twice rowed with golden oars it is entirely due to Michael's guidance. I would also like to thank Keith Ansell-Pearson, Graham Parkes and Lexington's anonymous reviewer for their sharp and insightful criticisms and suggestions. In the last stages of my research, I benefited from the conviviality of my colleagues at the Centre for the History of European Discourses (University of Queensland). Ian Hunter's inquisitorial interventions proved to be particularly challenging. I am exceedingly grateful to Russell Downham for his sterling work on the index. Needless to say, I am solely responsible for the book's many flaws.

Finally, if I may be permitted to misquote Herr Nietzsche, "life consists of those rare moments of the highest significance and countless intervals of time in which at best the shadowy images of those moments hover about us." If not for Anita Harris and my son, Lucius Harris-Ure, I would never have experienced such moments at all. Life without them would be an error. They supported me in every imaginable way, and then invented new ones to see me complete this book.

Versions of chapters 2, 5 and 6 appeared respectively in *Foucault Studies*, no. 4, 2007, 19–52; *Nietzsche-Studien*, Bd 34, 2005, 186–216; and Michael Ure, "The Irony of Pity," *The Journal of Nietzsche Studies*, 32, Autumn 2006, 68–91. Copyright 2006 by the Pennsylvania State University Press. Reproduced by the permission of the publisher. I am grateful to the editors for their permission to reproduce versions of those essays here.

Abbreviations

WORKS BY FRIEDRICH NIETZSCHE

Translations of major works are by Walter Kaufmann and/or R. J. Hollingdale, with the exception of *The Birth of Tragedy*, translated by Shaun Whiteside, and *Philosophy in the Tragic Age of the Greeks*, translated by Marianne Cowan, and *Thus Spoke Zarathustra*, translated by Graham Parkes. Gary Handwerk's translation of *Human, All Too Human*, vol. 1, is used where indicated in the notes. References to the original German are taken from *Nietzsche Werke: Kritische Gesamtausgabe*, edited by Giorgio Colli and Mazzino Montinari (1967–1978, Walter de Gruyter, Berlin). References to the translations of Nietzsche's essays that are only cited infrequently can be found in the main bibliography. The following abbreviations of translated works are used in the notes:

A   *The Antichrist*, translated by R. J. Hollingdale, 1985, Penguin, Harmondsworth, UK.

BGE   *Beyond Good and Evil: Prelude to a Philosophy of the Future*, translated by Walter Kaufmann, 1966, Random House, New York.

BT   *The Birth of Tragedy Out of the Spirit of Music*, translated by Shaun Whiteside, 1993, Penguin, London.

CW   *The Case of Wagner*, translated by Walter Kaufmann, 1967, Vintage, New York.

D   *Daybreak: Thoughts on the Prejudices of Morality*, translated by R. J. Hollingdale, 1985, Cambridge University Press, Cambridge.

EH   *Ecce Homo: How One Becomes What One Is*, translated by R. J. Hollingdale, 1985, Penguin, Harmondsworth, UK.

GM   *On the Genealogy of Morals*, translated by Walter Kaufmann and
        R. J. Hollingdale, 1969, Vintage, New York.
GS   *The Gay Science*, translated by Walter Kaufmann, 1974, Vintage,
        New York.
HAH1   *Human, All Too Human: A Book for Free Spirits*, vol. 1, translated
        by R. J. Hollingdale, 1991, Cambridge University Press, Cam-
        bridge.
HAH2   *Assorted Opinions and Maxims*, translated by R. J. Hollingdale,
        1991, Cambridge University Press, Cambridge.
MW   "On Music and Words," translated by Walter Kaufmann, in Carl
        Dalhaus, *Between Romanticism and Modernism*, 1980, University
        of California Press, Berkeley, 106–19.
NCW   "Nietzsche Contra Wagner," translated by Walter Kaufmann, in
        The Portable Nietzsche, 1969, Penguin Books, London.
PT   *Philosophy and Truth: Selections from Nietzsche's Notebooks of the
        early 1870s*, translated by Daniel Breazeale, 1979, Humanities
        Press, Atlantic Highlands, N.J.
PTG   *Philosophy in the Tragic Age of the Greeks*, translated by Marianne
        Cowan, 1987, Gateway, Washington, D.C.
RWB   *Richard Wagner in Bayreuth*, translated by R. J. Hollingdale, 1985,
        Cambridge University Press, Cambridge.
SE   *Schopenhauer as Educator*, translated by R. J. Hollingdale, 1985,
        Cambridge University Press, Cambridge.
TI   *Twilight of the Idols or How to Philosophize with a Hammer*, trans-
        lated by R. J. Hollingdale, 1985, Penguin, Harmondsworth, UK.
TSZ   *Thus Spoke Zarathustra: A Book for Everyone and Nobody*, trans-
        lated by Graham Parkes, 2005, Oxford University Press, Oxford.
UM2   *On the Uses and Disadvantages of History for Life*, translated by R.
        J. Hollingdale, 1985, Cambridge University Press, Cambridge.
WS   *The Wanderer and His Shadow*, translated by R. J. Hollingdale,
        1991, Cambridge University Press, Cambridge.

WORKS BY MICHEL FOUCAULT

References to the translations of Foucault's essays that are only cited infrequently can be found in the main bibliography. The following abbreviations of translated works are used in the notes:

AE   "An Aesthetics of Existence," in Sylvère Lotringer (ed.), *Foucault
        Live: Interviews 1966–1984*, translated by John Johnston, 1989,
        Semiotext(e), New York, 309–16.
BHS   "About the Beginning of the Hermeneutics of the Self," *Political
        Theory* 21, no. 2, May 1993, 198–227.

CS   *The Care of the Self*, translated by Robert Hurley, 1986, Pantheon, New York.

ECS   "The Ethics of the Care of the Self as a Practice of Freedom," translated by J. D. Gauthier, *Philosophy and Social Criticism* XII, no. 2–3, 1984, 113–31.

GE   "On the Genealogy of Ethics: An Overview of Work in Progress," in Paul Rabinow (ed.), *The Foucault Reader*, 1984, Penguin Books, London, 340–72.

HS   *The Hermeneutics of the Subject: Lectures at the Collège de France 1981–1982*, translated by Graham Burchell, 2005, Palgrave Macmillan, New York.

RM   "The Return of Morality," in Sylvère Lotringer (ed.), *Foucault Live: Interviews 1966–1984*, translated by John Johnston, 1989, Semiotext(e), New York, 317–31.

TS   "Technologies of the Self," in L. H. Martin, H. Gutman, P. Hutton (eds.), *Technologies of the Self: A Seminar with Michel Foucault*, 1988, University of Massachusetts Press, Amherst, 16–49.

UP   *The Use of Pleasure*, translated by Robert Hurley, 1985, Pantheon, New York.

WE   "What Is Enlightenment?" in Paul Rabinow (ed.), *The Foucault Reader*, 1984, Penguin Books, London, 340–72.

WORKS BY SIGMUND FREUD

References to the translations of Freud's essays and case studies that are only cited infrequently can be found in the main bibliography. The following abbreviations of Freud's translated works are used in the notes:

AS   "An Autobiographical Study," translated by James Strachey, in *Psychoanalysis: Its History and Development*, Penguin Freud Library, vol. 15, 1992, Penguin, London.

BPP   "Beyond the Pleasure Principle," translated by James Strachey, in *On Metapsychology: The Theory of Psychoanalysis*, Penguin Freud Library, vol. 11, 1991, Penguin, London.

CD   *Civilization and Its Discontents*, translated by Joan Riviere, 1975, Hogarth Press, London.

EI   "The Ego and the Id," translated by James Strachey, in *On Metapsychology: The Theory of Psychoanalysis*, Penguin Freud Library, vol. 11, 1991, Penguin, London.

GP   *Group Psychology and the Analysis of the Ego*, translated by James Strachey, 1989, W. W. Norton and Co., New York.

IV   "Instincts and Their Vicissitudes," translated by James Strachey, in *On Metapsychology: The Theory of Psychoanalysis*, Penguin Freud Library, vol. 11, 1991, Penguin, London.

MM   "Mourning and Melancholia," translated by James Strachey, in
         On Metapsychology: The Theory of Psychoanalysis, Penguin Freud
         Library, vol. 11, 1991, Penguin, London.
OH   "On Humour," translated by James Strachey, in *Art and Litera-
         ture*, Penguin Freud Library, vol. 14, 1985, Penguin, London.
ON   "On Narcissism," translated by James Strachey, in *On Metapsy-
         chology: The Theory of Psychoanalysis*, Penguin Freud Library, vol.
         11, 1991, Penguin, London.
OP   "Outline of Psychoanalysis," translated by James Strachey, in
         Psychoanalysis: Its History and Development, Penguin Freud Li-
         brary, vol. 15, 1992, Penguin, London.

WORKS BY ARTHUR SCHOPENHAUER

The following abbreviations of Schopenhauer's translated works are used in
the notes:

OBM   *On the Basis of Morality*, 1965, translated by E. F. J. Payne, Bobbs-
         Merrill, Indianapolis.
WWR1   *The World as Will and Representation*, vol. 1, 1969, Dover Publi-
         cations, New York.

WORKS BY LUCIUS ANNAEUS SENECA

References to Seneca's letters are taken from Robin Campbell's translations
in *Letters from a Stoic*, 1977, Penguin, Harmondsworth; occasional uses of
C. D. N. Costa's translations in *Seneca: 17 Letters* (1988, Aris and Phillips,
Warminster) are indicated in the notes. All other references to Seneca's
works are taken from *Minor Dialogues*, translated by Aubrey Stewart (1902,
George Bell and Sons, London). The following abbreviations of Seneca's
works are used in the notes:

De Ira   *De Ira*
Helvia   *Consolatio ad Helviam Matrem*
L   *Epistulae Morales*
Marcia   *Consolatio ad Marciam*
OM   *De Clementia*
OT   *De Tranquillitate Animi*

Introduction

Knowing one's "individuality" [Einzelheit].—We forget too easily that in the eyes of people who see us for the first time we're something quite different from what we take ourselves to be—usually nothing more than a single trait which strikes the eye and determines the whole impression. In this way, the gentlest and most reasonable person, if he wears a big moustache, can sit in its shade and feel safe—ordinary eyes will take him to be the accessory of a big moustache, a military type, quick to fly off the handle, sometimes even violent—they'll behave themselves in his presence.

Daybreak, 381

Friedrich Nietzsche here pokes fun at his own use of defensive masks, a joke that turns not only on his willingness to tease himself, but on his characteristic love of punning: his big moustache (*Schnurrbart*) becomes what it is: nothing other than a funny tale (*Schnurre*). Nietzsche, then, makes light of his own defences in both senses of the phrase: he illuminates his defensive strategies and reduces their weighty seriousness through comic relief. His gentle self-irony illustrates a positive, comic self-relation. This is not a Nietzsche we easily recognise. Nor is it a slant on becoming who one is that we readily identify as Nietzschean.

Rather, the Nietzsche who appears in this epigraph and the Nietzsche of the middle works, more broadly, have sat in the shade of his "big moustache," or, in slightly less figurative terms, in the shadows of the grandiose, never completed, and mostly unpublished ideas he had ruminated on during the late 1880s under the proposed title of *The Will to Power*.[1] This book aims to bring Nietzsche's middle period out of the shade from which it has been undeservedly consigned. For the point Nietzsche makes here in his

1

comical act of self-unmasking has proven prescient when applied to the reception of his works: we have been obsessed with their grand distractions. Often, for example, interpreters have been riveted to a single trait of his early or late works—the scenes of Dionysian ecstasy that pepper *The Birth of Tragedy* or the concept of the will to power that explodes across the pages of his late notebooks.

Located between the drumming thyrsi of his Bacchanalian revellers and the booming cannons of great politics that Nietzsche unwisely discharges in the late works and notebooks, his comparatively calm investigation of "small, unpretentious" psychological truths has never garnered the critical attention it so richly deserves.[2] Set against the opening of *The Birth of Tragedy* with its wild scenes of Dionysian voluptuaries losing themselves in orgiastic revelry, Nietzsche's turn to the patient labour of self-analysis was always destined to appear lifeless and pallid. By contrast with the *Sturm und Drang* of *The Birth of Tragedy*, he begins *Human, All Too Human* on a distinctly cool note, exhorting us to awaken from our metaphysical dreams and their "spinning out of forms and symbols."[3] In place of the grand metaphysical systems that had so enchanted German idealists and romantics, he proposes a modest labour of psychological observation "that does not weary of heaping stone upon stone, brick upon brick."[4]

Nietzsche acknowledges that his own patient labour of psychological analysis cannot yield the "splendid, intoxicating," perhaps even "enrapturing" illusions of metaphysics.[5] But such modest investigations, he maintains, are not without their own charm.[6] Revealingly he confesses that a "very seductive scent" clings to this genre of psychological investigation, the perfume of its former home: the seventeenth-century French salon.[7] In the manner of La Rochefoucauld Nietzsche begins his middle period as a quiet analyst of the human comedy and tragedy. Like La Rochefoucauld and the aristocratic *habitués* of the French salon, Nietzsche turns inward and undertakes the painstaking, unending work of plotting what remains concealed from ordinary eyes: the complex pathways traversed by our affects and judgements. La Rochefoucauld, we might recall, spent six or seven years refining and arranging his thoughts on the almost invisible, intricate world of human motives and feelings into a form combining the maximum of clarity with a minimum of words: the *maxime*.[8]

In the middle period, which spans his break with Wagner in 1876 through to the completion of the fourth book of *The Gay Science* in 1882, Nietzsche too works and reworks his insights and explanations of inner processes and drives.[9] While Nietzsche often finds the *maxime* form too constraining to capture the complexity, dynamism and multiplicity of the psyche, he nevertheless seeks the same kind of psychological clarity as his French predecessors.[10] From *Human All Too Human* on, he expends his intellectual energy on finding "secret paths" into the unknown, well-defended and mobile realm on the other side of consciousness. In doing so he enriches and refines our linguistic resources for expressing the minute feelings and minor keys of the soul.[11] However, Nietzsche undertakes this work not simply for the sake of the "intellectual coquetry" that fuelled the conversations of the French salon, nor for the aesthetic pleasure of composing finely honed maxims or aphorisms. Rather, what looms large in Nietzsche's thinking is the question of psychological health and sickness, and the light one sheds on the other. In the middle period, in other words, he conceives the patient, piecemeal labour of psychological self-observation as a therapy of the soul.

For Nietzsche the mere fact that it requires a difficult struggle to subject oneself to such analysis proves illuminating. That the labour of self-analysis is countered and often defeated enables him to identify and theorise both the existence of an internal censor and the linguistic obstacles that thwart self-scrutiny. We are not only "well-defended" against any "surveillance or besiegement" by ourselves; our language too, he claims, puts up barricades, for it has words only for our extreme affects while "the milder, middle degrees, not to speak of the lower degrees which are continually in play [and] which weave the web of our character and our destiny" constantly elude us.[12] Yet, according to Nietzsche, we construct the "*so-called 'ego'* [*'Ich'*]" through these misconceptions, which allow us to recognise ourselves only in those "extreme outbursts" or those "violent exceptions" that are "consequent on built-up congestions."[13] For Nietzsche, this crudely pathic *Ich* is only the psyche *in extremis*, in those highly charged emotional states of "anger, hatred, love, pity" through which it expels the affects accumulated as a consequence of delayed gratification.[14] It is because of our psychologically and linguistically induced blindnesses, he argues, that we see ourselves in, and only dignify with, the name *Ich*, this crudely explosive mechanism. "[H]ow easy it is," he remarks, "for these [extreme outbursts] to mislead the observer! No less easy than it is for them to mislead the person in whom they occur."[15]

Nietzsche argues that without careful work of self-observation, remembrance and analysis we misrecognise ourselves and remain in the thrall of an immature or infantile form of egoism or subjectivity. If we fail to overcome our amnesia regarding its origins and genesis and do not dispel the errors on which it is based, he suggests, we find ourselves limited to an archaic *Ich*, a loose cannon, so to speak, which merely serves to discharge a congested mass of affects.[16] When such an *Ich* weaves our "destinies," he observes, our lives must amount to little more than a series of compulsive reactions and projections. Through his analysis of the infantile *Ich*, then, Nietzsche cautions us against continuing to make the mistake of seeing ourselves as nothing more than appurtenances of a big moustache, to borrow once again from the epigraph. In other words, he points to another kind of egoism or, better still, another kind of self-relation, one that is premised on understanding and analysing the roots of this so-called *Ich* as an affective symptom of suffering and loss.

Here I shall examine Nietzsche's analysis of the psychodynamics of the forms of egoism and their intra- and intersubjective consequences. I argue that in the middle works he critically explores what we might call, borrowing from psychoanalytic parlance, the pathological symptoms of wounded narcissism. I show how Nietzsche draws on the Hellenistic and Stoic traditions to conceptualise a therapeutic art of self-cultivation oriented toward treating such pathologies. We have witnessed an extraordinary flourishing of philosophical and historical research on the Hellenistic philosophies as arts of living in the past two decades. Two of the central figures in this field of research, Pierre Hadot and Michel Foucault, have suggested that historians of philosophy have failed to recognise the extent to which the Greco-Roman therapeutic model of philosophy has shaped important strands of modern European philosophy. In this context, they both very briefly hypothesise that we might comprehend Nietzsche's philosophical project if we conceptualise it as an attempt to reconstitute the Hellenistic model of philosophy and its ethics of the care of the self.[17] "The philosophies of Schopenhauer and Nietzsche," as Hadot notes, "are . . . invitations to radically transform our lives."[18] Similarly, Foucault locates Nietzsche as one among a disparate group of the nineteenth-century German philosophers whose *implicit* goal, so he claims, was to revive the Greco-Roman model of philosophy as an art of living against longstanding efforts to expunge it from philosophy.[19]

Hadot and Foucault claim then that Nietzsche adopted a specifically Hellenistic conception of philosophy as an art or *technē* of living. In this model of philosophy systematic discourse only has a point and purpose insofar as it contributes to the formation of a certain ethos or character. To give this a slightly more technical flourish, we might say that the Hellenistic schools understand philosophy as an ethical *technē*—a practice of self-formation—that combines theoretical principles (*logos*) with *askēsis*. To practice philosophy is to construct a certain kind of self and mode of conduct as a result of accepting a set of beliefs, not merely to formulate or dispute ideas. On this account philosophers are more admired for their manner of living and dying than for the doctrines they construct. David's famous neoclassical depictions of Socrates' philosophic poise or Seneca's stoic nonchalance in confronting death illustrate this Greco-Roman belief that philosophy demonstrates itself through *argumentum ad oculos* (visible proof); they also testify to the ongoing cultural valence of this model of philosophy in late eighteenth- and early nineteenth-century Europe. Philosophy, in short, is a way of transforming one's life, and so it is how one lives and dies that is the measure of the value of philosophy.

Following this line of thought, one of Nietzsche's most significant borrowings from Hellenistic philosophy might be said to lie in his very conception of philosophy and the philosopher. We might take our initial bearing here from Nietzsche's furious and witty polemics against contemporary German university philosophy that he first expressed in *Schopenhauer as Educator*. Here he speculates that contemporary academics would be too ashamed of themselves to dare use the title "lovers of wisdom" (*Weisheit*) or "wise men" (sages) given that they practice philosophy as a specialised professional discipline that has no direct bearing on their own manner of living or on their wider culture. "The aim of wisdom," as Nietzsche defines it in distinctly Hellenistic terms, "is to enable a man to face all the blows of fate with equal firmness, to arm him for all times."[20] In resuscitating the Hellenistic notion of philosophy, Nietzsche recognises that it principally concerns the transformation of the self and its relationship to chance events (Epicurean) or fate (Stoic), a concern far removed it seems from modern philosophers' specialised academic preoccupations, which, so he argues, have no bearing at all on their character or actions.[21] "No one," as Nietzsche laments, "dares venture to fulfill the philosophical law in himself, no one lives philosophically with that simple loyalty that constrained a man of antiquity to bear himself as a Stoic where ever he was, whatever he did, once he affirmed his loyalty to the Stoa."[22] In the Hellenistic model, philosophers do not engage in reasoning for its own sake, but in order to shape characters capable of right action. If *logos* is important in this context, it is so only to the extent that it contributes to forming individuals capable of maintaining equanimity in the face of the storms of chance or fate.

We can already glimpse Nietzsche's identification with the Hellenistic tradition in his lament that modern German academic philosophers do not practice philosophy as an art of living, and do not therefore practice "a special manner of living." Rather, according to him, they treat philosophy as a "mere science" (*Wissenschaft*) concerned either with professional border patrolling or recounting its own history. Nietzsche draws on the Hellenistic notion of philosophy as an art of living to criticise this separation of *logos* and *ethos*, which, he claims, is especially marked in modern university philosophy. He identifies the modern transformation of philosophy into a "science" as a betrayal of, or at least as a falling away from, the Hellenistic school's "love of wisdom," which required philosopher's to have the courage to live according to their school's sayings and precepts. "To turn *philosophy* purely into a science," as he puts it, "is to throw in the towel."[23] Nietzsche complains that if we transform philosophy into a science we give up practising it as a method of spiritual progress that demands a radical conversion and transformation of our individual way of being.[24] By contrast, he assumes that philosophy ought to aim at the flourishing of life, or the exercise of a special manner of living, as it did in the Hellenistic tradition. For

Epicureans, Cynics-Stoics and Skeptics, philosophical work is a means of constructing a particular style of life and of achieving *eudaimonia*. Nietzsche follows this tradition insofar as he maintains that any philosophy that does not have as its goal the transformation of the subject and the realisation of *eudaimonia* does not warrant the appellation "philosophy" in its etymological sense of "love of wisdom." He makes his adoption of this Hellenistic notion of philosophy as a way of life quite explicit:

> the philosopher's product is his *life* (which occupies the most important position, *before* his *works*). His life is his work of art.[25]

With his trademark hyperbole he unequivocally confirms his commitment to this model of philosophy by claiming that Brutus' tyrannicide did more to demonstrate the dignity of (Platonic) philosophy than all of Plato's written doctrines.[26] Philosophy on Nietzsche's account is above all else a way of life, and it is only through the enactment of its principles that it has any value or significance. According to Hadot, this is one of the defining features of the ancient model of philosophy. What differentiates ancient from modern philosophy, he claims,

> is the fact that in ancient philosophy, it was not only Chrysippus or Epicurus who, just because they had developed a philosophic discourse, were considered philosophers. Rather every person who lived according to the precepts of Chrysippus or Epicurus was every bit as much a philosopher as they. A politician like Cato . . . was considered a philosopher and even a sage, even though he wrote and taught nothing, because his life was perfectly Stoic.[27]

If we take the ancient perspective as our guiding light, we are philosophers not because of the originality or abundance of philosophical discourses we conceive or invent, but as a function of the way we live.[28] In celebrating Brutus as a better Platonist than Plato, Nietzsche unmistakably subscribes to this classical notion of philosophy as an art of living. In the middle period, then, Nietzsche quite explicitly commits himself to the notion that "true" or "genuine" philosophy is an art of living and that to engage in philosophy entails practical or existential self-transformation.

In this current study I show that Hadot and Foucault are right to frame Nietzsche's philosophical project, at least his project in the middle period, as an experiment with the moral schools of antiquity, while bracketing the issue of whether or not he successfully addresses the philosophical-historical difficulties that accompany such a project.[29] Of more immediate concern to this study is identification of the psychological concerns that motivate Nietzsche to take up and attempt to renovate the Hellenistic *therapeia*. I explore how Nietzsche's ethics of self-cultivation springs from his analyses of the pathological forms of narcissism and his attempts to conceive a mature individualism that is free of their damaging, unhealthy effects for both the self and its relations with others. Mature individualism, as Nietzsche conceives it, tempers the pathologies of narcissism and establishes a positive place and function for that longing for plenitude that we inherit from the condition of primary narcissism.[30] If I am correct, Nietzsche is a subtle analyst of the psychological phenomena borne of the desire for majestic plenitude, which, as Freud suspected, individuals can only learn to temper and transform, since they can never fully abandon it.

In other words, the value and integrity of Nietzsche's middle period resides in its acute analysis of the transformations of narcissism. His psychological insights into the complex permutations of narcissism lead him to build on and renovate a tradition of philosophical therapy that aims to temper the excesses of its pathologies. It is through this work of renovation that Nietzsche formulates a notion of mature individualism. For Nietzsche mature individualism requires a labour of self that can mitigate the pathological excesses—the rage and vengefulness—that spring from wounded narcissism.[31]

To sum up, then, I argue that Nietzsche develops his idea of self-cultivation first and foremost on the basis of his incisive understanding of infantile narcissism, its pathological symptoms, and its possible healthy modulations and transformations. I stake a claim for treating the works of *Human, All Too Human*, *Daybreak* and *The Gay Science* (books 1–4) as a distinctive grouping in Nietzsche's corpus on the basis of their psychological insights into our narcissistic maladies and their treatment. In this regard, I demonstrate that the middle period is neither an intermezzo between *The Birth of Tragedy* and *Thus Spoke Zarathustra*, nor simply a prelude to his later works, as is often claimed, but a period whose integrity resides in its philosophical psychology and its ethics of self-analysis and self-cultivation.[32] The middle works crystallise a significant moment in Nietzsche's philosophy where his understanding of the Greco-Roman care of the self coalesces with the insights of the modern depth psychology that he trailblazes.[33]

However, this view of Nietzsche as a subtle psychologist who contributes to our theoretical grasp of the genesis and forms of narcissism has not been recognised by those contemporary interpretations that dwell on his "aestheticism" or the psychoanalytic tradition. The aestheticist interpretation of Nietzsche rightly recognises his concern with the nature of self-cultivation and self-making, but unfortunately it empties his philosophy of its psychological content. As we shall see in the first two chapters, both Alexander Nehamas's conception of the Nietzschean self as a literary composition and Michel Foucault's linking of the Nietzschean project to Baudelairean Dandyism overlook the theoretical and psychological matrix of his idea of self-cultivation. Nietzsche's concern with the artful shaping of the soul emerges from the work of self-analysis that he undertakes in order to understand and treat his own psychological maladies; the middle works, as he plainly states, embody his own antiromantic self-treatment. In other words, Nietzsche defines the shaping of the soul as the construction of a healthy psychological configuration, premised on identifying and treating its maladies and malaises. Self-cultivation is not therefore merely an aesthetic game governed by formal rules or by the aesthetic modernist drive to innovation for its own sake.

If, by contrast, the psychoanalytic tradition has been more ready to acknowledge Nietzsche as a psychologist of sorts, it generally misconstrues him as an unabashed celebrant of narcissism. In doing so, it blinds us to the manner in which Nietzsche contributes to our understanding of the analytic work the self can perform on itself—the very work that lies at the heart of the psychoanalytic enterprise. Only recently have psychologists recognised the debt the tradition owes to Nietzsche on this score and even then only partially.[34] In some recent works, for example, psychoanalytically inclined philosophers have accentuated Nietzsche's idea of self-overcoming in terms of sublimation, and construed the *Übermensch* as a sublimator par excellence.[35] For the most part, however, psychoanalytic theorists interpret Nietzsche's philosophy as an unabashed celebration of primary narcissism, rather than an acute psychological *analysis and therapy* of its various maladies.

Unfortunately, the general thrust of the psychoanalytic treatment of Nietzsche as a symbol of narcissistic regression also now freely circulates, albeit in a different register and with different aims, among the contemporary philosophical defenders of the new orthodox theory of subjectivity: that is, the dialogic or intersubjectivist perspective. Partly because he fails to acknowledge Nietzsche's middle period, Jürgen Habermas, ironically in company with the so-called French Nietzscheans whom he attacks, also misses Nietzsche's distinctive conception of the work of the self.[36] In *The Philosophical Discourse of Modernity*, for example, Habermas identifies Nietzsche's philosophy with an irrationalist championing of Dionysian self-dissolution.[37] In fact, it would be fair to say that it has now become something of a cliché to identify Nietzsche with un-adult-erated narcissism.

We need to briefly consider the origins and validity of the psychoanalytic depiction of Nietzsche as a narcissist par excellence, therefore, in order to clear a space for investigating the middle period's contribution to our understanding of narcissistic pathologies and their *therapeia*. Undoubtedly Freud's unmastered ambivalence toward Nietzsche has shaped the psychoanalytic tradition's interpretation of his philosophy. Freud both underlines one of the fundamental premises of this thesis—that is, that Nietzsche lays some of the foundations for the modern notion of the analytic work of the self on itself—and obfuscates his own insight by caricaturing Nietzsche as an unreconstructed narcissist. For our purposes, dispelling Freud's ambivalence serves to clarify the psychological underpinnings of Nietzsche's idea of self-cultivation.

On the one hand, in his quarrelsome history of the psychoanalytic movement Freud explicitly concedes what many of his followers had been clamouring for him to acknowledge—namely, that in many cases psychoanalysis merely confirms Nietzsche's (so-called) intuitions about the unconscious psychodynamics of subjectivity:

> In later years I have denied myself the very great pleasure of reading the works of Nietzsche, with the deliberate object of not being hampered in working out the impressions received in psycho-analysis by any sort of anticipatory ideas. I had therefore to be prepared—and I am so, gladly—to forgo all claims to priority in the many instances in which laborious psychoanalytic investigation can merely confirm the truths which the philosopher recognised by intuition.[38]

In his exhaustive study of Nietzsche's direct influence on Freud and the profound similarities between their psychological theories, Ronald Lehrer underlines the extent to which Freud's concession to Nietzsche's theoretical priority, albeit in the form of an undeniably backhanded compliment, holds true of *Human, All Too Human, Daybreak* and *The Gay Science*. In his appraisal of the psychological insights and concepts of the free-spirit trilogy Lehrer makes the following observation:

> As regards the general or overarching concepts and the territory being explored, Nietzsche was explicitly discussing material directly related to Freud's formulations of psychoanalytic concepts. Nietzsche discusses the nature of instincts and drives, the relationship of consciousness to unconscious processes, dynamic psychic conflict, the development of conscience, sublimation, the nature of dreams, that our actions are determined by multiple motives, including gratification, defence and the assuaging of conscience, and so on.[39]

On the other hand, however, Freud's acknowledgement of Nietzsche's pioneering understanding of unconscious psychodynamics is not reflected in the treatment and characterisation of Nietzsche's philosophy in his own theoretical works. Indeed, it almost seems as if in his theoretical speculations Freud takes the opportunity of revenging himself on Nietzsche for his own anxiety of influence, an anxiety which Jung and Rank did their level best to exacerbate.[40] This is especially evident in the way Freud first caricatures the Nietzschean image of the *Übermensch*. Freud maintains that in the image of the *Übermensch* Nietzsche celebrates a return to what he (Freud) claims is our originary condition of primary narcissism, which in his late structural model he defines as a condition of objectless plenitude. Freud caricatures Nietzschean philosophy in one of his speculative passages on the irrational origins of group psychology:

> The members of the group were subject to ties just as we see them today, but the father of the primordial horde was free. His intellectual acts were strong

and independent even in isolation, and his will needed no reinforcement from others. Consistency leads us to assume that his ego had few libidinal ties, he loved no one but himself, or other people only insofar as they served his needs. To objects his ego gave away no more than was barely necessary. *Here, at the very beginning of history of mankind, was the "superman" whom Nietzsche expected from the future.* Even today the members of a group stand in need of the illusion that they are equally and justly loved by their leader; but the leader himself need love no one else, he may be of a masterful nature, absolutely narcissistic, self-confident and independent.[41]

Freud vividly paints Nietzsche's *Übermensch* using the theoretical framework he develops in his metapsychological account of primary narcissism. In terms of this framework Freud positions the *Übermensch* as an idealised incarnation of the return to that objectless condition of plenitude that precedes the emergence of a differentiated subject-object world. Although a complete return to this condition is unsustainable for dependent creatures, Freud implies here that Nietzsche comes as close as possible to anticipating such a regression in the figure of an *Übermensch*. Freud depicts the *Übermensch* as the way across (*über*) to the narcissistic infancy of humankind. According to Freud, in his account of mass psychology even we supposedly rational and civilized moderns give way to the seductions of the crowd and willingly sacrifice ourselves to its leader/*Übermensch* because he realises our own narcissistic fantasy of monadic, unloving but entirely beloved majesty. Mass intoxication is a narcissistic miasma.

But even as Freud criticises his Nietzschean straw-man, he must acknowledge the profound grip narcissism has on the human imagination and its capacity to return in different guises. In this regard, even as Freud casts his analysis as a swipe against Nietzsche's idea of the *Übermensch*, his analysis of the lure of origins remains close to Nietzsche's critical insights. Both Nietzsche and Freud maintain, on the basis of a similar understanding of narcissism, that our desire for "food," for mere self-preservation or bodily gratification, exercises far *less* power over us than the "intoxication" supplied by the "laurel wreath" of victory, as Nietzsche expresses the point in *Daybreak* (188) in terms that deliberately conjure up the image of the Roman emperor, or *Fürst*, celebrating a triumph.[42] The "dream food" that the Roman circuses once supplied in abundance, Nietzsche implies, proves far more seductive and intoxicating than mere bread.[43]

Both Nietzsche and Freud suggest, moreover, that we can satisfy this need for intoxication through sacrificing ourselves to a grandiose narcissist. Freud's criticism of Nietzsche thus strangely turns back on itself and confirms Nietzsche's own fear in *Daybreak*. For if Freud is right, what we strive for is a return to the beginning of history, to the condition of monadic narcissism, which we can indirectly satisfy through submission to another who embodies this condition in our name—*der Fürst*. Even the most composed mind can be disturbed by the recrudescence of its originary narcissism. The question for both Nietzsche and Freud therefore is not how we can *surpass* narcissism once and for all, since it is an eternally recurring dream, but how we can temper and transform its pathological excesses. As Joel Whitebook points out, this dream of the origin-as-goal, the compulsive force of which Nietzsche and Freud both identify, can result in the most calamitous as well as the most sublime consequences in human affairs.[44]

Freud is right then that Nietzsche understood the lures of narcissistic regression, especially, as we shall see, in the middle works, but he is mistaken in his suggestion that Nietzsche *endorses* this regression as the goal of history. In the middle works Nietzsche sharpens our understanding of the pathologies of narcissism, and he does so not through mere "intuition," as Freud alleges, in a rhetorical gesture that perhaps calls up the ghost of Nietzsche's first scholarly tormentor, Wilamowitz.[45] Rather, he hones our self-comprehension through precisely the method Freud employs to such great effect in *The Interpretation of Dreams*: that is, through the difficult work of self-analysis.

Yet many psychoanalytic critics merely repeat or, at best, vary Freud's critical theme. Paul-Laurent Assoun, the author of the first book-length monograph comparing Nietzsche and Freud's psychological theories, simply reiterates Freud's basic charge. Nietzsche's idea of self-overcoming or "health," Assoun asserts, represents a regression to "the narcissistic scheme of omnipotence."[46] In his recent psychoanalytic exploration of Nietzsche, Victor Wolfenstein borrows from Kleinian discourse to reiterate this charge, extending its application to neo-Nietzscheans like Foucault. Nietzsche's genealogy of morals, he claims, depicts a "paranoid-schizoid" situation "replete with the narcissistic trends that are characteristic of that psychic position," a problem which plagues "Foucault's conception of human subjectivity" which, he asserts "is virtually as monadic as Nietzsche's."[47]

Elliot Jurist gives a much more nuanced assessment of Nietzsche in his attempt to achieve a rapprochement between Nietzsche and Hegel, or between what he describes as the strong affirmation of narcissism that arises from decentred notions of agency and the accent on mutuality that derives from intersubjectivist notions of agency. In the context of discussing *Thus Spoke Zarathustra* (book 3, III), where Zarathustra gives his blessings to a healthy *Selbstsucht*, Jurist ventures the following judgement:

> Nietzsche demands that we take into account narcissism, not that we endorse it. Yet he is clearly attracted to the healthy aspect of narcissism (the investment in self-gratification) and he does not have much to say about the unhealthy aspect (that others are reduced to mirrored reflections of the self).[48]

Jurist's first two claims are undeniably correct, though we need to specify more precisely what might count as the "healthy" aspect of narcissism.

However, the last claim Jurist makes here, that Nietzsche has little to say regarding its "unhealthy aspect," runs counter to one of the basic threads of analysis that Nietzsche weaves through the middle period.

Indeed, one of my central aims is to show that Nietzsche's psychological analysis identifies three main symptoms of the failure to treat the narcissistic loss of plenitude: melancholia, revenge and pity. I reconstruct his psychological critique of unhealthy narcissism in terms of its three symptoms: (1) the melancholic longing for death, which is the most radical form of this disease; (2) the phantasy of revenge through which we attempt to restore the magisterial illusion of our omnipotence and secure the realm of our pure-pleasure ego from the painful intrusions of the not-me world; and (3) the kind of *pitié* or *Mitleid* that Rousseau and Schopenhauer defend on philosophical and ethical grounds. By contrast, as we shall see, Nietzsche interprets the ethics of *pitié/Mitleid* as a means through which we assuage the painful loss of plenitude rather than as a step we take toward genuine mutuality or recognition.

To enter into Nietzsche's middle period then is to enter into the spirit of a thinker and a philosophical universe whose style, tenor, and conceptual foundations bear no resemblance to the straw man we find Nietzsche portrayed as in much of the psychoanalytic literature and the critical literature that emerges from the intersubjectivist camp: that is, the Schopenhauerian metaphysician who celebrates ecstatic self-dissolution. Human vanity, Nietzsche jokes, is the only "thing in-itself" he recognises.[49] To be human is to be incorrigibly narcissistic. And yet in the middle works we also find no signs of Freud's Nietzsche, the unreconstructed advocate of regression to the enchanted kingdom of "His Majesty the Baby."

Rather, Nietzsche engages in a sober attempt to analyse the dreams and perversions born of wounded vanity. Through his philosophical psychology he arrives at an understanding and treatment of unhealthy narcissism via his engagement with the Hellenistic and Stoic *therapeia* of loss and transience. Nietzsche's middle works, so I claim, provide the pivot between the two great philosophical *therapeia* in the Western tradition: the Stoic and psychoanalytic registers.[50] I suggest that in exploring the pathos of the soul that elicits these therapies Nietzsche maps out much of the conceptual terrain of Freud's psychodynamic metapsychology. Nietzsche deepens the Hellenistic tradition through his subtle grasp of the psychodynamics of wounded vanity, which Stoicism attempts to soothe and cure; and he goes beyond classical Freudianism insofar as he grapples with the problem of *transforming* narcissism. Whereas Freud tends to view narcissism in a predominantly negative light, Nietzsche, while aware of the dangers of omnipotence and grandiosity, seeks to temper and transform narcissism as part of a mature individualism.[51]

I begin by critically assessing the shortcomings of the aestheticist interpretation of Nietzschean self-fashioning. I suggest that this interpretation of Nietzsche systematically occludes his psychological analysis and its therapeutic concerns. In order to prepare the way to exploring the psychological analysis and self-analysis he undertakes in the middle period I critically examine the interpretive limitations of conceiving his ideal of self-cultivation in exclusively formal, aesthetic terms and metaphors. Nietzsche may well be concerned with how to compose a beautiful soul, but he defines a beautiful composition partly in terms of how it overcomes the excesses of melancholia, revenge and pity.

With this blind spot removed, I turn directly to Nietzsche's first self-avowal as a psychologist in *Human, All Too Human*. I examine the conceptual shift from metaphysics to psychology, and from ecstasy to *askēsis* that marks his break with the Schopenhauerian and Wagnerian foundations of his early work. In particular I demonstrate that a Stoic conception of the labour of the self enables Nietzsche to understand and criticise his Dionysian yearning for ecstatic self-dissolution and its metaphysical underpinnings. After rejecting his early artist's metaphysics and with it his celebration of Dionysian *Rausch*, Nietzsche investigates an ethical *topos*, which draws on various motifs and practices of the Hellenistic arts of existence. Alluding to the Cynic and Stoic practice of *askēsis*, he describes this ethics of self-cultivation as a "gymnastics" of the soul, something far removed from Schopenhauer and Wagner's Siren song of self-oblivion.[52] In making this case I especially draw on the work of Lucius Annaeus Seneca, the Roman Stoic philosophical physician who, as Nero's tutor and advisor, found himself charged with the unenviable task of seeking to temper this infamously malignant narcissist. I argue that Nietzsche understands the ideal of self-cultivation as a therapeutic tempering of wounded narcissism that can create a robust, mature form of individualism. I suggest that he defines the work on the self required to achieve mature individualism in terms similar to those dimensions of the Stoic and psychoanalytic work on the self that aim at bearing separation, loss and transience.

This book thus illuminates the nature and purpose of Nietzsche's conception of self-cultivation by showing its conceptual and ethical affinities to Stoicism and its invention of the conceptual territory now occupied by psychoanalysis. It closes by suggesting that Nietzsche provides plausible reasons for supposing that it is this work on the self that gives us the capacity for friendship. The closing sections thus delve into an area that largely remains a hidden continent on the map of Nietzsche studies: his conceptualisation of the positive dimensions of our relations to others.[53]

OUTLINE OF CHAPTERS

Chapter 1 examines Alexander Nehamas's influential interpretation of Nietzschean self-fashioning as an exemplification of the purely aestheticist interpretation of Nietzschean self-cultivation. Nehamas defines the latter as a practice of treating one's own life (or *bios*) as material for fashioning and shaping based on a literary model of organic wholeness. Paying close attention to the tone of Nietzsche's texts, the chapter argues that Nehamas's interpretation of Nietzschean self-fashioning takes an initial misstep by remaining deaf to Nietzsche's ironic deflations of the grandiose, hyperbolic claim we make to weaving our lives into such perfect totalities. It demonstrates that Nehamas's exclusively aestheticist notion of self-fashioning cannot escape the charge of immoralism—a point, as we shall see, that he reluctantly concedes.

Rather than imposing an organic literary metaphor on Nietzsche's conception of self-cultivation, as Nehamas does, this chapter examines Nietzsche's *own* analysis of literary figures in the middle works, especially his analysis of the appeal of tragic characters. Once Nietzsche's treatment of literary characters is brought into the foreground it becomes clear that he does not hold them up as models of an organic unity that we should emulate in order to meet the lofty requirements of a life lived as literature. Rather he analyses these characters in order to reveal the comical weakness and childish self-inflation involved in the notion that human beings are capable of such absolute self-composition and transparent self-knowledge.

Chapter 2 aims to move beyond the strangely monochromatic depiction of the aestheticist interpretation of Nietzschean self-cultivation. It does so by showing that Foucault's attempt to salvage a positive notion of subjectivity, or of the self's relation to itself, from the fragments and ruins of Hellenistic and Roman antiquity can be used as a portal to the ideal of self-cultivation in Nietzsche's middle period. It suggests that the late Foucault's Senecan mood, style, and, more importantly, *ethos* echoes Nietzsche's middle period. While the common Foucault-Nietzsche discussions find similarities in their ideas of power and knowledge, genealogy and interpretation, this chapter focuses on resonances between Foucault's resurrection of the ethics of the care of the self and Nietzsche's recovery of Hellenistic *therapeia* in his middle works.

However, it also shows that Foucault clouds the true nature and significance of the Hellenistic and Stoic care of the self by presenting it as a purely aesthetic project akin to nineteenth-century Dandyism. Once we see beyond his superficial aesthetic gloss it becomes apparent that Foucault retrieves from Hellenistic and Roman sources a positive conception of subjectivity that is better understood as therapeutic rather than aesthetic. For our purposes, Foucault's ethics of the care of the self is important because it clarifies the philosophic and therapeutic ethos that informs Nietzsche's ideal of self-cultivation. By setting aside the excesses of the aestheticist interpretation we can move toward achieving a better grasp of Nietzsche's debt to the medical-*cum*-therapeutic discourse of Hellenistic and Stoic philosophy, and the rich vein of psychoanalytic insight that he develops in renewing the ideal and ethics of self-cultivation.

Chapter 3 investigates the famous volte-face Nietzsche performs in *Human, All Too Human*: his painful repudiation of his former philosophical and cultural mentors, Schopenhauer and Wagner. It is in this work that Nietzsche first declares his intention of bracketing the kind of metaphysical philosophy for which he had been acclaimed by the Schopenhauerians and Wagnerians, and reviled by his former philological colleagues. Instead, he devotes the free-spirit trilogy to developing and refining the art of psychological observation and analysis. Nietzsche brings his penchant for self-analysis into the foreground by making Schopenhauerian ascetic self-mortification and Wagnerian musical ecstasy central objects of his psychological investigations. In doing so, as he puts it in the most excruciating terms, he "skins" himself alive for the sake of psychological knowledge.[54]

This chapter demonstrates that through this psychological analysis Nietzsche came to see asceticism and intoxication, or melancholia and mania, to borrow from the psychoanalytic vocabulary, as manifestations of one and the same narcissistic pathology. Here the chapter expounds and then employs Freud's theory of narcissism in order to illuminate Nietzsche's attempt to understand the oscillation between melancholia and mania, which constitutes the most radical outbreak of the narcissistic malady. It suggests that Nietzsche conceives the unremitting therapeutic work of self-cultivation as the means of tempering and cooling down these twin excesses.

Chapter 4 suggests that Nietzsche forges this therapy of the soul on the basis of what we might call the "postsirenian philosophy" of his middle period.[55] It shows that in developing his philosophic therapy, Nietzsche stands at the crossroads of Hellenistic and psychoanalytic therapy. He argues that self-cultivation requires the difficult labour of self-knowledge and self-analysis, which he conceptualises and explores through the images, metaphors and practices of Cynicism and Stoicism. In a Stoic vein, he claims that self-knowledge is the heavy burden we must bear if we are to achieve a temperate, composed individualism. We can see this shift in Nietzsche's thinking in his critique of Schopenhauer's all-too-quick dismissal of Stoic equanimity.

However, the chapter also suggests that Nietzsche moves beyond the limitations of the Stoic notion of the rational subject and that he does so by opening up a much richer understanding of the intrapsychic world, an understanding that lays the groundwork for much of the psychoanalytic conception of subjectivity. Unlike the Stoics, Nietzsche investigates our emotions and moods as symptoms whose roots lie in our earliest, largely forgotten, unconscious conflicts and traumas. It is for this reason that Nietzsche consecrates practical reason to the goddess of memory, Mnemosyne. Finally, this chapter illustrates how Nietzsche puts his psychological insights to work by interpreting metaphysical systems as symptoms of our psychological maladies. Nietzsche comes to see the dreams of metaphysics as the royal road to the unconscious. What he claims to discover along this road, as we shall see, is that our neuroses are inflections of a narcissistic flight from loss, separation and finitude.

Chapter 5 examines Nietzsche's analysis of what we might conceptualise, again borrowing from Freud, as the first modulation of narcissism: that is, the incipient ego's attempt to restore a phantasised condition of majesty and plenitude through vengefully projecting outward every source of unpleasure. It recollects Freud's famous vignette on the *fort-da* game in order to illustrate the psychology of revenge, which in this case manifests itself as a *Spiel* aimed at establishing an illusion of omnipotence and sovereignty. Freud shows that the infantile ego's rage for securing the illusion of omnipotence is symptomatic of its fear of annihilation, a fear that accompanies its discovery of the independence of the other.

This chapter employs Freud's analysis of the psychopathology of narcissism and revenge to illuminate Nietzsche's critique of heroism. It challenges the common claim that Nietzsche lionises the pre-Platonic hero and his manic, triumphant laughter in the face of tragedy. By contrast, it shows that Nietzsche joins with the Roman chronicler Suetonius, and the Roman Stoics Seneca and Epictetus, in satirising the follies of the hero and his overblown pathos. In the middle period Nietzsche treats the hero as material fit only for comedy. This chapter suggests that a combination of the neglect of his middle works and a certain tone deafness to his ironic satire partly accounts for the occlusion of Nietzsche's critique of the infantile hero.

Moreover, this chapter demonstrates that Nietzsche not only *employs* comic satire to illuminate the psychopathologies of heroism, he also *analyses* the psychological significance of our use of comedy and laughter. The chapter reconstructs Nietzsche's identification of three comic stratagems, which he conceptualises as expressions of different responses to or treatments of narcissistic loss. It elaborates his analyses of the cruel, manic laughter of melancholia, the self-humouring of Stoicism and, finally, the comic self-acknowledgement of human limitedness and finitude that he sees as a sign of maturity. It closes by suggesting that for Nietzsche, at least in the middle period, the wisdom of suffering lies not in heroic affirmation and the "solitary laughter of the mountaintops," as is often assumed to be the case, but in comic, antiheroic self-acknowledgement.[56] On the phenomenological plane, Nietzsche conceives this self-acknowledgement as a sorrowful smile at the desperately funny measures we employ to soothe our childish anxieties and fears.

Chapters 6 and 7 form companion pieces. It has almost become an un-written law among those who defend Nietzschean ideals of self-cultivation to skirt the issue of his critique of pity, dismissing it as an extraneous dia-tribe or an embarrassing fulmination. On the other hand, critics who de-nounce Nietzsche's ideal of self-cultivation as a dangerous solipsism that all too easily gives license to indifference or outright contempt for others seize on this aspect of his thought as cut and dried evidence for the claim that, as Charles Taylor coyly phrases it, "Nietzsche's influence was not entirely for-eign [to fascism]."[57]

Rather than dismissing or denouncing the "pitiless" Nietzsche, chapter 6 carefully examines his subtle psychological analysis of *pitié/Mitleid*. It trains the spotlight on Nietzsche's principal object of criticism: Rousseau and Schopenhauer's ethics of pity. This chapter demonstrates that Nietzsche's psychological analysis presents a compelling case for interpreting Rousseauian and Schopenhauerian pity not as a sign of living *for* others, or as a form of mutuality and recognition, as its defenders routinely assume, but as a veiled means of assuaging narcissistic loss at the other's expense. His analysis reveals pity as the third and, for our purposes, final pathologi-cal expression of narcissism alongside melancholic self-hatred and phanta-sised revenge.

Nietzsche shows that through pity the other becomes once again a means through which we conceal ourselves from ourselves, rather than a part of an independent not-me world that we acknowledge as such. The chapter thereby underlines the broader claim of this book that Nietzsche's ethics of self-cultivation is a meeting point of Stoic and psychoanalytic ethics and *therapeia*.[58] Nietzsche joins hands with and strengthens Stoic arguments and anxieties, exemplified by Seneca, to the effect that pity breeds venge-fulness and cruelty, and he does so by drawing on his psychoanalytic in-sights into our subterranean intrapsychic and intersubjective stratagems for restoring to ourselves the illusion of majestic plenitude.

Chapter 7 aims to demonstrate that Nietzsche identifies friendship as the counterpoint to these damaged forms of intersubjectivity. It suggests that he conceptualises the therapeutic work of self-cultivation as a crucial step to-ward living well with others. The chapter argues that his idea of solitude, which he conceives as an integral part of the work of the self, should not be mistaken as a contraction into solipsism. Rather, it suggests that Nietzsche develops a subtle account of solitude as a practice of the self that makes possible a relatedness to others that does not fall prey to the pathology of pity and envy. It shows how Nietzsche conceptualises his education in soli-tude in terms of the Stoics' metaphorical depiction of the work of the self as a digestion of the bitter affects that spring from loss and separateness. Seen in this light, Nietzschean solitude can be understood as a therapy of the self aimed at bearing separateness, finitude and loss, which enables us to accede to the separateness and independence of others and to rejoice in their joy. For Nietzsche, then, the work of self-cultivation can take the individual beyond both the zero-sum game of pity and envy, and the irrational miasma of group intoxication. His ideal of self-cultivation thereby points in the direction of a kind of friendship borne of a mature individualism, which he defines by its capacity to share in the other's joy (*Mitfreude*).

NOTES

1. Rüdiger Bittner outlines Nietzsche's complex, shifting publication plans as they appear in his late notebooks. Here Bittner draws on Montinari's analysis of the *Nachlass*. According to Montinari, in September 1888 Nietzsche abandoned his longstanding plan to publish a book with the title *The Will to Power* and instead moved toward the idea of a major work with the portentous title *Revaluation of all Values*, the first book of which he regarded as *The Antichrist*. Bittner's account of the change in the relationship between Nietzsche's notebooks and his publications after 1885 also underlines the importance of distinguishing between his published and unpublished writings, a distinction most famously and flagrantly violated by Martin Heidegger: "The relationship between Nietzsche's handwritten notes and his publications changed over his lifetime. While the published works never exhausted the contents of the notes, it was only after 1885, after the completion of *Thus Spoke Zarathustra*, that the disparity between what Nietzsche wrote down in his notebooks and what he brought to a definitive form for publication grew radical"; see Rüdiger Bittner, "Introduction," in Friedrich Nietzsche, *Writings from the Late Notebooks*, edited by Rüdiger Bittner and translated by Kate Sturge, 2003, Cambridge University Press, Cambridge, esp. ix–xv, x, emphasis added. Apart from the very occasional use of unpublished notes, and in these cases only where the notes are clearly a rough-hewn version of what Nietzsche later polished for publication, I will only draw on material Nietzsche chose to publish.

2. HAH1, 3; on Dionysus' drumming with his thyrsus, see Euripides, *The Bacchae and Other Plays*, translated by Philip Vellacott, 1973, Penguin Books, London, l. 237. The work of interpretation specifically devoted to Nietzsche's middle works would make a very slim volume, especially when measured against the extraordinary amount of literature devoted to the early and late Nietzsche. Rüdiger Safranski's wonderfully insightful philosophical biography of Nietzsche, in which he grants far more significance to the middle period than is conventionally the case, and Ruth Abbey's impeccably thorough and scholarly treatment of this period, which argues that on some axes the writings of the middle period are superior to what follows, stand as welcome and notable exceptions to this rule; see Ruth Abbey, *Nietzsche's Middle Period*, 2000, Oxford University Press, London; Rüdiger Safranski, *Nietzsche: A Philosophical Biography*, translated by Shelley Frisch, 2003, W. W. Norton & Co., New York.

3. HAH1, 3.

4. HAH1, 37.

5. HAH1, 3.

6. HAH1, 3.

7. HAH1, 37.

8. On this point, see L. W. Tancock, "Introduction," in La Rochefoucauld, *Maxims*, 1959, Penguin Books, Harmondsworth, UK, 13–14.

9. In his comprehensive publication history of Nietzsche's works, William Schaberg suggests that the comment he wrote for the back cover of the first edition of *The Gay Science* clearly shows that Nietzsche himself was the author of the three phases classification of his oeuvre. Here Nietzsche orders *Human, All Too Human* (including *Assorted Opinions and Maxims* and *The Wanderer and His Shadow*), *Daybreak* and *The Gay Science* in a series, observing that "[w]ith this book [GS] we arrive at the conclusion of a series of writings by Friedrich Nietzsche whose common goal it is to erect a new image and ideal of the free spirit." Hence I use the term "free-spirit trilogy" throughout this thesis to denote Nietzsche's own grouping together of these works into a self-contained series. Though rarely credited with it, as Ruth Abbey observes, Lou Salomé was the first interpreter to classify Nietzsche's oeuvre into three periods, the middle period of which consisted of HAH, including AOM and WS, D and the first four books of GS only, since Nietzsche did not compose the fifth book of GS until 1887; see William H. Schaberg, *The Nietzsche Canon: A Publication History and Bibliography*, 1995, University of Chicago Press, Chicago, 85–86; Lou Andreas-Salomé, *Nietzsche*, 1988, translated by Siegfried Mandel, Black Swan Books, Redding Ridge, 8–9; and Ruth Abbey, "Beyond Misogyny and Metaphor: Women in Nietzsche's Middle Period," *Journal of the History of Philosophy* 34, no. 2, April 1996, 233–56, 235, fn. 15.

10. Gary Handwerk makes this point deftly:

Nietzsche's aphorisms typically carry a continuous line of thought from one section to the next. . . . Although he often deploys the condensed formulations favored by his French predecessors, these aphoristic nodes typically serve as a starting point for reflection rather than as a detached distillation of it. . . . He takes up aphorisms by Lichtenberg and La Rochefoucauld not in order to outdo their stylistic flourish, but to explicate the psychological logic behind their spare observation[s].

In Gary Handwerk, "Translator's Afterword," in *Human, All Too Human: A Book for Free Spirits*, vol. 1, 1995, Stanford University Press, Stanford, Calif., 361–79, 377–78.

11. I deliberately echo here Nietzsche's description of Wagner as a musical miniaturist in an homage that is one of Nietzsche's most ravishingly beautiful prose passages, GS, 87, which he later included, with a minor addition, in the compilation NCW, "Where I Admire."

12. HAH1, 491; D, 115.

13. D, 115.

14. D, 115.

15. D, 115.

16. This colloquial metaphor is apposite. In *GS*, 49, Nietzsche claims that the *Egoismus* symptomatic of certain kinds of psychopathologies is best conceived as "a powerful centrifugal force [*Schleuderkraft*]." *Schleuder* is the German word for sling or catapult. We shall touch on this point again in chapter 5.

17. Horst Hutter attempts to see Nietzsche's philosophy through the lens of Hadot's account of ancient model. He explores with great clarity Nietzsche's recovery

of *askēsis*; see, *Shaping the Future: Nietzsche's New Regime of the Soul and Its Ascetic Practices*, 2006, Lexington Books, Lanham, Md.

18. Pierre Hadot, *Philosophy as a Way of Life: Spiritual Exercises from Socrates to Foucault*, translated by Michael Chase, 1995, Blackwell, Oxford, 272. Julian Young convincingly argues that despite Schopenhauer's argument that we ought to abandon the classical assumption that philosophy can be a guide to life, Schopenhauer's work in fact exemplifies practical philosophy insofar as it attempts to "transform life and character in ways which may be of moral relevance"; see Julian Young, *Willing and Unwilling: A Study in the Philosophy of Arthur Schopenhauer*, 1987, Martinus Nijhoff Publishers, Dordrecht, 103–7, 107.

19. HS, 28; see also 251.

20. PT, 109.

21. In his contextualist historiography of philosophy, Ian Hunter asserts that we can conceive all philosophies, not just Greco-Roman philosophies, as ensembles of intellectual arts for the cultivation of specific kinds of philosophical selves or personae. If this is so, he claims, it is possible to empirically investigate all modes of philosophy as techniques of existential self-transformation. Hunter uses this framing device to explore how philosophies that are commonly thought to fall outside the scope of the "practical" or "existential" model are actually extensions or variations on this theme. However, even if we grant that all philosophies entail the construction of a certain kind of persona, this claim should not conceal the radical divide that separates the Hellenistic schools from modern "university" philosophy. Hadot, of course, accepts that "university philosophy" constructs a certain kind of persona—the philosophy professor capable of training others for scholarship or public office—but he claims that this is not "existential" or "practical" in the sense in which this applies to ancient philosophy. That is to say what distinguishes the Greco-Roman model of philosophy from modern university philosophy is that it cultivates and transforms the *whole* of the individual's life and aims to show him/her how to overcome suffering and achieve *eudaimonia* or beatitude. On this basis, Hadot is right to claim that there is a radical opposition between the ancient philosophical schools, which addressed individuals in order to transform their entire personality, and university philosophy, with its focus on accreditation and training. "The goal" as he puts it "is no longer, as it was in antiquity, to train people for careers as human beings, but to train them . . . as specialists, theoreticians, and retainers of specific items of more or less esoteric knowledge. Such knowledge, however, no longer involves the whole life, as ancient philosophy demanded"; see Pierre Hadot, *What Is Ancient Philosophy?* translated by Michael Chase, 2002, Harvard University Press, Cambridge, Mass., 260; and Ian Hunter, "The History of Philosophy and the Persona of the Philosopher," *Modern Intellectual History* 4, 3, 2007, 571–600.

22. UM2, 5.

23. PT, 111. Nietzsche specifically cites Trendelenburg's work as an example of the kind of university philosophy he is castigating. In the context of analysing the political dimensions of Nietzsche's critique of university philosophy, Tamsin Shaw observes that "Trendelenburg's Kantian critique of Hegel's *Logic* inspired many German thinkers to return to Kant and in particular to the first *Critique*. This transition from a *weltanschaulich* mode of philosophy to a more limited *Erkenntnistheorie* struck Nietzsche as an abdication of philosophical responsibility"; Tamsin Shaw, *Nietzsche's Political Skepticism*, 2007, Princeton University Press, Princeton, N.J., 26.

24. See Pierre Hadot, *Philosophy as a Way of Life*, op. cit., 265.

25. PT, 109, original emphases.

26. SE, 193. David Sedley argues that contrary to what is often supposed, philosophically Brutus was a Platonist, a follower of the Old Academy, not a de facto Stoic. Sedley argues that Brutus committed tyrannicide on the basis of a proper understanding of Platonic political philosophy. "When we watch Brutus' role in the events of the Ides of March, it is Platonist political thought that we are seeing enacted." See David Sedley, "The Ethics of Brutus and Cassius," *Journal of Roman Studies* 87, 1997, 41–53.

27. Pierre Hadot, *Philosophy as a Way of Life*, op. cit., 272.

28. Pierre Hadot, *What Is Ancient Philosophy?*, op. cit., 172–73.

29. On the philosophical and historical difficulties of reviving the Greco-Roman therapeutic model of philosophy in modernity see, Pierre Hadot, *Philosophy as a Way of Life*, op. cit., 272–73; *What Is Ancient Philosophy?*, op. cit., 277–81; and John Cottingham, *Philosophy and the Good Life*, 1998, Cambridge University Press, Cambridge.

30. See for example HAH1, 95, for Nietzsche's use of the notion of mature individualism and its morality.

31. See Lou Salomé, *Nietzsche*, op. cit., 15.

32. On the first point regarding the integrity and value of the middle period, see Ruth Abbey, "Beyond Metaphor and Misogyny: Women in Nietzsche's Middle Period," op. cit., 236.

33. See the collection of essays in Jacob Golomb, Weaver Santaniello and Ronald Lehrer (eds.), *Nietzsche and Depth Psychology*, 1999, SUNY, Albany.

34. I consider below some of those psychologists who claim that Nietzsche makes a fundamental contribution to psychoanalysis. For an excellent survey of the history of the reception of Nietzsche as a psychologist, see Graham Parkes, *Composing the Soul: Reaches of Nietzsche's Psychology*, 1994, University of Chicago Press, Chicago, "Introduction," esp. fn. 1.

35. Jacob Golomb develops the most philosophically sophisticated version of this interpretation of Nietzschean philosophy; see Jacob Golomb, *Nietzsche's Enticing Psychology of Power*, 1987, Iowa University Press, Ames. Danielle Chappelle's playfully serious essay also illuminates some thought-provoking connections between the thought of eternal recurrence and the work of analytic therapy; see Danielle Chapelle, *Nietzsche and Psychoanalysis*, 1993, SUNY, Albany.

36. Apart from discussing the late Foucault's ethics of the care of the self I do not directly address the French Nietzscheans who came to prominence (and notoriety) in the 1960s and 1970s. This is so for two reasons: not only is there already an avalanche of literature on the French Nietzscheans, but more importantly they add little to our understanding of Nietzsche's middle period.

37. Jürgen Habermas, *The Philosophical Discourse of Modernity: Twelve Lectures*, translated by Frederick Lawrence, 1987, MIT Press, Cambridge, Mass., 99–105.

38. Sigmund Freud, *On the History of the Psychoanalytic Movement*, translated by Joan Riviere, 1967, W. W. Norton & Co., New York, 15–16. Freud repeats these points in his later *Autobiographical Study* (AS, 1924), adding that Nietzsche "anticipates" him to an "astonishing" degree, an anticipation that Freud now construes not just as "intuition," but as Nietzsche's apparent facility for making good "guess[es]." For a full analysis of the circumstances within the psychoanalytic movement that compelled Freud to make this concession to Nietzsche, and the history of Freud's re-

sistances, "half-truth[s]" and evasions in admitting the extent of his knowledge of Nietzsche's texts, see Peter Heller, "Freud in His Relation to Nietzsche," in Jacob Golomb (ed.), *Nietzsche and Jewish Culture*, 1997, Routledge, London, 193–217; Ronald Lehrer, *Nietzsche's Presence in Freud's Life and Thought: On the Origins of a Psychology of Dynamic Unconscious Mental Functioning*, 1995, SUNY, Albany; and Paul Roazen, "Nietzsche and Freud and the History of Psychoanalysis," in T. Dufresne (ed.), *The Return of the French Freud: Freud, Lacan and Beyond*, 1997, Routledge, London, 11–23.

39. Ronald Lehrer, *Nietzsche's Presence in Freud's Life and Thought*, op. cit., 41. Peter Heller also makes the passing observation that it is *specifically* in Nietzsche's "middle phase" that his psychological analysis and therapy proceeds in a very similar manner to Freud's and is closest to the psychoanalytic kind of veracity; Peter Heller, "Freud in His Relation to Nietzsche," op. cit., 210.

40. Jacob Golomb recounts the story of how Jung and Rank utilised Nietzsche in an attempt to free themselves from Freud's authority; see Jacob Golomb, "Freudian Uses and Misuses of Nietzsche," *American Imago* 37, no. 4, Winter 1980, 371–85.

41. GP, 71, emphasis added.

42. D, 188, 189.

43. Nietzsche uses this phrase in D, 119.

44. Joel Whitebook, *Perversions and Utopia: A Study in Psychoanalysis and Critical Theory*, 1995, MIT Press, Cambridge, Mass., 64.

45. For the details of the bitterly personal and poisonous Wilamowitz-Nietzsche *Streit* over *The Birth of Tragedy* (BT), see William Musgrave Calder III, "The Wilamowitz-Nietzsche Struggle: New Documents and a Reappraisal," *Nietzsche-Studien* 12, 1983, 214–54; and M. S. Silk and J. P. Stern, *Nietzsche on Tragedy*, 1981, Cambridge University Press, Cambridge, 90–107.

46. Paul-Laurent Assoun, *Freud and Nietzsche*, translated by Richard L. Collier Jr., 2000, The Athlone Press, London, 176.

47. Victor Wolfenstein, *Inside/Outside Nietzsche: Psychoanalytic Explorations*, 2000, Cornell University Press, Ithaca, N.Y., 212. On Klein's notion of the paranoid-schizoid position, see her essay "Notes on Some Schizoid Mechanisms," in Melanie Klein, *Envy and Gratitude and Other Works, 1946–1963*, 1990, Virago, London, 1–24.

48. Elliot L. Jurist, *Beyond Hegel and Nietzsche: Philosophy, Culture, and Agency*, 2000, MIT Press, Cambridge, Mass., 220.

49. HAH2, 46.

50. It is beyond the scope of this book to examine the fate of the Stoics and Stoicism in Nietzsche's later writings. However, it is plausible to suggest that in his later works Nietzsche's understanding of Stoicism tends to become little more than a caricature, especially when compared with his rich evocation of Stoic thought and psychology in the middle period. Indeed, ironically, as the classical scholar Thomas Rosenmeyer observes, in caricaturing Seneca as a "Toreador of Virtue" in *Twilight of the Idols* Nietzsche falls "victim to what must be regarded as a Christian narrowing of the Stoic legacy." It should be noted, however, that even as Nietzsche's vision of Stoicism suffers this "Christian narrowing" there is a certain ambivalence in his image of Seneca, for surely in Nietzsche's thinking a "Toreador"—regardless of the type—counts as a figure of some nobility, especially, as Duncan Large points out, in view of his love of Georges Bizet's opera *Carmen* and the toreador Escamillo; see

Thomas G. Rosenmeyer, *Senecan Drama and Stoic Cosmology*, 1989, University of California Press, Berkeley, 12; TI, "Expeditions of an Untimely Man," 1; and Duncan Large, "Introduction," in *Twilight of the Idols: Or How to Philosophize with a Hammer*, translated by Duncan Large, 1998, Oxford University Press, Oxford, 98, fn. 43.

51. Heinz Kohut, "Forms and Transformations of Narcissism," in *Self Psychology and the Humanities: Reflections on a New Psychoanalytic Approach*, 1985, W. W. Norton & Co., New York, 97–123; and Joel Whitebook, *Perversions and Utopia*, op. cit., 5. Arguably, however, it is a something of an overstatement to say that Freud's view of narcissism is *predominantly* negative, and that he especially objects to it on the grounds that it is an opponent of object love. For even in his celebrated essay on the topic Freud identifies a range of narcissistic symptoms stretching from the severest psychopathologies to the "moving and, at bottom, so childish" phenomenon of parental love. Parental love, he claims, "is nothing but the parents' narcissism born again, which, transformed into object love, unmistakably reveals its former nature"; ON, 85. If Freud is correct, parental love is not an abandonment, but a transformation of narcissism. We shall return to this point in chapter 5 when we consider Nietzsche and Freud's analysis of humour and comedy.

52. WS, 305.

53. Elliot Jurist devotes a very short chapter to this subject, though he does not alert us to the important point that in doing so he draws almost exclusively on notes from *Human, All Too Human* and *Daybreak*, as does Jacques Derrida in his treatment of Nietzsche in *The Politics of Friendship*. Elliot L. Jurist, *Beyond Hegel and Nietzsche*, op. cit.; and Jacques Derrida, *The Politics of Friendship*, translated by George Collins, 1997, Verso, London.

54. HAH2, Preface, 1: "[T]he desire awoke within me" as he later described this period "to skin, exploit, expose, 'exhibit' . . . for the sake of knowledge something I had experienced and survived, some fact or fate of my life." This is one of many uncanny, seemingly preternatural moments in Nietzsche's writings. After his collapse Nietzsche would be literally exhibited for the sake of knowledge by the psychiatrist Otto Binswanger in his lectures at the University of Jena in the winter semester of 1888–1889. One of Binswanger's students, Sascha Simchowitz, gives a powerfully moving account of Nietzsche's exhibition in Binswanger's lecture room; see Sander L. Gilman and David Parent (eds.), *Conversations with Nietzsche: A Life in the Words of His Contemporaries*, translated by David J. Parent, 1987, Oxford University Press, New York, 222–25.

55. Rüdiger Safranski, *Nietzsche*, op. cit., 20.

56. Simon Critchley, *Ethics, Politics, Subjectivity*, 1999, Verso, London, 235.

57. Charles Taylor, "The Immanent Counter-Enlightenment" in Ronald Beiner and Wayne Norman (eds.), *Canadian Political Philosophy*, 2001, Oxford University Press, Ontario, 396. Jurist illustrates the manner in which Nietzsche's critique of pity is often casually associated with the act of casting others into oblivion: "[Nietzsche's] repeated condemnation of pity offers tacit justification for discounting the feelings of others." See Elliot Jurist, *Beyond Hegel and Nietzsche*, op. cit., 258.

58. Martha Nussbaum identifies and elaborates this particular link between Stoicism and Nietzsche's ethics, especially as he develops it in *Human, All Too Human* and *Daybreak*. This chapter can be regarded as pursuing some of the interpretive possibilities that she has made possible through her astute sense of the Hellenistic and

Roman Stoic motifs and ideas that are indeed central to the middle works; see Martha C. Nussbaum, "Pity and Mercy: Nietzsche's Stoicism," in Richard Schacht (ed.), *Nietzsche, Genealogy, Morality: Essays on Nietzsche's Genealogy of Morals*, 1994, University of California Press, Berkeley, 139–67; and Martha C. Nussbaum, *Upheavals of Thought: The Intelligence of Emotions*, 2001, Cambridge University Press, New York, 358–59, 361–64, 366–67.

1

The Aesthetic Game of the Self

> So far as *praxis* is concerned, I view the various moral schools as experimental laboratories in which a considerable number of recipes for the art of living have been thoroughly practiced and lived to the hilt. The results of all the schools and of all their experiments belong legitimately to us.
>
> Nietzsche, *Posthumous Fragments*, Autumn 1881, 59

In his classic defence of Nietzsche's humanist credentials, Walter Kaufmann argues that Nietzsche's philosophy affirms nothing more than the solitary individual's pursuit of self-mastery through the art of sublimation. "[T]he *leitmotif* of Nietzsche's life and thought," he contends, "[is] the theme of the antipolitical individual who seeks self-perfection far from the modern world."[1] Kaufmann's portrait of Nietzsche as the advocate of a relatively uncontroversial brand of creative individualism has been amplified in a number of recent interpretations of Nietzsche as primarily an advocate of aesthetic self-fashioning rather than a political or social reformer. This amplification of Kaufmann can be seen in Alexander Nehamas's interpretations of Nietzsche. Kaufmann's rehabilitation of Nietzsche resonates in his claim that Nietzsche conceives self-constitution as an exclusively aesthetic game the self plays with itself.

Nehamas's interpretation is of particular interest here because he frames Nietzsche's philosophical project as a continuation of the Greco-Roman conception of philosophy as a practice or *askēsis* of self-shaping and reshaping. In line with Hadot and Foucault, Nehamas distinguishes between two philosophical traditions: theoretical philosophy, which focuses

exclusively on ascertaining true answers to supposedly perennial philosophical questions, and practical philosophy, which assumes that philosophy is a practice that shapes our character and mode of life.[2] In the
Greco-Roman tradition, as he notes, the essence of the philosophical
project is practical activity, a way of life, and the philosopher *qua* philosopher is principally concerned with living the life of a sage, not with formulating or disputing doctrine for its own sake. In *The Art of Living* he
shows how aspects of this Greco-Roman conception of philosophy as a
way of life survive in some major modern philosophers, including Montaigne, Nietzsche and Foucault.

Nehamas aims not only at the historical recovery or reconstruction of a
practical tradition that most modern philosophers have forgotten and
which has as a consequence passed into a state of desuetude. On the positive side of the ledger, he argues that we ought to consider it an "alternative,
though not necessarily a competitor, to the manner in which philosophy is
generally practised in our time."[3] In this regard, Nehamas follows Nietzsche
in seeking to reclaim the Greco-Roman model of philosophy for modern
culture. Nehamas's framing opens the way to understanding Nietzsche's
project in terms of his desire to revive the classical concern with philosophy
as a means of acting upon ourselves and moulding our character. If this is
correct, then we might say that for Nietzsche philosophy's essential purpose
is to shape our character and cure it of the emotional turmoil that prevents
us from achieving the sage's cheerful affirmation of life as it is. We can see
that this is the case from the way Nietzsche extols Montaigne's engagement
with Stoic, Epicurean and Sceptic philosophical therapies, whose common
goal is to use reason to combat and conquer suffering. According to Nietzsche, in the *Essais*, which constitute one of the most sustained modern ex-
perimentations with the Hellenistic *therapeia*, Montaigne attains the kind of
cheerful wisdom that is the goal of Greco-Roman philosophy. Philosophers
like Montaigne, he claims, are "victors who, precisely because they have
thought most deeply, must love what is most living, and, as sages [*weise*],
incline in the end to the beautiful."[4] In acclaiming Montaigne, Nietzsche
adopts Hellenistic philosophy's eudaimonistic goal in his claim that philosophy realises itself in and through the cheerful affirmation of fate.

Unlike Nehamas, however, Nietzsche is a radical critic of the theoretical
or "scholastic" style of philosophy that he claims had corrupted modern
philosophy. For this reason he does not share Nehamas's intramural concern with persuading contemporary university or academic philosophers to
open up the discipline to its various historical modalities, including its
practical, therapeutic mode. Rather Nietzsche denounces contemporary
philosophy as a profound corruption of the Greco-Roman tradition. All
that we encounter in the modern university he claims "is a feeble phantom
bearing the name of philosophy, a scholarly lecture-hall wisdom and lecture-

hall cautiousness" that, especially in its neo-Kantian form, makes philosophers little more than "the frontier-guards and spies of the sciences."[5] In *Schopenhauer as Educator* he unequivocally maintains that the Greco-Roman model alone defines the proper task of philosophy. Modern university philosophy, he argues, is an abdication of philosophy's responsibilities.

Indeed, in his polemical obloquy Nietzsche goes so far as to suggest that philosophy should be banished from universities and philosophers deprived of recognition and offices, so that it can only be pursued by those who practice it as an art of living rather than as a profession.[6] In this respect Nietzsche again shows his fidelity to the Greco-Roman philosophical school's conception of philosophy. Classical philosophers, we might recall, criticised the sophists for charging students for instruction in the political art of rhetorical persuasion. Following Plato, most classical philosophers conceived the sophists' commercialisation of pedagogy as symptomatic of a perversion or hatred of reason (*misology*) insofar as it entailed the transformation of *logos* into an instrument for manipulating others and securing political power.

Nietzsche levels similar criticisms at modern, state-funded university philosophers. In his judgement they are modern practitioners of sophistic *misology*. Contemporary university philosophers, he maintains, fatally compromise the independence of philosophical thought by treating it as an office of profit. On the one hand, Nietzsche indicts these modern philosopher-functionaries, whom he depicts as slavish ideologues of the state or idle and irrelevant sceptics. On the other, he applauds "the sages of ancient Greece who were not paid by the state but at most were, like Zeno, honoured with a gold crown and a monument in the Ceramicus."[7] He condemns "poor-seeming" university philosophers because like the sophists they use discourse as a means to secure recognition and office rather than as a practice through which they form their own and their students' characters and lives. It is worth noting here that Nietzsche draws his account of Zeno from a passage in Diogenes Laertius' *Lives* where, as Hadot points out, he reports that the founder of Stoic philosophy was posthumously honoured by the Athenians "not for his theories but for the education he gave to young people, the kind of life he led, and the harmony between his life and his discourses."[8]

Nietzsche founds his criticism of "university philosophy" on his commitment to the Greco-Roman belief that philosophical discourse is a means by which philosophers can act upon themselves. In the classical model of philosophical discourse, as Hadot observes, "[discourse] always has . . . a function which is formative, educative, psychagogic, and therapeutic. It is always intended to produce an effect, to create a *habitus* within the soul, or to provoke a transformation of the self."[9] Nietzsche extols Schopenhauer's philosophy precisely because he construes it principally as a means through which Schopenhauer addressed himself and by engaging in this discourse with himself sought to transform himself and his conduct.[10] By contrast, Nietzsche claims that in order to satisfy their institutional and political obligations, modern state-funded philosophers must turn philosophy into a rhetorical and ideological exercise that is antithetical to the classical model.

Clearly, Nietzsche is far more uncompromising in his rejection of "theoretical" or university philosophy than Nehamas. For Nietzsche, as we have seen, the Greco-Roman model is not an alternative to modern university philosophy, but in fact the only valuable form of philosophy. Despite this divergence Nehamas captures the spirit of Nietzsche's philosophic project by identifying it as one of several modern attempts to reclaim philosophy as a way of life. Indeed, these very differences merely underscore Nehamas's central interpretive claim that we should see Nietzsche as an advocate of the ancient conception of philosophy as an art of living. It is after all Nietzsche's fidelity to their Greco-Roman model of philosophical practice that underpins his animadversions against modern academic philosophy. Nehamas shows that Nietzsche conceives of philosophy along classical lines as a practice through which we can construct for ourselves a coherent, harmonious character. As Nietzsche himself puts it, a proper philosophical education should give individuals "creative sovereignty" over themselves.[11] The task of our philosophical educators is to mould our inner forces so that they form a dynamic structure analogous to "a living solar and planetary system."[12] Even Nietzsche's choice of metaphors for representing the order of the soul bears the stamp of the classical tradition. His metaphors echo the Stoics' belief that philosophy is a way of making our inner world mirror the rational necessity immanent in the cosmos. Nietzsche reclaims the Greco-Roman model of philosophy as a practice of ordering or composing our character or personality so that we can, in the manner of the Stoic sage, love everything that is willed by fate.

Yet though Nehamas demonstrates that Nietzsche belongs to a fugitive tradition in modern philosophy that struggles to revive philosophy as a way of life, arguably he misinterprets the way in which Nietzsche's modifies this classical tradition. Indeed, in many ways, as I shall argue at length in the remainder of this chapter, Nehamas's "aestheticist" interpretation misleadingly attributes to Nietzsche's ethics of self-cultivation a romantic or modernist interest in forging a unique and unforgettable personality. This interest in expressing and memorialising a unique self is not only anathema to the classical philosophical tradition, more importantly for our purposes, it is also at odds with Nietzsche's reinvention of the philosophical art of living.[13] In the middle period especially, Nietzsche is much closer to the spirit of the Greco-Roman tradition than to these romantic and aesthetic modernist currents. We might take an initial bearing on this issue by briefly exploring how Nietzsche's conception of the purpose and value of philosophical discourse and writing and its relationship to life is at odds with some essential aspects of the romantic cult of personality that Nehamas attributes to him.

According to Nehamas, the philosophical art of living is practiced through writing, and in what he calls its specifically aestheticist mode the purpose of writing is to construct an unforgettable character, one that is unlike any other character before or after.[14] In the aesthetic version of the philosophical art of living, as Nehamas understands it, we construct a unique, memorable personality specifically through the investigation, criticism and production of philosophical views.[15] It follows, as he points out, that the content of the philosophical life is the body of written work—made up of reflections on philosophical views—through which philosophers aim to construct their own unique, inimitable character.[16] If we examine the aestheticist strain of philosophy as an art of living, which Montaigne, Nietzsche and Foucault allegedly represent, we can see that their most important accomplishments "are the self-portraits that confront us in their writings."[17] The true significance and value of philosophy in this aestheticist mode is not to be discovered in philosophers' lives, but in their writings where as readers we can find convincing models of how to construct a unified and unique life. According to Nehamas, whether or not Montaigne, Nietzsche and Foucault managed to apply this model to themselves or to embody it in lived practice is a *biographical* matter; the only matter of truly *philosophical* import concerns "the image of life contained in their writings."[18] "[T]he most important accomplishment of these modern thinkers," as he puts it, "are the self-portraits that confront us in their writings."[19] In this case, the philosophical issue we must evaluate is whether the philosophers in this aestheticist tradition succeeded in constructing a coherent and unique identity in and through their writings; how they lived their lives outside their texts is a nonphilosophical, biographical issue.[20] How Nietzsche or Foucault, for example, conducted their "outward" life is philosophically irrelevant; all that counts is whether an interesting or memorable character, one exhibiting "aesthetic" unity or coherence, emerges from their philosophical commentaries on earlier philosophical commentaries. As Nehamas himself explains:

> Perhaps [Montaigne, Nietzsche, and Foucault] succeeded in applying these models to themselves; perhaps they did not. Whether they did is a matter of biography, and it will most likely remain a matter of contention. . . . But the image of life contained in their writings is a philosophical matter, and though it too will remain a matter of contention, the contention will be over whether that image is or is not coherent or admirable. . . . The art of living . . . is therefore practiced in writing. The question whether its practitioners applied it successfully to themselves is secondary and in most cases impossible to answer.[21]

If, however, we turn to Nietzsche's account of the purpose of philosophical discourse as he develops this in the mid-1870s, we can see that he treats this so-called aestheticist version of philosophical living as a perversion, not a continuation of the Greco-Roman tradition he seeks to resuscitate. As Nietzsche is at pains to point out, he takes Schopenhauer as his philosophical educator on the basis of his life rather than his philosophical theories and writings. Schopenhauer's true philosophical importance, he claims, lies in his exemplary life, not his writings. Nietzsche believes that in every case we should understand and evaluate philosophers on the basis of their lives, indeed that we should take their writings as of little account philosophically speaking compared with their public, external conduct. For Nietzsche, philosophers who do not enact the principles they express in their writings do not live philosophically; perhaps more precisely, he holds that philosophers' principles are those they embody in action and conduct, not those they express in writing or speaking. Compared with their conduct, what philosophers write has little probative value in identifying their philosophical position and significance.

Nietzsche not only explicitly states that actions not discourse are the primary form of philosophical expression, he also applies this criterion in assessing his contemporaries: he judges Kant's philosophical import in terms of his conformity to university life, his external conformity to conventional religious belief and his timidity before the state rather than his three *Critiques* and Schopenhauer in terms of his "heroic" solitude and unremitting introspection rather than the systematic doctrine he elaborates in *The World as Will and Representation*. In line with the philosophical priority he accords the exemplary life over written discourse, he suggests that it was a great deficiency to learn of Schopenhauer only in the form of his magnum opus, and for this reason he "strove all the harder to see through the book and imagine the living man whose great testament I had to read and who promised to make his heirs only those who could be more than his readers: namely his sons and pupils."[22] We might illuminate Nietzsche's point here by applying it to a more recent case. If we adopted his criterion we would take as the object of our philosophical appraisal Martin Heidegger's actions as rector of Freiburg University rather than his account of historicity in *Being and Time*. How philosophers live is the very content of their philosophy. If we are to comprehend and learn from a philosopher we should therefore take as our object of analysis their lives, not their writings, and *a fortiori* not the literary character that emerges from these writings. As Nietzsche explains, it is a philosopher's life that is of true philosophical import:

> I profit from a philosopher only insofar as he can be an example. . . . But this example must be supplied by his outward life and not merely his books—in the way, that is, in which the philosophers of Greece taught, through their

bearing, what they wore and ate, and their morals, *rather than* by what they said, *let alone by what they wrote.*[23]

Nietzsche affirms as one of the key points of the Greco-Roman philosophical model that the central purpose of philosophy is to live well, and that written discourse, if it is a part of the philosophical life at all—and, as the earlier cited examples of Cato or Brutus indicates, it need not be—it is so only as an instrument for working on and transforming ourselves so that we can achieve in and through our actions the good life as defined by our chosen philosophical school. The value of philosophical writing lies in the manner of living it enables the philosopher to lead; without this life it is valueless. In other words, Nietzsche affirms the Greco-Roman notion that what is philosophically important or valuable is the way one lives, not the literary persona one construct through one's philosophical discourse.

If a philosopher like Schopenhauer, who Nietzsche considers a practitioner of the philosophical art of living, does write, Nietzsche claims, it is strictly only to and for himself with the goal of achieving his own self-transformation. Schopenhauer, he claims, sought to maintain a "pure and truly antique attitude toward philosophy."[24] Nietzsche believes that Schopenhauer's philosophical writings preserve this antique attitude because they are primarily a spiritual exercise, to borrow Pierre Hadot's phrase, the purpose of which is to transform his own life. From Nietzsche's perspective, philosophical writing is one of the exercises or *technai* through which philosophers seek to realise the sage's simple and cheerful mode of living; it is not the substance or core of philosophy, but an instrument through which the self can work upon and transform itself. In other words, in the classical model Nietzsche affirms, writing is an exercise of philosophical reason through which the self can work on itself and free itself from or combat its own "sufferings" and "monsters."[25] If Schopenhauer's philosophical writing matters to others this is not because it constructs a fascinating, unique, unrepeatable character, but because it shows them how they too might engage in the kind of philosophical exercises—the dialogue of the self with itself—through which philosophers have sought to realise the cheerfulness and simplicity of the ancient sage.

As we saw earlier, Nietzsche censures modern philosophers for failing to live their philosophical convictions in the way that the Stoics bore witness to their philosophical precepts in all of their actions. Taking the Stoic model of philosophy as a lived practice as his standard of judgement, Nietzsche condemns modern philosophers for giving priority to discourse over action:

All modern philosophising is political and official, limited by governments, churches, academies, customs and the cowardice of men to the appearance of scholarship. . . . One may think, write, speak, teach philosophy—to that point more or less everything is permitted; only in the realm of action, of so-called "life," is it otherwise: there only one thing is ever permitted [i.e., conformity] and everything else is simply impossible: thus will historical culture have it. Are there still human beings, one then asks oneself, or perhaps only thinking-, writing- and speaking-machines?[26]

Nietzsche takes it as sure sign that the antique attitude to philosophy has been consigned to the past when philosophers take their vocation to consist of developing commentaries on commentaries, or continuous critique of past views, rather than in fulfilling their chosen philosophical law in the conduct of their lives. In resuscitating the Greco-Roman philosophical model Nietzsche takes aim at the view that philosophy is merely the construction of a textual persona through philosophical commentary:

The only critique of a philosophy that is possible and that proves something, namely, trying to see whether one can live in accordance with it, has never been taught at universities: all that has ever been taught is a critique of words by means of other words.[27]

Taking stock of this initial assessment of Nehamas's interpretation, we might say that he demonstrates the importance of framing Nietzsche as one of those modern philosophers who attempt to recreate the Greco-Roman notion of philosophy as an art of living. In many respects, as we have noted, Nietzsche commits himself to the Greco-Roman model much more strictly than Nehamas. Nietzsche's antique attitude is evident in the way he conceives philosophical *discourse* as a therapeutic exercise of the self upon itself that aims to conquer suffering and *philosophy* itself as a way of life or mode of conduct that embodies one's chosen philosophical attitude.[28] Once we follow Nehamas in recognising Nietzsche's commitment to the Greco-Roman model, however, we can also begin to see how this commitment makes Nietzsche a critic of the aestheticist model that Nehamas constructs.

As we have seen, Nietzsche rejects the idea that the content of philosophy is written discourse, let alone the discursive construction of a fictive persona. In the first place, he does so because this aestheticist model betrays the ancient conception of philosophy as a lived practice. Nietzsche diagnoses the modern displacement of the antique model of philosophy by the "scholastic" idea that philosophy consists of the writing of commentaries on commentaries as a symptom of the forgetting of the classical model of philosophy as art of living. Nehamas's notion that the philosophical practice consists in the artful construction of a fictive philosophical persona rather than in the actual conduct of life shares with this scholasticism the displacement of action that Nietzsche disdains as a betrayal of the classical legacy. If Nietzsche rejects this modern displacement of action and conduct by representation, his concern with philosophy as a therapy of the affects also implies a rejection of the romantic valorisation of "aesthetic difference and multiplicity."[29] In line with the Greco-Roman tradition, Nietzsche takes the philosophical work of the self on itself as a therapeutic and moral concern insofar as it aims to "turn men once and for all into contented inhabitants of the earth" and to educate them in the cheerful wisdom of the sage:

> Never have moral educators been more needed. . . . [W]here are the physicians for modern mankind? . . . A true philosopher as an educator who could raise me above my insufficiencies insofar as these originated in the age and teach me to be *simple* and *honest* in thought and life.[30]

On the basis of Nietzsche's adherence to the Greco-Roman model of philosophy, then, we have reasons for thinking that Nehamas's claim that Nietzsche makes aesthetics—in this case the construction of a unified, discursive persona—the pivot of philosophical self-fashioning is not a compelling interpretation of Nietzsche's notion of self-cultivation as he develops it from the mid-1870s onward.

However, Nietzsche is critical of the aestheticist model of self-fashioning not only on the basis of his return to the Greco-Roman conception of philosophy as a way of life, but also on the basis of his psychological insights. In the remainder of the chapter, I shall demonstrate (1) that Nietzsche's work of the self should not be understood as an aesthetic game based on a literary model, but as a therapy of the affects or emotions that Nietzsche derives from his psychological insights; and (2) that because Nehamas screens out the psychological analyses at the basis of Nietzsche's conception of self-cultivation, he fails to recognise its therapeutic dimensions and the implications it has for the self's engagement with others. Nehamas defends the idea that Nietzsche's art of living is simply a private relationship of the self to itself lacking any particular implications for the interaction between self and other. Ultimately, this involves Nehamas pressing the notion of aesthetic self-fashioning to the point where it becomes apparent that the presuppositions of this art clash with ethical or normative considerations. Despite his initial enthusiasm for the individualist and aestheticist genre of the art of living, Nehamas reluctantly concedes that by making aesthetics the pivotal point of self-fashioning, he cannot avoid justifying a kind of subjectivity that undermines sociability, reciprocity or intersubjectivity. On the other hand, because Nietzsche's own model of philosophical self-fashioning is a therapy of affects it has positive ethical implications, which I shall explore in later chapters.

NEHAMAS: LIFE AS LITERATURE

Nehamas asserts that Nietzsche's concept of self-fashioning hinges on a literary model of the perfectly organised, unified and coherent literary character. "Nietzsche," he writes, "always depended on literary and artistic models for understanding the world."[31] Nietzsche recommends, so Nehamas maintains, that individuals fashion their lives on the model of complete works of literature. According to Nehamas, Nietzsche orients his philosophy of self-fashioning around the question: "How does one become both a literary character who, unlike either the base Charlus or the noble Brutus, really exists and also that character's very author?"[32] If Nehamas is right, to be the author of one's own character is the aim of Nietzschean self-fashioning. It is this fascination with literature, he believes, that explains Nietzsche's "peculiar" and "original" views about what counts as a valuable or worthy life.[33] Nietzsche's "essentially aesthetic attitude toward life and the world," he suggests, "involves a radical formalism."[34] What is primarily important for the type of person who adopts Nietzsche's radically formalistic approach to life, he claims, "is the *organisation* of its experiences and actions and *not their intrinsic or moral character*."[35] In a life lived as literature, therefore, the value of an action lies not in its specific content, but in the place it has in the construction of a "totally integrated" character.[36] Above all else, it seems, Nietzsche's self-fashioners are virtuosi of organisation.

According to Nehamas, while Nietzsche challenges the "dogmatism" of all previous moralities, his own formalistic model of life as literature cannot prescribe a positive moral code that dictates how one should or should not live, or what is licit or illicit. On this reading, Nietzsche does not object to the specific content of previous moral views, but disagrees with the assumption that such views make about their own status—that is, that the view in question is true for everyone. He objects not to the specific principles or modes of life that Christianity advocates, for example, but to the fact that this morality claims to be unconditional.[37] On Nietzsche's model, whether a drive or quality counts as a strength or weakness, virtue or vice, depends on the contribution it makes to the overall composition of that life. One may, for example, adopt an ascetic mode of life, not because one believes that asceticism expresses the metaphysical truth of subjectivity, as Schopenhauer suggests, but simply because it contributes to the execution of one's aesthetic project. By the same token, Nehamas suggests, Nietzsche admires the (imaginary) nobles he depicts in the *Genealogy* not because of their cruelty or any other substantive trait, but because of their *mode of valuation*, which is explicitly nonabsolutist or perspectivist—it does *not* demand that everyone obey the same principles.[38] Hence, Nehamas maintains that "Nietzsche admires the barbarian nobles" not "*because* they are cruel," but "primarily for their lack of absolutism, for their attitude that it is impossible for everyone to be bound by the same rules of conduct."[39] Moral absolutism, by contrast, implies that a given feature, quality or ability of an individual is either acceptable in every case or in none.[40] Nietzsche adopts as his own the noble mode of valuation or moral perspectivism, as Nehamas calls it, which assumes that the value of a given feature, quality, passion or drive is not fixed once and for all, but is only determined by its setting or context. Like the novelist inventing a character, the Nietzschean artist of life does not disown or eliminate any given character trait, but freely exploits each one in the process of self-creation.

It is partly this rejection of moral dogmatism, Nehamas argues, that makes it possible for Nietzsche to advocate life as a literary practice. He brings Nietzsche's model of life as literature into close alliance with the idea of the eternal recurrence, which, he claims, Nietzsche formulates not as a cosmological doctrine, but as a test one applies to oneself to determine whether one has succeeded in organising one's life to achieve the formal unity and coherence demanded by the literary model.[41] Nehamas believes that living life as a literary composition entails nothing more (or less) than weaving together the discordant parts of one's contingent, inessential self into a unified and unique whole that one could affirm eternally.[42] He takes the ability to affirm the eternal recurrence as the measure of one's success in achieving aesthetic integration.[43] "The eternal recurrence is not," he asserts, "a theory of the world but a view of the ideal life. It holds that a life is justified only if one would want to have the same life one already had, since, as the will to power shows, no other life can ever be possible. The eternal recurrence therefore holds that our life is justified only if we fashion it in such a way that we would want it to be exactly as it had been already."[44]

Only a life lived as a literary narrative, Nehamas argues, could meet the test of the eternal recurrence. It is the literary text conceived of as a perfect organic unity, he claims, that supplies Nietzsche with his model of the artistic self. In the teaching of the eternal recurrence, then, Nietzsche assimilates the ideal person to an ideal literary character and the ideal life to an ideal story.[45] Just as nothing is superfluous or inconsequential in the perfect literary narrative, so the test of the eternal recurrence is meant to determine whether one affirms every aspect of one's life as an integral, essential part of the whole. Similarly, just as every detail about a literary character is equally essential, so individuals who apply the test of the eternal recurrence aim to construct a narrative of self in which each fragment and "accident" is woven into a definitive whole that they would not wish to be otherwise. To meet the test of the eternal recurrence means shaping one's life and actions like a literary character, an "object so organised that every single part of it is equally essential and in which, therefore, any alteration would bring about a breakdown of the whole."[46] According to Nehamas, therefore, the great life lived *as* literature deserves the epithet "great literature" not because of its specific content, but because it is "internally coherent and highly organised," because, in other words, it measures up to certain purely formal qualities.[47] To want the eternal recurrence of the same, he asserts, presupposes that "I have assembled all that I have done and all that has led to it into a whole so unified that nothing can be removed without that whole crumbling down. Being, for Nietzsche, is that which one does not *want* to be otherwise."[48]

Nehamas smuggles in one further criterion into his conception of Nietzschean self-fashioning—that is, that the literary life should not only be organised and coherent, such that the alteration of one part would essentially transform the whole, but that it should be *radically unique* or *original*. Nietzsche, he argues, eschews a positive moral code on the grounds that just as no code or set of rules can guide an artist in the creation of a radically new genre of art, equally no set of rules can guide one in becoming incomparable:

> A true individual is precisely one who is *different from the rest of the world*, and there is no formula, no set of rules, no code of conduct . . . no principles that we can follow in order to become, as Nietzsche wants us to become, *unique*. On the contrary, *it is by breaking the rules that such a goal* . . . *can ever be reached*. And it as impossible to specify in advance the rules that must be broken for the process to succeed as it is, say, to specify in advance the conventions that must be violated for a new and innovative genre in music or literature to be established.[49]

However, for Nietzsche himself in contrast to Nehamas's Nietzsche, there simply is no logical entailment that radical artistic originality and its rule breaking is necessary to passing the test of the eternal recurrence. It is logically possible for one to wish for the repetition of one's life exactly as it was regardless of whether or not it managed to be as different from every other person's life as neoclassical painting is from abstract expressionism. The testing of the self that Nietzsche's doctrine of the eternal recurrence enacts is not a test of one's radical originality. Nehamas, it seems, has smuggled into his formalistic conception of self-fashioning a substantive criterion of radical originality that derives from nineteenth-century aesthetic modernism.[50] Nehamas's addition of aesthetic originality to the criteria of Nietzschean self-fashioning has important repercussions on how we understand Nietzsche's work of the self, and we shall return to this issue in the following chapter when we consider Foucault's reconceptualisation of aesthetic self-fashioning.

Indeed, Nehamas tendentiously suggests that the eternal recurrence hinges on the question of whether one would want to repeat all that one *did*, or, as he puts it tautologically, "all of *my* doings as *my* own."[51] However, this emphasis leaves aside the more difficult and troubling side of the stance that the affirmation of the eternal return demands—that is, the self must be willing to will the return of all the accidents of existence, the sufferings and losses over which it had no control, to will the return, in short, of precisely that which it did not author or authorise.[52] "It signifies," as Staten puts it, "my ability to want my life . . . insofar as the world impinges on *me*, insofar as it is hard for *me* to swallow, to be repeated just as [it is]."[53] In *The Gay Science*, Nietzsche considers a version of self-fashioning similar to Nehamas's concept of the self constantly reweaving its self-narrative to integrate all the events of its life into a well-organised and coherent pattern in which nothing that happens is contingent or inessential. But he does so only to suggest that we should not form too high a valuation of this dexterity. Indeed, he implies that such dexterity may simply be a consoling rationalisation. Nietzsche contends that "we" face our hardest test after we have reached a high point in our existence and have "faced up to the beautiful chaos of existence and denied it all providential reason."[54] At this high point in life, he says, we are tempted by the idea that providence or a designing hand is at work organising our lives into a beautiful pattern. What makes such an idea seductive to us is precisely our own literary facility, a facility which Nehamas thinks defines Nietzschean self-fashioning:

> For it is only now that the idea of personal providence confronts us with the most penetrating force, and the best advocate, the evidence of our eyes speaks for it—now that we can see how palpably always everything that happens to us turns out for the best. Every day, every hour, life *seems* again to have no other wish than to prove that proposition again and again. Whatever it is, bad weather or good, the loss of a friend, sickness, slander, the failure of some letter to arrive, the spraining of an ankle, a glance into a shop, a counter-argument, the opening of a book, a dream, a fraud—either immediately or very soon after it proves to be something that "must not be missing"; it has profound significance for *us*.[55]

Nietzsche beautifully summarises here the essence of the model of life as literature, which turns on the idea that self-fashioning means "accepting everything we have done . . . and blending into a perfectly coherent whole" such that every single detail is essential and must not, as Nietzsche puts it, be missing.[56] Nietzsche argues that this facility in weaving a coherent, integrated narrative about ourselves might tempt us to abandon our faith in the Epicurean gods who are indifferent to our fate and embrace the Christian notion of providential design.[57] Instead of giving way to this temptation, he suggests, we should "rest content with the supposition that our own practical and theoretical skill in interpreting and arranging events has now reached its high point."[58] If Nietzsche left matters at this point, we might have a prime facie case for thinking that Nehamas's literary model accurately elaborates some aspects of his notion of self-fashioning. However, Nietzsche immediately throws this interpretation of self-fashioning into doubt with the following observation:

> *Nor should we conceive too high an opinion of this dexterity of our wisdom* when at times we are surprised by the wonderful harmony created by the playing of our

instrument. . . . Indeed, now and then *someone plays with us*—good old chance; now and then *chance guides our hand*, and the wisest providence could not think up a more beautiful music than that which our *foolish* hand produces then.[59]

Nietzsche here diminishes the significance of the subject's ex post facto rationalisations of the contingent events that shape its life, an art that Nehamas assumes exhausts the practice of self-fashioning. "To become who you are" in the sense Nietzsche intends, Nehamas claims, "is to be engaged in a constantly continuing and continually broadening process of the appropriation of one's experiences and actions, of enlarging the capacity for assuming responsibility for oneself which Nietzsche calls 'freedom.'"[60] Provocatively, but accurately, Ansell-Pearson suggests that Nehamas's portrait of Nietzsche lacks any appreciation of the anxieties Nietzsche felt and expressed about the possibilities of self-creation. What Nehamas offers instead, he observes, "[Is] a classic, archetypal account of the artist of genius, the figure who is in control, who is master of his own destiny, and who is able to construct for himself a coherent identity in the absence of a stable 'metaphysical' self."[61] According to Ansell-Pearson, Nietzsche airs his doubts about this project in the 1886 *Prefaces* where he assumes a mocking tone of self-parody regarding his own heroic efforts of self-overcoming. Nehamas glosses over this problem by placing the accent of self-fashioning on the narrative appropriation and organisation of all "that I have done" into a coherent whole.[62]

Nietzsche's positive views, Nehamas concludes, amount to the abstract view that one should strive to become a unified, consistent and unique whole, but the actual content of that whole remains radically indeterminate. For the artist of life, just as there is no single genre or style of great art, Nehamas reasons, there is also "*no* single type of life that can be commended or damned."[63] Since what counts as a great artwork, the elements of which it is composed, and the manner in which they are linked together are all radically indeterminate, Nietzsche therefore cannot "commend any general view of conduct that can apply to everyone and also be specific and interesting."[64]

Assuming for the moment that Nietzsche does adopt such a literary framework as the model of an ideal life, Nehamas is then confronted with the issue of the "immorality" of Nietzschean aestheticism. He very briefly examines the collision between his literary model and moral judgements. We can understand the conflict Nehamas confronts by teasing out the implications of treating the self as an integrated text or narrative. What counts in our evaluation of literary characters, Nehamas argues, is a purely formal factor—their organisation into a perfect unity—and not the content of their actions.[65] By applying this literary model of character to life, Nietzsche separates out the formal question of whether one has composed all of one's disparate qualities and drives into a perfect style from the issue of the moral content of one's actions. From the aesthetic point of view, what matters is whether one's actions fit into or perfectly express one's character; for Nietzsche, it seems, it is this criterion *alone* that determines a person's worth. As we evaluate literary characters, Nehamas claims, so the Nietzschean aestheticist evaluates life: "virtue does not depend on what one does but on whether what one does is an expression of one's whole self."[66] In the art of living, then, the self is solely concerned with its own coherence and unity.

At this point, Nehamas develops several arguments to downplay the significance of possible moral objections to this model of living well. In the first place, he does so by leaning on Kaufmann's classic defence of Nietzsche's humanism. Nietzsche's critique of moral absolutism, Nehamas suggests, consistently rejects the Calliclean view that we must give our impulses, whatever they are, free rein; rather, his view simply enables individuals to exploit *all* of their passions rather than excising some of them on the "false" assumption that they are essentially immoral. In this respect, he claims, Nietzsche's "ideal character is a master of moderation."[67] Indeed, like Kaufmann he attempts to associate Nietzschean self-making with Freud's concept of sublimation, though it should be noted that Nehamas supplies nothing in the way of an elaboration of what is, after all, an essentially contested concept in psychoanalytic literature.[68]

Instead, he links Nietzschean moderation with the aesthetics of classicism. Nehamas quotes from Nietzsche's *Nachlass* to define this moderation; it amounts to possessing "*all* the strong, seemingly contradictory gifts and desires—but in such a way that they go together beneath one yoke."[69] According to Nehamas, then, "[t]o be beyond good and evil is to combine all of one's features and qualities, whatever their traditional moral value, into a controlled and coherent whole."[70] However, his appeal to "moderation" simply sidesteps the issue. Because Nehamas defines "moderation" in strictly formal terms, it does not preclude the commission of acts that otherwise might be excluded by moral judgements, as long as these acts are done with sufficient style and as the expression of a well-organised self. It is precisely the evasion of this crucial point that leads exasperated critics of such a "troublingly formalistic" approach to rhetorically ask, "What would a stylish rape look like?"[71] Nor, it should be noted, does Nehamas clarify exactly how this kind of moderation fits with the modernist ethos of breaking with all past conventions that, as we have seen, he smuggles into the notion of self-fashioning.

Although Nehamas attempts to sidestep the moral critique of aestheticism through this invocation of moderation, ultimately he recognises that if formal, aesthetic criteria are the only basis of one's judgements then it is perfectly possible for one to esteem a character despite its "immorality." In this respect, Nehamas refers to the literary villains Richard III, Fagin, Don

Giovanni, Fyodor Karamazov and Charlus, and claims that the fact that we admire such artistically perfect characters regardless of the actual content of their actions is the best argument for Nietzsche's view that a person's character is important to us independent of their moral qualities:

> In their case we freely place our moral scruples in the background. What concerns us about them is the overall manner of their behaviour, the very structure of their minds, and not primarily the content of their actions. . . . Once again, literature emerges as the model behind Nietzsche's view of the importance of character and the nature of the self. Because organisation is the most crucial feature of literary characters, the quality of their actions is secondary: the significance and nature of a character's action is inseparable from its place in that organisation.[72]

If one applies aesthetic principles not just to literary figures, but to oneself and others, he admits, then it is perfectly possible to applaud even "evil" characters since one's eye is trained exclusively on the "unity" and "coherence" of the character in question, and not their "moral" worth. Blurring the boundaries between text and life means embracing an immoralism that gives priority to aesthetic considerations over moral concerns.[73] Among the many possible types of characters that one might esteem for their unity and coherence, he concedes, some may exhibit scant concern for the welfare of others. "The totally integrated person [Nietzsche] so admires," he acknowledges, "may well be morally repulsive."[74] Nehamas thus recognises that pure aesthetic judgements of form do not coincide with our conventional moral "scruples."

Nehamas responds to moral problems of the radical formalism he attributes to Nietzsche by falling back on ad hominem speculations: "I think Nietzsche realises that his framework is compatible with more types of life than he himself would be willing to praise," but this he assures us "is a risk he is willing to take."[75] Nehamas's point seems to be that despite deploring certain character types, Nietzsche remained committed to a literary model of life that does not always fit these personal preferences. He suggests that while Nietzsche could have found reasons to "*condemn*" many "vicious lives" he does not do so simply because his attention is not focused on this issue but on "the formidable problem of constructing a single type that falls within it."[76] Nehamas does not (and cannot) tell us which characters Nietzsche personally censured, nor can he adduce any grounds from within the aestheticist perspective for drawing such distinctions. And in the absence of Nietzsche's comments, Nehamas confesses that he does not know how we might overcome this apparent lacuna in his thinking and accomplish the task of ruling out "immoral" lives on grounds that remain compatible with the aesthetic orientation to life.[77]

Nehamas's recourse to the rhetoric of condemnation strikes an odd, discordant note, drawing as it does on the semantic resources of a moral discourse that his perspectivism explicitly disavows. Moreover, if the eternal re-currence is the principal test of the artistic life, then one must ask whether, or in what sense, it remains possible to "condemn" another person's life, since the testing of the self that the eternal recurrence enacts can only be un-dertaken and answered in the first person. In other words, *unlike* whether or not a literary character's actions "fit together into a coherent, self-sustaining, well-motivated whole," whether a life passes the test of the eternal recur-rence is a matter that only individuals who enact this test on their own life decide, and it therefore excludes third-person judgements.[78] If the eternal recurrence is the test of an ideal life then individuals can only applaud or condemn their *own* life, since the issue is decided by whether they could want this life again, not whether others find it worthy. If individuals are "crushed" by the thought of the eternal recurrence, they are so because of their *own* judgement that they could not bear its repetition, not by the judgements of others.

Recognising his failure on this score, Nehamas appends the weaker argu-ment that constructing a life that passes the test of the eternal recurrence is an extremely difficult task, and therefore not *every* vicious person would sat-isfy it. To learn that only a few vicious characters are sufficiently perfect in their self-organisation to meet with Nehamas's [Nehamas's Nietzsche's] ap-proval, would, one suspects, prove cold comfort to their victims. However, such facetious observations aside, Nehamas's claim once again leans on theoretical assumptions that his formalism explicitly disavows.

In the first place, if he is correct, then using the literary trope to evaluate life means that what counts as "vicious" is exclusively context dependent. "Nietzsche generalises the relatively uncontroversial point that no artistic feature is in itself beautiful or ugly," as Nehamas puts it, "to the radical view that *no actions or characters* . . . can be in themselves good or evil. He insists that their quality is the product of interpretation. It depends on the contri-bution they are taken to make to a whole that consists of such features that are equally devoid of value in themselves but that are construed as parts of a single complex."[79] Secondly, Nehamas once again slips into the assump-tion that the test of the eternal recurrence can function as an objective cri-terion for judging the worth of lives and practices. Yet, as has been argued, if the eternal recurrence is the principal test of Nietzsche's ideal life, then only individuals can determine for themselves whether their lives satisfy this test. If Nehamas's Nietzsche is to "condemn" "vicious" lives his case must be based on something other that the doctrine of the eternal recur-rence. Even if we overlook this criticism, however, Nehamas's claim that not every vicious life would pass the test of eternal recurrence glosses over its corollary: the difficulties of passing this test must surely apply to both "vir-tuous" and "vicious" characters alike, and so the test merely restricts the *number* of lives that count as "perfect" rather than serving to differentiate between them on substantive moral grounds. Indeed, Nehamas's argument leaves open the logical possibility that more "vicious" characters would satisfy it than "virtuous" ones.

If Nehamas's vision of Nietzschean self-fashioning is correct, it can affirm and admire "morally repulsive" lives on the grounds of their perfect "form" or "coherence." Neither his ad hominem speculations, nor his appeal to the difficulty of achieving the aesthetic ideal, enables Nehamas to defeat the claim that his formalist conception of Nietzschean self-fashioning cannot provide grounds for condemning or censuring individual actions and lives.[80]

NEHAMAS'S OEDIPAL DREAM

It remains an open question whether Nehamas develops a plausible interpretation of Nietzsche's own conception of self-cultivation. We can identify the limitations of his formalist interpretation by considering some aspects of Nietzsche's philosophy of art. Nehamas builds his notion of Nietzschean self-perfection on an anodyne, idealist and strikingly *un-Nietzschean* philosophy of art.[81] The concept of beauty or perfection that underpins Nehamas's account of self-fashioning turns on an idealist notion that judgements of beauty express a "liking" based on the form of the object without any interest based on charm or emotion.[82] If, however, we examine Nietzsche's treatment of literary characters it becomes apparent that he challenges the idealist view that their appeal lies in their pure form or organisation, and that he does not take the formal aesthetic qualities of these characters as the model for his notion of self-fashioning.

Strangely, despite his claim that Nietzsche's ideal of self-fashioning depends on a literary model, Nehamas never investigates in any detail Nietzsche's analysis of literary characters, or more precisely the tragic heroes and villains on whom he trains his critical gaze. Had he done so, he would have realised that Nietzsche attributes the appeal of such characters not to formal considerations, but to the way they pander to the spectator's narcissism. Nietzsche would surely claim that assuming spectators derive pleasure from the formal unity of Richard III or Don Giovanni's character is of a piece with the naïveté that defines all idealist aesthetics. ("If our aestheticians never weary of asserting in Kant's favor," Nietzsche jokes, "that, under the spell of beauty, one can *even* view undraped female statues 'without interest,' one may laugh a little at their expense: the experience of *artists* on this ticklish point are more 'interesting.'"[83] Art, Nietzsche insists, tickles our interest).

A brief examination of Nietzsche's analysis of these literary figures can show how it forms part of his exploration of narcissism. In *Daybreak* he attempts to explain the spectator's delight in tragic characters. Nietzsche challenges the notion that spectators derive their pleasure from the formal qualities of these literary creations (symmetry, unity, integration, and so on). Rather, he contends that the dramatic images of the heroes' reckless desire to satisfy their passion constitute a phantasised wish fulfillment. In psychoanalytic terms, tragic spectators stand to the dramatic spectacle as dreamers do to their dreams: in both cases the phantasy is a disguised fulfillment of a wish. The tragedians stage our dreams. It is the tragic characters' untrammeled will to satisfy their passion that, as Nietzsche expresses it, constitutes "the *sharpest spice* in the hot draught of this joy."[84] Nietzsche deliberately represents aesthetic spectators as gourmands or gluttons feasting on the pleasures of the spectacle in order to mark the distance between his own philosophy of art and the idealist tradition and its disinterested, passionless spectator. According to Nietzsche, it is themselves as they wish to be that spectators imbibe, so to speak, through the tragic spectacle. Illustrating his point, Nietzsche suggests that spectators take pleasure in Macbeth's willingness to risk annihilation to satisfy his raging ambition. The same is true, Nietzsche says, of Sophoclean heroes like Ajax, Philoctetes and Oedipus.[85] In his raging pursuit of majestic omnipotence, Macbeth is "royally" indifferent to the possibility of his own extinction. Spectators find his tragic fall powerfully intoxicating, he argues, precisely because it resonates with their own narcissistic desire for omnipotence, which, in its most inflamed form, is utterly heedless of self-preservation.[86]

Reframing Nietzsche's interpretation of literary characters in terms of his own philosophy of art has two significant consequences for understanding his notion of self-cultivation. In the first place, Nietzsche examines the seductiveness of tragic characters not in order to specify the formal criteria of his own model of self-fashioning, as Nehamas implies, but for the sake of explicating the psychopathologies of narcissism. Secondly, he uses his analysis of these characters' narcissism and its appeal as a source for understanding the different trajectories through which the self attempts to reclaim its narcissistic self-love. Nietzsche uses the insights of these analyses in formulating a mode of self-cultivation that aims to treat these pathologies of self-affection and their poisonous effects on the self's engagement with others. In other words, Nietzsche does not define his ideal of self-cultivation as an attempt to apply formalist aesthetic criteria to personal existence. Rather, he conceives self-cultivation as a philosophical *therapy* of the pathological forms of self-affection, some of whose forms he discovers through his psychological dissections of tragic characters and tragic spectatorship.

Nietzsche implies that it is an idealistic sleight of hand to displace the appeal of tragic characters onto their formal qualities, or to explain it in terms of the moral lessons one might read into their tragic fate. In this respect, Freud comes much closer to understanding Nietzsche's conception of the appeal of such literary figures than does Nehamas. This should not surprise us, since Nietzsche underpins his explanation with a substantive psychological thesis that challenges the idealist notion of aesthetic judgement. In his paper on narcissism, Freud claims that great literary criminals compel our interest because of a certain consistency, but he does not mean by this the formal consistency Nehamas discusses. Rather, Freud claims their appeal lies in the consistency with which such characters maintain an undiminished narcissism.[87] According to Freud, such characters are the fictional embodiment of the spectators' longing for a narcissistic condition they have reluctantly abandoned:

> [I]t seems evident that another person's narcissism has a great attraction for those who have renounced part of their own narcissism . . . even the great criminals and humorists, as they are represented in literature, compel our interest by their narcissistic consistency with which they manage to keep away from their ego anything that would diminish it. It is as if we envied them for maintaining their blissful state of mind—an unassailable libidinal position which we ourselves have since abandoned.[88]

As with Freud, however, it would be misleading to suggest that because Nietzsche recognises the seductive power of such images he therefore affirms the great criminal's blissful narcissism as the aim of self-fashioning. Rather, Nietzsche claims that the tragedian concocts such intoxicating, spicy draughts to satisfy the needs "of a restless, vigorous age which is half-drunk and stupefied by its excess of blood and energy."[89] Indeed, as we shall see, like Freud, Nietzsche uses such insights into the narcissistic sources of subjectivity to formulate the work the self can undertake on itself in order to achieve a greater degree of self-composure.

The account Nietzsche gives of tragedy and tragic spectatorship in *Daybreak* marks a dramatic shift in his philosophical orientation, a shift that demanded of him an equally radical transformation in the style, tone and tempo of his writing. Covering the same territory in *The Birth of Tragedy*, a decade earlier, Nietzsche proclaimed that the tragedian invents tragic figures to convey a metaphysical lesson about the artistic nature of the noumenal realm. Aeschylus and Sophocles create tragic heroes as shining images of the "world of phenomena," as he puts it, "in order, behind it and through its destruction to give a sense of the supreme artistic primal joy within the womb of the primal Oneness."[90] Stripped of this bombastic, quasi-Schopenhauerian metaphysics, in the middle works Nietzsche no longer concerns himself with intuiting metaphysical truths in tragedy, but with the psychology of its characters and the psychological significance of their undeniable appeal. Framing his inquiry with these concerns, Nietzsche now suggests that tragedies are symptomatic of an intoxication with images of narcissistic glory.

With this shift from metaphysical to psychological questions, Nietzsche transforms the style and tempo of his prose from the sluggish *lento* of earnest German metaphysics to the *presto* and lightness of the French aphorism and Roman satire. With this change of style, Nietzsche gives his analysis of tragic heroism a radically different cast and tenor from that which defined his early works. In the middle works, he infuses his analyses with a comic, ironical jauntiness designed to satirise both the narcissists drunk on these images of their own idealised selves, and the moralists who read into the heroes' fall nothing but stern moral lessons. ("Do you suppose," he wryly quizzes, "that Tristan and Isolde are preaching *against* adultery when they both perish by it?").[91] Nietzsche aims his jibes at both the moralist interpretation of tragedies as glorified Aesopian fables, and narcissists who gratify themselves through the hero's "exciting, changing, dangerous, gloomy and often sun-drenched existence."[92] Nietzsche, it might be said, aims to make his reader smile at the self-deceit of moralists who blind themselves to the seductive narcissism of the tragic hero, and the narcissist who becomes self-intoxicated at the sight of the hero's gloomy and sun-drenched adventures.

Recognising Nietzsche's comic style and tempo has important consequences for understanding his notion of self-fashioning, for it reveals Nietzsche as an *analyst*, rather than an *advocate*, of narcissism. In the middle works, Nietzsche is not seduced by narcissism, but performs a series of acute, satirical dissections of the processes of seduction and the many masks assumed by the longing for narcissistic bliss. These analyses form an integral part of the practice of self-cultivation he sees as necessary to cure the pathologies of narcissism.

Nehamas's attempt to duck the issue of the immoralism of an aesthetic ideal singularly misses the fact that Nietzsche approaches literary characters and models not as ideals to be emulated, but as objects of analysis from which he thinks it is possible to discover something about the psychology of narcissism and the ruses and conceits by means of which human beings conceal both their narcissistic wishes and defeats from themselves. Nietzsche does not hold up literary characters as models of unified selves or ideal figures who combine all of their features and qualities into "a controlled or coherent whole."[93] Rather, his analyses of these characters reveal the comical weakness and falseness of the notion that human beings are capable of such absolute, unimpeded self-composition and the untroubled self-knowledge that it demands.

Whereas Nehamas merely unpacks and describes the formal qualities that define a unified literary character, Nietzsche explores the broader psychological issue of why this literary model of the self as the author of its own character exercises such a powerful hold on the human imagination. By accentuating merely formal matters, Nehamas puts into the shade what Nietzsche identifies as the more pressing issue of understanding the appeal that lies in seeing oneself as the author of one's own character. To be the author of one's character, according to Nehamas, requires the self to continuously and retrospectively reintegrate whatever it has experienced as something that it authorised as essential to its identity, rather than as a contingent event that disrupted its cherished hopes, projects and dreams. In a life lived as literature, as Nehamas defines it, the self can never experience loss—whatever happens is a fulfillment of its deepest wish.

According to Nietzsche, by contrast, the idea that we freely compose ourselves is a deceit borne of the wish to experience oneself as the powerful, masterful executor of our own fate. Nietzsche draws on the Oedipal myth to make this case:

> You are willing to assume responsibility for everything! Except that is for your dreams! What miserable weakness, what lack of consistent courage! Nothing is *more* your own than your dreams! Nothing *more* your own work! Content, form, duration, performer, spectator—in these *comedies* you are all of this yourself! And it is precisely here that you rebuff and are ashamed of yourselves, even Oedipus, the wise Oedipus derived consolation from the thought that we cannot help what we dream! From this I conclude that the great majority of mankind must be conscious of having abominable dreams. . . . Do I have to add that the wise Oedipus was right, that we are really not responsible for our dreams—but just as much for our waking life, and that the doctrine of freedom of the will has human pride and the feeling of power [*Machtgefühl*] for its father and mother?[94]

Nietzsche here conceives the dreamer as analogous to the figure of Oedipus, and the dream itself as analogous to a tragicomic artwork. Nietzsche's cheerfully satirical gaze reveals the comedy of this Oedipal dreamer. According to Nietzsche, dreamers deceive themselves by disavowing what is *most* themselves, their *abscheuerlicher Träume*, which in Oedipus' case is the dream of becoming his own father and possessing his mother's body. Nietzsche adds the following paradoxical twist to this comic self-deception: one is not responsible for what is most one's own either in dreaming *or* waking life. Nietzsche claims that by attributing the power of self-composition or auto-genesis to ourselves, conceiving of ourselves as both mother and father to ourselves, so to speak, we engage in a comic, childish self-inflation designed to satisfy our *Machtgefühl*.

For Nietzsche, then, the desire to be one's own author, or one's own father, as it were, cannot be severed from its psychological roots in the narcissistic desire to experience oneself as omnipotent. To satisfy its narcissistic desire the self attempts to avoid anything impinging on it by imagining that it authorises everything that happens to it. It thus experiences itself as an utterly self-sufficient, self-propelling wheel. By opening onto this psychological analysis of the dream of self-authorship, Nietzsche suggests that its connections with pathological phenomena might not simply be the contingent relation that Nehamas would like us to believe. Rather, if Nietzsche is right in his analysis of Macbeth and Oedipus, the goal of being the author of one's own character is fuelled by the desire for omnipotence, and this desire can easily generate a murderous rage against all that threatens the illusory feeling of omnipotence, the resistant, independent "not-me" world of others.

Indeed, according to Nietzsche, it is precisely this narcissistic dream of omnipotence that generates a series of intersubjective pathologies: melancholia, revenge, and that kind of pity in which the self demotes everyone to "last place" in order to avoid any one disputing its claim to "first place."[95] For both Nietzsche and Freud, narcissism in its *fullest sense*, as Staten rightly points out, "encompasses the whole field of libidinal economy: the transit of libido through other selves, aggression, infliction and reception of pain, and something very much like death."[96] Nietzsche conceives self-cultivation as a treatment for these pathological expressions of the desire for narcissistic wholeness or plenitude.

In sum, Nehamas's construal of self-fashioning confuses what is in essence a psychological theory of the subject and its treatment, with a literary model. In doing so, he fails to capture two of the most important aspects of Nietzsche's understanding of the self in the middle works: (1) Nietzsche's psychological claim that the dream of self-composition is symptomatic of a desire for narcissistic plenitude, and (2) his conception of self-cultivation as a therapeutic response to the pathological affects or emotions that are borne of narcissistic loss. According to Nietzsche, it is the failure to treat this loss, or to cultivate oneself, that generates a range of pathological intersubjective phenomena, phenomena through which the ego consoles and compensates itself for its losses. How one bears narcissistic loss, Nietzsche claims, has profound implications for the dynamics and possibilities of social intercourse, and he identifies self-cultivation as a therapy that tempers these pathological excesses. He sees self-cultivation as a means of overcoming the pathological forms of intersubjectivity in which the self engages with others exclusively for the sake of alleviating itself of painful affects of narcissistic loss.

Finally, then, Nehamas's model fails to see how Nietzsche conceives self-fashioning *not* as a narrowly private, individualistic project, but as a means of refashioning and modulating the affects that shape the self's relationships with others. Nehamas correctly observes that Nietzsche does not propose a positive moral code, but he wrongly infers from this that his concern with self-fashioning has no ethical or intersubjective implications. For, according to Nietzsche, it is the affects that derive from our narcissistic losses, rather than formal codes, that dominate the self's manner of relating to others. The work the self undertakes on itself must therefore stand at the centre of Nietzsche's ethics. By restricting the scope of self-fashioning to formalist aesthetic concerns Nehamas's model blinds us to Nietzsche's analysis of the affective structures of subjectivity, our "nature as a moving sphere of *moods*," as Nietzsche puts it, and to his claim that it is the manner in which one interprets and works on these affects that fundamentally shapes the structure and dynamics of the self's intercourse with others.[97] Nehamas's exclusively literary conception of the self thus fails to recognise that for Nietzsche self-cultivation entails working on how the self plays out its affects in and through its relationships with others. For Nietzsche, in short, self-fashioning also refashions the affective basis—pity, rage, envy, anger and so on—of the self's relations with others.

The philosophical and conceptual sources of Nietzsche's ideal of self-cultivation do not lie in idealist formalism or its offshoots such as the aesthetic modernist's obsession with formal innovations, but, as we shall see in chapter 4, in a very different tradition. In his penetrating critique of Nehamas, James Conant foreshadows this point by claiming that Nietzsche seeks to revive the central preoccupation of Hellenistic and Roman philosophy: its ethical concern with the formation of character.[98]

NOTES

1. Walter Kaufmann, *Nietzsche: Philosopher, Psychologist, Antichrist*, 1974, Princeton University Press, Princeton, N.J., 418.

2. Alexander Nehamas, *The Art of Living: Socratic Reflections from Plato to Foucault*, 1998, University of California Press, Berkeley, 1–2.

3. Ibid., 2.

4. SE, 136.

5. SE, 193, 188.

6. SE, 190.

7. SE, 184. See Diogenes Laertius, *Lives of Eminent Philosophers*, vol. II, translated by R. D. Hicks, 1931, Harvard University Press, Cambridge, Mass., VII, 5–6, 10–11.

8. Pierre Hadot, *What Is Ancient Philosophy?*, op. cit., 100–101.

9. Ibid., 176.

10. SE, 134.

11. SE, 137. Nietzsche's reflections on the antinomy of freedom have been the subject of much dispute. For an overview of this debate see Tamsin Shaw, *Nietzsche's Political Skepticism*, op.cit., chs. 4 and 5.

12. SE, 131.

13. On this issue see also, Martha C. Nussbaum, "The Cult of Personality," *The New Republic*, January 4 and 11, 1999, 32–37.

14. Alexander Nehamas, *The Art of Living*, op. cit., 11.

15. Ibid., 6.

16. Ibid.

17. Ibid., 7.

18. Ibid., 8.

19. Ibid., 7.
20. Ibid., 7–8.
21. Ibid., 7–8.
22. SE, 136.
23. SE, 136–37, emphasis added. Cf R. Lanier Anderson and Joshua Landy, "Philosophy as Self-Fashioning, Alexander Nehamas's Art of Living," *Diacritics*, Spring 2001, 25–54. Following Nehamas, they argue that we should see Nietzsche as a philosophical self-fashioner whose goal was to achieve "by means of writing, a coherent persona which [stood] above and apart from the intractable features of [his] everyday self"; 37. Judging by Nietzsche's statement here, however, he thought that we could only construct a philosophically significant persona through our actions and that philosophy is precisely a practice for working on and transforming our everyday self and conduct, not the construction of an exclusively literary or fictive persona that is independent of lived practice. As we have seen, Nietzsche would be mortified by the aestheticist idea that in practising philosophy we aim to construct a textual/authorial persona and that we value this literary persona over and above our actual moral conduct. We might concede, therefore, "that when we nowadays use the name Nietzsche, we almost always mean the postulated author Nietzsche, rather than, or in addition to, the illness-ridden former Basel professor" (37). But from Nietzsche's perspective this fact does not demonstrate that aim of philosophical self-fashioning is to be "consubstantial" with an authorial persona; it merely testifies to the fact that modern philosophy has forgotten the absolute priority the Greco-Roman tradition gave to exemplary practice as the goal and measure of the philosophical art of living.
24. SE, 139.
25. SE, 135.
26. UM2, 85.
27. SE, 187.
28. Hadot elaborates this Stoic distinction between philosophical discourse and philosophy itself. See Pierre Hadot, *Philosophy as a Way of Life*, op. cit., 266–67.
29. Alexander Nehamas, *The Art of Living*, op. cit., 10.
30. SE, 133.
31. Alexander Nehamas, *Nietzsche: Life as Literature*, 1985, Harvard University Press, Cambridge, Mass., 194.
32. Ibid., 195.
33. Ibid., 195.
34. Ibid., 136.
35. Ibid., 136, emphasis added.
36. Ibid., 167.
37. See, for example, Nehamas's discussion of the purpose of Nietzsche's critique of asceticism: "What Nietzsche eventually comes to attack directly is not any particular judgement but the very tendency to make general judgements about the value of life"; Alexander Nehamas, *Nietzsche: Life as Literature*, op. cit., 135.
38. Ibid., 214, emphasis added.
39. Ibid., 215. Nehamas comments in this context that Nietzsche admires the nobles *because* they do not think the "base" should act in the way they themselves act; they are thus apparently good perspectivists refusing to give credence to the selfish demand that everyone act as they do. But this surely glosses over the fact that for

these fictitious nobles, the question of how the "base" should or should not act is simply irrelevant since they treat them as mere instruments to be used, destroyed or devoured. It also ignores the counter-argument, developed by Nussbaum among others, that Nietzsche does not in fact celebrate these nobles at all. See Martha Nussbaum, "Pity and Mercy: Nietzsche's Stoicism," in Richard Schacht (ed.), *Nietzsche, Genealogy, Morality: Essays on Nietzsche's Genealogy of Morals*, 1994, University of California Press, Berkeley, 139–67, esp. 166, fn. 44.

40. Ibid., 215.

41. In his notebooks Nietzsche devotes considerable space and energy to various proofs of the eternal recurrence, but, apart from one minor and oblique exception in *Zarathustra*, Nietzsche chose not to publish any of these proofs. Robin Small points out that the basic argument of the attempted proof appear in *Zarathustra*, "On the Three Evils"; see Robin Small, "Three Interpretations of Eternal Recurrence," *Dialogue* XXII, 1983, 91–112, 96. For contrasting views on the significance of Nietzsche's decision to exclude such proofs from his published works for our understanding the nature of the doctrine of the eternal recurrence, see Bernd Magnus, *Nietzsche's Existential Imperative*, 1978, Indiana University Press, Bloomington; and Rüdiger Safranski, *Nietzsche: A Philosophical Biography*, op. cit.

42. Alexander Nehamas, *Nietzsche: Life as Literature*, op. cit., 136.

43. Ibid., 190–91. Following a "deconstructionist" approach, Gary Shapiro challenges Nehamas's claim that Nietzsche intends the thought of eternal recurrence to inspire self-integration. He criticises Nehamas for applying a conception of texts as organically unified to Nietzsche's notion of identity; see Gary Shapiro, *Nietzschean Narratives*, 1989, Indiana University Press, Bloomington, 86–96.

44. Ibid., 7, and ch. 5.

45. Ibid., 165.

46. Ibid., 136.

47. Ibid., 197.

48. Ibid., 191.

49. Ibid., 225, emphasis added.

50. In a later work Nehamas distinguishes two different conceptions of self-fashioning, between Montaigne who, at home in his world, does not believe that fashioning himself requires an agonistic struggle against his own culture and its "table of values," and Nietzsche who believes that such agon is a sine qua non of self-composition. "Montaigne's example," Nehamas writes, "shows that the project of fashioning the self does not necessarily require the opposition that Nietzsche and Foucault may have considered essential to it. To fashion a self, to become an individual, one has to do something that is both significant and very different from whatever has been done before. But that need not be accomplished only by objecting to the tenor of one's time"; Alexander Nehamas, *The Art of Living*, op. cit., 183.

51. Alexander Nehamas, *Nietzsche: Life as Literature*, op. cit., 190, emphasis added.

52. On this point, see also Robin Small's sharp critique of Nehamas's interpretation of Nietzsche, "Nietzsche and Time Consciousness," unpublished paper (with author's permission), 13–14.

53. Henry Staten, *Nietzsche's Voice*, 1990, Cornell University Press, Ithaca, N.Y., 76.

54. GS, 277.

55. GS, 277, emphasis added.

56. Alexander Nehamas, *Nietzsche: Life as Literature*, op. cit., 188–89.

57. On the Epicurean gods, see Lucretius, *On the Nature of the Universe*, translated by R. E. Latham, 1951, Penguin, Harmondsworth, UK.

58. GS, 277.

59. GS, 277, emphasis added. It should be noted too that in conceptualising the notion of self-fashioning here Nietzsche develops an analogy between *musical improvisation* and self-making, rather than between *novel writing* and self-making. Undoubtedly, as with many of Nietzsche's aphorisms, this metaphor of life as a risky musical improvisation taps into his personal experiences, in particular to the harsh criticisms that his "Manfred Meditation" received at the hands of the composers Hans Von Bülow and later Friedrich Hegar, both of whom pointed out that his improvisational technique, that was carried by spontaneous emotions, did not enable him to master musical composition. See Helmut Walther "Nietzsche as Composer," Lecture at a Seminar of the *Gesellschaft für kritische Philosophie* held on the weekend of October 15–17, 2000, in Kottenheide, Germany.

60. Alexander Nehamas, *Nietzsche: Life as Literature*, op. cit., 190, emphasis added.

61. Keith Ansell-Pearson, "Towards the *Übermensch*: Reflections on the Year of Nietzsche's *Daybreak*," *Nietzsche-Studien* 23, 1994, 123–45, 145.

62. Alexander Nehamas, *Nietzsche: Life as Literature*, op. cit., 190.

63. Ibid., 190.

64. Ibid., 229.

65. Ibid., 193–94.

66. Ibid., 166.

67. Ibid., 221.

68. Alexander Nehamas, *The Art of Living*, op. cit. 139.

69. Ibid., 139.

70. Alexander Nehamas, *Nietzsche: Life as Literature*, op. cit., 227.

71. Terry Eagleton, *The Ideology of the Aesthetic*, 1990, Basil Blackwell, Oxford, 394.

72. Alexander Nehamas, *Nietzsche: Life as Literature*, op. cit., 193–95.

73. Thomas Mann's poignant critique of Nietzsche's elevation of aesthetic over ethical concerns remains the *locus classicus* of this argument; see Thomas Mann, "Nietzsche's Philosophy in the Light of Recent History," from *Last Essays*, translated by Richard and Clara Winston and Tania and James Stern, 1959, Alfred A. Knopf, New York, 141–77.

74. Alexander Nehamas, *Nietzsche: Life as Literature*, op. cit., 167.

75. Ibid., 167.

76. Ibid., 167, emphasis added.

77. Ibid., 167.

78. Ibid., 166. In GS, Nietzsche stresses that this test takes place in one's loneliest loneliness, and is set by a *daimon*, modeled on the Greek idea of the *daimon* not as a separate and distinct being, but rather as an "other *self*." On the importance of the Greek notion of the *daimon* to the thought of the eternal recurrence, see Robin Small, "Three Interpretations of Eternal Recurrence," op. cit., esp. 102–3.

79. Alexander Nehamas, *Nietzsche: Life as Literature*, op. cit., 230, emphasis added.

80. In a later essay Nehamas briefly attempts to address the moral issues raised by his own brand of Nietzschean aestheticism. He does so by examining whether or not his position might supply reasons for rejecting the "evil hero." Are there "Nietzschean"

grounds, he asks, for rejecting "the great individual who still, by any reasonable standard, may be a completely unacceptable human being"? He answers this question in the affirmative. Reduced to its essentials, his argument seems to be as follows:

(1) Noble souls have duties only to their peers.
(2) In some cases, however, our peers include every other individual.
(3) Therefore in such circumstances we have a duty to every person.

However, it does seem that Nehamas's first premise is extraneous to the aestheticist perspective that he originally outlined in *Life as Literature*. Within Nietzsche's aesthetic formalism, as he conceives it, whether one has a "duty" to another depends entirely on whether or not the action it entails fits into the singular "literary" unity one is attempting to construct, and nothing at all to do with the merit, value or status of the other person. After all, from Nehamas's literary perspective, Don Giovanni remains an admirable character even as he betrays his peers in the pursuit of sexual conquest. As Nehamas was at pains to establish, for the Nietzschean aestheticist *"who"* performs a deed rather than the content or moral quality of that deed is the *only* source of value. See Alexander Nehamas, "Nietzsche and 'Hitler,'" *The Southern Journal of Philosophy* XXXVII, Supplement, 1999, 1–17.

81. For an excellent, if highly critical, resumé of the different philosophies of art Nietzsche develops across the early, middle and late periods, see Julian Young, *Nietzsche's Philosophy of Art*, 1993, Cambridge University Press, New York. In what follows, we are primarily concerned with the grounds on which he criticises idealist aesthetics in the middle period.

82. See Immanuel Kant, *The Critique of Judgement*, translated, with an Introduction, by Werner S. Pluhar, with a foreword by Mary J. Gregor, 1987, Hackett Publishing Company, Indianapolis and Cambridge, §1–5, especially §2, "The Liking That Determines a Judgement of Taste Is Devoid of All Interest" (hereafter CJ).

83. GM, Bk 3, 6.

84. D, 240.

85. D, 240.

86. Among psychoanalysts, Heinz Kohut comes closest to this Nietzschean perspective:

> The art of the tragic . . . is concerned with man's attempt to live out the pattern of his nuclear self. . . . Surrounded by the incessant flux of the human condition, confronted by the necessity of admitting the impermanence of all things dear to him, compelled finally to acknowledge the finiteness of individual existence not only in the abstract but also as it concerns his own beloved self, man comes closest to narcissistic fulfillment when he is able to realise the pattern of his most central self. The effacement or death of the tragic hero is thus not an accidental occurrence. Its essential meaning is not to be seen as a punishment for a code-transgressing deed, which sets in motion the pattern of guilt and retribution. It is instead a necessary component of the hero's achievement, for it is only in death that the hero's narcissistic fulfillment attains permanence. The survivors weep about the hero's fate, but the raised body of the hero . . . is admired as the symbol of the hero's narcissistic triumph which, through his death, has now become absolute.

See, Heinz Kohut, "On Courage" in *Self Psychology and the Humanities: Reflections on a New Psychoanalytic Approach*, 1985, W. W. Norton & Co., New York, 5–50, 37–38.

87. In her brilliant discussion of Plato and Freud's critique of art as a "pseudo-cure," Iris Murdoch captures Freud's nonformalist, psychological theory of art: "One of the subtleties of Freud's definition [of art] is that it is indifferent to the 'formal value' of the art work, since what is really active and really attractive is the concealed fantasy"; see Iris Murdoch, *The Fire and the Sun: Why Plato Banished the Artists*, 1977, Oxford University Press, Oxford, 42, 40.

88. ON, 83. We shall examine Freud's seemingly odd conception of the humorist as a narcissist in chapter 5.

89. D, 240; see also BT, 22.

90. BT, 22.

91. D, 240.

92. D, 240.

93. Nehamas, *Nietzsche: Life as Literature*, op. cit., 227.

94. D, 128. Cf GM and TI on the birth of the doctrine of freedom of the will from the spirit of *ressentiment*.

95. Jean-Jacques Rousseau, *Émile*, translated by Barbara Foxley, 1974, Dent, London, 187.

96. Henry Staten, *Nietzsche's Voice*, op. cit., 98–99.

97. HAH1, 376; In a later essay, Nehamas briefly makes a related point, but he does so only in passing: "Nietzsche is perfectly aware that in making something out of oneself, even if one tries to do so in the most private of terms, one also changes . . . what many others will think and do as well. . . . What we take ourselves to be is essentially connected to how we propose to treat one another: the public and private intermix and philosophy, for better or worse, often has political implications"; see Alexander Nehamas, "Nietzsche, Aestheticism and Modernity" in Bernd Magnus and Kathleen M. Higgins (eds.), *The Cambridge Companion to Nietzsche*, 1996, Cambridge University Press, Cambridge and New York, 238.

98. James Conant, "Nietzsche's Perfectionism: A Reading of *Schopenhauer as Educator*," in Richard Schacht (ed.), *Nietzsche's Postmoralism: Essays on Nietzsche's Prelude to Philosophy's Future*, 2001, Cambridge University Press, Cambridge, 181–257. Conant dates this turn to Hellenistic and specifically Roman conceptions of self-cultivation as early as 1874, and certainly he develops a compelling case for interpreting the third untimely meditation, *Schopenhauer as Educator*, along these lines.

2

Senecan Moods: Foucault and Nietzsche on the Art of the Self

> It is well known that self-examination and the guidance of conscience was widespread among . . . the Stoics and the Epicureans as a means of daily taking stock of the good or evil performed in regard to one's duties. . . . *The guidance of conscience* was also predominant in certain cultured circles, *but as advice given . . . in particularly difficult circumstances: in mourning, or when one was suffering a setback.*
>
> Foucault[1]

In this epigraph, taken from a lecture he gave during the early stages of his research into the practices of the self, we find Foucault, the archaeologist of culture, at work excavating and reconstructing the fragments of the Hellenistic practices of the self. What he unearths beneath two millennia of Christian civilization are practices of the self that differ "radically," as he puts it, from Christian conscience-vivisection. Nor, as the epigraph makes clear, do the cultural practices of self-cultivation he pieces together from the fragments of antiquity bear much resemblance, if any, to the vain self-display and preciosity of the nineteenth-century dandy. Rather Foucault uncovers a "golden age of self-cultivation" in which individuals undertook the work of the self not in order to attain salvation from this world or aristocratic distinction within it, but as a therapy that enabled them to remain composed in the face of the sufferings and losses of mortal life.[2]

According to Didier Eribon, this excavation of the Hellenistic and Roman care of the self left an unmistakable mark on Foucault's writing style. In his last two works, Eribon notes, many of his former admirers and fellow travellers found themselves disappointed by this change of style, much as a century earlier Nietzsche's readers and erstwhile friends were alienated by the dramatic transformation that Nietzsche's own turn to Hellenistic philosophy had wrought on his style. Indeed, this parallel goes further, for Foucault's interpreters describe his stylistic shift in almost identical terms to those that Nietzsche's critics had employed to define his transformation from disciple of Dionysus to sober positivist. Foucault's interpreters, Eribon reports, contrasted the "fiery" style of his early works with the calm, dispassionate, "sober" style of his late research on antiquity.[3] Eribon claims that the style of Foucault's life and work in his last years bears testimony to the extent to which he assimilated Stoicism, especially in its Senecan moods:

> It is as if approaching death and the foreboding he had of it for several months had led Foucault onto the path of serenity. Seneca, whose works were among his favorite reading, would have praised such a model of "the philosophical life." Foucault seemed to have internalised the ancient wisdom to such a point that it had become imposed upon his style itself—his style as a writer and his style as a man.[4]

The sober, dispassionate style of Nietzsche's middle works and Foucault's late works signpost their return to the conception of the philosophical life and practice that dominated philosophy from Epicurus to Seneca, that is to say, to the idea of philosophy as a therapy of the soul. Both turned back to the Hellenistic therapies as the question of the self, or more specifically and pressingly, of their *ego ipsissimum* took centre stage in their thinking.[5] Nietzsche in his middle works and Foucault in his last, incomplete researches both draw on the Hellenistic and Stoic traditions that analyse and treat the pathologies which threaten to arise from "setbacks" to our wishes, especially from that "most touchy point in the narcissistic system": the mortality that shadows our lives and loves and which compels us to learn how to work on ourselves and mourn our losses.[6] Toward the end of his own life, Foucault himself was evidently captivated by this motif of Greco-Roman philosophy: "That life, because of its mortality, has to be a work of art is a remarkable theme."[7]

Of course, the more common Foucault-Nietzsche discussions turn on perceived similarities or linkages in their ideas of power and knowledge, genealogy and interpretation, will and agency. Indeed, on this latter point, there is almost universal agreement that the critique of the metaphysics of subjectivity that forms the theoretical underpinning of Foucault's thinking in the 1970s largely derives from Nietzsche's genealogical analysis of the fabrication of subjectivity. The disagreements in this debate do not concern the extent of Nietzsche's influence on Foucault, but the philosophical validity and political implications of his Nietzschean-inspired critique of the "magisterial illusions of subjectivity."[8] There is also widespread agreement that in his late texts Foucault once again returns to Nietzsche, but this time to rescue a positive model of the exercise of subjectivity from his own unrelenting critique of the illusions of agency; as Keith Ansell-Pearson explains:

> [I]n his later works on ethics Foucault was to recognise that his notion of the subject as a mere effect of power constituted one of the major deficiencies in his thinking, and it was precisely to a Nietzschean *aesthetic* conception of ethics that he turned in his thinking about an alternative non-juridical model of selfhood.[9]

However, as we have noted, the shift in Foucault's philosophical orientation and style derives from a tradition that can be better understood in *therapeutic* rather than *aesthetic* terms. Foucault clouds the true nature and significance of the Hellenistic and Stoic care of the self insofar as he presents it as a purely aesthetic project akin to nineteenth-century dandyism.[10] On the other hand, if we bracket Foucault's comments glossing these practices as purely aesthetic, and examine instead his historical analyses of the care of the self we discover the clear outlines of Hellenistic philosophy and Stoicism as philosophic *therapeia* of the soul.[11] In other words, Foucault's research reveals a much richer conception of the work of the self than he can capture with this aesthetic gloss. As we shall see, it is this richer conception of the self that stands at the centre of Nietzsche's middle works. Once we suspend Foucault's misleadingly aestheticised rendering of the Hellenistic and Roman tradition, therefore, we can use his historical excavation of the practices of the self to clarify the ethics of subjectivity (or agent-centred ethics, to use analytic parlance) that lies at the heart of Nietzsche's middle works. Indeed, in his 1981–1982 lectures Foucault himself suggests in passing that it might be possible and fruitful to reread Nietzsche's thought as a difficult attempt to reconstitute the Hellenistic ethics of the self.[12] Finally, as we saw above, the care of the self addresses the psychological traumas of loss and transience, and it is for this reason that Nietzsche's renovation of this tradition can be explicated as a treatment that addresses the loss of narcissistic plenitude and its pathological manifestations, which, in one way or another, seek to restore the magisterial illusions of subjectivity.

Foucault's recuperation of the Hellenistic care of the self establishes two points that clear the way to comprehending Nietzsche's ethics of subjectivity: (1) that the Christian hostility to pagan self-love blocks our comprehension of Hellenistic ethics and continues to pervert the critical reception of its modern renovations, and (2) that the ethics of the care of the self, properly conceived, is a philosophical therapy guided by the notion that the self constitutes itself through the voluntary exercise of a range of reflexive techniques and practices oriented towards treating the affects of revenge, envy and anger. In sum, Foucault's recuperation of Hellenistic ethics clarifies both the general conception of ethical practice and some of the substantive ethical and psychological issues at stake in Nietzsche's middle works.

For our purposes, the significance of Foucault's resurrection of the Hellenistic and Roman practices of self-cultivation lies in the way he clears several obstacles that stand in the path of comprehending Nietzsche's own concern with these practices. In the first place, Foucault demonstrates the extent to which the reception of Hellenistic self-cultivation has been marred by Christian polemics against self-love, which its early theologians consider the besetting sin of all paganism. These polemics, Foucault shows, have cast a long shadow over every attempt to recover a positive notion of the work of the self on itself. In other words, one of the great merits of Foucault's excavation of the Hellenistic practices of the self lies in the way it frees the reception of this tradition from the incrustations of Christian polemics. He demonstrates that Christianity wrongly interprets Hellenistic self-cultivation as closely connected, either historically or analytically, with a "conceited ontology" that gives license to various brands of hyper-individualism.[13]

Foucault's interpretation of Hellenistic self-cultivation sets it apart from individualism understood either as a solipsistic withdrawal into the private sphere, a crude exaltation of singularity, or, as indeed Augustine saw it, an inflamed self-love that blossoms into a love of power over others.[14] According to Foucault, an intense labour of the self on itself can, as it did with the Stoics, fuse with fulfilling one's obligations to humankind, to one's fellow citizens and to a denunciation of social withdrawal.[15] Once it emerges from the shadows of Christianity, he argues, the Hellenistic tradition can be rightfully seen as a rich vein of philosophical therapy that takes as its starting point a conception of the subject as a series of reflexive spiritual and material exercises. We can then recover the remnants of a philosophical therapy, "a treasury of devices, techniques, ideas and procedures," focused on analysing how the self can work on itself in such a way that it does not rage vengefully either against the mortal losses it suffers or against those who brim with such vengefulness.[16]

It follows that if Nietzsche anchors his middle works in the Stoic tradition's intensification and valorisation of the practices of the care of the self then his ethical project must also be sundered from any necessary connections with the chain of synonyms that Augustine associates with this tradition: perverse self-love, love of domination, apostasy from God and the sin of pride.[17] If this can be established then it is also plausible that those critics who equate Nietzsche's ideal of self-cultivation with narcissistic self-involvement and/or grandiose exaltation of the self over others merely reprise Christianity's moral and hermeneutic prejudices against the Hellenistic arts of living.

Secondly, Foucault's schematic presentation of the concepts and practices of Hellenistic self-cultivation, especially his analysis of the Roman Stoics, can be used to clarify the extent to which Nietzsche takes up not just its general ethical orientation, but also its substantive conception of the work of the self.[18] Like the Hellenistic thinkers, Nietzsche conceives this ethics as a continuous, difficult and sometimes painful *labour* that the self performs on itself, rather than as a heightening of narcissistic self-preoccupation. We can measure the distance between narcissistic self-absorption and self-cultivation by the fact that both the Hellenistic thinkers and Nietzsche see it as a labour mediated through social practices that draw on and enrich the bonds of friendship.[19] Nietzsche's ethics of self-cultivation also rests on the *central* organising principle of Hellenistic discourse: its analogy between the arts of medicine and philosophical therapy. Nietzsche follows the Epicureans, but especially the Stoics, in charting the movements of the soul as a series of cycles of illness, convalescence and health, in conceptualising philosophers as doctors to the soul, and in employing medical metaphors to designate the operations necessary to perform the care of the soul.

Foucault's research opens up an ethical perspective that, with the exception of Nietzsche's middle works, modern philosophy has until very recently neglected.[20] Yet his reconstruction of the ethics of the care of the self is marred by the conceptual limitations and blindnesses of his own formulations of an aesthetics of existence. Foucault's recasting of the work of the self in terms of Baudelairean dandyism or the freedom of undefined, unrestricted self-invention, elides something fundamental to this ethics: that is, the fact that it addresses the *pathos* that arises from mortality and loss, and that it does so in order to identify, temper and overcome the individual and political pathologies that arise from these wounds to our narcissistic wish for immortality and omnipotence. In closing, this chapter suggests that we can establish a better grasp of Stoic and Nietzschean ethics of subjectivity by framing their central concerns in terms of the psychoanalytic problem of narcissism, its pathologies and cures, rather than, as Foucault does, in terms of aesthetic modernism's ideal of radical creativity. Both the Stoics and Nietzsche's ethics of the care of the self, it is argued, can be seen as attempts to analyse and overcome various pathological expressions of the desire for narcissistic omnipotence. If this is so, then we must sharply demarcate both from the aesthetic modernist currents that Foucault advocates. By framing his aesthetics of existence in terms of the Baudelairean dandy's feline "cult of oneself as the lover of oneself," I argue, Foucault reduces the idea of the self as a work of art to a personality tour de force, and in the process he suppresses the important therapeutic and psychological concerns that both the Hellenistic thinkers and Nietzsche made central to the work of the self on itself.[21] To state the difference in bold terms, the Stoic and Nietzschean ethic of self-constitution analyses and attempts to treat narcissism, whereas Foucault's Baudelairean aesthetic self-fashioning is merely a symptom of narcissism.

FOUCAULT: CLASSICAL, ROMAN, AND MODERN ARTS OF LIVING

Foucault's critics and defenders in philosophy and social theory rarely, if ever, recognise that his historical investigation of subjectivity uncovers a series of quite different practices of ethical self-constitution, rather than a single, uniform art of living.[22] They devote most of their interest to demonstrating that his history of practices of self-constitution contradicts his earlier genealogical unmasking of humanist notions of a centred, self-determining subject. As a result, they have shown much less discernment in mapping the historical terrain that Foucault covers in this research.

Yet an examination of his history of the self suggests that he detects three quite distinct forms of the artistic elaboration of the self: the Greek or classical arts, the Roman Stoic practices of self-cultivation, and the distant echoes of antiquity he claims to discover in Baudelaire's dandyism.[23] His critics particularly neglect the distinction he draws between classical and Roman arts of living. In casting doubt on the contemporary significance or desirability of these ancient practices commentators invariably frame their concerns in terms of the *classical Greek* practices. "In what way," as one critic asks, "is the liberty of the *Greeks* ours?"[24] According to Foucault, however, the Stoics of the imperial age significantly modified the classical Greek arts of existence. Stoicism, so he argues, refined and reworked pre-existing classical forms. It did so, he suggests, by refashioning the way in which subjects recognised themselves as ethical subjects, the ascetic practices that they used to constitute themselves as subjects, and the very *telos* of these practices.[25] Unlike the classical practice of self-fashioning, as he sees it, Stoic self-cultivation was not pursued for the sake of exercising domination over others or attaining personal glory. For the Stoics, caring for oneself was not a prelude to, a primer for, or an analogical representation of political authority.[26] Rather, he claims that Roman Stoics like Seneca and Epictetus conceived self-cultivation as an occupation that revolved around "the question of the self, of its dependence and independence, of its universal form and of the connections it can and should establish with others."[27] Importantly, yet seldom noted, Foucault describes this Stoic art of living as *"the summit of a curve, the golden age in the cultivation of the self."*[28] Foucault, in other words, chronicles Stoicism as the crowning glory of the ancient ethics of the care of the self.

While his critics devote much of their attention to contextualising Foucault's history of the different practices of the self in terms of its place in his overall philosophical development and its significance for contemporary critical theory, they give less attention to his efforts to reshape the assumptions that frame the reception of Greek and Roman practices of the self, and to his conceptualisation of these practices themselves.[29]

Foucault contributes to this neglect by blurring the lines that separate the ancient practices of the self from aesthetic modernist cults of self-fashioning. He emblematises modern self-fashioning through Baudelaire's figure of the dandy. Baudelaire's decadent self-absorption is, he claims, "the attitude of modernity."[30] Glossing over the differences separating Greco-Roman technologies of the self from the aesthetic modernist's manner of fusing life and art, he describes Baudelaire's attitude as "a way of thinking and feeling . . . [a] bit, no doubt, like what the Greeks called an *ethos*."[31] Foucault makes the same casual association in lamenting the demise of the Greco-Roman *ethos* of self-stylisation:

> We have hardly any remnant of the idea in our society, that the principal work of art which one has to take care of, the main area to which one must apply aesthetic values, is oneself, one's life, one's existence. . . . We find this in the Renaissance . . . and yet again in nineteenth century dandyism, but those were only episodes.[32]

Encouraged, no doubt, by such cavalier associations, when they analyse Foucault's late works his critics also tend to neglect the radical differences between the Greco-Roman arts of living and aesthetic modernism. As Foucault does in this passage, they are inclined to reduce the arts of living to one undifferentiated category, the "aesthetics of existence." However, Foucault's historical analyses demonstrate that this category conceals a number of disparate conceptions of the self, each of which demands analysis on its own terms. This becomes apparent if we examine the philosophical and ethical chasm dividing the self-fashioning of Baudelaire's dandy and the ethical practices of Stoicism. Between Baudelaire's "exclusive cult of the passions" and Stoicism one could reasonably admit only the very faintest, *if any*, family resemblance.[33] It is true that in defining dandyism, Baudelaire briefly touches on its penchant for stoic *gestures*, but the accent he places on originality and excess demonstrates just how far removed this *ethos* is from Stoic philosophy and morals. The grandeur of folly and excess Baudelaire describes in the following passage is antithetical to the Stoic ideal of rational self-mastery:

> It is, above all, the burning desire to create a personal form of originality, within the external limits of social conventions. It is a kind of cult of the ego. . . . A dandy may be blasé, he may even suffer pain, but in the latter case he will

keep smiling, like the Spartan under the bite of the fox. Clearly, then, dandy-ism in certain respects comes close to spirituality and to stoicism, but a dandy can never be a vulgar man. If he were to commit a crime, he might perhaps be socially damned, but if the crime came from some trivial cause, the disgrace would be irreparable. Let the reader not be shocked by this mixture of the grave and the gay; let him rather reflect that there is a sort of grandeur in all follies, a driving power in every sort of excess.[34]

Here we might invoke one of Foucault's own rhetorical strategies to cor-rect his tendency to gloss such differences: while some of the dandy's asce-tic precepts and gestures might distantly echo the classical and Stoic arts of living, the dandy's moral *ethos* in fact defines a very different modality of the relation to the self.[35] Even if Foucault occasionally *fails* to adhere to them, and his philosophic critics rarely recognise them, it is important to acknowledge the significant differences between the various artistic prac-tices of the self.[36] Stoicism's philosophical therapy should not be confused with the dandy's project of elaborating one's existence according to the principles of aesthetic formalism, a project fuelled by the desire to establish aristocratic social distinctions against the rising tide of democratic vulgar-ity.[37] Nor, as we shall see below, should Stoicism simply be equated with the classical Greek practices of the self.

In truth, however, Foucault only slides over such crucial distinctions in his pronouncements about the contemporary relevance of the arts of the self.[38] By contrast, his historical analyses of these practices, especially his 1981–1982 lectures published as *The Hermeneutics of the Subject*, identify and reinforce the notion that there are significant discontinuities between these practices of the self. Indeed, in mining the philosophical, moral and medical texts of Hellenistic antiquity, Foucault discovers the lineaments of a conception of the self's relationship to itself that seems more properly called *therapeutic* than *aesthetic*, or, in which "aesthetic" practices merely serve as part of a larger philosophical therapy. It is this account of Hellenis-tic therapy, especially the Roman Stoics' care of the self, rather than his fleet-ing glances towards Baudelairean self-invention, that provides a schema for interpreting what Nietzsche identifies, self-consciously advertising its Latin foundations, as his *disciplina voluntatis*.[39]

THE FLAMING GAZE OF VANITY

In order to excavate and then distinguish the classical Greek and late Ro-man technologies of the self, Foucault first had to challenge the Christian polemics against the immorality of pagan "self-pleasers."[40] Such criticisms, he observes, first appeared among the early church fathers, who cast a sus-picious eye on pagan self-love. The early church fathers, he recollects, saw the care of the self as a source of diverse moral faults, and gladly denounced it as "a kind of egoism or individual interest in contradiction to the care one must show others or the necessary sacrifice of the self."[41] As the inheritors of the Christian traditions and their secularised derivatives, Foucault claims, "we" moderns easily fall into the trap of conceiving the care of self as intrinsically immoral:

> We find it difficult to base rigorous morality and austere principles on the precept that we should give ourselves more care than anything else in the world. We are more inclined to see taking care of ourselves as an immorality, as a means of escape from all possible rules. We inherit the tradition of Christian morality which makes self-renunciation the condition of salvation. . . . We also inherit a secular tradition which respects external law as the basis of morality. How then can respect for the self be the basis of morality?[42]

Erich Fromm supports Foucault's historical point. According to Fromm, beginning with Christian theology and reaching through Protestantism, German Idealism and psychoanalysis, the notion of caring for oneself or self-love has been maligned and salvation associated exclusively with austere self-renunciation. Freud's assertion that the more love the ego reserves for itself the less it has for others, he argues, merely sums up in quasi-positivistic terms the entire drift of the dominant strand of moral discourse:

> The doctrine that love for oneself is identical with "selfishness," and that it is an alternative to love for others has pervaded theology, philosophy and the pattern of daily life. . . . According to Freud, there is an almost mechanical alternative between ego-love and object-love. The more love I turn toward the outside world the less love I have for myself, and vice versa. Freud is thus moved to describe the phenomenon of falling in love as an impoverishment of one's self-love because all love is turned to an object outside of oneself.[43]

Fromm claims that the Christian construction of self-love as a negation of altruism has shaped the very foundations of philosophical thinking about the self's relationship to itself, including the psychoanalytic conception of the subject. He argues, as Foucault does in his later works, that Christianity's highly charged critique of self-love profoundly distorts modern ethical discourse. It has impaired our philosophical and ethical thinking, he suggests, by conflating all self-love with a disavowal or negation of others.[44] One legacy of Christianity, therefore, is the presumption that anything other than the self's abasement before God (or his secular representatives) is a symptom of the pagan vice of pride or self-love. Foucault sets out to demonstrate that the Christian conception of the self's relationship to itself, a relationship in which the self submits itself to a divine law, is not the only practice through which the self can constitute itself as an ethical subject.[45] "[T]here is," he hypothesises, "a whole rich and complex field of historicity in the way the individual is summoned to recognise himself as an ethical subject."[46]

However, unlike Fromm, Foucault also establishes specific historical sources that make it possible to theorise different practices and discourses of self-love. His excavation of classical and Hellenistic practices enables him to flesh out the claim that, at least in this theoretical and historical context, self-love takes the form of a complex work of the self on itself. Christianity's polemical interpretation of classicism and Hellenism, he maintains, elides from our philosophical and ethical heritage a fertile tradition that offers us alternative images, techniques, ideas and practices for theorising the self's relationship to itself. In Greco-Roman antiquity he discovers an ethical tradition which accentuates the self's relationship to itself as its central concern, and whose philosophies and schools elaborate or invent a series of practices through which the self becomes an ethical agent. Here the self's fashioning of itself is not considered antithetical to, but *constitutive* of, ethics. For the classical and Hellenistic philosophers, he argues, ethics *is* self-cultivation.

Fromm and Foucault, then, trace to Christianity a peculiar torsion in our ethical discourse: the condemnation of self-love as the "sin" of self-deification. Foucault adds that this torsion has erased the Greco-Roman ethics of the care of the self from our ethical landscape. Foucault believes contemporary attempts to renovate various Greek and Roman conceptions of the arts of living continue to be stymied by this Christian polemic. In our conception of the self, according to Foucault, we still live in the shadows of the Christian God. "There is a certain tradition," as he puts it, "that dissuades us (us, now, today) from giving any positive value to all [the] expressions, precepts, and rules" concerned with caring for the self, and "above all from making them the basis of a morality."[47] (If in political theory we have yet to cut off the king's head, as Foucault claims, then in the theory of the self we have yet to kill God).

THE ETHICS OF THE CARE OF THE SELF: FROM CLASSICAL GREECE TO IMPERIAL ROME

Foucault's first step toward throwing off the constraints of Christian prejudices against the care of the self is methodological. In order to understand antique ethics he introduces a tripartite framework for interpreting the history of morality. In *The Uses of Pleasure*, he distinguishes three fields of inquiry, which, he claims, encompass three different realities: moral codes, moral behaviours and what he calls ethics. The history of moral codes studies the system of values, rules and interdictions operative in a given society, the history of behaviours investigates the extent to which the actions of individuals and groups are consistent with these rules, and the history of ethics examines the "way in which individuals are urged to constitute themselves as subjects of moral conduct" and concerns itself "with the models proposed for setting up and developing relationships with the self, for self-reflection, self-knowledge, self-examination, for the decipherment of the self by oneself, for the trans- formations that one seeks to accomplish with oneself as object."[48] Simplify- ing this framework, Foucault identifies a field of "moral" problems concern- ing codes or interdictions and their application, and another field of "ethical" problems about how the self turns itself into a moral agent.

According to Foucault, the decisive transformations in the history of moral experience lie not in the history of codes, which reveals only the "poverty and monotony of interdictions," but in the history of ethics, where this is understood "as the elaboration of a form of relation to self that en- ables an individual to fashion himself into a subject of ethical conduct."[49] In concrete historical terms, he suggests that we can distinguish the Greek, Roman and Christian traditions not so much in terms of their moral pre- scriptions, which, he claims, remain "formally alike," but in terms of the different forms of self-relationships which they encourage individuals to practice.[50] Although Foucault acknowledges that in any attempt to identify the break between Christianity and antiquity "the topography of the part- ing of the waters is hard to pin down," he nonetheless selects two key points of differentiation.[51]

In the first place, he claims that although the necessity of respecting the law and customs was often underscored in Greek and Roman antiquity,

> more important than the content of the law . . . was the attitude that caused one to respect them. The accent was placed on the relationship with the self that enabled a person to keep from being carried away by the appetites and pleasures, to maintain a mastery and superiority over them, to keep his senses in a state of tranquility, to remain free from interior bondage to passions, and to achieve a mode of being that could be defined as full enjoyment of oneself, or the perfect supremacy of oneself over oneself.[52]

While Foucault clearly compresses many different conceptions of the prac- tices of the self into this passage, he nevertheless believes they share a close family resemblance insofar as they place the accent not on the strict codifi- cation of conducts or the authority that enforces it, but on what is required of individuals in their relationship to themselves, to their actions, thoughts, and feelings as they seek to form themselves as an ethical subjects.[53] In Greco-Roman culture, he argues, both the codes and the practices through which the self constitutes itself, its forms of self-examination and self- elaboration, were *supplements* or *luxuries* that individuals voluntarily adopted. Its various schools proposed rather than imposed "different styles of mod- eration or strictness, each having its specific character or 'shape.'"[54]

Secondly, Foucault claims that in the Greco-Roman tradition the choice to apply these codes and practices to the shaping of one's existence, and the constitution of oneself as a self-disciplined subject, was determined by the aim of transforming one's existence into a work of art. "From Antiquity to Christianity," he asserts, "we pass from a morality that was essentially a search for a personal ethics to morality as obedience to a system of rules."[55] For the classical Greeks, for example, sexual austerity was not a matter of internalising, justifying or formalising general interdictions imposed on everyone; rather, it was a means of developing an "aesthetics of existence," or "a stylisation of conduct for those who wished to give their existence the most graceful and accomplished form possible."[56] In the Greco-Roman world, this aesthetic care for the self was, as Foucault puts it, "the manner in which individual liberty . . . considered itself as ethical."[57]

However, if we narrow our focus to Foucault's treatment of ethics *within* antiquity, it quickly becomes apparent that he differentiates between the classical Greek practices of liberty and the late Roman Stoics' care for the self. During the golden age of self-cultivation, so he claims, important shifts occur in the mode in which the self recognises itself as an ethical subject, the ascetic practice through which it constitutes itself, and the goal of its work on itself. In the classical Greek perspective, he claims, the self defines its relationship to rules or norms as the means through which it achieves "beauty, brilliance, nobility, or perfection."[58] Foucault describes this as an aesthetic mode of adjustment to norms. The Stoics, by contrast, recognise norms as those that apply to all rational beings.[59] Between classical Greek ethics and Stoicism, he claims, there is also a dramatic shift in the range and type of ascetic or self-forming practices. Indeed, he associates Stoicism with a veritable burgeoning of self-forming activities, exercises and practices. Finally, Roman Stoicism changes the *telos* of ethical subjectivity.[60] While the Roman Stoics, in conformity with the classical tradition, still define the art of the self in terms of achieving the rule of the self over itself, "this rule broadens out into an experience in which the relation to self takes the form not only of domination but also of an enjoyment of oneself without desire or disturbance."[61] Foucault correlates this shift toward the enjoyment of oneself with a shift away from the goal of domination over others:

I think that the difference is that in the classical perspective, to be master of one-self meant, first, taking into account only oneself and not the other, because to be master of oneself meant that you were able to rule others. So the mastery of one-self was directly related to a dissymmetrical relation to others. . . . Later on . . . mastery of oneself is something which is not primarily related to power over others: you have to be master of yourself not only in order to rule others . . . but you have to be master of yourself because you are a rational being. And in this mastery of yourself, you are related to other people, who are masters of themselves. And this new kind of relation to the other is much less non-reciprocal than before.[62]

STOICISM AND NIETZSCHE:
THE GOLDEN AGE OF SELF-CULTIVATION

A brief examination of Foucault's schematic depiction of the golden age of Stoic self-cultivation suggests that it is precisely this kind of self-cultivation that provides the groundwork for Nietzsche's conception of the art of living.[63] Foucault follows in Nietzsche's footsteps by identifying the origin of the tradition of caring for oneself, the organising principle of the classical art of existence, in the early Socratic dialogues. It is the neglect of this Socratic tradition, Nietzsche asserts, that "transforms the earth for so many into a 'vale of tears.'"[64] Like Foucault, Nietzsche takes the figure of Socrates in the *Apology* as the seminal source of the Greco-Roman ethic of caring for oneself. Unfortunately, Nietzsche laments, the Christian orientation to the "salvation of the soul" has buried this tradition:

> Priests and teachers, and the sublime lust for power of idealists of every description . . . hammer into children that what matters is . . . the salvation of the soul, the service of the state, the advancement of science, or the accumulation of reputation and possessions, all as a means of doing service to mankind as a whole; while the requirements of the individual, his great and small needs within the twenty-four hours of the day, are to be regarded as something contemptible or a matter of indifference. Already in ancient Greece Socrates was defending himself with all his might against this arrogant neglect of the human for the benefit of the human race, and loved to indicate the true compass and content of all reflection and care with an expression of Homer's: it comprises, he said, nothing other than "that which I encounter of good and ill in my own house."[65]

According to Foucault, this Socratic ethic of caring for the self reaches its summit in Roman Stoicism. In the Hellenistic and imperial periods, he observes, the Socratic notion of "taking care of oneself" became a common philosophical theme. The Roman Stoics, in particular, conceived the care of the self as an end in itself and transformed it into a way of living that extended across the whole of the individual's life.[66] In Seneca and Marcus Aurelius, Foucault contends, the thematic of caring for oneself, their "meticulous attention to the details of daily life, with the movements of the spirit, with self-analysis," became the centre of philosophical life and "gradually acquired the dimensions of a veritable 'cultivation of the self.'"[67] Indeed, they defined human existence as a permanent exercise of the self on itself. As the imperative to care for oneself assumed centre stage in Roman philosophic culture it organised itself around a conception of the self as a reflexive exercise, an exercise of the self on itself mediated through certain forms of self-examination and ascetic practices. A brief analysis of Stoicism's care for the self, as Foucault presents it, suggests that in the middle works Nietzsche self-consciously assumed its conception of the self, its ethics and its practices, as his own.[68]

Like Seneca, Epictetus and Marcus Aurelius, Nietzsche extracts the principle of caring for oneself as the key Socratic legacy, and he identifies the chief cause of all psychical frailties as the failure to attend to this principle and undertake the continuous, careful observation of the most minute and closest details of one's mode of life.[69] In common with the Stoics, Nietzsche conceptualises self-observation as labour of the self on itself. The Greek term *epimeleia*, as Foucault points out, designates not a preoccupation with oneself, or an "idle" gazing at oneself, but a whole set of occupations, a work of the self on itself.[70] *Epimeleia heautou*, Foucault observes, describes the activities of the master of the household, the work of agricultural management, and a doctor's treatment of patients. Nietzsche's middle works are studded with examples of these forms of labour being used as metaphors for the work of the self on itself.[71] In criticising those who take pity on others, for example, he alleges that their actions and prescriptions prevent the pitied from properly managing their own domestic economy.[72] In other places, he takes gardening as the metaphor of the self's cultivation of itself, and the flourishing garden as the image of its purpose:

> *Gardener and garden.*—Out of damp and gloomy days, out of solitude, out of loveless words directed at us, *conclusions* grow up like fungus: one morning they are there, we know not how, and they gaze at us, morose and grey. Woe to the thinker who is not the gardener but only the soil of the plants that grow in him![73]

In the 1886 preface to the second volume of *Human, All Too Human*, he recasts the entire enterprise as a work he undertook on himself in order to weed out Schopenhauer's pessimistic judgements from his own soul. Here he brings together Stoic notions of the exercise of the self, its insistence on constant inward vigilance, with the Stoic emphasis on self-composure and equanimity in the face of loss and sorrow, and its resolute defence of life against the judgements of melancholia. Nietzsche confronts what we might describe as Schopenhauer's revolt against mourning—or against the possibility of coming to terms with loss—with the Stoic endurance of separation and solitude.[74] In this context, he portrays himself *as* a Stoic and the work he undertakes on himself as a Stoic spiritual exercise:

> [In *Human, All Too Human*, volume 2, and *The Wanderer and His Shadow*] there is a *determination* to preserve an equilibrium and composure in the face of life and even a sense of gratitude towards it, here there rules a vigorous, proud, constantly watchful and sensitive will that has set itself the task of defending life *against* pain and of striking down all those inferences that pain, disappointment, ill-humour, solitude and other swampgrounds usually cause to flourish like poisonous fungi.[75]

But Nietzsche, again following the Stoics, in whom this tendency reaches its zenith, reserves a privileged place for *medical* metaphors in his articulation of the art of living. The Hellenistic schools, and most comprehensively Roman Stoics, correlate the care of the self with medical thought and practice. Indeed, as Nussbaum observes, this correlation had become so pervasive in Stoic thought that Cicero felt the need to complain of their "excessive attention" to such analogies.[76] Cicero succinctly expresses the medical analogy on which Hellenistic philosophy pivots:

> There is I assure you, a medical art for the soul. It is philosophy, whose aid need not be sought, as in bodily diseases, from outside ourselves. We must endeavour with all of our resources and all our strength to become capable of doctoring ourselves.[77]

Like his Hellenistic predecessors, Nietzsche obsessively returns to the idea that philosophy is a therapeutic art that heals the sufferings and diseases of the soul.[78] Unsurprisingly, therefore, he contests or challenges other philosophic perspectives by accusing them of quack-doctoring or medical negligence.[79] Nietzsche adopts the collectively shared view of the Cynics, Epicureans and Stoics that such maladies are often perpetuated and reinforced by erroneous beliefs and value judgements that translate into disorders or affects that carry the soul away from itself. Nietzsche interprets his own philosophy as so many signs and symptoms in his soul's cycle of illness, convalescence and health. He frames his writings in much the same way as Seneca, who reports to Lucilius that he is recording the stages in his self-treatment for those who "are recovering from a prolonged spiritual sickness" and on "behalf of later generations":[80]

> I am writing down a few things that may be of use to them; I am committing to writing some helpful recommendations, which might be compared to formulae of successful medications, the effectiveness of which I have experienced in the case of my own sores, which may not have been completely cured but have at least ceased to spread.[81]

In recounting his own middle works, Nietzsche adopts Seneca's rhetorical pose, describing them as "the history of an illness and recovery," "a spiritual cure" and "self-treatment," which teach *"precepts of health* that may be recommended to the more spiritual natures of the generation just coming up as a *disciplina voluntatis."*[82] Nietzsche, like Seneca, recommends these precepts, and he also counsels that these spiritual natures "in whom all that exists today of sickness, poison and danger comes together" become doctors to their own soul. Permanent medical care, as Foucault relates, is one of the central features that the Stoics introduced into the practice of self-cultivation. In the imperial age, he explains, *paideia* increasingly took on a medical coloration that was absent in Platonic pedagogy.[83] "One must," according to the Stoics, "become the doctor of oneself."[84]

In the 1886 preface, in what is indisputably an homage to Stoic and Cynic practices of the self, Nietzsche describes how he forged his philosophy as an attempt to become the doctor of his own soul. In a passage overloaded with allusions to the figure of Diogenes and to the Stoic soul-doctors, Nietzsche reports that it was their disciplines that enabled him to overcome that pessimistic malaise, whose main symptom he identifies as an oscillation between extreme denial and manic affirmation. It is worth quoting this passage at length in order to gauge the full extent to which Nietzsche identifies his philosophy with Cynicism and Stoicism from this passage:

> Just as a physician places his patient in a wholly strange environment so that he may be removed from his entire "hitherto," from his cares, his friends, letters, duties, stupidities and torments of memory and learn to reach out with new hands and senses to new nourishment, a new sun, a new future, so I as physician and patient in one compelled myself to an opposite and unexplored clime of the soul, and especially a curative journey into strange parts, into *strangeness* itself, to an inquisitiveness regarding every kind of strange thing. . . . A protracted wandering around, seeking, changing followed from this, a repugnance towards all staying still, toward every blunt affirmation and denial; likewise a dietetic and discipline designed to make it easy as possible for a spirit to run long distances, to fly to great heights, above all again and again to fly away. A *minimum* of life, in fact, an unchaining from all coarser desires, an independence in the midst of all kinds of unfavourable outward circumstances together with pride in being *able* to live surrounded by these unfavourable circumstances; a certain amount of cynicism, perhaps, a certain amount of "barrel," but just as surely a great deal of capricious happiness, capricious cheerfulness, a great deal of stillness, light, subtler folly, concealed enthusiasm—all this finally resulted in a great spiritual strengthening, an increasing joy and abundance of health. Life itself *rewards* us for our tough will to live, for the long war that I then waged with myself against the pessimism of weariness with life, even for every attentive glance our gratitude accords to even the smallest, tenderest, most fleeting gift life gives us.[85]

Nietzsche spells out here his debt to the philosophic therapy of Cynicism and Stoicism without any reservations, a debt so great that a complete interpretation of this passage would entail an exposition of almost every significant aspect of these two philosophical schools. For the moment, we need only note that Nietzsche explicitly affirms the Stoic medical analogy and its notion that philosophic practice should act as a tonic to the soul, a means of overcoming the torments of memory and the violent oscillation between melancholia and mania that disturbs the soul's equanimity and composure.

The Stoics took the medical analogy with sufficient seriousness that they could designate the procedures of the care of the self with a whole array of medical metaphors. Foucault reports a series of medical metaphors that they regularly employed: "put the scalpel to the wound; open an abscess, amputate;

evacuate the superfluities, give medications; prescribe bitter, soothing or bracing potions."[86] Nietzsche borrows many of these metaphors to describe his art of psychological examination and its objects; confirming his commitment to reviving their therapeutic model of philosophy. In *Human, All Too Human,* he proposes that we see his work as a "psychological dissection table" and his analyses as the "knives and forceps" he uses to remove diseased moral, religious, aesthetic, and social "sensations"; and he writes of applying conceptual "icepacks" to reduce the fevers of the soul produced by metaphysical and religious errors.[87] This conception of philosophic procedures and the ethics of the care of the self it carries with it pervades Nietzsche's thinking, down to the most minute details, which are easily lost in the polemical storm that surround his work. We can see this, for example, in the way Nietzsche urges a medical response to the treatment of human suffering. Following the Stoics, Nietzsche believes individuals must cure themselves of pity and self-pity; otherwise, they will be incapable of enabling others to overcome their own sufferings. Nietzsche makes this case against pity in the name of an alternative medico-philosophic therapy. In doing so, he leans on the Stoic conception of the philosopher as physician who skilfully employs various procedures in search of a cure:

> to serve mankind as a physician *in any sense whatever* will have to be very much on guard against pity—it will paralyse him at every decisive moment and apply a ligature to his knowledge and his *subtle helpful hand.*[88]

Finally, to complete this picture Nietzsche, along with the Stoics, believes this medical practice of the self is best pursued through the application of tests that function as diagnostic procedures for assessing the health of the soul and, if applied frequently and rigorously, as partial cures or tonics for the soul. The Stoics famously counsel the practice of *praemeditatio* as a means of testing the extent to which the soul has risen above the tumult of anger, vengeance and envy, and as a way of moving toward achieving the goal of philosophical therapy.[89] The practice aims to establish a rational soul whose self-composure is founded on a joy in itself that cannot be perturbed by the sufferings and deprivations fortune ceaselessly inflicts on mortals. Foucault correctly notes that the purpose of these testing procedures "is to enable one to do without unnecessary things by establishing a supremacy over oneself that does not depend on their presence or absence. The tests to which one subjects oneself are not successive stages of privation. They are ways of measuring and confirming the independence one is capable of with regard to everything that is not indispensable and essential."[90] Seneca exhorts Lucilius to "rehearse" poverty, suffering and death not because he ought to value renunciation or mortification for their own sake, but so that he can maintain his equanimity in the face of all circumstances.[91] Foucault correctly observes that this relationship of the self to itself is antithetical to the Christian hermeneutic of self-decipherment and self-renunciation.[92] In Stoic self-testing, one does not seek to decipher a hidden truth of the self for the sake of self-renunciation. Rather, in the philosophic tradition dominated by Stoicism, *askēsis* "means not renunciation but the progressive . . . mastery over oneself, obtained not through the renunciation of reality, but through the acquisition and assimilation of truth."[93]

Nietzsche explicitly recalls the Stoic tradition of self-testing to explain the philosophic therapy he undertook in the middle works. Like the Stoics, he claims that if we wish to "return to health, we have no choice: we have to burden ourselves more heavily than we have ever been burdened before."[94] He explains his own exploration of a resolutely post-metaphysical perspective as part of a campaign that "I conducted with myself as a patient," or as a form of "self-testing" that all pessimists should use as a signpost to the health of their soul.[95] Nietzsche's most famous test of the soul, the potentially crushing burden of the eternal recurrence, the "greatest weight," as he calls it, is cut from the Stoic cloth: it is both diagnostic and curative.[96] Bernd Magnus's groundbreaking study of Nietzsche's doctrine of eternal recurrence (unwittingly) discloses the close link between the goals of Stoic *askēsis* and Nietzsche's doctrine. He structures his entire account of Nietzsche's philosophy in terms of the Stoic medical analogy without, however, acknowledging its Hellenistic and Stoic provenance.[97] According to Magnus, Nietzsche's philosophy centres on the diagnosis of a particular disease, "kronophobia," the identification of its various symptoms (Platonism, Christianity, and romantic pessimism) and its treatment or therapy. He conceives Nietzsche's philosophy, in short, as a therapeutic treatment of the kronophobic malaise. Platonism and Christianity and romantic pessimism, each in their own way, express the kronophobe's "need to arrest becoming, the need to make transience abide. The flux cannot be endured without transfiguration. Time, temporality must be overcome."[98] In this context, Magnus claims that the "value of eternal recurrence . . . lies primarily in its diagnostic thrust"; that is to say, he sees it as a test that the self applies to itself to determine the extent to which it suffers from the disease of kronophobia.[99] Indeed, he sees the idea of eternal recurrence as a diagnostic tool that enables us to become aware of suffering from a disease, a morbid suffering that we would otherwise fail to detect in ourselves.

For Nietzsche the testing of the self that the eternal recurrence enacts shares a goal in common with the ethical practices of his Hellenistic and Stoic predecessors. According to Foucault, they aim at a "conversion to the self" that expresses itself in a certain relationship or disposition of the self to itself.[100] This conversion succeeds where the self takes joy in itself in the same way that one takes pleasure in a friend. "What progress have I made?" Seneca writes to Lucilius, "I am beginning to be my own friend."[101] "Such a person," he adds, "will never be alone, and you may be sure he is a friend of all."[102] The Hellenistic thinkers believe that the labour of establishing this friendship between the self and itself enables individuals to sustain themselves without vengefulness, and take joy in their existence regardless of the blessings or curses of fortune. Hellenistic ethics is not about fortifying oneself against loss, which, if the Stoics are right, is an impossible, self-defeating and anxiety inducing project, but about fortifying oneself against a vengeful *response* to loss. "The geometrician teaches me how to keep my boundaries intact," Seneca quips, "but what I want to learn is how to lose the whole lot cheerfully."[103]

In formulating the doctrine of eternal recurrence, Nietzsche echoes the Stoic notion that the aim of self-testing is to transform one's relationship to oneself, or to become, as Seneca puts it, one's own friend: "[H]ow well disposed to yourself and to life," Nietzsche remarks in the concluding line of his famously dramatic invocation of recurrence, "to crave nothing more fervently than this ultimate eternal confirmation and seal."[104] It is a test, in other words, that is designed to measure and move one toward acquiring the virtue of being well disposed or friendly towards oneself. Here the point of Foucault's distinction between morality and ethics, and its application to the Stoics and Nietzsche becomes apparent: their ethics of the care of the self principally concerns the manner in which agents or subjects relate to, and transform themselves in the process of becoming agents or subjects of action, rather than with establishing or adjudicating normative codes. How the self relates to itself, especially to "the greatest weight" it is burdened with, its memories and its losses, lies at the heart of Nietzsche's and Stoicism's *therapeia*.[105] Like the Stoics, then, Nietzsche's conception of the self's work on itself is more properly speaking therapeutic than "aesthetic." In elaborating the nature and purpose of the specifically "artistic" elements of the self's work on itself Nietzsche makes it clear that they are subordinate parts of a therapeutic task or work (*Aufgabe*) that treats outbreaks of psychical fears and torments:

> *Against the art of works of art.*—Art is above and before all supposed to beautify life, thus make ourselves endurable, if possible pleasing to others: with this task in view it restrains us and keeps us within bounds, creates social forms. . . . Then art is supposed to *conceal* or *reinterpret* everything ugly, those painful, dreadful, disgusting things which all efforts notwithstanding, in accord with the origin of human nature again and again insist on breaking forth: it is supposed to do so especially in regard to passions and psychical fears and torments. . . . After this great, indeed immense task of art, what is usually termed art, that of the work of art, is merely an appendage.[106]

It is not surprising therefore that when Foucault turns to elaborating a new perspective on Hellenistic philosophy in his 1981–1982 lectures, he very briefly identifies Nietzsche's philosophy as one of several nineteenth-century German attempts at reconstituting the Hellenistic and Roman arts of living.[107] Indeed, it seems that Foucault undertook his journey back to the golden age of self-cultivation for the sake of understanding how Nietzsche and other representatives of modern German philosophy sought to resurrect the Hellenistic conception of philosophy as a way of life, to borrow Pierre Hadot's term.[108] Foucault claims that this strand of German philosophy attempted to recover the Hellenistic model by once again connecting the "activity of knowing" with "the requirements of spirituality."[109] Following Hadot, Foucault draws a sharp divide between this Hellenistic therapeutic-practical conception of philosophy, on the one side, and the strictly cognitive understanding of philosophy that has dominated the discipline since Descartes, on the other.[110] Both Hadot and Foucault share the view that Hellenistic and Roman philosophy differs dramatically from post-Cartesian philosophy insofar as it pivots on the assumption that the activity of philosophic knowing is always tied "to a transformation of the subject's being."[111] If they are correct, the acrimonious contemporary conflict between "Continental philosophy" and analytic philosophy revolves around the issue of whether the practice of philosophy can and ought to transform the whole of the individual's way of being, or, in Hadot's words, whether wisdom should not merely cause us to know, but to make us "be" in a different way.[112]

As we have seen, Foucault is undoubtedly correct to identify Nietzsche as a key figure in the German philosophic movement that sought to reanimate the spiritual-*cum*-therapeutic ambitions of Hellenistic philosophy, though errs slightly in claiming that Nietzsche and his fellow travellers do so only "implicitly."[113] It is clear that in his middle works Nietzsche explicitly assumes the stance of a philosophical therapist on the model of the Hellenistic and Roman examples. Indeed, as early as his inaugural Basel lecture (1869), Nietzsche memorably invokes Seneca's lament that rise of sophistic teaching had transformed philosophy, the study of wisdom, into philology, the study of mere words.[114] In what he calls a "confession of faith," Nietzsche declares his intention of performing the reverse operation: turning philology into philosophy; that is to say, of transforming a discipline that teaches us how to commentate into one that teaches us how to live.[115] Nietzsche self-consciously models his philosophic enterprise on the Senecan/Stoic notion of philosophy as a mode of knowing that transforms who one is.

In his 1981–1982 lectures Foucault follows Nietzsche's lead: his positivistic account of the shifts and transformations in the history of the ancient care of the self is fuelled by a similar enchantment with the prospect of rekindling a mode of knowing that transfigures or liberates the self. Like Nietzsche, Foucault seems to lament the fact that philosophy after Descartes came to be conceived as a purely cognitive activity that ought to be purged of the misguided Hellenistic notion that the acquisition of truth must transform one's being. In one of the rare moment of pathos in these lectures, Foucault conjures up the lonely figure of Faust lamenting that all his scholarly lucubrations, "philosophy, jurisprudence, medicine and theology," have yielded nothing "by way of his own transfiguration."[116] Foucault himself clearly sympathises with this Faustian nostalgia for the ancient figure of knowledge as a source of spiritual transfiguration.[117]

At the same time, however, he remains sceptical about the possibility of any attempt to reconstitute an ethics of the self. Though he declares that establishing a contemporary care of the self is "an urgent, fundamental and politically indispensable task," Foucault suspects that not only are all nineteenth-century German attempts like Nietzsche's, "blocked and ossified," but that despite our recent efforts in this direction we may well simply find it "impossible to constitute an ethics of the self."[118] Regrettably, Foucault never had the opportunity to explore the different ways German philosophy sought to renovate and recover the ancient arts of living and their spiritual modalisation of knowledge. We will never know, therefore, the exact reasons for his scepticism about both Nietzsche's and his own efforts to restore philosophy as a spiritual and therapeutic adventure. It seems reasonable to suppose, however, one of the central difficulties that may have prompted this note of doubt is the collapse of the cosmological and mythical beliefs that were essential to the conceptual structure and psychological efficacy of the Hellenistic *therapeia*. It is a problem Nietzsche also faces insofar as he found it impossible to frame his key "spiritual exercise," the thought of eternal recurrence, without recourse to Stoicism's cyclical cosmological doctrine.[119] We might surmise that Foucault saw how problematic it is to think that Stoicism's spiritual exercises are philosophically sustainable or psychologically plausible in the absence of the Stoa's foundational belief in a providential or divine *logos*.[120]

Foucault's account of the Hellenistic and Roman *therapeia* remains then a prolegomenon to a study of their modern renovations that he never had the opportunity to undertake. As we have seen, in the 1981–1982 lectures he goes along way to establishing that their fundamental point of convergence between the ancient and modern ethics of the self is the link they establish between knowledge and self-transformation. However, these lectures only give us a tantalising intimation of the manner in which Nietzsche and others sought to rework the Hellenistic *therapeia* and to challenge the Cartesian separation of knowledge and spirituality, truth and subjectivity. It is perhaps because Foucault only had the opportunity to gloss these issues that he never fully comes to grips with the possibility that some of the currents of thought he considers reinventions of the ancient care of the self, most notably Baudelaire's aestheticism, seem to radically diverge from the normative assumptions of the Hellenistic and Stoic traditions. Indeed, from the

Stoic and Nietzschean perspective (or at least the Nietzsche of the middle works), the limitless, perpetual self-transformation that Foucault champions must surely count as one of the pathologies that the care of the self is designed to cure, that is, the restlessness that Stoics refer to as *stultitia*, and which they argue derives from a lack of self-sufficiency.

THE LIMITS OF FOUCAULT'S LIMIT-ATTITUDE

Foucault's re-examination of the Stoic practices of the self, then, makes it possible to see one of the key philosophical sources of Nietzsche's ethics of subjectivity. However, Foucault's own approach to self-fashioning as the continuous estrangement of the self from itself, as an *askēsis* aimed at *nothing* other than getting "free of oneself" or "straying afield of (one)self," also strays far from the Stoics' and Nietzsche's *therapeia*.[121] Foucault's aesthetic modernist conception of self-fashioning as a release from all pregiven limits is too often and too easily identified as a continuation of Nietzsche's project:

> The work of Foucault . . . explicitly adopted Nietzsche's advocacy of aesthetic fashioning as an ideal. Rather than being true to the alleged "authentic" self advocated by existentialists like Sartre, he insists, "we have to create ourselves as a work of art." The result might well resemble the elite and narcissistic world of the nineteenth century dandy, who deliberately rejected the *telos* of a natural self in favour of a life of contrived artifice, and did so with minimal regard for others.[122]

Yet, as we have seen, Nietzsche's primary debt lies with Hellenistic and Stoic philosophical therapy, not Baudelaire's aesthetic modernism. By anchoring Nietzsche in this tradition it becomes apparent that his conception of the self and self-fashioning must in fact be distinguished from Foucault's Baudelairean fantasy of "unrestricted," open-ended self-invention. The differences can be seen by comparing this tradition with Foucault's conceptualisation of aesthetic self-fashioning:

> What strikes me is the fact that in our society, art has become something which is related only to objects and not to individuals, or to life. . . . But couldn't everyone's life become a work of art? Why should the lamp or the house be an art object, but not our life? . . . From the idea that the self is not given to us, I think that there is only one practical consequence: we have to create ourselves as a work of art.[123]

The analogy Foucault draws here between life and the raw materials of artistic *poiesis* immediately indicates the gulf separating him from the conceptual framework of Stoic and Nietzschean therapy. Foucault appears to be advocating "an *arbitrary* stylisation of life," as one commentator expresses it, a stylisation that eschews the possibility that the material it shapes has an intrinsic *telos* and that is independent of all external or objective norms.[124] He claims that the justification for this notion of aesthetic fashioning lies in the fact that the self is "not given to us." In other words, Foucault challenges the notion that liberation is the discovery and expression of an authentic self that pre-exists the exercise of liberty.[125] If, however, as Taylor points out, the self is not given to us in this sense, it is not clear what justifies Foucault's normative judgement that we *have to* (or "*must,*" as he says elsewhere) create ourselves as a work of art.[126]

More importantly, while Nietzsche might also eschew the notion that the self is given to us in the sense of an "authentic" or natural self, his philosophical therapy implies that the self *is* given to us in another sense: the "self" that is already there consists of the powerful affects and moods that derive from the loss of our phantasy of majestic plenitude. Nietzsche does not therefore conceptualise the material of self-fashioning as analogous to the indifferent, indeterminate material of artistic *poiesis*, as Foucault sometimes does, rather he describes this material as the "passions and psychical fears and torments" which break forth from human nature.[127] Nietzschean self-cultivation is not the all too easy and purely cognitive acknowledgement of the self's historical "contingency." What the self confronts in the "immense task of art," Nietzsche suggests, is not an abstract, contingent "otherness," but its own powerful desire for narcissistic plenitude and the history of its attempts to console itself for the loss of this ideal state. For Nietzsche, then, self-fashioning is the working-through of those affects or passions that derive from the human subject's loss of its narcissistic majesty and which, so he claims, engender an array of pathological modes of interaction through which it consoles itself for this loss:

> *The oldest means of solace.*—First stage: man sees in every feeling of indisposition or misfortune something for which he has to make someone else suffer— in doing so he becomes conscious of the power he still possesses and this consoles him.[128]

Foucault's purely aesthetic and formalistic conception of self-fashioning empties the Nietzschean and Hellenistic tradition of this psychological significance.[129] Rather than being oriented toward the "aesthetic" achievement of an original "personal" style, Nietzschean and Stoic philosophic therapy attempts to overcome the social and psychological pathologies that derive from the loss of narcissistic wholeness. As we shall see, for Nietzsche the necessity of self-cultivation is established in the face of the pathologies generated by the narcissistic origins of subjectivity.

What the Stoics and Nietzsche confront is the *pathos* or suffering that arise from the self's discovery of its powerlessness and the phantasies through which it allays this suffering, the earliest primitive forms of which Nietzsche nominates as compensatory vengeance and the exchange logic of guilt and atonement.[130] The pathologies that Stoicism attempts to cure, as Foucault's account already implies, derive from what we might call the narcissistic problem of separation and individuation. Stoic therapy focuses on how the self can negotiate the tension between dependence and independence, or "presence" and "absence"—to use the terms Foucault finds himself compelled to adopt in describing this therapy.[131] Recast in these terms, Stoicism investigates how the self can establish supremacy over itself, or perhaps more accurately, joy in itself. Through Stoic therapy the self seeks to constitute itself so that it can experience the uncontrollability and potential absence of cherished objects as something other than its own annihilation.

In his failure to take seriously the ethical implications of the Stoic and Nietzschean critique of the emotions, Foucault not only fails to recognise, or at least fully acknowledge and define, the extent to which his own aesthetics of self-transformation is something quite different from this Stoic and Nietzschean therapeutic work on the self, he leaves himself without the conceptual resources for understanding the maladies that these *therapeia* seek to treat. Indeed, by presupposing rather than critically probing the feeling of powerlessness and restlessness that fuels the transgressive drive to flee from oneself or tear oneself from oneself, Foucault transforms what the Stoics and Nietzsche conceive of as a compulsive malady, explicable in terms of narcissistic wounding, into a virtue.[132]

Despite Foucault's backward glances to the Stoics and Nietzsche's philosophical therapy, his own model of the work of the self is in fact one of the pathologies for which they seek a diagnosis and cure. For Stoic therapy aims at establishing a sovereignty over oneself that abolishes all striving to become other to oneself, and it achieves this composure through weeding out the emotional attachments or investments that hold us in bondage to chance events. If we fail to achieve this sovereignty, this state of self-completion, the Stoics argue, we must suffer from *stultitia*, a kind of restlessness or irresolution that compels the *stultus* to "constantly chang[e] his way of life."[133] Ironically, Foucault's analysis of the Stoic goal of self-completion and self-sufficiency reveals exactly how his own version of *askēsis*, which makes a virtue of constantly seeking to become other to oneself, is at odds with Stoicism's fundamental normative and therapeutic orientation.

From the Stoic perspective, Foucault's *askēsis* of constantly losing oneself is symptomatic of a failure to care for oneself. Foucault himself recognises the Roman care of the self was "not a way of marking an essential caesura in the subject."[134] As he observes, the Stoics deployed a series of terms to refer to a break between the self and everything else, but these terms did *not* refer to a "break of the self with the self."[135] Foucault's own notion of *askēsis*, in other words, seems to take up the Hellenistic and Stoic therapeutic-practical conception of philosophy, but to sever it from its central normative ideal of self-sufficiency and the analysis and critique of the emotional agitations or pathologies on which this ideal is premised. In the Stoic scheme Foucault's celebration of the limit experiences that create radical caesuras within the self can only be seen as symptomatic of a failure to understand, analyse and treat the emotional agitations which compel us to constantly seek out another place, another time or another self.

By contrast with Foucault, as we shall see in the following chapters, Nietzsche frames his account of the self in terms of the problem of the loss of majestic plenitude. He identify the pathologies of the self as borne of the loss of this phantasy of plenitude, which, according to Freud, the self first experiences in its inability to control objects and ensure their eternal presence. Nietzsche critically examines the array of consolations that reproduce, displace and exacerbate, rather than temper, the problem of narcissistic loss. Unlike Foucault, then, Nietzsche draws on the Stoic and Hellenistic schools not as a remnant of a purely aesthetic program of self-fashioning, but as a philosophy that identifies the narcissistic foundations of subjectivity and which elaborates a therapy, a work of the self on itself, designed to address these narcissistic excesses and pathologies. In the middle period, Nietzsche discovers in the Hellenistic and Stoic arts of the self-models for the work of memory and mourning which is integral to the analysis and cure of the self.

NOTES

1. Michel Foucault, "*Omnes et Singulatum*: Toward a Criticism of 'Political Reason,'" in *The Tanner Lectures on Human Values II*, Sterling McMurrin (ed.), 1981, University of Utah Press, Salt Lake City, 238, emphasis added. The published essay is the text of two lectures Foucault delivered at Stanford University on October 10 and 16, 1979.

2. CS, 45.

3. Didier Eribon, *Michel Foucault*, trans. Betsy Wing, 1991, Harvard University Press, Cambridge, Mass., 331. Eribon quotes from Deleuze and Blanchot, respectively. In his last interview Foucault himself discusses his stylistic change in strangely enigmatic terms; see Michel Foucault, RM 317–31. Paul Veyne also notes that Seneca's Stoicism played an important role in Foucault's "interior life" in his last years as he was living under the threat of AIDS; see Paul Veyne, *Seneca: The Life of a Stoic*, trans. David Sullivan, 2003, Routledge, New York, ix–x.

4. Eribon, *Michel Foucault*, 331. According to Paul Veyne, in the last stages of his life Foucault himself practised this Stoic mode of philosophising and writing of the self: "Throughout the last eight months of his life, writing his two books played the

same part for him that philosophical writing and personal journals played in ancient philosophy—that of the work performed by the self on the self, of self-stylization" (quoted in Eribon, *Foucault*, 325). By contrast, James Miller attempts to downplay the importance of this Stoic turn in Foucault's work; James Miller, *The Passion of Michel Foucault*, 1994, Flamingo, London, 342.

   5. HAH2, Preface §1. Hollingdale translates *ego ipsissimum* as "my innermost self." Nietzsche's use of this phrase deliberately underlines the Latin roots of his idea of the care of the self.

   6. ON, 85.

   7. Michel Foucault, quoted in Timothy O'Leary, *Foucault and the Art of Ethics*, 2002, Continuum, London, 175, fn. 14.

   8. Michael Janover, "The Subject of Foucault," in Clare O'Farrell (ed.), *Foucault: The Legacy*, 1997, Queensland University Press, Queensland, 215–27. The nature and extent of Foucault's debt to Nietzsche's critique of the metaphysics of subjectivity has been rehearsed too often to require further elaboration here; for a lucid discussion of this issue, see Peter Dews, *Logics of Disintegration: Post-structuralism and the Claims of Critical Theory*, 1987, Verso, London; and Peter Dews, "The Return of the Subject in the Late Foucault," *Radical Philosophy* no. 51, Spring 1989, 37–41.

   9. Keith Ansell-Pearson, "The Significance of Michel Foucault's Reading of Nietzsche: Power, the Subject, and Political Theory," in Peter Sedgwick (ed.), *Nietzsche: A Critical Reader*, 1995, Blackwell, Oxford, 13–30, 26–27, emphasis added.

   10. In his remarkable systematic reconstruction of Foucault's ethics, Timothy O'Leary makes a similar point. He claims that Foucault often imposes a nineteenth-century aestheticist cult of beauty onto a Greco-Roman philosophic tradition that was preoccupied with aesthetics in the much narrower sense of a series of *technai* (techniques) for working on and transforming the self, and that he overstates the extent to which beauty was the *telos* or aim of these techniques; see O'Leary, *Foucault and the Art of Ethics*, 14–15, 86, 102–4, 172. For a rigorous account of the Stoics' *technical* conception of philosophy—that is, its understanding of philosophical wisdom as a technical knowledge analogous to the expert knowledge of the craftsmen—which functions to transform one's *bios* or way of living, see John Sellars, *The Art of Living: The Stoics on the Nature and Function of Philosophy*, 2003, Ashgate, Aldershot, UK.

   11. David M. Halperin develops another angle on why we should avoid reducing Foucault's aestheticism to Baudelairean or Wildean dandyism; see *Saint Foucault: Towards a Gay Hagiography*, 1995, Oxford University Press, New York.

   12. HS, 251.

   13. Romand Coles constructs pagan subjectivity as founded on a "conceited ontology"; see Romand Coles, *Self, Power, Others: Political Theory and Dialogical Ethics*, 1992, Cornell University Press, Ithaca, N.Y.

   14. CS, 42–43; and GE, 350.

   15. CS, 42.

   16. GE, 349.

   17. John M. Rist, *Augustine: Ancient Thought Baptised*, 1994, Cambridge University Press, Cambridge, 190.

   18. The analysis here follows CS, 39–68.

   19. For an excellent synopsis of Nietzsche's shifting reflections and on evaluations of friendship, see Ruth Abbey, "Circles, Ladders and Stars: Nietzsche on

Friendship," in Preston King and Heather Devere (eds.), *The Challenge to Friendship in Modernity*, 2000, Frank Cass, London, 50–73.

20. On this point, see Martha C. Nussbaum, *The Therapy of Desire: Theory and Practice in Hellenistic Ethics*, 1994, Princeton University Press, Princeton, N.J., 4–5.

21. See Charles Baudelaire, *Intimate Journals*, translated by Christopher Isherwood, 1983, City Lights Books, San Francisco, 49.

22. For an exception to this rule, see O'Leary, *Foucault and the Art of Ethics*, ch. 3.

23. Foucault twice mentions the Renaissance arts of living as distant echoes of antiquity, but this remains nothing more than a gesture. It is impossible, therefore, to assess whether he believed that a study of these Renaissance practices might yield a distinct form of self-cultivation; GE, 362, 370.

24. Christian Bouchindhomme, "Foucault, morality and criticism," in *Michel Foucault: Philosopher*, trans. Timothy J. Armstrong, 1992, Harvester, New York, 317–27, 324; Andrew Thacker also claims that "[p]erhaps the main problem with Foucault's map is that it is a Greek one"; see Andrew Thacker, "Foucault's Aesthetics of Existence," *Radical Philosophy* 63, Spring 1993, 19.

25. Of the four structural features of the practices of the self that Foucault identifies, Stoicism leaves only the "ethical substance" unchanged; see GE, 357.

26. See HS, 75, 82–83.

27. CS, 238.

28. CS, 45, emphasis added; see also CS, 238–39; GE, 348, 357–58; and HS, 81. Foucault seems to have Hegel's deprecation of Hellenistic philosophy in his sights. Hegel treats the Hellenistic schools and the Stoic care of the self as little more than poor substitutes for civic participation in the *polis*; see Georg Wilhelm Friedrich Hegel, *The History of Philosophy*, translated by J. Sibree, 1900, George Bell and Sons, London, 328; the editors of Foucault's 1981–1982 lectures elaborate this point; see HS, 23, fn. 47.

29. See for example Rainer Rochlitz, "The Aesthetics of Existence: Postconventional Morality and the Theory of Power in Michel Foucault," in *Michel Foucault: Philosopher*, trans. Timothy J. Armstrong, 1992, Harvester, New York, 248–59.

30. WE, 33–50.

31. WE, 39.

32. GE, 362.

33. GE, 421.

34. Charles Baudelaire, "The Painter of Modern Life," in *Baudelaire: Selected Writings on Art and Artists*, translated by P. E. Charvet, 1972, Penguin Books, Harmondsworth, UK, 420.

35. This is how Foucault argues that despite the presence of similar precepts in the Late Hellenistic practices of the self and early Christianity, they are in fact radically different ethical systems and practices; see CS, 239.

36. Martin Jay rightly claims that the analysis of every "aestheticisation" of politics or existence must begin by identifying what notion of aesthetics it is invoking; see Martin Jay, "'The Aesthetic Ideology' as Ideology; Or, What Does It Mean to Aestheticize Politics?" *Cultural Critique*, Spring 1992, 42–61, 43.

37. Cesar Grana, *Modernity and Its Discontents: French Society and the French Man of Letters in the Nineteenth Century*, 1967, Harper Torchbooks, New York, 148–54.

38. On this point, see also Thacker, "Foucault's Aesthetics of Existence," *Radical Philosophy* 63, Spring 1993, 13.

39. HAH2, Preface, 2.

40. Augustine, *City of God against the Pagans*, translated by Henry Bettenson, 1984, Penguin, Harmondsworth, UK, Bk XIV, ch. 13.

41. ECS, 113–31, 115–16.

42. TS, 22.

43. Erich Fromm, "Selfishness and Self-Love," first published in *Psychiatry: Journal for the Study of Interpersonal Process*, William Alanson Psychiatric Foundation, Washington, vol. 2, 1939, 507–23; reprinted in *The Yearbook of the International Erich Fromm Society*, vol. 5, 1994, LIT-Verlag, Münster, 173–97.

44. Heinz Kohut's challenge to the psychoanalytic tradition also supports this point. See Heinz Kohut, "Forms and Transformations of Narcissism," op. cit., 97–123.

45. See BHS, 198–227.

46. UP, 32.

47. HS, 12.

48. UP, 29.

49. UP, 251.

50. UP, 250; see also GE, 355.

51. Foucault quotes Peter Brown in "The Battle for Chastity," in Phillipe Aries and André Béjin (eds.), *Western Sexuality: Practice and Precept in Past and Present Times*, trans. Anthony Forster, 1985, Basil Blackwell, Oxford, 14–25, 25.

52. UP, 31.

53. UP, 29–30.

54. UP, 21.

55. AE, 309–16, 311.

56. UP, 253, 250–51.

57. ECS, 115.

58. UP, 27.

59. UP, 354, 356. The classicist Pierre Hadot correctly observes that in treating the Hellenistic and Stoic spiritual exercises as sources for his own idea of aesthetic self-fashioning Foucault fails to "sufficiently stress" the connection the between self-cultivation and the exercise of reason that was integral to these traditions. By contrast with the Hellenistic traditions, Hadot maintains, Foucault's own notion of the cultivation of the self was "too purely aesthetic—that is to say, I fear, a new form of dandyism, a late twentieth-century version," and for that reason could not legitimately claim descent from ancient sources. In this respect, Hadot confirms one of the central claims of this chapter: that Foucault anachronistically attributes a late twentieth-century dandyism to the ancient practices of the self; see Pierre Hadot, "Reflections on the Notion of the 'Cultivation of the Self,'" in *Michel Foucault, Philosopher*, trans. T. J. Armstrong, 1992, Harvester, London, 225–32, 230.

60. Timothy O'Leary correctly observes that while in volumes 2 and 3 of the *History of Sexuality* Foucault clearly distinguishes between the *teloi* of classical and late-Stoic ethics—the former aiming at political power, and the latter at self-composure and self-enjoyment—in his interview he nevertheless insists on attributing a single, purely aesthetic *telos*, the cultivation of beauty, to these two ethical traditions.

O'Leary claims that Foucault deliberately engaged in this mystification for the sake of a contemporary project, that is, jolting his readers out of a habitual acceptance of a particular form of universalist morality. See O'Leary, *Foucault and the Art of Ethics,* op. cit., 7, 86, and 172.

61. CS, 68; see also, UP, 63, 70.

62. GE, 357–58. Gretchen Reydams-Schils amplifies and clarifies this quick gloss on the connection the Stoics drew between the care of the self and relationality; see Gretchen Reydam-Schils, *The Roman Stoics: Self, Responsibility, and Affection,* 2006, University of Chicago, Chicago, ch. 2.

63. Jim Urpeth makes a similar claim about the "fundamental, though largely implicit, contribution" Foucault's history of the ancient care of the self makes to arriving at a clear understanding of Nietzsche's idea of *askēsis.* Urpeth, however, conceives Nietzsche's "affirmative ascesis" as in some sense "Dionysian" rather than Stoic. See Jim Urpeth, "Noble Ascesis: Between Nietzsche and Foucault," *New Nietzsche Studies* 2, no. 3–4, Summer 1998, 65–91, 72.

64. WS §6.

65. WS §6; see Plato, *Apology* 29e; Homer, *Odyssey,* trans. E. V. Rieu, 1985, Penguin Books, Harmondsworth, UK, Bk IV, 1. 392; Foucault cites this passage from the *Apology* as the fountainhead of the ethics of the care of the self in CS, 44, and TS, 20.

66. See HS, Lecture 5.

67. TS, 28; CS, 44.

68. Günter Gödde demonstrates that the Hellenistic *therapeia* are the starting point for Nietzsche's (and Freud's) notion of the work of the self; see Günter Gödde, "Die Antike Therapeutik als Gemeinsamer Bezugpunkt für Nietzsche und Freud," *Nietzsche-Studien,* Bd 32, 2003, 206–25.

69. WS §6; see also D §462.

70. CS, 50.

71. GE, 49–50. Graham Parkes gives a brilliant and exhaustive treatment of Nietzsche's metaphors of the soul; see Graham Parkes, *Composing the Soul,* op. cit.

72. GS §338.

73. D §382; see also D §560.

74. For Schopenhauer's Augustinian-inspired critique of Stoic *eudaimonism,* see WWR 1, §16, especially 86–91, and WWR 2, vol. 2, ch. XVI.

75. HAH2, Preface, §5.

76. Cicero, *Tusculan Disputations,* quoted in Nussbaum, *The Therapy of Desire,* 316.

77. Ibid.

78. Nietzsche mines this seam of Hellenistic thought in countless places and contexts; for just a few examples, see D §52, §449, §534 and the 1886 Prefaces to HAH1 and HAH2, and GS.

79. WS §83.

80. L VIII, 2.

81. L VIII.

82. HAH2, Preface, §2, §5.

83. CS, 55.

84. TS, 31.

85. HAH2, Preface, §5. Nietzsche also touches on Diogenes the Dog at HAH1, §34, §275. For a recent account of Nietzsche's relation to the Cynic tradition, see

84 Chapter 2

Heinrich Nichues-Pröbsting, "The Modern Reception of Cynicism," in R. Bracht Branham and Marie-Coile Goulet-Gaze (eds.), *The Cynics*, 1996, University of California Press, Berkeley, 329–65, 354ff.

86. CS, 55.

87. HAH1, §37, §38; D §53.

88. D §134; for the Stoic critique of pity, see Seneca, OM, esp. ch. 6

89. See *Helvia*, 324–25. Foucault treats the Stoic practice of *praemeditatio* in HS, Lecture 23, 468–73.

90. CS, 59. Foucault elaborates the Stoic notion of life as a test in HS, Lecture 22.

91. See L XVIII, XXIV and XXVI, where he counsels Lucilius to rehearse poverty and death so that he can maintain his liberty and equanimity should he in fact lose his fortune or suffer the threat of the emperor's sword.

92. Foucault develops this point in BHS.

93. TS, 35. Foucault spells out the difference aims of Stoic and Christian *askēsis* in HS, Lecture 16, esp. 321–27.

94. HAH2, Preface, §5.

95. HAH2, Preface, §5.

96. GS §341.

97. Bernd Magnus, *Nietzsche's Existential Imperative*, op. cit., 42–43.

98. Ibid., 194.

99. Ibid., 156.

100. CS, 64.

101. L VI.

102. L VI.

103. L LXXXVIII.11 in C. D. N. Costa's translation, *Seneca: 17 Letters*, 1988, Aris and Phillips, Warminster; Seneca here takes the loss of property as an allegory for all the losses we must endure, including mortality. His point then is that Stoics must *learn* how to lose their property, and ultimately their ownmost property, *cheerfully*; it is thus the difficult art of learning how to lose without bitterness or vengefulness that is central to the Stoic's practices.

104. GS §341, emphasis added.

105. Commentators often neglect the Stoics' account of the therapeutic function of memory in the composition of the soul. As Gretchen Reydam-Schils observes, "[b]ecause memory is ranked among the indifferents, and time is one of the incorporeals in the Stoic system, the importance of these two notions has been overlooked in assessments of the Stoic idea of selfhood. But they are, in fact, revealing and crucial to the question." See Reydam-Schils, *The Roman Stoics*, op. cit., 29 and 29–34.

106. HAH2, §174.

107. HS, 28 and 251.

108. See Pierre Hadot, *Philosophy as a Way of Life*, op. cit., esp. ch. 11.

109. HS, 28.

110. HS, 14–16. Foucault actually refers to the "Cartesian moment" rather than Descartes. Foucault uses this phrase merely as a convenient signpost for a broad shift in the conception of philosophy rather than as a comment upon Descartes' philosophy. His caution here relates to the fact that even in Descartes philosophy, as Hadot observes, elements of the ancient spiritual exercises such as *meditatio* survive;

see Hadot, *Philosophy as a Way of Life*, op. cit., 271 and *What Is Ancient Philosophy?*, op. cit. 263–65.

111. HS, 14–16.

112. Hadot, *Philosophy as a Way of Life*, op. cit., 265. Simon Critchley takes up Hadot's distinction in his attempt to mediate the debate between analytic and "Continental" philosophy; see Simon Critchley, *Continental Philosophy*, 2001, Oxford University Press, Oxford, ch. 1.

113. HS, 28.

114. L CVIII, 23; "*Itaque quae philosophia fuit facta philologia est.*"

115. "*Philosophia facta est quae philologia fuit.*" The passage is from Nietzsche's inaugural Basel lecture (May 1869), later privately published as "Homer and Classical Philology"; quoted in James I. Porter, *Nietzsche and the Philology of the Future*, 2000, Stanford University Press, Stanford, Calif., 14 and 35.

116. HS, 310.

117. In UP Foucault puts the point in the form of a rhetorical question: "After all, what would be the value of the passion for knowledge if it resulted in a certain amount of knowledgeableness and not *in one way or another* . . . in the knower's straying afield of himself?" The answer obviously is that pursuing knowledge would have very little value unless it put at stake the very being of the knower. The question Foucault does not raise here, and which I discuss below, is whether his way of straying afield of himself is compatible with Stoicism's fundamental normative assumptions; see UP, 8 (emphases added).

118. HS, 252, 251.

119. The exact nature of Nietzsche's doctrine of eternal recurrence remains a matter of considerable dispute. It is still a matter of debate whether Nietzsche considered it a cosmological doctrine or an existential test that one could undertake without committing oneself to belief in the literal eternal return of all things. For the latest installment in this debate, see Lawrence J. Hatab, *Nietzsche's Life Sentence: Coming to Terms with Eternal Recurrence*, 2005, Routledge, New York.

120. Pierre Hadot attempts to address this problem in *Philosophy as a Way of Life*, op. cit., 273, 282–84.

121. UP, 8, see 8–9. For an excellent treatment of Foucault's notion of "limit experiences" as a transgression of the limits of coherent subjectivity see Martin Jay, *Songs of Experience: Modern American and European Variations on a Universal Theme*, 2005, University of California Press, Berkeley, 390–400.

122. Martin Jay, "The Morals Of Genealogy: Or Is There a Post-structuralist Ethics?" *The Cambridge Review*, June 1989, 73.

123. GE, 350–51.

124. See Dews, "The Return of the Subject in Foucault," op. cit., 40.

125. Foucault warns that there is a danger that liberation "will refer back to the idea that there does exist a nature or a human foundation which, as a result of a certain number of historical, social or economic processes, found itself concealed, alienated, imprisoned in and by some repressive mechanism. In this hypothesis it would suffice to unloosen these repressive blocks so that man can be reconciled with himself, once again find his nature or renew contact with his roots and restore a full a positive relationship with himself"; ECS, 113.

126. "If I was interested in Antiquity it was because, for a whole series of reasons, the idea of morality as disobedience to a code of rules is now disappearing, has already disappeared. And to this absence of morality corresponds, *must* correspond, a search for an aesthetics of existence"; AE, 311, emphasis added; and Charles Taylor, "Foucault on Freedom and Truth" in D. C. Hoy (ed.), *Foucault: A Critical Reader*, 1986, Basil Blackwell, Oxford, 69–102. O'Leary claims that we should read Foucault's imperative as a historical, rather than a moral necessity. However, if we recall that both philosophically and methodologically Foucault is deeply committed to an antiteleological perspective, it seems highly implausible to believe that he would resort to the notion of historical necessity to support his normative judgements or intuitions. We might be better served seeing Foucault's imperative as illustrating Nietzsche's quip: "There is a point in every philosophy when the philosopher's 'conviction' appears on the stage—or to use the language of an ancient Mystery: *Adventavit asinus/Pulcher et fortissimos* (The ass arrived, beautiful and most brave)"; see O'Leary, *Foucault and the Art of Ethics*, op. cit., 7, and BGE, 8.

127. HAH2, §174. There is significant debate about how Foucault might have understood basic material from which a subject is formed; see, for example, O'Leary, *Foucault and the Art of Ethics*, op. cit; Chris Falzon, "Foucault's Human Being," *Thesis Eleven*, no. 34, 1993, 1–16; Paul Patton, "Taylor and Foucault on Power and Freedom," *Political Studies* XXXVII, no. 2, June 1989; and Paul Patton, "Foucault's Subject of Power," *Political Theory Newsletter* 6, no. 1, May 1994, 60–71.

128. D §15.

129. Joel Whitebook brilliantly analyses Foucault's theoretical and personal resistance to psychoanalytic theories, and cogently argues that many of the philosophical and ethical problems of Foucault's notion of self-fashioning result from this resistance; see Joel Whitebook, "Freud, Foucault and the Dialogue with Unreason," *Philosophy and Social Criticism* 25, no. 6, 1999, 29–66; and "Against Interiority: Foucault's Struggle with Psychoanalysis" in Gary Gutting (ed.), *Cambridge Companion to Foucault*, 2005, Cambridge University Press, New York, 312–49.

130. D §15.

131. CS, 59 (quoted above).

132. Paul Patton argues that Foucault must presuppose "something like a feeling of powerlessness" in order to account for the desire to constantly transform oneself and enhance one's feeling of power. See Patton, "Foucault's Subject of Power," op. cit, 71.

133. HS, 132.

134. HS, 214.

135. HS, 212.

3

Beyond Melancholia and Mania: Nietzsche's Middle Works

> Now the Sirens have a still more fatal weapon than their song, namely their silence. And though admittedly such a thing has never happened, still it is conceivable that someone might possibly have escaped from their singing; but from their silence certainly never.
>
> Franz Kafka, *The Silence of the Sirens*

Drawing on metaphors derived from the Roman baths, Nietzsche's scholarly friend and advocate, Erwin Rohde, observed that coming to *Human, All Too Human* after experiencing Nietzsche's earlier writings was like being chased from the *calidarium*, the steamy waters, into an icy *frigidarium*, a "rather shocking experience."[1] Rohde's metaphorical description expresses with unequalled beauty and concision the fundamental change Nietzsche made to the philosophical cast and style of his work in the later 1870s. The shocking drop in temperature that Rohde experienced in reading *Human, All Too Human* can be understood as the effect wrought on him by Nietzsche's coolly detached dissection of the feverish symptoms of narcissism. Fusing together the languages of Stoicism and psychoanalysis we might state the matter as follows: in the middle period, Nietzsche comes to realise that we need a touch of Stoic ice running through our veins if we are to bear with equanimity the painful wound inflicted on us by the loss of our narcissistic plenitude.[2]

This chapter examines Nietzsche's critique of what he began to conceptualise as opposed manifestations of *one and the same* narcissistic complex:

melancholia and mania. Freud's theory of narcissism crystallises the origins, characteristics and psycho-dynamics of these two pathological symptoms of narcissistic loss. We can benefit from this theory in unpacking Nietzsche's middle works because it identifies precisely the melancholic and manic diseases that he seeks to understand, criticise and supplant with an alternative solution to the problem of narcissism. Nietzsche formulates an alternative to the melancholia/mania complex in his notion of self-cultivation. Framed in this way, we can begin to see this idea of self-cultivation as an attempt to delineate a concept of mature egoism, rather than, as his critics argue, an expression of the manic pole of pathological narcissism.

Nietzsche broaches the melancholic side of the narcissistic complex in his critique of Schopenhauer's ascetic philosophy of self-abjection. In line with the sceptical, antimetaphysical stance he takes up in the middle works, Nietzsche criticises the metaphysical account of the world that Schopenhauer uses as the philosophical foundation of his melancholic asceticism. However, and more importantly for our purposes, he also reproaches Schopenhauer's ascetic ethics as a botched therapy for the narcissistic wound, a therapy, that is to say, which inflames rather than cures this wound. Indeed, he holds that by exacerbating the narcissistic malady of the ideal, as it is called in the psychoanalytic discourse, Schopenhauer's asceticism serves not only to intensify the subject's self-hatred, but also fuels its enmity to intersubjectivity.[3] To put it another way, Nietzsche treats Schopenhauerian asceticism as a perverse *Bildungsroman*: a work through which the self systematically deconstructs the psychological foundations and resources that enable it to bear its narcissistic loss and to live with others without vengefulness, or *ressentiment*.

In the late 1870s, Nietzsche also reconsiders and rejects much of the philosophic basis and tenor of his own early work, especially its Dionysian celebration of ecstasy and mania. Most significantly, Nietzsche conceives melancholic self-abjection and ecstatic self-dissolution as the two extreme poles of one and the same malady: pathological narcissism. In the middle works, then, he acknowledges that the psychological root of melancholia *and* mania derive from the failure to work through the loss of narcissistic plenitude. Far from celebrating manic dedifferentiation, as he had in some moments of *The Birth of Tragedy*, in *Human, All Too Human* he brusquely dismisses it as another symptom of the narcissistic malady. In order to find remedies for this malady, and its wildly compulsive oscillation between despair and elation, Nietzsche turns to the Hellenistic and Roman practices of the self. He recalls the Hellenistic and Stoic *therapeia* for the sake of investigating the psychological work that might enable us to forge a strong ego capable of bearing separation and finitude. In other words, Nietzsche conceives the work of self-cultivation as a means of tempering or cooling down the worst excesses that derive from the suffering or pathos of narcissistic loss:

Schopenhauerian self-mortification and its opposite number, Dionysian ecstasy.

In order to establish the theoretical groundwork for elaborating and clarifying Nietzsche's philosophical therapy of narcissism, this chapter briefly sketches the main outlines of Freud's theory of narcissism, accentuating those aspects that illuminate the psychological source of melancholia and mania. It then elaborates Schopenhauer's defence of ascetic self-abnegation and resignation. By transposing Schopenhauer's defence of asceticism from the metaphysical to the psychological register, Nietzsche convincingly shows that it is a symptom of the malady of the ideal, to borrow from the psychoanalytic lexicon. Finally, this chapter demonstrates that in the middle period Nietzsche applies his sudden passion for coolly detached psychological analysis to his own Dionysian longing for "being-outside-oneself." In doing so, he argues that it belongs among those flights from suffering that make us burdensome companions for ourselves and others.

PATHOLOGICAL NARCISSISM: NIRVANA AND MANIA

In his metapsychological speculations on narcissism, Freud introduces the notion that the entire development of the ego can be understood in terms of its enforced departure from a condition of primary narcissism and its vigorous attempts to recover that state.[4] Freud conceptualises primary narcissism as a state of perfection and wholeness that precedes the differentiation of the ego from the world; it is for this reason that he describes it as a "pre-ego" or nonindividuated condition. As he conceives it, primary narcissism is a condition in which there can be neither subject nor object, only the oceanic dispersal of libido. Freud uses the metaphor of an "oceanic feeling" to describe the blissful condition of plenitude that we phantasise as the condition that comes before the emergence and differentiation of the ego agency from the external world.[5] It can thus be understood as a condition in which the limitless pre-ego experiences itself as encompassing and effortlessly "directing" the world, if we can be permitted to apply concepts of volition to a condition that precedes the formation of the subject-object poles. On this basis, Freud claims that memory traces of primary narcissism revive a feeling of plenitude and that later narcissistic maladies take the shape of phantasies of magically orchestrating the world.[6] It is only terminated when a separate ego agency emerges as the dawning awareness of the object world's resistant otherness. In *Group Psychology* Freud lucidly expresses the shocking, never fully stabilised transition human creatures must negotiate from the all-encompassing plenitude of primary narcissism to the shrunken condition of individuation, and the potential for illness that it harbours:

Thus, by being born we have made the step from an absolutely self-sufficient narcissism to the perception of a changing external world and the beginnings of the discovery of objects. And with this is associated the fact that we cannot endure the new state of things for long, that we periodically revert from it, in our sleep, to our former condition of absence of stimulation and avoidance of objects.[7]

According to Freud, then, primary narcissism is not simply a developmental phase that is gradually surpassed, but the ego's fundamental, animating project.[8] He conceives the ego as engaged in a tenacious, complex campaign to regain some vestiges of the organism's original undifferentiated condition of plenitude. Since the ego never overcomes the search for narcissistic gratification, Freud distinguishes between the normal and the pathological not in terms of whether the ego relinquishes the aim of self-enjoyment, but in terms of the paths and forms through which it seeks to re-experience the "oceanic feeling."

It follows that for Freud the ordinary feeling of the self as "autonomous and unitary" is not a natural or essential fact of subjectivity, but a fabrication that emerges from the struggle and conflict that is required to break up the narcissistic monad.[9] "[O]riginally," Freud claims, "the ego includes everything, later it separates off an external world. Our present ego-feeling is, therefore, only a shrunken residue of a much more inclusive—indeed, an all-embracing—feeling which corresponded to a more intimate bond between the ego and the world about it."[10] With the introduction of the thesis of primary narcissism, as Whitebook points out, Freud's concept of reality acquired the connotations of harshness, as "something opposed to the nexus of our wishes and to our narcissism," that it had hitherto lacked.[11] "When during the stage of primary narcissism, the object makes its appearance," as Freud puts it, "hating . . . appears. . . . At the very beginning, it seems, the external world, objects, and what is hated are identical. . . . Hate, as a relation to objects, is older than love. It derives from the narcissistic ego's primordial repudiation of the external world with its outpouring of stimuli."[12]

Importantly, for reasons we shall explore in later chapters, Freud speculates that the separation and gradual delimitation of narrower ego boundaries is not just imposed on the subject by the intrusions of the external world, for he suggests the narcissistic pleasure ego also *creates* this reality by projecting into the external world all of the internal sources of unpleasure. Where the ego maintains the inner world as a site of pure pleasure through such projections, he observes, it must confront a strange and hostile "outside" that is largely of its own making. The narrower ego thus forms and demarcates itself through a combination of enforced reality testing *and* the projection of disavowed or unintegrated aspects of itself into the world, a method which Freud sees as the source of significant pathological disturbances.[13] It is this casting out of bad feelings or "unpleasure" into the external world in the attempt to retain a pure-pleasure ego that allows Freud to assume that the basic tendency of the psychical system is the avoidance of pain and tension.[14]

To recapitulate the main points, Freud argues that memory traces of the "oceanic feeling" persist to a lesser or greater degree alongside the narrower and more sharply demarcated ego feeling of maturity.[15] He claims that this memory trace and the phantasies associated with it fuel the ego's desire to reclaim that condition of primary narcissism, which can be figured either in terms of the pre-Oedipal, infant-mother symbiosis, or, in some perspectives, the prenatal "experience" of womb-like security.[16] In other words, Freud asserts that the longing for narcissistic plenitude can never be fully relinquished, only displaced or reconfigured.

In his analysis of the genesis of the human creature's complex, differentiated psychical system, then, Freud does not simply draw a topographical division between the expansive, oceanic feeling and the shrunken, instrumentally oriented ego that forms itself through separating and differentiating itself from the outer world. Rather, he contends that the relationship between the originary experience of limitlessness and the shrunken ego is dynamic; that is to say, the memory of this more expansive, unbounded condition acts as a counterpressure on the differentiated, unitary ego. Freud conceives the residue of the pre-ego's more intimate bond with the world as an affectively charged force within the psyche that presses toward ego dedifferentiation.[17] He believes that the gradual differentiation and consolidation of ego functions is maintained only against a constant retrogressive pressure toward dedifferentiation.

According to Freud, the mature ego, haunted by memory-traces of oceanic limitlessness, is always susceptible to the lure of dissolution. It is haunted in this way, he believes, because the narcissistic pleasure of infancy is never given up but carried forward and projected into the future by a spectral agency that he calls the ego ideal. Anamnesis therefore has a conative force that can never be entirely vanquished; rather, as we shall see, it can generate either various pathological attempts at regression to the prereflective state of wholeness, which in extreme cases is sought in psychosis or death, or, at best, it can be sublimated into culturally exalted achievements.[18] Freud depicts the ego's nostalgia for the psyche's imagined state of majestic glory as both a malaise and a potential source of self-overcoming.[19] Indeed, for Freud the narcissistic longing for plenitude has an ambivalent status as the source of both the debased and the sublime.[20] The ambivalence, which is an essential feature of the ego ideal, "refers to the manner in which the individual can seek to recover lost omnipotent perfection once primary fusion has been dissolved" and differentiation from others and within the psyche have been introduced.[21]

Freud identifies one of these debased configurations of narcissism in the melancholic malaise of self-abnegation. It is this malaise, as we shall see, which is conceptually embodied in Schopenhauer's philosophic affirmation of ascetic self-mortification. For Schopenhauer self-mortification is a step toward "nirvanic" bliss, as he calls it. By weakening and ultimately destroying the ego through cruel mortification, Schopenhauer claims, we abolish that agency whose constantly thwarted pursuit of plenitude only serves to recall and aggravate the painful anguish of narcissistic loss.[22]

For our purposes, then, Freud's theory of narcissism illuminates the psychodynamics that explain the ascetic's compulsive attempt to achieve a condition of nirvanic quiescence. Indeed, Christopher Lasch claims that is precisely the theory of narcissism that leads Freud to formulate the nirvana principle, the idea that human beings harbour a longing for absolute repose, for the cessation of all stimulation and with it a contentment that lies beyond libidinal gratification. Cast in terms of Freud's theory, Lasch observes, we can treat the longing for nirvana as an attempt to reclaim something of the originary feeling of plenitude that comes from the infant's symbiotic fusion with the mother. In seeking nirvana the ascetic is reawakening the infantile ego's protest against its helplessness before an independent and resistant world. In the psychoanalytic framework, it is the infant's discovery of its own helplessness that obliges it to recognise the not-me world and thus begin its reluctant departure from its original, undifferentiated symbiosis with the (maternal) world. According to Lasch, because narcissism dates "from a stage of mental life that antedates any sense of the distinction between the self and the outside world, [it] has no knowledge of death and therefore remains indifferent to the possibility of its own extinction."[23]

Lasch suggests that this need to overcome the pain of separation and abandonment can become so intense that it overwhelms even the self-preservative instinct. Freud's theory of primary narcissism thus raises the disturbing possibility, he writes,

> that something in the self longs to regress to a condition anterior to all tension and striving and cares nothing for the welfare of the bodily ego. The nirvana principle as Freud came to call it, seeks absolute release from the tension and thus experiences even the promptings of the pleasure principle as a disturbing intrusion on the womblike contentment it wishes to restore.[24]

In short, he argues, the "nirvana principle" originates "in primary narcissism, with its illusion of everlasting life and its indifference to bodily demands."[25] As we shall see, it is this narcissistically fuelled quest for nirvana that underpins and explains Schopenhauer's defence of self-abnegation.

SCHOPENHAUER'S MELANCHOLIA: DEADLY SELF-LOVE

Schopenhauer's defence of self-mortification as the means to nirvanic bliss hinges on the assumption that the psyche's *exclusive* goal is to recover the state of complete repose or quiescence. Borrowing from Buddhism he describes this goal as a longing for nirvana, for "a final satisfaction of the will, after which no fresh willing would occur; a last motive of which would give the will an imperishable satisfaction."[26] He therefore equates all psychical tension arising from the ego's striving for particular goals or objects with displeasure or privation. Freud also specifies "the final goal of all organic striving" as the return to "an *old* state of things, an initial state from which the living entity has at one time departed and to which it is striving to return by circuitous paths along which its development leads . . . *the aim of all life is death.*"[27] "The tension which . . . arose in what had hitherto been an inanimate substance," he speculates, "endeavoured to cancel itself out. In this way the first instinct came into being: the instinct to return to the inanimate state."[28]

Schopenhauer and Freud both postulate that at its deepest level the human psyche pursues the fundamentally nirvanic aim of escaping from the pain of desire and the release of all tensions. Because narcissistic or oceanic contentment is Schopenhauer's sole measure of value he conceives any delay between wish/desire and gratification as a painful disruption of the original condition of unbroken plenitude. If "nirvana" constitutes the only complete form of satisfaction for human beings, then the ego must experience its own constant strivings as painful disruptions of its former state of quiescence. By affirming its "will to life" through the pursuit of self-preservation or transient pleasures the ego therefore condemns itself to constant suffering. Schopenhauer's absolutist requirement means that the admixture of pleasure and pain that accompanies any act of will or desire is itself sufficient to deny it any worth.

According to Schopenhauer, the ego repeatedly wills its own will, or seeks its own gratification, only because it suffers under the misapprehension that its next action must finally deliver the longed for condition of permanent satisfaction. Schopenhauer states axiomatically that the ego suffers from desire or willing. For Schopenhauer desire is a *pathos* in the strict sense of the term. "The basis of all willing," he claims, "is need, lack, and hence pain, and by its very nature and origin is therefore destined to pain."[29] The ego attempts to alleviate this pain, he claims, by satisfying the wish to return to the condition of narcissistic plenitude that lies at its source. In doing so, however, it only succeeds in reproducing the original suffering by generating a fresh desire and so on ad infinitum. It is the very nature of the will as a constant striving (i.e., will as will) that each particular satisfaction only serves to generate that painful sense of lack from which it springs.[30]

"Thus that there is no ultimate aim of striving," he asseverates, "means that there is no measure or end of suffering."[31] Nevertheless, the ego is constantly seduced into pursuing new objects on the ill-founded hope that success—the consumption or incorporation of the object—will yield the ultimate state of repose it so intensely desires. Schopenhauer argues that while the ego suffers from each desire, this suffering rarely deters it from ceaselessly pursuing the mirage of integral gratification.

Schopenhauer leans on his metaphysical conception of the ego as the highest phenomenon of the will to life in order to explain its constant, painful striving. This metaphysics depicts the ego as trapped in a diabolical game the will plays with itself: through its objectifications the will to life seeks a final satisfaction that, because of its very nature as endless willing, it cannot achieve.[32] If the will to life is an insatiable lack that nonetheless constantly presses for the impossible—a gratification that would bring it to a final halt—the ego as its highest objectification is condemned to a life of ever renewed suffering. "For all striving," Schopenhauer asserts,

> springs from want or deficiency, from the dissatisfaction with one's own state or condition, and is therefore suffering so long as it is not satisfied. No satisfaction, however, is lasting; on the contrary, it is always merely the starting point of a fresh striving. We see striving everywhere impeded in many ways, everywhere struggling and fighting, and hence always as suffering. Thus that there is no ultimate aim of striving means that there is no measure or end of suffering.[33]

What keeps the ego committed to willing itself as will is just this recurring failure to achieve complete tension reduction. Schopenhauer therefore depicts the ego's constant striving not as symptomatic of its joy in willing, but as testimony to its chronic failure to realise its own death.

According to Schopenhauer, the best the ego can hope for is occasional pauses, the complete absence of stimulation or tension, in the constant stream of painful desires. Even in the case where all conceivable bodily desires are sated, the will persists without an empirical object, a condition he describes "as a fearful, life-destroying boredom, a lifeless longing without a definite object, a deadening languor."[34] "Hence," Schopenhauer writes, "life swings like a pendulum to and fro between pain and boredom, and these two are in fact its ultimate constituents."[35] From the proposition that the ego is the phenomenon of an eternal will to life that has no ultimate satisfaction that would bring it to end, he reaches the conclusion that it is destined to a continuous reeling between pain and boredom.

Schopenhauer argues that the only way to still this pendulum is the melancholic "solution" which turns against the very source of its animation: the desiring ego. On this basis, he defends a radical cure of the narcissistic malaise: abolishing or extinguishing every stirring of desire or will.

In view of the nature of the ego as the phenomenon of an insatiable will to life, Schopenhauer claims that there is only one salvation from suffering: that is, the path of ascetic saints who deliberately mortify their own will. In this context, he maintains that

> [t]he absolute good, the *summum bonum*, [is] the complete self-effacement, and denial of the will, true will-lessness, which alone stills and silences for ever the cravings of the will; which alone gives that contentment that cannot again be disturbed; which alone is world-redeeming . . . and we may regard it as the only radical cure for the disease against which all other good things, such as fulfilled wishes and all attained happiness, are only palliatives, ano-dynes.[36]

Schopenhauer's radical asceticism aims to weaken the ego's willingness to will itself, to cast a shadow over the life of desire so that the ego voluntarily relinquishes all of its desires. He recommends ascetic self-mortification as the only means of diminishing the vehemence of the will to life. By asceticism he understands the "deliberate breaking of the will by refusing the agreeable and looking for the disagreeable, the voluntarily chosen way of life of penance and self-chastisement, for the constant mortification of the will."[37] Taken to its limit, the ascetic subject deliberately seeks out suffering and pain, chastising and mortifying its own will, so that it can find its "highest joy and delight in death."[38] The ascetic "cure" is radical in the proper sense of the word: it goes to the root of the problem, which for Schopenhauer is the will to life conceived of as a pathos.

Put in psychoanalytic terms, Schopenhauer's radical cure springs from the painful loss of the original condition of narcissistic plenitude that precedes the emergence of an ego aware of itself as separate from and dependent on a world of recalcitrant objects. Rather than accepting this loss of plenitude and seeking ways to fashion an ego capable of tolerating the inevitable interweaving of pain and pleasure, Schopenhauer's melancholic ascetic demands nothing less than to revert to this original condition. He reasons that since human beings seek permanent, untroubled gratification, and since the ego's inextinguishable desiring constantly opens the psyche to new, painful stimulation, the ego itself must be abolished.

In other words, Schopenhauer believes that because the desiring ego does not satisfy the narcissistic yearning for archaic plenitude it should be annihilated through ascetic practices. He thus embraces the melancholic solution to narcissistic suffering: the ascetic's practice of mortifying rather than gratifying the desiring ego. Rather than making the futile effort to secure plenitude through consuming transient or perishable goods, an effort which only serves to keep the ego oscillating between pain and boredom, the ascetic solution wards off all pain by denying its source: the pathos of desire. In those who have freely denied their will, Schopenhauer says,

instead of the restless pressure and effort; instead of the constant transition
from desire to apprehension and from joy to sorrow, we see that peace that is
higher than all reason, that *ocean-like calmness of the spirit*, that deep tranquillity . . . whose mere reflection in the countenance, as depicted by Raphael and
Corregio, is a complete and certain gospel.[39]

The ascetic who has annihilated the desires, Schopenhauer explains, "is
then left only as pure knowing being, as the undimmed mirror of the world.
Nothing can distress or alarm him any more; nothing can move him; for he
has cut all the thousand threads of willing which hold us bound to the
world, and which as craving, fear, envy, and anger drag us here and there in
constant pain."[40] It is through this melancholic self-abasement that
Schopenhauer believes the subject can gratify its most ardent desire for the
complete, undisturbed quiescence or repose which is entirely indifferent to
the welfare of the ego. Self-mortification to the point of indifference to the
preservation of the ego is the high price we must pay to achieve the painless
condition that the ego inevitably fails to attain when it attempts to gratify
rather than renounce its wishes. In *The Wanderer and His Shadow*, Nietzsche
gives a lyrical description of the melancholic's self-negation: "he wants
nothing, he is troubled by nothing, his heart stands still, only his eyes are
alive—it is death with open eyes."[41] Ultimately, according to Nietzsche and
Freud, Schopenhauer's melancholic wants to revert to the narcissism of
dreamless sleep through the work of self-mortification and self-depletion.
The work of mortification is complete, he maintains, when the ego reaches
a state of resignation in which death itself appears as a blessing. "Even in
your folly and despising, you despisers of the body," as Zarathustra puts this
point, "you are serving your Self . . . your Self wants to die and turns away
from life."[42]

Nietzsche not only criticises the metaphysical and psychological basis
of Schopenhauer's defence of melancholia, points we shall return to
shortly, he also expresses this critique through comic satire. By adopting
this satirical style Nietzsche implies that we need comic relief from ourselves and our suffering if we are to penetrate to the core of, and treat,
the narcissistic suffering that holds us in its grip. In counselling the troubled Serenus, Seneca reflects on how to avoid the pathological oscillation between melancholia and mania, or, as he puts it, "how the mind
may always pursue a steady, unruffled course, may be pleased with itself,
and look with pleasure upon its surroundings . . . *without being either
elated or depressed*."[43] In doing so, Seneca distinguishes between Stoic
self-composure, which he claims can sustain the subject's relatedness to
and pleasure in the world, and what we have described as nirvanic withdrawal. Seneca in fact classifies this weariness as among those diseases
that prevent us from attaining true tranquillity, and which therefore must

be treated by the Stoic philosophical physician. He identifies this distressed weariness by humorously observing that there are those "who, like bad sleepers, turn from side to side, and settle themselves first in one manner and then in another, until at last they find rest through sheer weariness."[44] Nietzsche borrows Seneca's jest to provide both insight into Schopenhauerian resignation as a symptom of the exhaustion generated by the melancholic self-torment, and, like Seneca, in order to supply the tonic of comic relief:

> *Resignation.*—What is resignation? It is the most comfortable position of an invalid who, having tossed and turned in his torment in an endeavour to *find* it, at last *grew tired* through this tossing and turning—and therewith found it![45]

FROM MELANCHOLIA TO MANIA

According to Freud, as we have seen, every subject is haunted by a nostalgia for the condition of primary narcissism in which the "great reservoir of libido" is accumulated in the undifferentiated ego-id. Primary narcissism, he claims, is never finally or wholly abandoned but simply displaced and reproduced in and through various disguises and symptoms. "To be their own ideal once more as they were in childhood," he emphatically declares, "this is what people strive to attain as their own happiness."[46] Freud develops this thesis by suggesting that on the intrapsychic plane this compulsion to reclaim narcissistic plenitude explains the genesis of a special agency within the psyche, the ideal ego or ego ideal, that can serve as the repository of our abandoned plenitude:

> This ideal ego is now the target of the self-love which was enjoyed in childhood by the actual ego. The subject's narcissism makes its appearance displaced on to this new ideal ego, which, like the infantile ego, finds itself possessed of every perfection that is of value. . . . What he projects before him as his ideal is the substitute for the lost narcissism of his childhood in which he was his own ideal.[47]

In other words, Freud suggests that it is the attempt to rescue the oceanic feeling that underpins the initial differentiation of the psyche into ego and ego ideal. It is a differentiation, as we shall see in later chapters, with profound implications for the odyssey of the subject and its relations with others. For this differentiation of the psyche places a new set of obstacles in the path of our attempt to recapture some vestiges of the archaic experience of narcissistic plenitude. In the first place, according to Freud, while we are compelled to form an ego ideal, and to seek our satisfaction by fulfilling its demands, the mere issuing of such imperatives by this agency, as he observes, does not supply us with the psychological resources for satisfying them:

> A man who has exchanged his narcissism for homage to a high ego ideal has not necessarily on that account succeeded in sublimating his libidinal instincts. It is true that the ego ideal demands such sublimations, but it cannot enforce it; sublimation remains a special process which may be prompted by the ideal but the execution of which is entirely independent of any such promptings.[48]

Secondly, the breakup of the narcissistic monad and its division into ego and ego ideal means that the ego "enters into a relation of an *object* to the ego ideal which has been developed out of it, and that all the interplay between an external object and the ego as a whole . . . may possibly be repeated upon this new scene of action within the ego."[49] Freud believes that it is the genesis of the ego ideal from an originally undifferentiated psyche which establishes the nucleus from which the melancholic malady of self-abnegation can develop, for it makes it possible for the ego to be treated as a mere object.

Indeed, it is precisely this reconfiguration of narcissism, we might say, that underlies Schopenhauer's melancholic self-mortification: because the ego ideal places the impossible demand on the ego to attain a state of plenitude it ultimately turns against and lacerates the ego as the source of its suffering and anguish. Just as the infant rages against and seeks to annihilate external objects when it discovers that they do not immediately yield to its wishes, so too, Freud claims, in melancholia the ego ideal replays this rage, but against the ego rather than an external object. "The reproaches and attacks directed towards the object," as he sums up the point, "come to light in the shape of melancholic self-reproaches."[50]

Freud argues that melancholic self-abasement develops when, rather than giving up its narcissistic investment in an external object, an investment, that is to say, made in the hope that the object might restore to it the feeling of plenitude, the ego withdraws this investment from the object and instead identifies itself with the abandoned external object. By identifying itself with the abandoned object in this way, Freud writes,

> the shadow of the object fell upon the ego, and the latter could henceforth be judged by a special agency, as though it were an object, a forsaken object. In this way object loss was transformed into ego loss and the conflict between the ego and the loved person into a cleavage between the critical activity of the ego and the ego altered by identification. . . . If the love for the object . . . takes refuge in narcissistic identification, then the hate comes into operation on this substitutive object [i.e., the ego], abusing it, debasing it, making it suffer and deriving sadistic satisfaction from its suffering.[51]

Schopenhauer arrives at the malaise of melancholia along exactly the pathway Freud identifies as the source of this disease: rather than mourning the loss of the loved object through which the ego had forlornly hoped to regain plenitude, it identifies part of itself with this object and then rages against this part of itself for failing to become the desired source of permanent satisfaction. According to Schopenhauer, we must eschew the delusion that we could ever find an object, or, as he puts it "something in life that is not to be found at all," namely, an object that could satisfy all of our needs, as if it were magically attuned to us, so that we could never again experience want, need or loss. Because we can never find such an object (or *refind* it, if we accept the psychoanalytic notion that this object is a phantasy generated on the basis of our lost fusion with the [m]other), Schopenhauer maintains, we are caught in the bind of constantly seeking that which we can never find.[52] The radical solution to this loss of the magical or transformational object, he argues, is the melancholic solution; we must, Schopenhauer says, "denounce our own inner nature," our ego, "as the source of our sufferings."[53] In the most extreme case of melancholia, Freud maintains, the ego can kill itself because through identification it treats itself as an object and thus can "direct against itself the hostility that relates to an object and which represents the ego's original reaction to objects in the external world."[54] It is just this extreme melancholia Schopenhauer gives full license to in his doctrine of ascetic self-mortification.

Now, according to Freud, it is this melancholic self-abasement that fuels the need for manic intoxication.[55] According to Freud, the misery of the melancholic

> cannot be borne for long . . . and has to be temporarily undone. . . . The Saturnalias of the Romans and our modern carnival agree in this essential feature with the festivals of primitive people, which usually end in debaucheries of every kind and the transgression of what are at other times the most sacred commandments . . . the ego ideal comprises the sum of all the limitations in which the ego has to acquiesce, and for that reason the abrogation of the ideal would necessarily be a magnificent festival for the ego, which might once again feel satisfied with itself.[56]

In other words, the ego finds temporary release from melancholic self-mortification in mania, or the abrogation of the harsh, censorious ego ideal. Freud sees melancholia and mania as opposing symptoms of the "sharp conflict between the two agencies of [the] ego" that emerge from the attempt to retain our narcissistic plenitude through such splitting. In Schopenhauerian melancholia, as we have seen, the ego ideal cruelly mortifies the ego in a quest to achieve the ultimate quiescence of dreamless sleep or death, whereas in mania the ego violently brushes aside its tormentor through carnivalesque transgressions in order to regain a sense of self-satisfaction.[57] Nietzsche with his signature pithiness and psychological acuity sums up this connection between melancholia and mania: "The mother of excess is not joy but joylessness!"[58]

MUSICAL INTOXICATION

In *Human, All Too Human* and *Daybreak*, Nietzsche attempts to liberate his thinking from the metaphysical, aesthetic and ethical presuppositions that he had absorbed from Schopenhauer and Wagner. One of the main points Nietzsche puts at stake in the self-critique he undertakes in the middle works is the narcissistic longing to regress to a condition anterior to the distinction between self and world, an absolute release from the tensions that disturb the subject in the wake of separation and individuation. In the middle works, Nietzsche comes to realise the extent to which his own thinking betrayed some aspects of this narcissistic nostalgia, a nostalgia that, in Schopenhauer's case, fuels his defence of the "nirvana" principle.

In his early works, however, Nietzsche accentuates and celebrates the other side of melancholia: what he characterises as ecstatic dedifferentiation of subjectivity, or what we have been describing, using Freud's terms, as the manic abrogation of the ego ideal for the sake of the momentary intoxication of an otherwise abject ego. Nietzsche, who famously remarks that life without music is an error, filters his understanding of this mania through his experience and interpretation of musical intoxication. In the middle works, however, far from affirming this manic intoxication, Nietzsche critically explores it as a symptom of pathological nostalgia for plenitude that haunts the subject. By criticising musical intoxication in *Human, All Too Human*, in other words, Nietzsche assails his early works for falling prey to the powerful allure of self-dissolution, whose flipside, as he comes to see, is precisely Schopenhauerian melancholia. It follows that the broader shifts in Nietzsche's conceptualisation of subjectivity must be understood as beginning with his analysis and rejection of the nostalgia for the condition of primary narcissism that, on the intrapsychic plane, gives rise to the twinned pathologies of melancholia and mania. A brief exegesis of Nietzsche's early debt to Schopenhauer and Wagner's musical metaphysics will illuminate the scope and nature of the reorientation that marks the middle period and its shift toward an ethics of self-cultivation.

In *The Birth of Tragedy* Nietzsche famously construes music as the Dionysian art par excellence. He explicitly grounds this conception of music on Schopenhauer's metaphysical account of musical phenomena, itself the theoretical culmination of German Romanticism's celebration of music's radical superiority over the other arts. Above all the other arts, the romantics hail music for its capacity to explore the depths of unconscious emotions and desires; as Wackenroder suggestively put it, "music teaches us to feel our own feeling."[59] "Music unlocks for man the gateway to an unknown realm," E. T. A. Hoffman wrote in his essay on Beethoven's instrumental music, "a world which has nothing in common with the eternal world of the senses that surrounds him, and in which he leaves behind all definable feelings so as to abandon himself to an ineffable yearning."[60] In the current context, however, the most significant aspect of this rich vein of romanticism in Nietzsche's early thinking is his attraction to Schopenhauer's assertion that the origins of music lie in the prelinguistic realm that precedes the formation of distinct subjects and objects. For Nietzsche, as we shall see, music becomes a cipher for the recovery of the primal unity and plenitude that precedes the formation of individuated phenomena.

Following Schopenhauer's lead, Nietzsche claims in the early, unpublished essay "On Music and Words" that "the origin of music lies beyond all individuation."[61] Nietzsche believes that Dionysian musical intoxication provides an intimation of an archaic realm free of the "fetters of individuation" and separation, and its "tangible" effect is to release the subject from the constraints of compulsive self-identity.[62] Music, he claims, transports the listener to a sphere in which "individuation is broken and annulled."[63] Music expresses the universal, undifferentiated ground of being, and it works its magic most powerfully when it "blinds" the subject to the illusion of individuated, separate phenomena.[64] According to Nietzsche, then, Dionysian musical ecstasy dissolves the *principium individuationis* and the boundaries it establishes within itself, and between self and other. In Dionysian musical experiences, the subject forgets itself as a distinct, discontinuous individual and recaptures the universal basis of human experience—which in *The Birth of Tragedy* he refers to with the Schopenhauerian notion of will to life.

Schopenhauer's metaphysical grounding of music enables Nietzsche to establish music's pre-eminence over vision. He claims that music not only discloses being in itself as a single, unified will to life, but he goes so far as to claim that the will to life should be conceived as analogous to the form of music: "we could just as well call the world embodied music as embodied will."[65] Nietzsche treats the *melody* of the voice as the primeval and richest mode of communication; images and words, on the other hand, are little more than impoverished "echoes" of this original music. He grants the world of tone a privileged position because it issues directly from the "heart of the world," from "the primeval ground [which] is the same in all human beings."[66] Dramatic images and linguistic representations, he claims, restrict us to a narrowly circumscribed sphere of experiences, supplying a "delight in seeing" which is only a "delight because nothing reminds us of a sphere in which individuation is broken and annulled."[67] Stating the matter paradoxically, the "seeing" of discrete, separate appearances is a means of blinding the self to this undifferentiated sphere; shining Apollonian images, Nietzsche says, are "light patches to heal the gaze seared by the terrible night."[68] Musical ecstasy, by contrast, submerges the ego in the fundamentally undifferentiated ground of being which is its original matrix. On the basis of this distinction, Nietzsche claims that we need to account for two opposed types of art; while dramatic and visual arts arouse pleasure in beautifully distinct, radiant images, music arouses pleasure in the breakdown or destruction of these bounded, individuated forms.[69] In Dionysian music, he writes, "the spell of individuation is broken and the path is open to the Mothers of Being, to the innermost core of things."[70]

In this early period, Nietzsche grants the state of undifferentiated fusion an ontological status that he denies the realm of individuation and representation. Nietzsche points to the ontological primacy of fusion through his repeated use of maternal metaphors to describe music's origins and effects.[71] These metaphors underline his claim that music emerges from and transports the listener to a sphere of experience where the separation or gulf between subject and object is absent or annulled. It is Dionysian music, he implies, which recalls the ego to its primordial experience of symbiosis with the maternal, and in doing so shatters the magic spell that keeps the individual imprisoned within its own narrow boundaries. If the metaphysical ground of life is one—the *Urmutter*, as Nietzsche calls it—then individuation can only be a source of suffering, a fetter from which the self seeks release. It is musical intoxication, according to Nietzsche, that supplies the key to this release by recalling the ego to the pleasures of the archaic, pre-individuated unity of the maternal world.[72]

In *The Birth of Tragedy*, Nietzsche is unequivocal that genuine joy in life is possible only when individuals lose themselves *as separate, differentiated individuals*:

> Dionysian art . . . wishes to convince us of the eternal delight of existence. . . . For a brief moment we really become the primal essence itself and feel its unbounded lust for existence and delight in existence . . . in Dionysian ecstasy . . . we are happy to be alive, not as individuals but as *the* single living thing, merged with its creative delight.[73]

It is only "the end of individuation" that "casts a ray of joy across the face of the world, torn and fragmented into individuals."[74] Nietzsche, in short, suggests that Dionysian musical intoxication (*Musikorgiasmus*) erases the ego's boundaries and enables it to merge with the "Primal Mother, eternally creative, eternally impelling into life, eternally drawing satisfaction from the ceaseless flux of the phenomena."[75] According to Nietzsche, it is not one's separate and distinct individuality—the individual's particular experiences or emotions—that one takes pleasure in through music, but the eternal will to life that remains untouched and undamaged by the continual creation and destruction of individual phenomena. In fact, the metaphysical fiction of an eternal will to life *consoles* the ego for the terrors of its own *individual* existence.[76] Since from the Dionysian perspective the *principium individuationis* is unbearable, the "eternal delight of existence" of which Nietzsche speaks is predicated on the ego overcoming itself through ecstatic identification with the "eternal life" or the "Primal Mother."

DIONYSIAN MANIA: THE OTHER SIDE OF MELANCHOLIA

In *The Birth of Tragedy* then Nietzsche follows Schopenhauer in maintaining that the condition of individuation or ego differentiation is the fundamental source of human suffering. He claims that the pain of individuation can be alleviated through the reflective consolation supplied by the metaphysical principle that an eternal will to life is present in all merely transient phenomena, or through the ecstatic self-destruction of the enclosed, bounded subject. In the middle works, however, Nietzsche abandons the metaphysical notion of a noumenal realm, and he therefore eschews any notion of being metaphysically consoled for the tragic and useless "squandering" of life.[77] At the same time, he also identifies the continuities between his own celebration of Dionysian "being-outside-oneself, or εκστασις, and the death-welcoming, nirvanic mood at the heart of Schopenhauer's asceticism.[78]

In *Human, All Too Human* and *Daybreak*, Nietzsche criticises his own early faith in the manic dissolution of the split, differentiated ego, the revelling in the loss of boundaries he associates with Dionysus, as a sickness of the soul stemming from an inability to bear separation and individuation. Nietzsche claims "self-relinquishment" is *neurotic* insofar as it engenders greater *ressentiment* toward one's bounded, differentiated ego and (importantly) toward one's neighbours, and in doing so deepens the longing for the narcissistic retreat into womb-like quiescence that lies at the heart of Schopenhauer's philosophy. As we shall see, this re-evaluation of his early thinking is integral to understanding the ethics of self-cultivation that he introduces in the middle works.

Nietzsche opens *Human, All Too Human* by announcing his intention of bracketing all metaphysical claims in the name of a historical and psychologically oriented investigation of the genesis of thought.[79] His critical suspension of metaphysical ideas includes "putting on ice" his own earlier Schopenhauerian assertion that music expresses being *an sich*. Alongside a sceptical, historicising turn against Schopenhauer's metaphysical claims he also repudiates the creative and transformative value of musical experiences of manic intoxication.[80] On the first issue, he relinquishes the Schopenhauerian notion that music is an unmediated "presencing" of the eternal ground of being, or that any direct presencing of the "thing-in-itself" is possible.[81] Nietzsche suspends all such metaphysical speculation for the sake of investigating the genesis of such claims. Briefly stated, he claims that it is the individual's sufferings—caused by either the "errors of reason" or by the inability to bear solitude, separateness and vulnerability—that give birth to all metaphysical visions of another eternal world.[82]

More importantly for our purposes, this scepticism with regard to Schopenhauer's metaphysics feeds his doubts about the value of musical intoxication as a source of artistic creativity or existential affirmation.[83] Nietzsche critically analyses the intoxicating effects of Wagner's "endless melody" as a vehicle for re-evaluating the creative promise and potential he had once attributed to manic self-dissolution:

> *How modern music is supposed to make the soul move.*—The artistic objective pursued by modern music in what is now, in a strong but nonetheless obscure phrase, designated "endless melody" can be made clear by imagining one is going into the sea, gradually relinquishing a firm tread on the bottom and finally surrendering unconditionally to the watery element: one is supposed to *swim*. Earlier music constrained one—with a delicate or solemn or fiery movement back and forth, faster and slower—to *dance*: in pursuit of which the needful preservation of orderly measure compelled the soul of the listener to a continual *self-possession*. . . . Richard Wagner desired a different kind of *movement of the soul*: one related, as aforesaid, to swimming and floating.[84]

Nietzsche, of course, later describes the birth of self-consciousness as analogous to forcing marine creatures into becoming land animals.[85] Couched in terms of this analogy, Wagner's music expresses and incites a longing for the reverse movement: from self-possession to the submersion of the ego in an all-engulfing, undifferentiated element.

In Nietzsche's view, Wagner's musical innovations intoxicate listeners with an experience of ecstatic self-dissolution, seducing them with the pleasures of the ego's reimmersion in an undifferentiated, "fluid" medium, a pleasure that in his early works he counsels as the only radical cure for the suffering caused by separation and differentiation. By contrast, in the middle works Nietzsche elucidates the dangers of modern Wagnerian music as analogous to the perils faced by Odysseus in his voyage of homecoming (*nostos*). It has been argued that the key symbol of Nietzsche's critique of Dionsyian intoxication is Odysseus' confrontation with the song of the Sirens.[86] In *Human, All Too Human* he frames his liberation from Wagnerian music as analogous to overcoming the seduction of immortality and the boredom of satiation with which Calypso ensnares Odysseus for seven long years:[87]

> *Music and sickness.*—The danger inherent in modern music lies in the fact that it sets the chalice of bliss and grandeur so seductively to our lips and with such

a show of moral ecstasy that even the noble and self-controlled always drink from it a drop too much. This minimal intemperance, continually repeated, can however eventuate in a profounder convulsion and undermining of spiritual health than any coarser excess is able to bring about: so that there is in the end nothing for it but one day to flee the nymph's grotto and to make one's way through the perils of the sea to foggy Ithaca and to the arms of a simpler and more human wife.[88]

If we see the adventures of Odysseus as "dangerous temptations removing the self from its logical course" of individuation and differentiation, and the episode of the Sirens as recounting the greatest threat of complete ego dedifferentiation and merger, then Nietzsche diagnoses the malady of his early works as a nostalgia for narcissistic bliss.[89] This allegorical interpretation of the *Odyssey* in terms of the process of self-formation underscores the regressive pull of primary narcissism: "The strain of holding the I together adheres to the I in all stages; and the temptation to lose it has always been there with the blind determination to maintain it."[90] Nietzsche clearly concedes that his own early works succumb to the temptation to allow the I to dissolve in and through manic intoxication.

In *Human, All Too Human*, then, Nietzsche treats this yearning for ecstatic self-dissolution inspirited by romantic music as among the sicknesses that his new model of philosophical therapy aims to cure. It is for this reason, Nietzsche recounts in the preface he later added to this work, that he began his *antiromantic* self-treatment,

> by *forbidding* [him]self, totally and on principle, all romantic music, that ambiguous, inflated, oppressive art that deprives the spirit of its severity and cheerfulness and lets rampant every kind of vague longing and greedy, spongy desire. "*Cave musicam*" is to this day my advice to all who are man enough to insist on cleanliness in things of the spirit; such music unnerves, softens, feminises, its "eternal womanly" draws *us*—downwards![91]

According to Nietzsche, then, what the subject who suffers from Schopenhauer's romantic melancholia needs to be rescued from is the musical intoxication that entices it to surrender to the compulsive desire for the manic dissolution of the differentiated, self-reflective self, or, as he put it, the downgoing or going to ground that is one of, if not *the*, dominant chord of *The Birth of Tragedy*.

For, as Nietzsche comes to recognise, this mania simply reproduces rather than cures the melancholic disease. In the 1886 preface to *The Birth of Tragedy*, Nietzsche claims that he had "obscured and spoiled Dionysian intimations with Schopenhauer's formulae"; in his final work, he asserts that its "formulas [are] infected with the cadaverous perfume of Schopenhauer."[92] Nietzsche's choice of metaphor alludes to Schopenhauer's embrace of a melancholic asceticism that takes the "highest joy and delight in death."[93] If *The Birth of Tragedy* is spoiled by a cadaverous perfume, then, it could only have one source: that is, Schopenhauer's morbid melancholia.

In the middle works Nietzsche makes explicit the connection between melancholia and mania that he only tacitly identifies in the early works. Here he unequivocally condemns Dionysian intoxication and ecstasy as, in psychoanalytic terms, the manic pole of pathological narcissism:[94]

> *Der Glaube an den Rausch*—Men who enjoy moments of exaltation and ecstasy and who, on account of the contrast other states present and because of the way they have squandered their nervous energy, are ordinarily in a wretched and miserable condition, regard these moments as their real "self" and their wretchedness and misery as the effect of what is "outside" the self [*Ausser-sich*] and thus harbour the feelings of revengefulness towards their environment, their age, their entire world. Intoxication counts as their real life, as their actual ego: they see in everything else the opponent and obstructor of intoxication. . . . Mankind owes much that is *evil* to these wild inebriates: for they are insatiable sowers of the weeds of dissatisfaction with oneself and one's neighbour, of contempt for the age and the world, and especially of world-weariness [*Welt-Müdigkeit*]. Perhaps a whole Hell of criminals could not produce an effect so oppressive, poisonous to air and land, uncanny and protracted as does this noble little community of unruly, fantastic, half-crazy people of genius who cannot control themselves and can experience pleasure in themselves only when they have quite lost themselves.[95]

Nietzsche directly targets his own early account of the Dionysian, in particular his celebrated analogy of Dionysian music, with the physiological state of intoxication. Nietzsche criticises not only the longing for Dionysian intoxication, but also its aftereffects, which he describes in *The Birth of Tragedy* as a feeling of disgust or nausea with everyday reality that leads to an ascetic, will-negating mood.[96] Nietzsche suggests that when individuals associate pleasure with intoxicated self-dissolution, or when, to go one step further, they identify their "true" self with this undifferentiated condition, they exacerbate the suffering whose source lies in ego differentiation. Temporarily abolishing the ego ideal through mania, he acknowledges, only serves to make each successive return to the differentiated self more difficult to sustain, and thus creates the condition for vengefulness toward all that exists outside oneself, or all that obstructs the intoxicated regression to the phantasy of plenitude. By surrendering to the longing for manic dedifferentiation, individuals transform the world into a living hell for themselves: they experience the separation and differentiation of the ego as a painful loss of plenitude.

Thus in the middle works Nietzsche acknowledges the Dionysian drive to manic fusion as a *neurotic* defence against the painful experience of ego differentiation and separation. He comes to see Dionysian mania as a symptom of pathological narcissism, a symptom that only heightens the ego's dissatisfaction with and vengefulness toward itself *and* its neighbours. In short, Nietzsche identifies how mania reproduces and exacerbates melancholia. He therefore treats intoxication as both a cause and symptom of melancholia and its resigned *Welt-Müdigkeit*.[97]

On the intrapsychic level, then, Nietzsche claims the pathological narcissism that strives to recuperate the feeling of pre-ego plenitude through manic intoxication simply exacerbates the melancholia from which it draws its impetus. Since the narcissistic quest for fusion with the *Urmutter* turns the individual against its differentiated, "shrunken" ego it eventually generates a desire to achieve a *permanent* annihilation of the differentiated ego. Nietzsche recognises that a death-welcoming mood, embodied in the nirvana principle, is the logical consequence of the manic drive to return to the phantasy of plenitude. Schopenhauer's melancholic asceticism simply takes this pathological narcissism to its ultimate conclusion; it equates pleasure and redemption with the submersion of the self-conscious, "willful" ego in ocean-like contentment or calmness.[98] Because pathological narcissists cannot tolerate the world of phenomena—of spatio-temporally demarcated subjects and objects—they seek the destruction of the *principium individuationis* as the only way of reclaiming the undifferentiated, presubjective condition that precedes the birth of the subject. "One effect of the incapacity to accept separation, individuality, and death," as Norman O. Brown puts it, "is to erotize death—to activate a morbid wish to regress to the prenatal state before life (and separation) began, to the mother's womb."[99]

After 1876, then, Nietzsche recognises that his own earlier notion of manic self-dissolution carries the risk of engendering in the subject the same nihilistic turn against "this world" of separate, finite selves that he reviles in Schopenhauer's melancholic asceticism. It is by way of a revival of the Hellenistic practices of the self, as we shall see in the next chapter, that Nietzsche explores the possibility that one can bear one's differentiated ego, rather than falling into the pathology of melancholia and mania. Indeed, he maintains that without bearing oneself as a separate, distinct individual one cannot avoid the perils of *ressentiment* toward oneself and one's neighbour. Drawing on the Hellenistic analogy between philosophy and medicine, Nietzsche seeks to articulate an ethics of self-cultivation that can treat narcissistic "soul-sicknesses":

> *Where are the new physicians of the soul?*.—It has been the means of comfort which have bestowed upon life that fundamental character of suffering it is now believed to possess; the worst sicknesses of mankind originated in the way in which they have combated their sicknesses, and what seemed a cure has in the long run produced something worse than that which it was supposed to

overcome. The means which worked immediately, anaesthetising and intoxicating, the so-called consolations, were ignorantly supposed to be actual cures; the
fact was not even noticed, indeed, that these instantaneous alleviations often
had to be paid for with a general and profound worsening of the complaint,
that the invalid had to suffer from *the after-effect of intoxication,* later from the
withdrawal of intoxication, and later still from an oppressive general feeling of
restlessness, nervous agitation and ill-health. Past a certain degree of sickness
one never recovered—the physicians of the soul, those universally believed in
and worshipped saw to that. It is said of Schopenhauer, and with justice, that after they had been neglected for so long he again took seriously the sufferings of
mankind: where is he who, after they have been neglected for so long, will again
take seriously the antidotes to these sufferings and put in the pillory the un-
heard of quack-doctoring with which, under the most glorious names, mankind
has hitherto been accustomed to treat the sicknesses of the soul?[100]

Nietzsche undoubtedly includes not only Buddha and Christ, but Dionysus too among the "glorious names" he pillories.[101] In *Human, All Too Human,* Nietzsche implies that Dionysian intoxication exacerbates the malady
it is meant to cure: that is, the suffering which individuals experience in and
through the process of separation from a condition of undifferentiated,
"primal Oneness."[102] In psychoanalytic terms, Nietzsche treats Dionysian
mania as a rebellion against the differentiated ego, a dissolution of the
bounded ego into a phantasy return to the pre-ego "oceanic feeling." However, as he makes clear in *Daybreak* (52), the "cure" of manic intoxication
only serves to engender the melancholic desire for ascetic self-abnegation.

Yet, for all of his fulminations against Schopenhauer, Nietzsche does
gives him credit for once again taking seriously the sufferings of humankind. With this backhanded compliment Nietzsche implies that
Schopenhauer's melancholic vision is worthy of consideration because it is
deeply attuned to the suffering caused by the destruction of the blissful state
of plenitude that is necessary for the formation of the ego. Paradoxically, as
we have seen, Schopenhauer's melancholic ascetics demand a much higher
form of pleasure than the ego can arrive at through the satisfaction of particular wishes and impulses; they demand oceanic contentment or the objectless plenitude of primary narcissism. According to Schopenhauer, those
who cling to the "illusion" of their separate, differentiated ego see the ascetic's "flowing away into nothing," into womblike, oceanic contentment,
as a supreme danger, whereas for those who have once experienced dedifferentiation it becomes the only desirable end.[103] Hence he closes *The World
as Will and Representation* with the following antinomy:

> We freely acknowledge that what remains after the complete abolition of the
> will is, for all who are still full of the will, assuredly nothing. But also con-
> versely, to those in whom the will has turned and denied itself, this very real
> world of ours with all its suns and milkyways, is—nothing.[104]

However, while Nietzsche gives Schopenhauer credit for identifying the pain of our narcissistic loss, he repudiates both melancholic self-mortification and manic self-dissolution as neurotic responses to this loss. Instead he proposes to renew the Hellenistic and Stoic practices of self-cultivation as the proper antidote for the malady of the ideal. In the middle works, the fruit of his own "long years of convalescence," Nietzsche argues for the merits of Hellenistic and Stoic *therapeia* as the propaedeutic to the establishment of a mature, healthy ego that can bear its separation and differentiation.[105]

CODA

Even in the middle works Nietzsche, an inveterate lover of music, does not entirely devalue the musical arts or musically mediated experience. Rather, he transforms his philosophy of music on the basis of his psychological insights into the pathological expressions of primary narcissism. We can chart this reorientation in his philosophical approach to music in two dramatic shifts. In the first place, he explicitly rejects his earlier philosophical hymn in praise of the ecstasies and intoxications of Wagnerian music and explicitly criticises what he came to see as the theoretical fallacies of Schopenhauer's and Wagner's metaphysics of music.[106] Secondly, he begins to examine music as a source and medium of self-cognition rather than as "the truly metaphysical art of this life" as he had proclaimed it in the original 1871 preface to *The Birth of Tragedy*.[107] Nietzsche now explains the magical effect of music in terms of his understanding of the relationship between acoustics and memory. He suggests the texture of our earliest sensory impressions is stored in acoustic memories. Our memory traces of childhood, he claims, are carried forward by our first "musical delights," which, he maintains, are the "strongest of our life."[108] If the past can be restored to us, he suggests, it is through the medium of musical impressions. What these acoustic impressions store, according to Nietzsche, are the qualities of the lived experiences of our own personal past. He believes that a single musical impression can be sufficient to conjure up the texture of this lost time. In *Human, All Too Human*, therefore, Nietzsche conceives certain kinds of musical experiences as soundscapes that reproduce and revive lost moments and modes of experience.[109]

In *The Wanderer and His Shadow*, he arrives at this insight by taking issue with those "Pharisees of good taste" or "the experienced connoisseurs" who deprecate the pleasures of simple music in the name of the formal, artistic reception of "serious and opulent music."[110] For no matter "however favorably inclined we may be to such [serious] music," he writes, "there are . . . hours . . . when we are overcome, enchanted and almost melted away by its opposite: I mean those utterly simple Italian operatic melismas which, in

spite of all their rhythmic monotony and harmonic childishness, sometimes seem to sing to us like the soul of music itself."[111]

Nietzsche sets out to solve the aesthetic riddle as to why we are enchanted
and haunted by such music, and he attempts to do so by investigating the link
between music and memory. In this context, he speculates that the textures,
tones and tastes of past experience are embedded in acoustic memories. It is
for this reason, he implies, that the concept of a nonlinguistic or "musical" aspect of the psyche, expressed in the metaphor of the "strings of the soul," is
more than simply a literary figure or affectation. According to Nietzsche, under the spell of brief, simple musical phrases we are reconnected to our earliest musical experiences, the "nurse's song" or the "organ grinder's tune," and
these in turn "touch" the "strings of our soul," bringing to life a whole lost
world of early experiences. It is because such simple, sentimental music re-
connects us with our earliest musical experiences that they have what at first
might seem to be an inexplicable power to enchant.[112] The magic derives
from the fact that they unlock buried treasure chests of precious memory
traces. Nietzsche maintains that this reconnection with our first musical delights, the repositories of "childhood bliss," brings with it a mixture of aesthetic joy and moral grief. The aesthetic pleasures of this musically mediated
recovery of the past is, he explains, mixed with grief over "the loss of childhood, the feeling that what is most irrecoverable is our most precious possession—this too touches the strings of our soul and does so more powerfully
than art alone, however serious and opulent, is able to do."[113] Indeed, Nietzsche generalises this psychological interpretation of musical enchantment to
cover "almost all music," which, he says "produces a magical effect only when
we hear the language of our own *past* speaking out of it."[114] Since Italian
melismas and other kinds of simple music are the most infused with the sensations of the past it follows that they are also the most magical.

This music, he argues, unlocks a particular aspect of our childhood, an aspect that we can explicate in terms of what Freud identifies as one of the earliest inflections and modulations of narcissism. When the monadic stage of
primary narcissism has been surpassed and the incipient ego begins to
emerge as an agency that mediates the psyche's relationship to the object
world, it either wards off what is painful or attempts to incorporate what is
pleasurable, or, as Freud explains:

> When the narcissistic stage has given place to the object stage . . . pleasure and
> unpleasure signify relations of the ego to the object. If the object becomes a
> source of pleasurable feelings, a motor urge is set up which seeks to bring the
> object closer to the ego and to incorporate it into the ego. We can then speak
> of the "attraction" exercised by the pleasure-giving object and say that we "love"
> the object. . . . Conversely, if the object is a source of unpleasurable feeling,
> there is an urge . . . to repeat in relation to the object the original attempt at
> flight from the external world with its emission of stimuli.[115]

We might illuminate Nietzsche's conception of the nexus of music and memory with the aid of these Freudian terms: simple Italian operatic music transports us back to this stage of the pure pleasure ego, or, as Bachelard puts it, to "the days of happiness when the world is edible."[116] Such music is mellifluous in the true sense of the word: it makes the honey of the past flow. Nietzsche's description of the enchantments of such music fits the first modulation of narcissism in which the ego seeks to incorporate and taste the world; it recalls us to the moment, as Nietzsche puts it,

> when we tasted the virgin honey of many things for the first time, and the honey never again tasted so good, it seduced us to life, to living as long as we could, in the shape of our first spring, our first flowers, our first butterflies, our first friendship.[117]

Unlike those hypocritical arbiters of good taste, Nietzsche says, we ought not haughtily dismiss the pleasures of that simple music which conjures up these remembrances of things past because therein lies the magical effect of almost all music. (Indeed, he implies, that those who take pleasure in art purely as artists, and who therefore dismiss the melting aesthetic of the melisma, lack precisely *good taste*).[118] It is this magical effect, as he notes, that Faust discovers to his benefit at the end of the first scene of Goethe's *Faust*.[119] Nietzsche's speculations on the acoustics of memory in fact owe much to Goethe's vision of Faust's rebirth. In the depths of his deadly depression, we might recall, Faust hears the chiming of the Easter bells, which, as Marshall Berman describes it,

> bring him into touch with the whole buried life of childhood. Floodgates of memory are thrown open in his mind, waves of lost feelings rush in on him—love, desire, tenderness, unity—and he is engulfed by the depths of a child-hood world that his whole adulthood has forced him to forget. . . . Faust has inadvertently opened himself up to a whole lost dimension of his being, and so put himself in touch with sources of energy that can renew him.[120]

Yet, if in the middle works Nietzsche is willing to concede that music might have a tonic effect on the soul it is not modern Wagnerian musical ecstasies and melodramas, but those simple musical phrases that serve as soundscapes of the past.[121] Nietzsche values them not because they draw us away from ourselves, but because they enable us to fathom that which we have lost, the pure pleasure ego that seeks to incorporate the world and that experiences its transient beauties as if they were eternal. After his disenchantment with Wagner's and Schopenhauer's metaphysics of music, Nietzsche thus turns to a notion of music as a mode of self-cognition. In his paradoxical language, simple musical experiences illuminate the losses that otherwise lie hidden, but not for that reason inactive, in the night of the unconscious. "[I]n music," as he writes in *Daybreak*, "men let themselves go,

in the belief that when they are *concealed* in music no one is capable of seeing them."[122] Musical self-cognition, he claims, gives us just enough distance from the painful loss of childhood that we can learn to laugh a little
at our grief. It is a little laughter, he implies, through which we acknowledge
and moderate our narcissistic losses rather than plunge into the eternal
night of melancholia:

> *As friends of music.*—In the last resort we are and remain well disposed towards
> music for the same reason we are and remain well disposed towards moon-
> light. Neither wishes to supplant the sun, after all—both desire only to the best
> of their ability to illumine our *nights*. And yet—may we not make fun of them
> and laugh at them nonetheless? Just a little, at least? And from time to time?
> At the man in the moon! At the woman in music![123]

NOTES

1. Erwin Rohde, Letter to Nietzsche, June 16, 1878, quoted in Erich Heller, "Introduction," in *Human, All Too Human: A Book for Free Spirits*, translated by R. J.
Hollingdale, Cambridge University Press, Cambridge, vii–xix, esp. xi.

2. Nietzsche's dedications for *The Birth of Tragedy* and *Human, All Too Human*
hint at the scope and nature of the transformation in his intellectual commitments
and sympathies: whereas Nietzsche wrote the former as a manifesto on behalf of
Wagner, and laces it with Schopenhauerian formulae, he composed *Human, All Too
Human* in honour of Voltaire's spirit of emancipated scepticism. On the significance
Nietzsche later gives to this Voltaire dedication see, EH "Human, All Too Human,"
1. After the first edition Nietzsche scrapped the Voltaire epigraph and the quotation
from Descartes' *Meditations* that accompanied it.

3. The "malady of the ideal" is the subtitle of Janine Chasseguet-Smirgel's book
on the perversions of narcissism. She uses it as a shorthand expression for the idea
that we are all afflicted with the desire to restore a phantasised pre-Oedipal condition of plenitude, a desire which, she argues, spawns various perversions designed
to bridge the gap between the ego and the ego ideal; see Janine Chasseguet-Smirgel,
The Ego Ideal: A Psychoanalytic Essay on the Malady of the Ideal, translated by Paul Barrows, 1985, Free Association Books, London.

4. ON, 95.

5. CD, 1–10.

6. ON, 67.

7. GP, 80.

8. On this point see also Lou Salomé's astute comment: "[Narcissism] accompanies all the strata of our experience, independently of them. In other words, it is not
only an immature stage of life needing to be superseded, but also the ever renewing
companion of all life"; Lou Andreas-Salomé, "The Dual Orientation of Narcissism,"
The Psychoanalytic Quarterly, 31, 1962, 3–30.

9. CD, 3.

10. CD, 5.

11. Joel Whitebook, *Perversions and Utopia*, op. cit., 70.
12. IV, 134, 137. The narcissistic stage thus develops two relations to the object:

(1) "hate," which is the attempt to destroy all sources of unpleasure by destroying threatening external objects or projecting painful internal stimuli outward, and
(2) "love," which attempts to incorporate or devour the pleasure giving object through identification and introjection and is thus consistent with abolishing the object's separate existence.

In the narcissistic organisation of the libido, therefore, love and hate are barely distinguishable, for they both attempt to deny the object's existence, one through destruction, the other through incorporation. Narcissistic love is therefore deeply marked by ambivalence; it easily slides over into hatred where the love object cannot be incorporated.
13. CD, 4.
14. Freud's account of the psychical system as oriented exclusively toward the removal of pain and disturbances has been the subject of much dispute. For a critique of this monadic conceptualisation of the prelinguistic subject, see Daniel N. Stern, *Interpersonal World of the Infant: A View from Psychoanalysis and Developmental Psychology*, 1985, Basic Books, New York; for a critical response to Stern's claim to have invalidated the assumption of primordial state of symbiosis, see C. Fred Alford, *Narcissism: Socrates, the Frankfurt School, and Psychoanalytic Theory*, 1988, Yale University Press, New Haven, Conn., and London, 8–9.
15. CD, 5.
16. Melanie Klein develops this notion of "the universal longing for the prenatal state" of womb-like security; see Melanie Klein, *Envy and Gratitude*, op. cit., 179.
17. Herbert Marcuse claims that "[t]he idea that mankind in general and in its individuals is still dominated by 'archaic' powers is one of Freud's most profound insights"; see Herbert Marcuse, *Five Lectures, Psychoanalysis, Politics and Utopia*, 1970, translated by J. J. Shapiro and Shierry M. Weber, Beacon Press, Boston, 8. In his great work on Freud's philosophical contribution, Paul Ricoeur suggests that if we interrelate all of the "modalities of archaism" we find in psychoanalytic theory "there is formed the complex figure of destiny in reverse, a destiny that draws one backward"; see Paul Ricoeur, *Freud and Philosophy: An Essay on Interpretation*, translated by Denis Savage, 1970, Yale University Press, New Haven, Conn., and London, 452.
18. Janine Chasseguet-Smirgel, *The Ego Ideal*, op. cit., 7.
19. For an attempt to introduce a plural and critical version of nostalgia, see Michael Janover, "Nostalgias," *Critical Horizons* 1, no. 1, 2000, 113–33.
20. For further elaboration of this point see C. Fred Alford, *Narcissism*, op. cit, 27, 68; and Joel Whitebook, "Mutual Recognition and the Work of the Negative," in William Rehg and James Bohman (eds.), *Pluralism and the Pragmatic Turn: The Transformation of Critical Theory, Essays in Honor of James McCarthy*, 2001, MIT Press, Cambridge, Mass.
21. Joel Whitebook, *Perversions and Utopia*, op. cit., 64.
22. Schopenhauer explicitly identifies a Buddhist conception of nirvana as the representation closest to his own metaphysical vision. See for example, WWR 1, §63, 356.

23. Christopher Lasch, "Introduction" in Janine Chasseguet-Smirgel, *The Ego Ideal*, op. cit., xi.

24. Ibid.

25. Ibid.

26. WWR1, §65, 362

27. BPP, 310–11, emphasis added.

28. BPP, 311.

29. WWR1, §57, 312.

30. WWR1, §56, 309.

31. WWR1, §56, 309.

32. See WWR1, §68, 392. It is for this reason that Nietzsche lampoons Schopenhauer's conception of the will, "which from the description [he gives] of this all-one-will, is as good as wanting to make God out to be the stupid Devil"; HAH2, 5.

33. WWR1, 309. Schopenhauer's account of the self-defeating will draws on Lucretius' use of the image of drawing water with the vessels of the Danaides. We should note, however, that Schopenhauer transforms the meaning of Lucretius' imagery: for Lucretius it serves as a caution against constantly seeking for what is not, rather than against seeking per se. In other words, this gloomy Epicurean, as Nietzsche describes Lucretius, does *not* argue, as Schopenhauer does, that the transience of feelings of pleasure is any reason to spurn it. On the contrary, Lucretius asserts that we should enjoy all the prizes of life without expecting permanent satisfaction, or, more precisely, that in order to enjoy these prizes we must in fact forego this narcissistic aim; see Lucretius, *On the Nature of the Universe*, op. cit., Bk 3, l. 1082, and ll. 931–52.

34. WWR1, §29, 164; see also WWR1, §57, 313–14, §65, 364.

35. WWR1, §57, 312. In HAH2 Nietzsche brilliantly satirises Schopenhauer's conception of the will's pendulum see HAH2, 349, and also WS, 308.

36. WWR1, §65, 362.

37. WWR1, §68, 392.

38. WWR1, §68, 398.

39. WWR1, §71, 411, emphasis added.

40. WWR1, §68, 390. As Nietzsche notes in the *Genealogy*, Schopenhauer imagines here a perspective-less eye, "an eye turned in no particular direction, in which the active and interpreting forces through which alone seeing becomes seeing something"; GM, Bk 3, 12. However, it should be noted that as Schopenhauer begins to accentuate the ascetic ethics in the final book of WWR1, he gives the notion of perspective-less seeing a different significance. In the final book he values it *not* for its (alleged) epistemological advantages, but because it satisfies the subject's wish for detached, serene composure.

41. WS, 308.

42. TSZ, 1, "On the Despisers of the Body."

43. OT, 255–56, emphasis added.

44. OT, 255–56.

45. D, 518.

46. ON, 95.

47. ON, 88.

48. ON, 89.

49. GP, 79–80.

50. GP, 83.

51. MM, 258, 260.

52. Freud discusses the anamnestic function of the ego, that is to say, its desire to *"refind"* its lost object, in his 1925 paper "On Negation," but the point stretches as far back as the 1895 *Project* where the object to be found is the mother's breast.

53. WWR1, 318; I borrow the concept "transformational object" from Bollas; see Bollas quoted in Martha Nussbaum, *Upheavals of Thought*, op. cit., 184.

54. MM, 261.

55. Freud identifies a spontaneous and a psychogenic explanation for the oscillation between melancholia and mania. In the former the ego spontaneously rebels against the ego ideal because of its severity, a rebellion that takes the shape of manic intoxication, and in the latter, the ego is incited to rebellion by ill-treatment on the part of its ideal, but this ill-treatment is one it encounters because it has become identified with an abandoned or lost object; see GP, 81–84.

56. GP, 81.

57. GP, 83.

58. HAH2, 77. On this point, see also D, 39:

> *Pure "spirit" a prejudice.*—Wherever the teaching of pure spirituality has ruled it destroyed nervous energy with its excesses: it has taught deprecation, neglect or tormenting of the body and men to torment and deprecate themselves on account of the drives which fill them; it has produced gloomy, tense and oppressed souls. . . . A general chronic over-excitability was finally the lot of these virtuous pure-spirits: the only pleasure they could still recognise was in the form of ecstasy and other precursors of madness—and their system attained its summit when it came to take ecstasy for the higher goal of life and the standard by which all earthly things stood condemned.

59. Heinrich Wackenroder, quoted in Hans Georg Schenk, *The Mind of the European Romantics: An Essay in Cultural History*, 1979, Oxford University Press, New York, 202.

60. E. T. A. Hoffman, quoted in ibid., 232.

61. MW, 111.

62. BT, 21.

63. MW, 110.

64. MW, 113.

65. WWR1, §52, 262–63. Nietzsche quotes this passage approvingly as part of his attempt to explain and defend the thesis that tragedy is born from the spirit of music; see BT, 16.

66. MW, 108.

67. MW, 110.

68. BT, 9.

69. BT, 16.

70. BT, 16.

71. Nietzsche's maternal metaphors also suggest that like post-Freudian psychoanalysts Nietzsche understands ecstatic dedifferentiation as a phantasised regression to the infant's primordial state of symbiosis with the mother. We might consider the following description of Dionysian manic self-dissolution in this light: "in the mystical

triumphal cry of Dionysus the spell of individuation is broken and the path is open to the Mothers of Being, to the innermost core of things"; and "[the Dionysian] takes the world of phenomena to its limits, where it denies itself and seeks to escape back to the womb of the true sole reality . . . [the] tremendous Dionysiac impulse . . . devours this whole world of phenomena, in order, behind it and through its destruction, to give a sense of a supreme artistic primal joy within the womb of the primal Oneness"; see, BT, 16, and BT, 2, respectively.

72. BT, 16.

73. BT, 17, emphasis added.

74. BT, 10.

75. BT, 16, 21.

76. See BT, 7: "The metaphysical consolation . . . that whatever superficial changes may occur, life is at bottom indestructibly powerful and joyful."

77. HAH1, 33

78. See also Nietzsche's 1869 Note: "In those orgiastic festivals of Dionysus there prevailed such a degree of being-outside-oneself, that men acted and felt like transformed beings"; quoted in John Sallis, *Crossings: Nietzsche and the Space of Tragedy*, Chicago University Press, Chicago, 1991, 53.

79. See, for example, HAH1, 1–3, 16–18.

80. In a fragmentary essay written in 1868 Nietzsche had already laid out the major analytic type arguments against both Schopenhauer's metaphysical principle of the *Wille zu Leben* in particular, and metaphysical claims in general. Despite this critique, however, Schopenhauer's notion of a primordial will to life seems to underpin the central argument of *The Birth of Tragedy*. Henry Staten convincingly demonstrates that Nietzsche tried to write this concept out of his first work, but failed because the whole argument pivots on the idea of an "eternal," metaphysical will to life. One of Schopenhauer's foremost contemporary interpreters, Christopher Janaway, argues that on the balance of evidence we must concur with Staten's understanding of the significance of Schopenhauer's metaphysics of the will for *The Birth of Tragedy*. John Sallis, by contrast, draws on Nietzsche's notebooks from the late 1860s and early 1870s to show that any interpretation that assimilates *The Birth of Tragedy* to Schopenhauer's metaphysical axis misunderstands the way in which his notion of Dionysian ecstasy "twists" free of the metaphysics of being and appearance. See Nietzsche, "On Schopenhauer," appendix 1, in Christopher Janaway (ed.), *Willing and Nothingness: Schopenhauer as Nietzsche's Educator*, 1998, Clarendon Press, Oxford, 258–65; Henry Staten, *Nietzsche's Voice*, op. cit., 192; Christopher Janaway, "Schopenhauer as Nietzsche's Educator," in Christopher Janaway (ed.), *Willing and Nothingness*, op. cit., 24; and John Sallis, *Crossings*, op. cit.

81. See, for example, HAH1, 215, 218, 220.

82. HAH1, 17, 27.

83. For Nietzsche's critique of the idea that intoxication and inspiration are the source of artistic creation, see, for example, HAH1, 155, 164.

84. HAH2, 134.

85. GM, 2, 16.

86. Rüdiger Safranski claims that this celebrated episode of Homer's *Odyssey* was Nietzsche's symbol of the chiastic nature of Dionysian musical intoxication and transgression. As Safranski explains: "From the vantage point of everyday conscious-

ness, the Dionysian is horrifying. By the same token, the Dionysian perspective regards everyday reality as horrifying. Conscious life moves between both outlooks, and this movement is tantamount to being torn in two. . . . It is hardly surprising that Nietzsche found the symbol for this precarious situation in the fate of Odysseus, who had himself bound to the mast in order to hear the song of the sirens without having to follow it to his own destruction"; see Rüdiger Safranski, *Nietzsche*, op. cit., 80.

87. Homer, *Odyssey*, Bk V.

88. HAH2, 159. It is perhaps worth speculating that among all of Odysseus' adventures he might have selected as an allegory of self-formation and its perils, Nietzsche chose the Calypso episode, rather than the more obvious symbol of the song of the Sirens, for peculiarly personal reasons: that is, like Odysseus, who was detained on the island of Ogygia by Calypso for seven years, Nietzsche came to feel that he too had been ensnared in a stifling friendship with Richard and Cosima Wagner, which also, as far he was concerned, lasted almost exactly seven years, from his first visit to Tribschen on May 17, 1869, to the months leading up to the first Bayreuth Festival in July 1876.

89. See Theodor W. Adorno and Max Horkheimer, *Dialectic of Enlightenment*, 1979, translated by John Cummings, Verso, London, 47.

90. Ibid., 33.

91. HAH2, preface, 3. Nietzsche conceptualises the recovery of oneself as, in part, a struggle to overcome the "feminine"; understood in this context as a metaphor for ecstatic dedifferentiation and the loss of ego-boundaries, that is, in terms of the condition of primary narcissism. The lure of the "feminine" that Nietzsche seeks to resist is the yearning for self-dissolution. In the 1886 preface to the second volume of *Human, All Too Human* Nietzsche sees his own struggle for self-mastery as one that requires an overcoming of his own "greedy desire" for primordial fusion. Nietzsche's metaphors of the feminine have been the subject of much recent discussion and dispute, along with his largely negative stance on the emerging feminist movement of the nineteenth century. Contemporary interpretations of Nietzsche on feminism range from deconstructionist attempts to salvage an affirmative account of his perspectivism for use by feminists through to readings that take Nietzsche at his word and see him as fundamentally antifeminist. However, it should be noted that in her detailed examination of Nietzsche's middle works, Ruth Abbey suggests that at least in part, "Nietzsche's middle period offers a nonessentialist, sympathetic reading of the female condition." The wide range of views and controversy on this issue are well represented in Paul Patton (ed.), *Nietzsche, Feminism and Political Theory*, 1993, Allen and Unwin, Sydney; see also Ruth Abbey, "Beyond Metaphor and Misogyny: Women in Nietzsche's Middle Period," op. cit., 233–56, 248; and Kathleen M. Higgins, "Gender in *The Gay Science*," *Philosophy and Literature* 19, no. 2, 1995, 227–47.

92. BT, preface, 6, and EH, "*The Birth of Tragedy*," 1.

93. WWR1, Bk 4, §68, 398, and §71, 411–12. The confusion of pleasure and death, *eros* and *thanatos*, has of course bedevilled psychoanalytic theory since Freud introduced these Schopenhauerian motifs in BPP; For a discussion of this issue, see Herbert Marcuse, *Five Lectures*, op. cit.

94. For Nietzsche's use of the term *verzuckten* to describe the Dionysian condition, see BT, 1 and 7.

95. D, 50.

96. BT, 7; see also Nietzsche's essay from June 1870, which he presented to Cosima Wagner at Christmas 1870, "The Birth of Tragic Thought," translated by Ursula Bernis in *Graduate Faculty Philosophy Journal* 9, no. 2, Fall 1983, 12–13.

97. Zarathustra, it should be recalled, twice encounters Schopenhauer's doctrine in the guise of the prophet of great weariness (*Müdigkeit*) whose teachings he parodies: "All is the same, nothing is worthwhile, the world is without meaning, knowing chokes"; TSZ IV, "The Cry of Need"; see also TSZ II, "The Prophet."

98. WWR1, §71, 411.

99. Norman O. Brown, *Life against Death*, op. cit., 107.

100. D, 52, emphasis added.

101. For Nietzsche's satirical treatment of Christ as a failed physician, see, for example, WS, 83.

102. BT, 1 and 7.

103. WWR1, §71, 411.

104. WWR1, §71, 411–12.

105. HAH1, preface, 4.

106. HAH1, 215: "[N]o music speaks of the 'will' or of the 'thing in itself.'"

107. BT 1871, preface to Richard Wagner.

108. WS, 168.

109. Nietzsche's contribution to the phenomenology of perception would make an interesting topic for another study. It is worth noting that in this aphorism Nietzsche, like Herder, treats hearing as the "inner sense," in contrast to the distancing and objectifying sense of sight. It is because in hearing it is more difficult for us to discern and maintain the separation between subject and object that acoustic phenomena are far better at conjuring up our intrapsychic or inner world, or, to put it another way, that we hear ourselves in music more than we see ourselves in objects. In this lies the secret of music as a source of self-cognition. Music enables us to hear what normally remains hidden from view, and thus it can become, paradoxically, a rich source of self-observation and self-revelation. Musical self-revelation is a constant in Nietzsche's own experience; see, for example, HAH1, 628, which we shall examine further in the next chapter, and D, 216, where Nietzsche plays on the paradox of seeing oneself in music. On the contrast between the phenomenology of sight and hearing, see Walter H. Sokel, "Freud and the Magic of Kafka's Writing," in J. P. Stern (ed.), *The World of Franz Kafka*, 1980, Holt, Rhinehart and Winston, New York, 145–58, 155.

110. WS, 168.

111. WS, 168. On the aesthetic notion of melting beauty, see Friedrich Schiller, *On the Aesthetic Education of Man, in a Series of Letters*, translated by Elizabeth Willoughby and L. A. Willoughby, 1967, Clarendon Press, Oxford, Letters 16–18. For a brief discussion of Schiller's influence on Nietzsche's conception of melting beauty, see Lesley Chamberlain, *Nietzsche in Turin: The End of the Future*, 1996, Quartet Books, London, 229, fn. 11. For the most recent broad-ranging and thorough comparative analysis of Schiller and Nietzsche's aesthetics, see Nicholas Martin, *Nietzsche and Schiller: Untimely Aesthetics*, 1996, Clarendon Press, Oxford.

112. This aphorism counterbalances those interpretations of Nietzsche that exclusively dwell on his genealogical tracing of memory as a crucial element in the forging of the self-disciplined, self-punishing subject. In fact, in WS, 168, Nietzsche

treats musical anamnesis here as a counterweight to what Herbert Marcuse describes, in the terms he borrows from the *Genealogy*, as "the one-sidedness of memory training in civilization: the faculty was chiefly directed toward remembering duties rather than pleasures; memory was linked with bad conscience, guilt and sin. Unhappiness and the threat of punishment, not happiness and the promise of freedom, linger in memory"; see Herbert Marcuse, *Eros and Civilisation*, 1969, Sphere Books, London, 185–86. For an attempt to draw a positive notion of memory from Nietzsche's work, see also Ofelia Schutte, "Willing Backwards: Nietzsche on Time Pain, Joy and Memory," in Jacob Golomb (ed.), *Nietzsche and Depth Psychology*, 1999, SUNY, Albany.

113. WS, 168.

114. WS, 168.

115. IV, 134–35; In a powerfully uncanny aphorism, D, 423, and more briefly again in the gem-like D, 541, Nietzsche acknowledges and analyses the seductions and lures of this latter inflection of narcissism: the flight into inorganic, mute indifference as an escape from the external world's emission of painful stimuli. For a discussion of Nietzsche's fascination with the return to the inorganic, especially at the time of *Daybreak*, see Graham Parkes, "Staying Loyal to the Earth: Nietzsche as Ecological Thinker," in John Lippitt (ed.), *Nietzsche's Future*, 1999, Macmillian Press, London, 167–88, 182–83; see also BPP, 310–11.

116. Gaston Bachelard, *The Poetics of Reverie*, translated by Daniel Russell, 1969, The Orion Press, New York, 141.

117. WS, 168.

118. Wolfgang Welsch argues that Nietzsche protests against what Welsch calls the "elevatory imperative" of German idealist aesthetics, that is to say, against its demand that philosophical aesthetics step above the immediately sensible to the non-sensible plane of the "higher" pleasures of reflection; see Wolfgang Welsch, *Undoing Aesthetics*, translated by Andrew Inkpin, 1997, Sage, London.

119. WS, 168.

120. Marshall Berman, *All That Is Solid Melts into Air: The Experience of Modernity*, 1983, Verso, London, 43. Faust's speech no doubt had an uncanny effect on Nietzsche, who was haunted by the bells of his father's church.

121. Nietzsche's aesthetic critique of dramatic music is one constant between the early and middle works; for his early critique of dramatic music, see MW, and for a brief restatement of it in the lighter, aphoristic style and tone of the middle works, see, for example, WS, 163.

122. D, 160.

123. WS, 169.

4

At the Crossroads of Hellenistic and Psychoanalytic Therapy: The Free-Spirit Trilogy

Measure and moderation.—Of two very exalted things—measure and moderation—it is best never to speak. Some few know their significance and power through inner sacred paths of experience and conversion: they revere in them something divine and refuse to speak of them aloud. All the rest hardly listen when they are spoken of, and confuse them with boredom and mediocrity: except perhaps for those who once did hear a premonitory echo from that domain but closed their ears to it. The recollection of it now makes them angry and agitated.

Human, All Too Human 2, 230

Apollo's oracle at Delphi dwelt high on the side of a sacred mountain with two mottoes carved over its portal: "Know Thyself!" and "Nothing too Much!" In his middle period, Nietzsche, albeit in his own idiosyncratic way, attempts to follow both mottoes. As we have seen, he repudiates both Dionysian ecstasy and Schopenhauerian mortification, diagnosing them as opposing sides of the same melancholic inability to mourn the loss of a phantasised condition of plenitude. In this way he identifies how our attempts to alleviate the pain of dismemberment through intoxications and balms can only engender deeper malaises and maladies. Casting his point in terms of Homer's Odyssean myth, Nietzsche discovers that succumbing to the song of the Sirens transforms individuated existence into a source of a melancholic discontent, a discontent that only serves to fuel a mania for self-dissolution. In quintessentially Stoic fashion Nietzsche observes that it is such "*alleviations* for which we have to atone the most! And if we want to return to health we have no choice: we have to burden ourselves *more heavily* than we have ever been burdened before."[1]

In the free-spirit trilogy, Nietzsche formulates what Rüdiger Safranski aptly describes as a "postsirenian philosophy" that attempts to understand, diagnose and treat the pathologies of this form of nostalgia.[2] In doing so, as we shall see, he renews some aspects of the Hellenistic philosophical therapies and their practices of self-cultivation. This turn is not particularly surprising in light of Nietzsche's classical education, his philological studies of Diogenes Laertius, and the fact that Seneca and Epictetus were among the most heavily read and annotated in his library.[3] Nietzsche was steeped in Hellenistic thought.

This chapter examines Nietzsche's postsirenian philosophy for the sake of clarifying his conception of the work of self-cultivation. For Nietzsche, self-cultivation entails the difficult work of knowing oneself; or, to put it in his Stoic language, self-knowledge is the heavy burden we must bear if we are to achieve a temperate, composed individualism. The chapter shows that he identifies self-cultivation with the difficult labour of self-analysis. We must undertake this self-cultivation, he suggests, in order to treat the pathologies that we suffer when we are overpowered by our nostalgia for a phantasy of lost majesty. Self-consciously borrowing Cynic and Stoic motifs, he holds that we can only return to health by exchanging the Saturnalias of slaves for an "athletic" training in, and sharpening of, the arts of self-observation, self-cultivation and self-endurance.[4] The first section of this chapter shows that Nietzsche gives us the first glimmerings of his renovation of Hellenistic and Stoic therapy by contesting Schopenhauer's dismissal of the Stoic belief that through rational therapy we might achieve a degree of composure and equanimity in the face of harsh necessity.

However, as the second section shows, Nietzsche's path to self-knowledge takes him beyond the Stoic notion of the rational subject toward a much richer understanding of the intrapsychic world, an understanding that lays the groundwork for much of the psychoanalytic conception of subjectivity. In particular it examines how Nietzsche moves beyond the Stoic notion of the emotions as false cognitions. Unlike the Stoics, that is to say, Nietzsche investigates our emotions and moods as symptoms whose roots lie in our earliest, largely forgotten conflicts and traumas. It is on the basis of this insight that Nietzsche refigures philosophical therapy as a work of recollection that struggles to overcome our amnesia about the genesis and sources of our dominant moods, sensation and judgements. Nietzsche, as we shall see, consecrates practical reason to the goddess of memory, Mnemosyne.

Finally, the third section shows that Nietzsche interprets and evaluates metaphysical systems as symptoms of psychological maladies. The section demonstrates that because he treats metaphysical philosophies as symptoms forged under the pressure of sickness, as "a prop, a sedative, medicine, redemption, elevation or self-alienation," they serve him as a privileged site for fathoming unconscious psychical desires.[5] For Nietzsche the dreams of metaphysics are the royal road to the (and his own personal) unconscious. What Nietzsche claims to discover through his investigations of the psychology of metaphysics, as we shall see in the close of this chapter, is that our neuroses and maladies are different inflections of the narcissistic flight from loss, separation and finitude.

NIETZSCHE'S SECRET PATH TO MODERATION: FROM SCHOPENHAUER TO STOICISM

It is with the aid of the Greco-Roman model of therapy that Nietzsche first begins to conceptualise an art of self-fashioning through which individuals could learn to maintain their composure in the face of what he describes, in terms reminiscent of Schopenhauer, as the inhuman "squandering" of life, a profligate expenditure of energy without any ultimate reconciliation or higher end.[6] Nietzsche gives us the first glimmering of his turn to the Hellenistic notion of philosophy as a therapy that aims to fashion a composed, moderate soul in the opening section of *Human, All Too Human*.

In the penultimate aphorism "Of First and Last Things," Nietzsche analyses two radically opposed responses to the squandering of life. In the first place, Nietzsche recalls Schopenhauer's figure of the petty egotist blind to the world of suffering. He exposes their splendid "self-isolation" as the conventional means by which most human beings recoil from the dangers of tragic insight into the realm of necessity (or *Ananke*) that is utterly indifferent to their personal wishes. Here Nietzsche sees this egotistical preoccupation with oneself as a defence against a painful psychological predicament that confronts us—it is a fearful denial of the tragic dimensions of the human condition. In this regard at least Nietzsche follows Schopenhauer. By blinding themselves to the universality of suffering, Schopenhauer claims, such egotists attempt to convince themselves that their own suffering is merely an idiosyncratic and easily resolved difficulty. By confining themselves to the realm of their own "private" suffering, and treating it as potentially solvable through instrumental action, they conceal from themselves the fact that suffering is "essential to this existence itself."[7] Following Schopenhauer Nietzsche *laments* the fact, as he sees it, that most individuals restrict their capacity for *Mitgefühl* in order to avoid confronting the inevitability and purposelessness of suffering:

> Every belief about the value and worth of life rests upon impure thinking; it is possible only because sympathy [*Mitgefühl*] for the common life and the suffering of humanity is very weakly developed in the individual.[8]

Nietzsche claims that the suffering of humanity is not redeemed by the realisation of any higher goal or ultimate redemption. In *Human, All Too Human*, he rejects all such metaphysical theodicies, including in these his earlier artistic-metaphysical consolations and romantic supernaturalism.[9] Faith in redemption, whether it is understood in terms of the realisation of individual geniuses or higher types of communities, is, so he claims, an illusion that conceals this "ultimate purposelessness."[10] Nietzsche "purifies" his tragic vision of both the "artist's metaphysic" of *The Birth of Tragedy* and the romantic supernaturalism that informs *Schopenhauer as Educator*: that is, the notion that nature presses for redemption through the production of a higher type: the saint, the artist and the philosopher.[11]

From this "purified" perspective, Nietzsche defines history as a "squandering" of forces that offers no compensations for or redemption from the losses it inflicts on humanity. It is in light of this tragic perspective that Nietzsche claims that free spirits must create new ways of living with themselves without seeking metaphysical solace or comfort. According to Nietzsche, however, most people avoid this predicament by elevating their own concerns above all other problems:

> [They] endure life without a great deal of complaining and thus *believe* in the value of existence, but precisely because each of them wills and affirms only his own life and does not step outside himself like those exceptions do: *everything outside themselves is either not noticeable at all for them or at most a faint shadow. Thus, for the ordinary, everyday person, the value of life rests solely upon him taking himself to be more important than the world.* The great lack of imagination from which he suffers makes him unable to empathise [*hineinfühlen*] with other beings, and hence he participates in their fate and suffering as little as possible.[12]

Nietzsche's thinking here bears the strong imprint of Schopenhauer's critique of that banal "egoism" in which we treat the momentary gratification of our own "vanishing person" as more important than the world. However, where Schopenhauer ultimately turns this critique in the direction of melancholic self-mortification, Nietzsche turns to another tradition to understand how individuals might live with the conflict between their narcissistic wishes and the harsh lessons of reality.

According to Schopenhauer, egotists retreat inward and restrict their attachments to others in order to blind themselves to the nature of that boundless, uncontrollable "will" that goads them to seek a state of complete satisfaction that constantly and necessarily eludes them, a cycle that can only be brought to an end by the living death of self-mortification (or actual death). In what Nietzsche evidently felt was one of his most powerful images, Schopenhauer describes this egotistic delusion in the following terms:

Just as the boatman sits in his small boat, trusting his frail craft in a stormy sea that is boundless in every direction, rising and falling with the howling, mountainous waves, so in the midst of a world full of suffering and misery the individual man sits, supported by and trusting the *principium individuationis*, or the way the individual knows things as phenomenon. The boundless world, everywhere full of suffering in the infinite past, in the infinite future, is strange to him, is indeed a fiction. His vanishing person, his extensionless present, his momentary gratification, these alone have reality for him; and he does everything to maintain them, so long as his eyes are not opened by a better knowledge.[13]

In *Human, All Too Human* Nietzsche pursues a similar train of thought: egoists value life only by contracting into themselves and reducing others to spectres whose fate they barely notice or feel. Such individuals, Nietzsche claims, experience any threat to their self-enclosure as a profound threat to their ontological security. He claims that in order to avoid this dread we blunt our imaginative sensitivity to what lies beyond our narrow sphere of private concerns. It is fear for ourselves, he suggests, that engenders the anxious need to transform others into "faint shadows" whose suffering can therefore have no reality or significance for us. Nietzsche conceives this insular egoism as a defence or fortification against the universality of suffering. Schopenhauer borrows Lucretius' celebrated metaphor to describe such egotists: they are like tranquil spectators observing from the safety of the shore the "shipwreck" of humanity.[14]

Nietzsche identifies one exception to this rule: those rare individuals whose imagination enables them to participate and enter into the sufferings of other beings. It is this ability to transport themselves into others that enables these exceptions to form a conception of the purposelessness that encompasses all humanity. Nietzsche could hardly draw a starker contrast between the egoist's defensive self-enclosure and the exceptional individual's imaginative *hineinfühlen* (literally, the imaginative capacity to enter into another's feelings). However, he recognises a limit to the latter's participation in suffering:

if such an exception did manage to conceive and to feel the total consciousness of humanity within himself he would collapse with a curse against existence—for humanity as a whole has no goal, and consequently the individual cannot find anything to comfort and sustain him by considering the whole process, but only despair.[15]

Even such exceptions, who, rather than contracting into themselves, participate in the fate and suffering of other beings, can do so only up to a certain point, beyond which poetic illusions and consolations become necessary. In what is doubtless an ironic jibe at his own earlier penchant for aesthetic consolations, Nietzsche observes:

> But to feel oneself as humanity (and not only as an individual) just as much squandered as we see individual blooms of nature squandered, is a feeling beyond all feelings—But who is capable of that? Certainly only a poet and poets always know how to comfort themselves.[16]

Nietzsche then considers how we can incorporate the pathos engendered by the sight of purposeless squandering of life, rather than, in manner of the poets, consoling ourselves by treating it, as he had in *The Birth of Tragedy*, as "merely an aesthetic game," or, like Schopenhauer's egoists, fearfully defending ourselves through strenuously avoiding the other's pathos.[17] Beyond the poet's metaphysical consolations, to which he had once subscribed, and the egoist's anaesthetics and blinkers, Nietzsche conceives another way of treating the pathos engendered by the destruction of the narcissistic dream that human losses could ever be fully compensated or that human beings might one day return to an (imagined) state of tranquil plenitude, and it is a way that entails a certain kind of *Bildung* or work on the self's temperament. Reflecting on the intensity of our pathos, Nietzsche turns to Stoicism for a response that avoids both the defensive contraction of the self into itself, on the one side, and Schopenhauerian melancholic self-mortification, on the other. In light of nature's squandering of life, Nietzsche poses the following question:

> Won't our philosophy thus turn into a tragedy? . . . Is it true, would there remain only a single way of thinking that yields despair as the personal result and a philosophy of destruction as the theoretical result?—I believe the decisive factor in determining what after-effect of knowledge will have is the *temperament* of a person: I could just as easily imagine an aftereffect for individual natures different from the one that has been described, one that would give rise to a much simpler life, more purified of affects than at present: so that even though the old motives produced by more intense desire would at first still have the strength of old, inherited habits, they would gradually become weaker under the influence of a purifying knowledge.[18]

The work of the self with which Nietzsche concerns himself, then, is one that aims to construct, as he says, "a stable, mild, and basically cheerful soul."[19] In his reference to a future simpler life in which our cravings or greed will be weaker than they are at present, Nietzsche unmistakably describes as the aim of *Bildung* the realisation of a cheerful Stoicism.

Schopenhauer occasionally acknowledges this Stoicism as a plausible therapeutic response to our painful loss of majestic plenitude. However, unlike Nietzsche, but very much like the early church fathers, Schopenhauer brusquely dismisses Stoicism as requiring too much of our rationality. Stoic therapy, as Schopenhauer sees it, principally aims at freeing us from the delusion that we could find something in life that is not to be met with, namely, the permanent satisfaction of our tormenting Hydra-headed desires. He claims that we are *not* sufficiently rational to acquiesce in the notion that suffering is ultimately ineradicable. The Stoic attempt to achieve equanimity through philosophical therapy must fail, he argues, because our longing to return to an originary state of perfection, a state free of all possible suffering, permanently abides within us and is much more powerful than our rational assessment of the impossibility of satisfying this longing. If the thought that suffering is a permanent rather than a contingent feature of life, and that only the *particular* shape of our personal suffering is a matter of chance "were to become a living conviction," he reasons, "then it might produce a considerable degree of stoical equanimity, and greatly reduce our anxious concern about our own welfare. But such a powerful control of the faculty of reason over directly felt suffering is seldom or never in fact found."[20]

Nietzsche is more sanguine about our capacity for employing reason to temper our suffering and the perversions to which it gives rise. Indeed, in criticising St. Augustine's brand of Christianity, Nietzsche explicitly draws on the Hellenistic and Stoic sages who had incurred the ire of this early church father:

> *Christianity and the affects.*—Within Christianity there is audible also a great popular protest against philosophy: the reason of the sages of antiquity had advised men against the affects, Christianity wants to *restore* them. To this end, it denies to *virtue* as it was conceived by the philosophers—as the victory of reason over affect—*all moral value*, condemns rationality in general, and challenges the affects to reveal themselves in their extremest grandeur and strength: as *love* of God, *fear* of God, as fanatical *faith* in God, as the blindest *hope* in God.[21]

By contrast with Schopenhauer (and St. Augustine), Nietzsche argues in a Stoic vein that it is the manner in which one cares for, explores and cures oneself that determines the aftereffects of the knowledge that for mortal creatures there can be no ultimate return to the womb of narcissistic plenitude and bliss. Nietzsche believes it may become a "purifying knowledge" whose effect is to make it possible,

> to live among human beings and with ourselves as if in *nature*, without praise, reproaches, or excessive zeal, or as if at play, feasting upon the sight of many things that had previously only made us afraid. We would be rid of *emphasis* and would no longer feel the pricking of the thought that we are only nature or are something more than nature.[22]

If, then, Nietzsche defends an ethics of caring for the self, it is an ethics that is radically opposed to both a rigidly defensive egocentricity and ascetic self-mortification. Both contracting and mortifying ourselves, Nietzsche maintains, express in opposed ways our desire to flee from inescapable dimensions of the human experience: separation, individuation and finitude. Reviving the Hellenistic and Roman techniques of self, he claims, may enable us to transform ourselves in such a way that we can bear these pains without either defensive contraction or melancholic mortification. In the middle works he concerns himself with how we can incorporate the loss of our narcissistic plenitude without contracting from others or turning resentfully against ourselves or life itself. As James Conant states correctly:

> [Nietzsche] urges that a prior preoccupation with the formation of character (rendering oneself capable of exercising practical wisdom)—which he identifies as formerly having been a central preoccupation of Hellenistic and Roman philosophy—once again be restored to its rightful place at the center of philosophy.[23]

Nietzsche turns to Greco-Roman philosophic therapies to find a way beyond the faith in an illusory ultimate reconciliation between human wishes and necessity. Taking his lead from the Hellenistic schools, Nietzsche develops a philosophical therapy that turns on resisting the seductions of the metaphysical and religious chimeras of a transcendent world. His therapy entails subjecting oneself to an unremitting work of self-analysis in order to comprehend both the lure of the song of the sirens and the pathologies to which to it can so easily give rise.

NIETZSCHEAN THERAPY:
FROM STOICISM TO PSYCHOANALYSIS

In the 1886 preface to *The Gay Science* Nietzsche retrospectively frames the works spanning his middle period—*Human, All Too Human: Assorted Opinions and Maxims, The Wanderer and His Shadow, Daybreak* and the first four books of *The Gay Science*—as a therapeutic drama that charts a course from illness, through convalescence to recovery. In *Human, All Too Human* Nietzsche begins this therapeutic drama with a historical and psychologically oriented investigation of the genesis of metaphysical, religious and aesthetic sensations.[24] As we saw in chapter 2, the wide range of medical metaphors he employs in *Human, All Too Human* to describe his art of psychological examination confirms his intention of reinventing the therapeutic model of philosophy.[25] By claiming that his own psychological probings of these "sensations" are practices in self-doctoring, exercises in diagnosing and curing his own maladies, Nietzsche inscribes himself in the Stoic tradition, which exhorts every individual to become doctor and patient in one.[26]

In his own Senecan mood, Nietzsche conceives his philosophy as an explication of the methods, styles and stages in his self-treatment. Like Seneca, Nietzsche wants to explicate this cure in a manner that will benefit his readers in their own attempt to find a path from suffering to joy.[27] Nietzsche's style(s) are thus bound up with his therapeutic intent. As with the Stoics, this therapeutic objective means that Nietzsche cannot achieve his end through ordinary, prosaic scholarly argumentation.[28] The prefaces that Nietzsche added to *Human, All Too Human, Daybreak* and *The Gay Science* in 1886 frame these works as self-revelations of his odyssey from the sickness of romantic pessimism, through the cure by means of cold, analytical sobriety and the return to health in the lyrical "yea saying" of the final work in the free-spirit trilogy.

Nietzsche sees himself as resolutely siding with the spirit of science in its attempts to reveal the origins and history of humanity's cognitive, moral and religious "faculties" and "sensations" against the precedent set by metaphysical philosophy of accepting the "most recent shape of human beings" as the "fixed form from which we must proceed."[29] A "higher culture," he proclaims, encourages historical and psychological dissection rather than continuing with the paltry evasions that have previously thwarted the investigation of the origin and history of "human" sensations: "It is the mark of a higher culture to value little unpretentious truths which have been discovered by means of a rigorous method more highly than the blissful and blinding errors that stem from metaphysical and artistic ages and human beings."[30] Perhaps, he concedes, it might be better for the total happiness of humanity that we remain blind to the genesis of the most "recent shape of human beings," perhaps, in fact, those psychological surgeons who dissect the moral, religious and aesthetic sensations are "almost inhuman" insofar as they reveal the origins of these sensations.[31]

Nietzsche's school of suspicion thus contains two premises that cut against the blissful errors into which human life has hitherto been deeply sunk.[32] His method of historical philosophising assumes, firstly, that in relation to human beings there is no *aeterna veritas*, no "secure measure for things," and secondly that the contemporary shape of human beings has been forged through metaphysical and religious errors. It is for this reason that Nietzsche takes Paul Rée's proposition that the "moral person does not stand any nearer to the intelligible (metaphysical) world than the physical person" as the ground bass for much of his analysis of the human, all too human.[33]

Having announced Rée's principle, Nietzsche immediately illustrates it by challenging Kant's metaphysics of morality. In one of his signature critical and rhetorical strategies, he first demonstrates that the "meaning" of "moral sensations" is extremely fluid and that the history of its metamorphoses has been obliterated by amnesia. According to Nietzsche, our amnesia about the ancient history of morality has the effect of making the current shape of moral sensations appear to us as if they were its intrinsic or essential form. Nietzsche seeks to undo our forgetfulness about the sources of our moral sensations and in doing so he implies that such sensations have no intrinsic, a priori shape or form.

Against Kant's attempt to explain and defend moral conscience through recourse to the metaphysical concept of intelligible freedom, Nietzsche offers a very different explanation of the origins and genesis of the moral sensations of guilt and sinfulness, one that does not hinge on any transcendental claims. Moral conscience, he asserts, is "a very changeable thing, tied to the evolution of morality and culture and perhaps present in only a relatively brief span of world history."[34] He assumes that moral "sensations" such as guilt are contingent products of history, which we can explain in psychological rather than metaphysical terms. The "fact" of moral conscience, he asserts, should not be misunderstood as an *aeterna veritas*, but as a historically constituted phenomenon that can be explained sociologically and psychologically.[35]

In developing a genetic explanation of moral conscience Nietzsche emphasises the archaic psychological sources of the categorical imperative ("I must do this, not do that") that Kant tries to justify as apodictic or synthetic a priori judgements.[36] On the ontogenetic plane, Nietzsche argues, we form our moral conscience through internalising the demands of authority figures, demands that are coloured by our ambivalent feelings of love and fear for these figures. Our moral conscience, as he puts it "is therefore not the voice of God in the heart of man, but the voice of some men in man."[37] According to Nietzsche, then, Kant's moral individuals do not stand any nearer to the metaphysical world, as he supposes, but live in the shadows of the archaic world of their earliest emotional conflicts, conflicts which have long since been forgotten, but whose product—the imperative voice of conscience—has been gilded and glorified by religious conceptions and rationalised by metaphysical philosophy.

For Nietzsche, mature individuals do not deploy metaphysical charms to block their ears to the siren song that continues to remind them of their lost plenitude. We must, he believes, pay heed to that which lies before and profoundly shapes the manner in which we internalise the voice of others. We need to pay heed, in short, to the archaic features that shape moral conscience. In this context, he conceives reason in terms of the work of reconstructing our traumatic loss, as it is idiosyncratically inflected in our personal histories, and its pathological consequences. He claims that through this kind of reason, attuned as it is to the music of the pre-Oedipal stage, to borrow from psychoanalytic language, we can construct a tempered, stable, mild self capable of enduring its exile without the hope of a definitive or final return.

In other words, Nietzsche conceives his historical and psychological observations as deepening and extending the Enlightenment critique of "religious and mythological monsters" that have hitherto blinded us to the complex evolution of our religious and moral sensations.[38] By dissecting these moral sensations, he claims, we can enlighten ourselves about the archaic sources of the "current shape of human beings," and begin the task of circumnavigating "that inner world called 'man.'"[39] For Nietzsche, as we shall see shortly, this circumnavigation of the soul takes shape through the art of remembrance of his own personal history. To the eye of earlier cultures, he acknowledges, this art of psychological examination may make our scientific form of life seem "*uglier,*" "but only because it is incapable of seeing how the realm of inner, spiritual beauty is continually growing deeper and wider, and to what extent we may now all accord the eye of insight greater value than the most beautiful structure or the most sublime construction."[40] Nietzsche self-consciously suspends the aesthetic concern with beauty and sublimity for the sake of this work of self-analysis and self-exploration.

According to Nietzsche, it is through our work of insight and analysis and the ugly little truths we perceive that we might become ethical subjects. In bracketing metaphysical speculations, Nietzsche aims to develop a psychological-genealogical investigation of the genesis of the affective structures and dynamics of the intrapsychic world.[41] In the middle period, his investigations have an objective that is rarely acknowledged: it is part of his attempt to transform practical reason into a therapeutic practice of "spiritual health."[42] "As yet we lack above all," he observes, "the physicians for whom that which has hitherto been called practical morality [is] transformed into an aspect of their art and science of healing."[43] Nietzsche aims to incorporate his insights about the complex psycho-dynamics that ensue from the loss of narcissistic plenitude into a therapeutic philosophy.[44] He thus sets the parameters of his morality of insight by combining Stoicism's therapeutic model of practical reason with his grasp of the narcissistic pathologies that afflict human beings. As chapter 2 argued, Nietzsche adopts as his guiding model for his own *Heilkunst* and *Heilwissenschaft,* the Hellenistic medical-therapeutic ethos.

Indeed, Nietzsche's assumption of the mantle of the Hellenistic therapist is more than merely a rhetorical gesture and personal exigency. In taking up this mantle his philosophical therapy adopts one of Stoicism's substantive points: it conceives the emotions as *beliefs* or *judgements,* indeed as, more often than not, false cognitions.[45] Following the Stoics, then, he contends that feelings are *not* blind, noncognitive impulses or nonreasoning movements:

> *Feelings and their origination in judgements.*—"Trust your feelings!" But feelings are nothing final or original—behind feelings there stand judgements and evaluations which we inherit in the form of feelings.[46]

It is precisely because feelings are judgements or value-laden ways of seeing, rather than brutish impulses or instincts, that Nietzsche claims a change in our thinking can lead to a change in emotion itself: "We have to *learn to think differently*—in order at last, perhaps very late on, to attain even more: *to feel differently.*"[47] Nietzsche suggests that, properly understood, our feelings are judgements and evaluations whose source lies not in our subrational or instinctual nature, but are the product of our primitive attachments and mimetic identifications. Applying the genealogical metaphor in a literal manner, Nietzsche describes these feelings as the "grandchildren of a judgement, and often a false judgement!"[48]

Nietzsche deploys the art of self-analysis to comprehend the genealogy of these emotions and in the process to dispel the phenomenological perception that they are something "final or original." Following the Stoics, Nietzsche believes we can achieve a degree of self-composure by analysing our emotions as false judgements. Nietzsche indicates that this is indeed the aim of his genealogical tracings by alluding to the Stoic conception of philosophical therapy. In one of his celebrated letters to Lucilius, Seneca counsels him to pursue rational self-command rather than submit to the fetishes of conventional Roman religion:

> The god is near you, with you, inside you. This is what I am saying to you Lucilius: a holy spirit is seated within us, a watcher and guardian of our good and bad actions. . . . Do you ask what that is? The soul, and reason fulfilled in the soul.[49]

Nietzsche echoes Seneca's declaration in developing his own conception of reason and therapy:

> To trust one's feelings—means to give more obedience to one's grandfather and grandmother and their grandparents than to the gods which are in *us*: our reason and experience.[50]

However, if in following Stoicism, Nietzsche conceptualises emotions as judgements and evaluations rather than blind natural forces, he also modifies Stoicism by seeing that what we might describe as our emotion thoughts or moods are deeply anchored in our past, especially in our earliest struggles with the object world.[51] Nietzsche's insight into the fact, at least as he sees it, that our moods are anchored in a distant past proves decisive for his conception of philosophical therapy. It opens up to him, as we shall see, the psychological phenomenon of narcissism. On the phenomenological plane, to return to our present point, Nietzsche claims that we are assailed by overpowering moods or feelings which seem to us to be *causa sui* and to "take [us] deep into the interior, close to the heart of nature."[52] It is these moods that we seek to transfigure with metaphysical origins. When we are under their sway, he argues, we are not conscious of the fact that through these moods we illuminate and colour our experiences in ways that bear the traces of our distant, ghostly selves:

> Have you not noticed what kind of will rules behind your seeing? . . . When you are physically tired you will bestow on things a pale and tired coloration, when you are feverish you will turn them into monsters. Does your morning not shine upon things differently from your evening? Do you not fear to re-encounter in the cave of every kind of knowledge your own ghost—the ghost which is the veil behind which truth has hidden itself from you?[53]

According to Nietzsche, our moods are the ghosts of our past selves, which unbeknownst to us illuminate and colour our experience of present objects. Even Plato's pure metaphysical vision, he believes, has almost imperceptible (but perhaps audible) sources in a complex group of forgotten, spectral thoughts. Our forgetfulness or amnesia of the origins and genesis of these ghosts, however, means that we cannot grasp or shape the moods and feelings, including powerful moral feelings, that rule our perceptions and interpretations of ourselves and our objects. Our strong moods, whose complex, diverse origins we have forgotten, become indivisible unities that overpower us:

> All *stronger* moods bring with them sympathetic resonance [*Miterklingen*] on the part of related sensations and moods. . . . Thus there comes to be constructed habitual, rapid associations of feelings and thoughts are formed, which finally, when they follow one another with lightning speed, are no longer even sensed as complexes, but rather as *unities*. In this sense, we speak of moral feelings . . . as if they were nothing but unities: in truth, they are streams with a hundred sources and tributaries.[54]

Nietzsche claims that we require a careful analytic mnemotechnique in order to bring to light the complex tissue of evaluations and judgements embodied in such seeming unities, otherwise the way the world appears to us is unconsciously governed by these emotion thoughts or moods. It is a memory work that reverses this process, disclosing the small, microscopic affects and the processes through which they have become fused into such powerful unities. It is this memory-work which partly explains Nietzsche's reliance on aphoristic constellations: the multiplicity and variety of his aphoristic texts reflect his attempt to slow down associations which otherwise move at lightning speed, and in doing so to show each individual frame of mood complexes that otherwise appear as indivisible wholes.

In this respect, Nietzsche consecrates reason to Mnemosyne, the Greek goddess of memory, and the mother of all arts. Hence he does not banish the arts from the realm of knowledge and self-knowledge. Rather he believes that the close link between art and memory can help us disclose the sources that shape our selves, and the unreason in our claims to reason. On the other hand, when practical reason is captivated by the metaphysical project, rather than constructed in terms of this art of memory, he argues, it becomes little more than a series of ex post facto rationalisations of these swollen moods that we have inherited from the past, and which, if we follow his metaphors, threaten to sweep away everything in their path. Through a lack of "self-observation," as he puts it, we have allowed the passions to develop into such "monsters," and it is now "up to us to take from the passions their terrible character and thus prevent them from becoming devastating torrents."[55]

In *Daybreak* (34) Nietzsche identifies his project as a *history* of such feelings. His history attempts to fathom the psychological sources in mimesis; sources which our moral accounting merely glosses:

> It is clear that moral feelings are transmitted in this way: children observe in adults inclinations for and aversions to certain actions, and as born apes, *imitate* these inclinations and aversions; in later life they find themselves full of these acquired and well exercised affects and consider it only decent to try to account for and justify them. This "accounting" however, has nothing to do with either the origin or degree of intensity of the feeling: all one is doing is complying with a rule that, as a rational being, one has to have reasons for one's For and Against, and they have to be adducible and acceptable reasons. To this extent the history of moral feelings is quite different from the history of moral concepts. The former are powerful *before* the action, the latter especially after the action in the face of the need to pronounce upon it.[56]

While Nietzsche might reject reason in the guise of such ex post facto rationalisations, he does not reject, as he makes clear in *Daybreak* (35), the gods in us, reason and experience, but recasts them in terms of a memory work that aims to fathom the sources and genesis of the moods and sensations we once constructed by means of such early mimetic identifications. Nietzsche describes his own anamnestic conception of reason as a "morality of insight." In *The Wanderer and His Shadow*, he claims that in its primitive stages morality is shaped around a fear of ancestral gods or everlasting punishment in the Beyond; it then proceeds to the commands of a god before ascending, as he puts it:

> further and higher still the commands of the concept of unconditional duty with its "thou shalt"—all still somewhat coarsely hewn but broad stages and steps, because men do not know how to place their feet on narrower, more delicate steps. Then comes a morality of *inclination*, of *taste*, finally that of *insight*—which is above and beyond all illusionary motive forces of morality but has a clear realisation of why for long ages mankind could possess no other.[57]

Nietzsche conceives his practical, therapeutic reason as a work of remembrance that discloses the psychological foundations of those emotion thoughts that have come to seem auratic or magical through the transfigurations of metaphysics.[58]

NIETZSCHEAN *BILDUNG*: FROM TROPICAL TO TEMPERATE SELVES

As Nietzsche understands it, philosophical therapy entails excavating and reshaping the sources of our self-identity rather than elaborating metaphysical rationalisations for the archaic judgements that well up into consciousness in the guise of overpowering moods, feelings or imperatives. Nietzsche claims that this analytic therapy can "cool" our excessive pathos and transform our moods. He believes this is possible because, following the Stoics, he contends that our pathos and moods are not brute nature, but value-laden ways of seeing and interpreting whose complex origins we have forgotten and, at the risk of being too cute, that we have mostly forgotten that we have forgotten.[59] However, while this tempering of the self is possible, he also believes we need to work hard against the pride, which demands that we forget our origins and to which we too often yield. It is for this reason that Nietzsche describes his psychological dissections as continuous with the enlightenment project of self-understanding:

> Because they dissect morality, moralists must now be content to be upbraided as immoralists. But he who wants to dissect has to kill; yet only for the sake of better knowledge, better judgement, better living; not so all the world shall start dissecting.[60]

For analytical purposes Nietzsche plays out his notion of philosophical therapy on both the cultural and the personal level, though, ultimately, as we shall see, he merges these two levels of analysis. What Nietzsche hopes to achieve is a "transition" (*Übergang*) from metaphysical interpretations of the world that "overburden the heart" with moods and sensations to a "truly liberating science" that analyses their genesis, and in doing so diminishes their force. He describes the work of analysis as a "wintry way of thinking": by revealing the illusions of metaphysics it "ices up" what hitherto counted as humanity's most profound sensations and passions.[61] For it is these metaphysical illusions, he claims, that embody and stoke the most powerful sensations and threaten us with the most violent and dangerous neuroses:

> We have Christianity, the philosophers, poets, musicians to thank for an abundance of profound sensations: if these are not to stifle us we must conjure up the spirit of science, which on the whole makes one somewhat colder and more sceptical and in particular cools down the scorching stream of a faith in final, definitive truths that has become so fierce principally due to Christianity.[62]

Nietzsche thus sees his psychological critique as a means of "extinguishing and cooling" an "age which is visibly becoming more and more ignited."[63] These metaphysical orientations may have induced heightened states of being, but—and this is his chilling antithesis—there is no higher truth inherent in these states.[64] For Nietzsche, it is no longer admissible for us to treat heightened religious or artistic states of being as mediums of hidden grand truths, but only as symptoms that can be overcome through cool sceptical analysis of their historical and psychological sources and sanctions. It is through the emergence of this sceptical, retroactive psychological analysis, he asserts, that modern culture can cross from one "geographic zone" to another, from a tropical to a temperate culture:

> In comparison with the temperate zone of culture into which it is our task to cross, the zones of the past give the impression of a tropical climate. Violent contrasts, abrupt changes between day and night, heat and splendid colours, the reverence for everything sudden, mysterious, terrible, the speed with which the storm breaks out, everywhere the lavish overflow of nature's cornucopia: and by contrast in our culture, a bright, yet not luminous sky, clear, generally unvarying air, sharpness, even occasionally coldness: thus the two zones contrast with each other. If in the former we see how raging passions are overpowered and shattered by the uncanny force of metaphysical conceptions, we feel as if savage tropical tigers were being crushed before our eyes in the coils of colossal serpents; our spiritual climate has no such occurrences, our imagination has been tempered, even in dreams we scarcely come close to what earlier people beheld while awake. . . . For us . . . the very *existence* of the temperate zone of culture counts as progress.[65]

According to Nietzsche, modern culture is still in a transitional zone or interregnum: "Our age gives the impression of being an interim state, the old ways of thinking, the old culture are still partly with us, the new not yet secure and habitual and thus lacking in decisiveness and consistency . . . we cannot return to the old, we *have* burned our boats."[66] He believes that this sceptical assault on religious and metaphysical commitments is in the process of icing up the "illusions, onesidednesses, passions" that once fired the old "tropical cultures."[67]

This notion of the self's *Übergang* (crossing, transition, bridging) makes it clear that the temperate culture he envisages depends on both analysing and mourning the loss of our most potent "errors" and illusions.[68] Nietzsche argues that the *Übergang* from a religious to a scientific mode of thought should not be a violent leap because the economy of the soul is such that it requires gradual transitions. Casting a glance at political phenomena, he suggests that we carefully note the "pathetic and bloody quackery" of the French Revolution. Using the bloody revolution as an allegory, he maintains that any hope for a "sudden recovery" in the politics of the soul must also unleash a devastating torrent of violence.[69] Nietzsche recognises that because the errors and illusions of religion and metaphysics have fundamentally shaped our affective being losing them threatens to bring about a dangerous "eclipse of the soul."[70] In other words, according to Nietzsche, for the sake of effecting a transition to a temperate culture we must both endure the gradual, piecemeal labour of self-analysis which dissects our feverish hopes for salvation or redemption and soothe ourselves for their loss with the "festive levity" exemplified by Horace's *Odes*.[71] In our worst hours, he acknowledges, we can do nothing but humour ourselves.

His psychological analysis lays the axe to the root of the "metaphysical need" and its "counsel of eternity."[72] According to Nietzsche, the intellectual conscience of an enlightened age will not allow us to remain in, or return to, a precritical philosophy that assumes, so to speak, "that the world turns toward us a legible face which we only have to decipher."[73] As far as metaphysical speculation is concerned he claims that we can only assert of "the metaphysical world that it is a being-other, an inaccessible, incomprehensible being-other; it would thus be a thing of negative qualities."[74] Nietzsche takes this metaphysical abstinence, which only allows us to conceive the "thing in-itself" as an unknowable not-X, one step further, for, as he writes, "[e]ven if the existence of such a world were never so well demonstrated, it is certain that knowledge of it would be the most useless of all knowledge: more useless even than knowledge of the chemical composition of water must be to a sailor in danger of shipwreck."[75]

In *Letter* (108) Seneca uses a similar metaphor: he praises therapeutic philosophers as acute steersmen/navigators and maligns grammarians, philologists and especially sophists, for whom reason/*logos* is merely a commercial skill of disputation, as seasick sailors. Because the philologist and the sophist teach us how to commentate and dispute rather than how to live, Seneca writes,

> [he] can be of no more help to me as an instructor than a steersman who is seasick in a storm—a man who should be hanging onto the tiller when the waves are snatching it from his grasp, wrestling with the sea itself, rescuing his sails from the winds. What good to me is a vomiting and stupefied helmsmen? And you may well think the storm of life is a great deal more serious than any which ever tosses a boat.[76]

The result of the rise of sophistic teaching, Seneca laments, has been the transformation of philosophy, the study of wisdom, into philology, the study of mere words (*Itaque quae philosophia fuit facta philologia est*).[77] Like Seneca, Nietzsche praises therapeutic philosophers; his antitype, however, are not the sophists, but the metaphysicians who threaten to sink the "ship of humanity" by intoxicating it with "the scent of blossoms."[78] Metaphysicians are drunken, intoxicated (*berauscht*) sailors who shipwreck humanity.[79] What we need to save ourselves from shipwreck, he implies, is not metaphysical speculation, but knowledge of our own psychical chemistry, as it were. He aims to supplant Plato's nonsensory vision of eternal, ideal forms with his therapeutic insight into the genesis of our moods, feelings or sensations, which we compress into unities and transfigure through metaphysical speculations.

With deliberate irony, Nietzsche describes the overcoming of metaphysics using the central metaphors of the foundational narrative of metaphysical philosophy, Plato's allegory of the cave. The free spirit, he says, recognises the expressions "punishments of Hell, sinfulness, incapacity for good . . . as being only the flickering shadow images cast by false views of the world and of life."[80] It is the theologians and metaphysicians, Nietzsche implies, who are the most successful artistic mountebanks: they have usurped the artists by convincing humanity that their ideas are far more than mere flickering illusions and chimeras. He explains his scepticism with regards to the truth of metaphysical assertions by drawing an analogy between metaphysics and painting: both seduce or dazzle the eye through their use of colour, contrast, and perspectival illusion. Philosophers, he claims, use painterly techniques for achieving verisimilitude and effect, and philosophy itself can therefore be in some respects recast as a perspectival artform.[81]

However, even as Nietzsche loses faith in the shadow images of metaphysics, he has not quite exhausted his philosophical, cultural or psychological interest in these speculations. In the first place, he exercises a great deal of circumspection about the possibility and promise of freeing humanity from the metaphysical assumptions that support the notion of salvation or the idea that moral conscience places human beings nearer to the "essence of the world."[82] Nietzsche argues that human beings can only free themselves from these metaphysical interpretations to a limited extent because it is these errors of the human intellect that have made the world "wonderfully bright, terrible, profoundly meaningful, soulful."[83] In the second place, he argues that the composure and mildness of a temperate self is only available through the difficult work of self-analysis, which "salve[s]" our "wounds" by enabling us to find alleviation and joy in the "smallest, tenderest, most fleeting gift[s] life gives us" rather than continuing to irritate these wounds with metaphysical dreams of redemption.[84] According to Nietzsche, simply taking away our metaphysical crutches without at the same time undertaking the work of self-analysis that enables us to comprehend why we needed them and what wounds they were meant to salve only leads to greater psychological distress or, as he puts it, an "eclipse of the soul."[85]

Finally then, and most importantly for our purposes, Nietzsche suggests that once we reach the negative goal of seeing "every positive metaphysics" as "an error," a "reverse movement" is necessary: "[we] must grasp the historical justification as well as the psychological one for such conceptions, [we] must recognise how the greatest advancements of humanity came from them and how [we] would rob [ourselves] of the best results that humanity has thus far produced without such a reverse movement."[86] In other words, Nietzsche claims that we can forge a temperate self only by remembering and reconstructing the temples at which we formerly worshipped.[87] It follows from his claim that hitherto metaphysics has borne "in its womb all happiness and unhappiness," or, to put it in slightly different terms, that it has been the repository for all that lies closest to our "heart[s]," that exploring its *psychological* genesis and justification must also take us to the very heart of our forgotten or unconscious wishes.[88] By fathoming the psychology of metaphysics, Nietzsche believes, we can come close to identifying the forgotten ghosts that project the shadows and flickerings images of our world. Indeed, as we shall see in a moment, for Nietzsche fathoming the unconscious of Platonic metaphysics enables him to fathom his own "heart."

In *Human, All Too Human* (628) Nietzsche gives an example of his therapy of self-recollection: here the chiming of bells awakens in him a painful nostalgia that serves him as a portal to self-understanding. Nietzsche's self-understanding begins with a musical experience that reawakens and reanimates layers of experience and sensations that had suffered amnesia:

> *Seriousness in play.* In Genoa, at the time of evening twilight, I heard from a tower a long chiming of bells, it refused to end and rang, as if insatiable for itself, above the noise of the streets and out into the evening sky and the sea air, so horrible and at the same time so childlike, so full of melancholy [*wehmutsvoll*]. Then I recalled the words of Plato and suddenly I felt them in my heart: *nothing human is worth taking very seriously: nevertheless—*[89]

Laurence Lampert makes the following observation about this aphorism:

> The evening bells that sound in one of the most beautiful aphorisms of *Human* also reminds Nietzsche of mortal things and turns his thought to Plato's judgement that their mortality makes them unworthy of the greatest seriousness. But "Seriousness in Play" questions Plato's judgement.[90]

Yet at first blush Nietzsche appears not to be questioning Plato's judgement so much as acknowledging the psychological force of Platonic idealism. He feels Plato's words in his heart. Nietzsche's use of the rhetorical figure of prosopopoeia is one of the most striking features of this aphorism: he personifies the sound of the bells, as if the chiming itself were refusing to end, as if it were insatiable for itself.[91] By projecting it into an inanimate object Nietzsche successfully dramatises his own wish for self-resounding. He hears his wish to resound eternally as something childlike and full of melancholy.[92] The reason the bells sound melancholic to Nietzsche can be explained perhaps in terms of the collision between their figurative and literal meaning: the chiming both expresses the mortal self's insatiable longing for itself and, as the sounding of the passage of time, the defeat of this wish.[93] Longing and loss are acoustically intermingled.

Hearing the sorrowful chiming of the bells, Nietzsche recalls Plato's critique of tragic poetry. In the run of argument from which Nietzsche quotes, Plato admonishes the tragedians for magnifying the seriousness of mortal losses and misfortunes and in so doing awakening that "lower" part of the soul that remembers our sorrows and inflames our grief.[94] By encouraging the love of mortal things, Plato warns, they expose us to loss and threaten to trigger in us an "epidemic of grief."[95] On the other hand, the good person, according to the Platonic Socrates, "will not lament for the death of a friend or child, calling out for pity," since such a person is "most self-sufficient in what is needed for the good life and of all men least dependent on others."[96] Nietzsche recalls this critique and is moved by it, we might surmise, because it appears to offer a way to soothe his own sorrowful affects, which he perceives in the tolling of the evening bells. Nietzsche finds Plato's metaphysical vision of imperishable, eternal Forms moving, he confesses, because it proposes to alleviate his own melancholic recognition of the knot that binds together love and loss, joy and sorrow.

However, Nietzsche recognises that Plato's idealism cures only by entirely removing us from the very possibility of loss and violation.[97] This becomes apparent in Plato's idealist notion of the ascent of love. In Plato's idealism it appears unthinkable to "pour out one's being toward merely mortal objects precisely *as* mortal, with no thought of any transcendence."[98] In the Platonic image of the ladder of love the particular object is therefore merely a step towards the vision of the ideal. Platonic love aims at realising a state of godlike self-sufficiency that closes the self from the possibility of loss. In other words, Platonic idealism appeals to our hearts because it gives measure to our grief, whereas as lovers of mortal things we are at risk of measureless sorrow. Putting this in the terms I have used to frame Nietzsche's middle works, we might say that Nietzsche construes Platonic idealism as an attempt to secure a state of narcissistic self-sufficiency and thereby escape the losses that make mourning unavoidable for mortals.[99] For Nietzsche the metaphysics of transcendence has its roots in the longing to close the circle of the self and prevent it from ever again becoming vulnerable to loss.[100]

Framed in this way, Plato's idealism could be said to appeal to Nietzsche's and our own hearts because it promises to restore us to self-sufficiency. It is the force of Plato's idealism as a consolation for our loss of self-sufficiency that he registers when he confesses that he is moved by Plato's judgement of the worthlessness of human or mortal things. It is his acknowledgement of the appeal of Plato's metaphysical idealism as a salve for the narcissistic wound.[101] Nietzsche's analysis of Plato is thus subtler than Lampert credits: he does not simply question Plato's judgement. Rather, he attempts to perform the "reverse movement" of grasping the psychological justification of Plato's metaphysics. In performing this reversal he discovers in his own heart a profound resistance to the pain of loss and temporality and a nostalgia for the timeless present of childhood experience. By examining the psychological roots of metaphysics, Nietzsche thus reveals the traces of a never fully extinguishable grief that the Platonic flight into the eternal is designed to assuage. It is this work of self-analysis that enables Nietzsche to identify many other pathological flights through which we attempt to soothe this narcissistic loss.

Indeed, Nietzsche develops this insight in the very next aphorism after "*Seriousness in Play.*" Nietzsche turns his attention to the artists and tragedians whom Plato banishes from the well-ordered psyche. In fact, he goes some way towards *agreeing* with Plato that they dangerously exaggerate the value of mortal loves and attachments. According to Nietzsche, "artists" have always made passions "the objects of idolatry."[102] Placing this artist's idolatry under the microscope, he asks whether "in subsequent cold sobriety" we must remain faithful to what we have promised in passion, and he answers in the negative:

> Because we have sworn to be faithful, though perhaps to a purely fictitious being such as a god, because we have given our heart to a prince, a party, a woman, a priestly order, an artist, or a thinker, in a state of blind madness that enchanted us and made that being seem worthy of every honour and sacrifice—are we now inescapably bound? Weren't we in fact deceiving ourselves at the time? Wasn't it a hypothetical promise, made under the admittedly unspoken assumption that those beings to whom we dedicated ourselves really were what we imagined them to be? Are we obligated to be true to our errors, even after we have seen that we are doing damage to our higher self as a result of this loyalty?—No, there is no law, no obligation of this kind; we must be traitors, act unfaithfully, forsake our ideals again and again.[103]

Here Nietzsche claims that we establish the ideals to which we consecrate ourselves through blindness and self-deception. Artists glorify passionate loves that are based on enchanting delusions: in such loves we honour and sacrifice ourselves to ideals that we project onto others, who become merely "fictitious beings." In the second volume of *Human, All Too Human*, Nietzsche targets this morbid self-love in what can only be described as a veritable tour de force of psychoanalytic self-analysis. In aphorism 37 he draws together almost all of the central concepts and leitmotifs of psychoanalytic theory, exploring what it translates into semi-technical notions of repression, censorship, amnesia, resistance and projection. We can see how Nietzsche puts these concepts to work in criticising a certain kind of love as an *unhealthy* expression of narcissism, or *Selbstsucht*:

> *Deception in love.*—We forget a great deal of our own past and deliberately banish [*schlägt*] it from our minds: that is to say, we want the image of ourself that shines upon us out of the past to deceive and flatter our self-conceit [*unserm*

Dünkel schmeichele]—we are engaged continually on this self-deception.—And do you think, you who speak so much of "self-forgetfulness in love," of "the merging of the ego in the other person," and laud it so highly, do you think this is anything essentially different? We shatter the mirror, impose ourself upon someone we admire, and then enjoy our ego's [*Ich*] new image, even though we may call it by that other person's name—and this whole process is supposed not to be self-deception, *not* egoism [*nicht Selbstsucht*]! A strange delusion! Those who conceal something of themselves from themselves . . . perpetrate a *robbery* in the treasure-house of knowledge: from which we can see against which transgression the injunction "know thyself" is a warning.[104]

Here Nietzsche identifies a self-forgetfulness that we achieve by forcefully and constantly working to banish the ugly truths about ourselves from our memory. His use here of the German verb to strike or beat—*schlagen*—conveys the violence of this psychical action, and hence the need for dynamic categories to explain the operations of the psyche. We exercise this censorship, he maintains, so that we only see the shining image of our perfection, or ego ideal, as it is called in the psychoanalytic vocabulary. It is our fear of narcissistic suffering that establishes a taboo against seeing ourselves and thus an inner resistance to self-analysis.

Nietzsche draws a parallel between the active, intrapsychic work of self-forgetfulness and the work we perform in relationships that masquerade as love. Through our projections onto others, he contends, we construct the loved other as a mirror whose paradoxical function is to conceal ourselves from ourselves; the other functions here to ensure we achieve the self *mis*recognition we so ardently desire. Love can be a flight from finitude and limitedness into the delusions of self-majesty. Thus Nietzsche conceives such love as a means by which we remain incognito to ourselves—or better still as the means by which one part of ourselves remains incognito from another. Punning on the similarity between *Dünkel* (self-conceit) and *Dunkel* (dark), Nietzsche implies that the light that shines to us from the past and from those on whom we impose our own ego ideal is a darkness that we use to cloud our self-understanding. Indeed, as Nietzsche observes in the next aphorism, it follows that the more "brutal" one's vanity, the more intensely one strives for this misrecognition that transforms the other into nothing more than a distorted mirror of the self, the greater one's need for the darkness of self-oblivion:

To him who denies his vanity.—He who denies he possesses vanity usually possesses it in so brutal a form he instinctively shuts his eyes to it so as not to be obliged to despise himself.[105]

Nietzsche thus uses his conceptual and rhetorical virtuosity to shed light on the soul's eclipses. By contrast, he treats the realm of ordinary language "communication" as one of concealment and blindness. In this realm, as he sees it, we may well acknowledge and recognise others by calling them by their correct name, but this act of linguistic recognition conceals a far more important and powerful realm of nonlinguistic, imaginary exchanges, a realm in which "treasures," not mere names, are won and lost. Ordinary language communication, Nietzsche implies, conceals a dream-like world of spells and magical transformations that we can best evoke, as he often does, through fairy-tale images and tropes. In order to glimpse ourselves we need to put these dream images on display.[106] In self-seeking love we magically transform the other *"into ourselves,"* or more precisely, into a mirror that shines back to us the image of our ideal self.[107] When we are enmeshed in this self-seeking love we reduce the other to a reflection of who we wish to be based on a phantasy of what we imagine we once were. We find ourselves by losing ourselves. By attempting to possess our ego ideal in this way, Nietzsche warns, we also transform ourselves into "the most inconsiderate and selfish [*selbstsüchtigste*]" of "dragon[s] guarding [our] golden hoard."[108]

In other words, Nietzsche takes cognisance of the dangers of losing sight of ourselves and of the enchanted world of our self-seeking projections. It is a danger that he believes looms large when we fail to recognise the extent to which the psyche remains enthralled to its image of plenitude and the manner in which these pictorial-based, nonlinguistic desires weave themselves into and through linguistic communication and interaction. Against the dangers of this dark art of self-deception, which is motivated by our desire to stave off the knowledge and feeling of narcissistic loss, Nietzsche calls up as his countercharm the first principle of Western, Socratic philosophy, the Delphic command "Know Thyself."[109]

For Nietzsche the philosophical therapy of self-recollection requires analysing the source of such ideals and enduring the pain of betraying them if they cannot be shown to have "intellectual significance."[110] Rather than forging attachments on such a basis, his therapy demands that we temper our narcissism by analysing our projections and idealisations—by knowing ourselves.[111] He sees this analytical self-dissection as part of a practice of self-cultivation that makes it possible for us to acknowledge and comprehend others in their individuality and singularity. When we remain captive to the artist's promise of enchantment, on the other hand, we treat others as mere means for loving ourselves. Indeed, Nietzsche maintains that if we remain wholly seduced by our enchanted world of projections we establish the conditions that make us unjust and cruel towards others.

Finally, in the last few aphorisms that follow *"Seriousness in Play,"* and which close *Human, All Too Human*, Nietzsche examines the psychological sources of fanatical religious devotion to an abstract idea or conviction:

> Conviction is the belief that we possess the absolute truth about some specific point of knowledge . . . countless human beings . . . have sacrificed themselves

for their convictions believ[ing] that they were doing it for absolute truth. They were all wrong in that . . . in reality, one wanted to be in the right because one thought one *had* to be right. Letting one's belief be torn away perhaps meant putting one's eternal salvation in question. In a matter of such extreme importance, the "will" was all too audibly the prompter of the intellect.[112]

If Nietzsche is right, the commitment to religious conviction has its deepest source in what Freud will later describe as "the most touchy point of the narcissistic system, the immortality of the ego."[113] Nietzsche evinces a particular anxiety about the damaging consequences of religious idealisation. Because religious believers wager the salvation of the soul on their absolute truth-value of these convictions, in order to protect them they "malign reason" and persecute nonbelievers. In the "blindness" of such religious love, as Freud puts it, "remorselessness is carried to the pitch of crime."[114] The remorselessness of religious love, Nietzsche suggests, is nowhere more apparent than in the Christian love of God. If these Christians could have been persuaded to examine the sources of their need for such convictions, he writes,

how peaceful human history would then appear! How much more knowledge there would be! We would have been spared all the cruel scenes resulting from the persecution of every sort of heretic, for two reasons: first, because the inquisitors would have inquired above all into themselves and would have gotten beyond the presumption that they were defending the absolute truth; and then, because the heretics themselves would not have given any further credence to propositions as badly grounded as the propositions of all religious sectarians and "true believers" are, once they had investigated them.[115]

It is this context, Nietzsche maintains, which makes discontent with "sceptical and relativistic positions" perfectly comprehensible, "but the scientific spirit in human beings must gradually bring to maturity the virtue of *cautious reserve*, the wise moderation that is more familiar in the sphere of practical life than in the sphere of theoretical life."[116] Ironically, Nietzschean self-cultivation (*Bildung*) entails performing a cruel work of *self-*inquisition. It is a self-inquisition that aims both to reveal the unassuaged grief that springs from our loss of narcissistic plenitude, and to comprehend how our grief continues to fuel our pathological stratagems and maladies. William Connolly nicely sums up this work of the self on itself:

When Nietzsche . . . commends the self as a work of art acting modestly and artfully on its own entrenched contingencies, the aim is not self-narcissism, as neo-Kantians love to insist. The point is to ward off the violence of transcendental narcissism. To modify the sensibilities of the self through delicate techniques . . . so that you no longer require the constitution of difference as evil to protect a precarious faith in an intrinsic identity or order. The goal is to modify an already contingent self . . . so that you are better able to ward off the

. . . temptation to transcendentalise what you are by constructing difference as heresy or evil.[117]

In Nietzsche's own words, the ideal of analytic self-cultivation entails comprehending oneself as *dividuum* rather than *individuum*.[118] Hitherto, he asserts, "being philosophically minded" meant "striving to acquire a single deportment of feeling, a single class of opinions for all the situations and events in life."[119] But in a postmetaphysical, sceptical culture, he suggests, our rigid, monological deportment might be able to give way to another philosophical ethos, one in which we attune ourselves to, and develop an ear for, different voices. It may have a "higher value for the enrichment of knowledge," he speculates, if, rather than making "ourselves uniform" or striving to acquire a single view that encompasses every possible situation, we instead

> listen to the soft voice of different situations in life; these bring their own particular view with them. Thus we take an attentive interest in the life and being of many things by not treating ourselves as fixed, stable, single individuals.[120]

Nietzsche thus links treating oneself as a *dividuum*, or as an "unknown and unknowable subject," to the cultivation of a rich sensibility for the specificity and singularity of experiences.[121] In the culminating sections of *Human, All Too Human* he argues that it is by cultivating a capacity to pass through many convictions that we might transcend the vengeful annihilation of differences that flows from clinging to convictions:

> Anyone who has not made his way through various convictions, but has instead remained attached to the belief in whose net he first became entangled, is at all events a representative of backward cultures precisely because of this constancy; in accordance with this lack of cultivation [*Bildung*] . . . he is hard, injudicious, unteachable, without gentleness, always suspicious, an unscrupulous person who seizes every opportunity for making his opinions prevail because he simply cannot comprehend that there have to be any other opinions.[122]

In the final aphorism of the first volume of *Human, All Too Human* Nietzsche encapsulates his alternative notion of mature individualism and self-cultivation in the emblem of the "wanderer."[123] Because they undertake the difficult labour of self-analysis and endure their own state of becoming, Nietzsche defines free spirited wanderers as geniuses of justice, who as "opponent[s] of convictions" attempt to "give everything its due."[124] This free-spiritedness might be a "cooling" of the spirit, but it is, Nietzsche stresses, a cooling of those raging fires that "make us unjust."[125]

Understood in this way, Nietzsche's wanderer is a fitting symbol for the mode of self-cultivation he formulates in *Human, All Too Human*. As this chapter has demonstrated, like his Hellenistic predecessors, Nietzsche conceives philosophy as a therapy that attempts to heal the diseases of the soul. It is thus with a view to transforming practical morality into a therapeutic art of self-analysis that he dissects the metaphysical tradition. His morality of insight combines Hellenism's medical model of self-cultivation with his psychoanalytic insights into the symptoms of narcissistic wounding. In this context, he conceives the work of self-analysis and remembrance as integral to a philosophical therapy that moderates the inflamed affects of wounded vanity. In his unpublished notes on his academic discipline, "We Philologists," Nietzsche remarks that "what is inexhaustible is the ever new accommodation of each age of antiquity."[126] In the middle period, as this chapter has shown, he transposes this proposition into the psychological register. Composing our souls, as he sees it, depends on how we accommodate ourselves to those geological upheavals—the soul's earthquakes and eruptions, as it were—in which "the ground upon which we live" is completely turned over "so that the dead rise up and our antiquity becomes our modernity."[127] Without the work of self-composition, he fears, the unassuaged grief of wounded vanity threatens to unleash the furies.

NOTES

1. HAH2, preface, 4. On this Stoic notion of therapy, see especially *Helvia*, chs. 1–4.

2. Rüdiger Safranski, *Nietzsche: A Philosophical Biography*, op. cit., 20.

3. Martha C. Nussbaum, "Pity and Mercy," op. cit., 149. Nussbaum draws on Oehler's account of Nietzsche's library.

4. In formulating the notion of *askēsis* the Cynic tradition drew on images of athletic training, emphasising the parallels between endurance athletics and their own art of living: "the Cynic trained . . . to ensure his capacity for endurance. . . . Diogenes trained himself against such adversities as exile, poverty, hunger and death. For him this was the only battle worth winning. Whereas civilized existence represents these trials as evil, the Cynic sought to endure them precisely by refusing to call them evil." As we have seen, Nietzsche calls up the spirit of Diogenes in his 1886 preface to HAH2, 5, by describing his discipline as one that makes it as easy as possible for the free spirit to run long distances; see R. Bracht Branham and Marie-Coile Goulet-Gaze (eds.), "Introduction" in their edited collection, *The Cynics: The Cynic Movement in Antiquity and Its Legacy*, 1996, University of California, Berkeley, 25–26.

5. GS, preface, 2.

6. HAH1, 33, 34.

7. WWR1, §57, 319.

8. HAH1, 33.

9. On romantic supernaturalism, see Meyer H. Abrams's classic discussion in *Naturalism and Supernaturalism: Tradition and Revolution in Romantic Literature*, 1971, W.W. Norton & Co., New York.

10. HAH1, 33. Both these cases, Nietzsche contends, still depend on "impure" thinking: i.e., they maintain a sense of life's value and avoid the grip of nihilism only by blinding their adherents to the common fate of humanity—its "ultimate purposelessness."

11. SE, 160-61, 142.

12. HAH1, 33, emphasis added.

13. WWR1, §63, 352-53. In an interesting twist on Kant, Schopenhauer implies that the allegedly (synthetic) a priori categories of space, time and causality are means through which the ego wards off such dread. These categories enable them to do so by shaping the ego's perception of the world as constituted by separate and distinct entities whose experiences are alien to one another. Insofar as a world seen through Kant's categories of reason excludes *Mitgefühl*, Schopenhauer implies, it is a world constructed according to the psychological exigencies of fear and dread of being contaminated by the other's suffering.

14. See WWR1, §57, 313; on the history of the shipwreck metaphor, see Hans Blumenberg, *Shipwreck with Spectator: Paradigm of a Metaphor for Existence*, translated by Steven Rendell, 1997, MIT Press, Cambridge, Mass.

15. HAH1, 33.

16. HAH1, 33.

17. BT, 22.

18. HAH1, 34.

19. HAH1, 34.

20. WWR1, §57, 315.

21. D, 58; Nietzsche here appears to draw this Christian list of cherished emotional agitations from the passages in the *City of God* where Augustine defends the moral worth of pathos against the impiety of Stoic *apatheia*; see Augustine *City of God*, op. cit., bk XIV, ch. 9, and bk XIX, ch. 4.

22. HAH1, 34; see also HAH1, 287.

23. James Conant, "Nietzsche's Perfectionism: A Reading of *Schopenhauer as Educator*," op. cit., 220.

24. HAH1, 35-38.

25. HAH1, 37, 38. Nietzsche echoes Seneca's startling claim that the Stoic attempts to effect a cure for grief "not by soothing measures, but by cautery and the knife"; Seneca, *Helvia*, ch. 2, 321-22.

26. HAH2, preface, 5; HAH2, 356; HAH1, 243.

27. See WS, 128: "He who reduces to paper what he suffers will be a *melancholy* author. A *serious* author, however, is one who tells us what he *has suffered* and why he is now reposing in joy."

28. On the relationship between Stoic medical, therapeutic philosophy and its stylistic devices, see Martha C. Nussbaum, *The Therapy of Desire*, op. cit., 35ff.

29. HAH1, 2.

30. HAH1, 3 (Handwerk translation).

31. HAH1, 1.

32. HAH1, 34.

33. HAH1, 37; Paul Rée completes the sentence thus—"because there *is* no intelligible world." Later, in the *Genealogy of Morals*, Nietzsche will stress his divergence from Rée's analysis of the *altruistic* origins of morality, but his starting point

nonetheless still rests on Rée's fundamental premise that morality does not have a metaphysical basis; see GM, preface, 4.

34. HAH1, 39.

35. HAH1, 37.

36. WS, 52; Nietzsche will later satirise Kant's notion of synthetic a priori judgments in BGE, 4, 5, and especially 11. In place of Kant's question "How are synthetic judgements a priori possible?" Nietzsche substitutes the question "Why is belief in such judgments *necessary?*"; see Immanuel Kant, *Groundwork of the Metaphysics of Morals*, translated by H. J. Paton, 1964, Harpers Torchbook, New York, 95.

37. WS, 52.

38. HAH1, 37

39. HAH1, preface, 7

40. HAH1, 3.

41. In his discussion of Kant's notion of moral autonomy and Nietzsche's critique Jay Bernstein suggests that Nietzsche's psychological model of reflection is internal to the logic of moral thought, not merely an unnecessary supplement. If Bernstein is correct, then moral reason becomes irrational when it excludes reflection on the conditions of its employment. See Jay M. Bernstein, "Autonomy and Solitude," in Keith Ansell-Pearson (ed.), *Nietzsche and Modern German Thought*, 1991, Routledge, London, 192–215, 199.

42. D, 202.

43. D, 202.

44. Ibid. On the Stoic notion of "spiritual well-being," see Seneca, Letter XLI.

45. Martha Nussbaum sums up the alternative to the Stoic's cognitive conception of the emotions: "The Stoic view of emotion has an adversary. It is the view that emotions are 'nonreasoning movements,' unthinking energies that simply push the person around, without being hooked up to the ways in which she perceives or thinks about the world. Like gusts of wind or the currents of the sea, they move, and move the person, but obtusely, without vision of an object or beliefs about it. In this sense they are 'pushes' rather than 'pulls'"; Martha C. Nussbaum, *Upheavals of Thought*, op. cit., 24–25.

46. D, 35.

47. D, 103.

48. D, 35.

49. L XLI.

50. D, 35.

51. Martha Nussbaum identifies the Stoics' blindness to the temporal constitution of the emotions:

> The Greek and Roman Stoics had no apparent interest in childhood, nor did they ever ask how early experiences shape the mature emotional life. Indeed, they appear to have had the implausible view that children, like animals, do not have emotions. We can see that this was an error—that the "geological upheavals of thought" that constitute the adult experience of emotion involve foundations laid down much earlier in life, experiences of attachment, need, delight, and anger. Early memories shadow later perceptions of objects, adult attachment relations bear the traces of infantile love and hate.

Martha C. Nussbaum, *Upheavals of Thought*, op. cit., 6.

52. HAH1, 15, 29.

53. D, 539.

54. HAH1, 14; on this point see also HAH1, 136. Nietzsche first tackles these issue in an early essay (1864), "On Moods." Here he broaches two questions that are prominent in HAH1 and 2—that is, how we might integrate the emotions and experiences which fuse with music, especially painful experiences, into what he describes, with obvious Platonic resonances, as the household of the soul; and how, in order to achieve this work of self-tuning, we need to find ways of transposing musical moods into the realm of visual images, or of building a "bridge," as he puts it, "from the mysterious castle of the musician" to "the free country of images"; see, "On Moods," *Journal of Nietzsche Studies* 2, 1991, 5–10, translated by Graham Parkes; MW, 109. See also Graham Parkes's illuminating discussion of this early essay, in which he draws out Platonic resonances of Nietzsche's notion of self-attunement; Graham Parkes, *Composing the Soul*, op. cit., 42–48.

55. WS, 37.

56. D, 34; see also HAH1, 608. Nietzsche develops his concept of mimetic identification at HAH1, 51, and D, 134.

57. WS, 44.

58. In this regard, Nietzsche's analysis of the disenchantment of sacred architecture can serve as an allegory for his analysis of the self. In the case of sacred spaces, Nietzsche's morality of insight is no longer seduced by the sense of the uncanny or exalted which once clung to the lines and figures of a temple, just as in his analysis of the self he is not seduced by the divine aura that surrounds archaic layers of the self, and which, if Kant's treatment of the holy will is any guide, some times still cloaks them; see HAH1, 218.

59. On the power of self-forgetting see for example, WS, 40. Of course, as we have seen, Nietzsche, again like the Stoics (and as Freud will later), describes passions, feelings, pathos with metaphors drawn from nature, often, indeed, "sublime" natural forces—storms, torrents, electrical charges etc. However, this does not imply that he conceives them as brute, instinctual nature. Rather, these metaphors serve him, as they served the Stoics, as convenient expressions for conveying the common phenomenological or lived experience of the power of moods and feelings. For an excellent discussion of this point see, Martha C. Nussbaum, *Upheavals of Thought*, op. cit., ch. 1.

60. WS, 19.

61. HAH1, 38.

62. HAH1, 244.

63. HAH1, 244.

64. D, 32. I borrow this phrasing from Rüdiger Safranski, *Nietzsche: A Philosophical Biography*, op. cit., 194–95.

65. HAH1, 236.

66. HAH1, 248; D, 453.

67. HAH1, 236.

68. HAH1, 109.

69. D, 534.

70. HAH1, 109; see also HAH2, 13.

71. HAH1, 109; Nietzsche quotes here from Horace, *Odes*, translated by G. Shepherd, 1985, Penguin Books, Harmondsworth, UK, Book II, 11. Nietzsche quotes

from two verses, which read: "The glory of vernal flowers is not/ forever, nor does the bright moon shine/ with one sole face. Why tire your mortal mind/ with counsels of eternity? Better to drink while we may,/ reclining insouciant beneath some/ lofty plane or pine." Nietzsche edits out Horace's reference to drowning our sorrows!

72. HAH1, 37.

73. Michel Foucault, "The Order of Discourse," in Michael J. Shapiro (ed.), *Language and Politics*, translated by I. Macleod, 1984, New York University Press, New York, 127; see also HAH1, 8. At the same time, however, Nietzsche recognises that absolute scepticism is trapped in an unresovable antinomy: it recognises that to judge, evaluate or measure is always illogical insofar as the values which drive our actions are always our own projections, and yet life itself is inconceivable without such illogical projections. "We are from the very beginning illogical and therefore unjust beings, *and can recognise this*: this is one of the greatest and most inexplicable disharmonies of existence"; HAH1, 32.

74. HAH1, 9.

75. HAH1, 9.

76. L, 108.

77. L, 108. In his inaugural Basel Lecture (May 1869), later privately published as "Homer and Classical Philology," Nietzsche memorably invokes Seneca's lament about the pursuit of wisdom being turned into the study of mere words. In what he calls a "confession of faith," Nietzsche declares his intention of turning philology into philosophy (*philosophia facta est quae philologia fuit*), or, as James Porter puts it, "encompassing . . . philology within a philosophical *Weltanschauung*." Paradoxically, Nietzsche chose his first ceremonial address as a professional philologist to announce *not* his entry, but his departure from conventional philology, and he did so by turning to Seneca's notion of the love of wisdom as a therapeutic art of life. In other words, Nietzsche *first* announces his break with conventional philology not in the guise of a Schopenhauerian metaphysician or a Wagnerian aesthete, but in the guise of a Senecan philosophical therapist for whom philosophy is analogous to the art of navigation (of life). Arguably, it this early confession of faith that Nietzsche returns to and explores in the middle period; see, respectively, L, 108; and James I. Porter, *Nietzsche and the Philology of the Future*, op. cit., 14, 35; and letter to Rohde, April 30, 1872, quoted in Porter, 298, fn. 11.

78. HAH1, 29.

79. HAH1, 29.

80. HAH1, 56.

81. D, 561; see also HAH1, 16, HAH2, 19, D, 426.

82. HAH1, 29; on this point we should note Nietzsche's quip in D, 338: "One man is another man's conscience: and this is especially important if the other has no other conscience."

83. HAH1, 16.

84. HAH2, preface, 5.

85. HAH1, 109; see also WS, 350.

86. HAH1, 20.

87. HAH1, 56, 274, and 602.

88. HAH1, 4, 29.

89. HAH1, 628. Nietzsche quotes from *The Republic*, Bk 10, 604b–c.

90. Lawrence Lampert, *Nietzsche's Teaching: An Interpretation of Nietzsche's Zarathustra*, 1986, Yale University Press, New Haven, Conn., 347, fn. 141.

91. Nietzsche claims that the rhetorical trope of prosopopoeia is fundamental to understanding the nature of our thought processes, including philosophical thinking, because in most thinking we personify our abstract ideas and then traffic with them as if they were individuals. For Nietzsche prosopopeia is a rhetorical device that is crucial to the work of self-analysis insofar as it transforms abstract, often musical impressions, into visible images; see HAH2, 26, and GS, 335. In the winter semester of 1872–1873 Nietzsche delivered a course on rhetoric, and he touched on all of the major rhetorical figures, including prosopopoeia. Hillis-Miller discusses the possible impact of this course on Nietzsche's conceptualisation of philosophic thought, see J. Hillis-Miller, "Nietzsche in Basel: Writing, Reading," *Journal of Advanced Composition* 13, no. 2, 1993, 311–22.

92. Freud also identifies the implacable demand for the endless repetition as a *childish* compulsion, one that comes to play a pivotal role in psychoanalytic treatment. He argues that in the case of *unpleasurable* experiences, the purpose of repetition is to master a powerful impression or to bind quantities of disruptive energy; see BPP, 307–9. For a compelling interpretation of children's need for repetition as the assimilation and deepening of their relation to the object rather than as a regressive drive to return to an earlier state of narcissistic plenitude, see Ernest Schachtel, *Metamorphosis: On the Development of Affect, Perception, Attention and Memory*, 1963, Routledge & Kegan Paul, London, 258–65. Danielle Chapelle provides the most sustained analysis of the parallels between Nietzsche's concept of the eternal return and the psychoanalytic notion of repetition compulsion. Chappelle argues that both Nietzsche's philosophy and psychoanalytic therapy are preoccupied with resentment over impermanence and aim at overcoming this resentment; see Danielle Chapelle, *Nietzsche and Psychoanalysis*, op. cit.

93. Nietzsche's use of the first person singular gives this aphorism its confessional, autobiographical air. In his precocious 1858 autobiographical sketch, "From My Life," Nietzsche recalls the chiming bells at his father's funeral: "At one o'clock in the afternoon the ceremonies began, with the bells pealing their loud knells. Oh, never will the sound of those bells quit my ears." It is well documented that Nietzsche felt he never fully recovered from his father's death, and his family's unhappy departure from the *Vaterhaus* at Röcken. Again, he connects this trauma with the ringing of evening bells: "The time approached when we were to leave Röcken. I can still remember the last day and the last night we spent there. That evening I played with several local children, thinking that it would be for the last time. The vesper bell tolled its melancholy peal across the meadow, dull darkness settled across the earth"; quoted in David Farrell Krell and Donald L. Bates, *The Good European: Nietzsche's Work Sites in Word and Images*, 1997, University of Chicago Press, Chicago, 14, 16–17.

94. *The Republic*, bk 10, 604e, 605b.

95. Henry Staten, *Eros and Mourning: Homer to Lacan*, 1995, Johns Hopkins University Press, Baltimore, xii.

96. *The Republic*, bk 3, 387d–e and bk 10, 603e.

97. D, 448.

98. Henry Staten, *Eros and Mourning*, op. cit, xii.

99. Rüdiger Safranski's analysis of Nietzsche notebooks from the mid-1870s bears out this point in slightly different terms; see Rüdiger Safranski, *Nietzsche*, op. cit., 153, 152.

100. Martha Nussbaum sums up the narcissistic orientation of the contemplative or idealist notion of love that Plato inaugurates and which, so she argues, Spinoza and Proust elaborate:

> All begin with an understanding of love that derives from a picture of infantile help-lessness and the infantile wish for omnipotence—that sees the wish of love in terms of a restoration of totality and a Golden Age needless state. We might say that they express . . . pathological narcissism: for they long for complete control over the world and they therefore refuse to abandon this wish in favour of more realistic wishes for interchange and interdependence. Their characterisation of what human life is like is distorted by their wish, for they see only agony and misery where there is incompleteness and lack of dictatorial control. . . . Rather than learning to live in a world where every lover must be finite and mortal, the contemplative lover finds marvellously ingenious devices to satisfy those desires of infancy. . . . Rather than renouncing the wish for totality in favour of a more appropriate human wish this lover continues to be motivated by infantile om-nipotence and has for this reason had to depart from a world in which a infant's wishes can never be satisfied.

Martha C. Nussbaum, *Upheavals of Thought*, op. cit., 524–25.

101. See also BGE, 14.

102. HAH1, 629

103. HAH1, 629.

104. HAH2, 37.

105. HAH2, 38.

106. Throughout his monumental study of Nietzsche's depth psychology, Gra-ham Parkes demonstrates the significance of images and imagery to Nietzsche's psy-chological explorations and experiments. "Nietzsche's psychology," he writes, "(is) above all imagistic, a discipline practised in *images* rather than in concepts"; see Gra-ham Parkes, *Composing the Soul*, op. cit., 7–8, and passim.

107. GS, 14.

108. GS, 14.

109. According to Socrates in the *First Alcibiades*, our first philosophic duty is to obey the Delphic command, "Know Thyself," "for once we know ourselves, we may learn how to care for ourselves, but otherwise we shall never shall"; quoted in W. K. C. Guthrie, *Socrates*, 1971, Cambridge University Press, Cambridge, 151. Guthrie discusses the modern dispute over antiquity's attribution of this dialogue to Plato, see 150, fn. 2.

110. HAH1, 629.

111. ON, 85.

112. HAH1, 630.

113. ON, 85.

114. GP, 57.

115. HAH1, 630.

116. HAH1, 631; see also HAH2, 230.

117. William E. Connolly, *The Augustinian Imperative: A Reflection on the Politics of Morality*, 1993, Sage Publications, Newbury Park, Calif., 145.

118. Hollingdale defines these scholastic terms: *individuum*—that which cannot be divided without destroying its essence; *dividuum*—that which is composite and lacks an individual essence; see his note to HAH1, 57.

119. HAH1, 618. One of Nietzsche's targets here is what we might call, following Graham Parkes's paraphrases of Nietzsche, Plato's "monotonocracy." Parkes develops a subtle and persuasive analysis of both Nietzsche's objections to the monochromatic simplicity of Plato's rational soul, and Nietzsche's alternative model, see Graham Parkes, *Composing the Soul*, op. cit., 355ff.

120. HAH1, 618.

121. WS, 267, emphasis added.

122. HAH1, 632.

123. For Nietzsche's use of the image of the traveller, see HAH2, 211, 223, 228, and WS, 307.

124. HAH1, 636.

125. HAH1, 637; Nietzsche thus closes HAH1 with an allusion to and subtle shift in Plato's conception of the just individual and the just accommodation within the soul; see Plato, *The Republic*, bk 4, 443c–d.

126. Nietzsche, "We Philologists," quoted in James I. Porter, *Nietzsche and the Philology of the Future*, op. cit., 14.

127. HAH2, 360.

5

The Comedy of Revenge

The human "thing in itself."—The most vulnerable and yet the most un-conquerable is human vanity: indeed, its strength increases, and in the end can become gigantic, through being wounded

Human, All Too Human 2, 46

This chapter examines Nietzsche's account of the psychological fuel of the raging fires that "make us unjust" and the analytic work on the self that might cool this spirit of vengeance.[1] In order to facilitate this exploration, the first section draws on Freud's analysis of one of the earliest modulations of narcissism: that is, the incipient ego's attempt to restore a phantasised condition of majestic plenitude. Freud suggests, as we shall see, that the infantile ego accomplishes this phantasy through vengeful projection. For the sake of explaining and clarifying Freud's psychology of revenge, the chapter recalls his famous vignette on the *fort-da* game, which he analyses as an infantile strategy to establish an illusion of sovereignty. Freud shows that the rage for securing this illusion is symptomatic of a fear that accompanies the discovery of the independence of the other: the fear of annihilation.

The second section argues that Freud's analysis of the psychological connections between this first narcissistic wounding and vengeful projection illuminates Nietzsche's critique of heroism. In this regard, it subverts the notion that Nietzsche lionises pre-Platonic heroes and their manic, triumphant laughter in the face of tragedy. Rather like Suetonius, the deadpan chronicler of the emperors' follies, and Seneca and Epictetus, Nietzsche satirises the overblown pathos of heroism. In the middle period Nietzsche treats the hero as material fit only for comedy. It demonstrates that he underpins this comic jesting through his protopsychoanalytic insights into the hero's desperate attempt to use vengeance as a means of securing a phantasy of omnipotence. In other words, Nietzsche satirises the hero's desire for the illusion of omnipotence as the exemplification of an infantile method of salving the narcissistic wound.

In the final sections, the discussion of Nietzsche's own use of satire opens onto a broader consideration of his analysis of the psychological significance of comedy and laughter. For Nietzsche laughter, jokes and humour are privileged points of access for theorising the intrapsychic world. He maintains that conceptualising the self as a comic genre, or, more precisely, as a series of comic stratagems, can serve as a rich source of self-knowledge. Like other explosive pathos, he uses laughter as a spy that can help to penetrate our psychic fortifications.

This chapter shows that Nietzsche analyses a series of comic stratagems as sources from which we can learn more about the psychodynamics of narcissism. In doing so, it suggests that he distinguishes between neurotic inflammations of narcissism and a mature form of individualism that tempers and incorporates the residues of narcissistic yearning into the work of self-composition and self-composure. In exploring the comedies of the soul, Nietzsche identifies three comic stratagems that he conceptualises as expressions of different responses to or treatments of narcissistic loss: manic laughter, melancholic humour, and what he, along with Freud, considers the positive self-humouring of Stoicism. Finally, the chapter examines what we might call, following Simon Critchley, comic self-acknowledgement, and demonstrates that Nietzsche treats this as a sign of mature individualism.[2] In the middle period, therefore, Nietzsche understands the wisdom of suffering to lie in comic, antiheroic self-recognition of human finitude.

FORT-DA: THE FIRST REVENGE

A brief examination of the psychoanalytic account of projection can serve as background for understanding Nietzsche's critique of narcissistic object relations. In his attempt to account for the genesis of the ego, Freud claims that a primitive ego-form emerges once repeated experiences of a lack of immediate gratification upset the infant's state of primary narcissism or symbiotic fusion with the mother.[3] Only its enforced exile from symbiotic fusion, and with it the loss of the feeling of narcissistic plenitude, compels the human creature to begin differentiating between itself and the world, between inside and outside. Freud calls the psychical agent that negotiates the transition from fusion to separation, from oceanic plenitude to terra firma, the "pleasure ego."[4] Even though the pleasure ego must negotiate this blow to infantile narcissism, he suggests, it nevertheless remains enthralled by the promise of blissful submersion; it is still seduced by the siren's music, so to speak. In its earliest incarnation, therefore, the ego attempts to find substitutive means for satisfying the desire for the lost state of primary narcissism. Its first strategy is to draw the boundaries between itself and the outside in such a fashion that it retains a feeling of narcissistic plenitude. It does so by projecting, or literally throwing out, all internal sources of unpleasure into the external world and incorporating or devouring the external sources of pleasure. "The original pleasure ego," Freud writes, "wants to introject into itself everything that is good and to eject from itself everything that is bad."[5]

Projection is thus the ego's primordial defence mechanism for restoring something of the feeling of plenitude that its discovery of the independence of the object world compels it to abandon. While Freud acknowledges that the boundaries between inside and outside established by the pleasure ego's projections and introjections cannot escape rectification through experience, he believes that the mechanism of projection continues to be active as a means through which the ego seeks to relieve itself of intolerable internal anxieties.[6] Projection is not just a symptom of pathological paranoia, according to Freud, since it also appears under other psychological conditions. "When we refer the causes of certain sensations to the external world, instead of looking for them . . . inside ourselves," he writes, "this normal proceeding, too, deserves to be called projection."[7] This mechanism, he suggests, allows the ego to defend itself against an internal anxiety as though it came from the outside, or from the direction of a perception. Projection is an attempt to transform an internal anxiety, which the ego is powerless to prevent or to shield itself from, into an external object against which it can defend itself. "[I]nternal excitations which produce too great an increase in unpleasure," he contends, "are treated as though they were acting not from inside, but from outside, so that it may be possible to bring the shield against stimuli into operation as a means of defence against them."[8] In the case of a phobia, for example, an external object takes the place of an internal anxiety, and the ego can thus "react against this external danger with attempts at flight by phobic avoidances."[9]

Freud conceives projection as one of the means through which the ego can repeat in relation to the phobic object what he see as its original relation to the world: that is, the attempt to flee or annihilate the external world with its overwhelming emission of stimuli.[10] However, by attempting to maintain itself as a site of pure pleasure through projection, Freud observes, the ego ultimately only succeeds in creating for itself a strange and threatening "outside."[11] It is, in short, a neurotic or pathological solution to the difficulties posed by internally driven anxieties. The projective defence mechanism not only fails to dissolve or cure the anxieties it sought to fend off, it recreates them in new and insidious forms. In this way, Freud argues, projection can be seen as the "starting-point of important pathological disturbances."[12]

Freud addresses the psychological issue of regaining the pleasure of omnipotence through projection in his famous vignette on the *fort-da* game. His little allegory affords a compelling insight into the psychological structure that underpins Nietzsche's critique of the vengefulness that springs from wounded narcissism. A brief examination of Freud's analysis of the *fort-da* game can therefore serve to illuminate the structure of the childish vengeance that Nietzsche identifies as the core of the heroic ethos.[13]

In the *fort-da* (gone-there) game, Freud speculates, the infant derives a yield of pleasure from becoming active in relation to a situation in which he was formerly passive: the situation of his dependence on his mother for his feeling of self-presence. According to Freud, the *fort-da* game, which consists in throwing away a spool and making it disappear (*fort*) and reeling it back into view (*da*), is the infant's imaginary act of vengeance on his mother for going away from him and the painful feeling of impotence and annihilation that her departure arouses in him. Through this game, he argues, the child reverses the balance of power between himself and his mother: in fantasy he becomes the active, powerful subject, capable of tossing away and annihilating the mother, and she becomes the needy, dependent child suffering the pain of being cast into oblivion. On the plane of phantasy, then, the child uses the *fort-da* game as a means of compensating himself for the pain of separation and the terrifying discovery of his impotence, and he does so by vengefully inflicting on a symbolic substitute the same kind of suffering he experiences when his mother's absence threatens him with annihilation.

Projection is thus central to the *Spiel*: the infant projects his own needy, dependent self and its painful feelings of loss and separation into an object, and then vengefully assumes the role of the powerful master who causes the object to suffer by making it disappear. Freud captures the essence of the vengeful strategy for regaining the illusion of omnipotence in the infant's use of projection to assuage its loss through the imaginary transfer of its pain and impotence to another. He sees this vengeful artifice at work in many games where the child creates a *Spiel* that re-enacts his sufferings, but in doing so makes himself the master and the other the victim: "As the child passes over from the passivity of the experience to the activity of the game, he hands on the disagreeable experience to one of his playmates and in this way revenges himself on a substitute."[14] If Freud is right, it is the infantile inability to bear separation and impotence that makes seeing or arousing suffering in others so addictively pleasurable for human beings, for it is this vengeance that enables us to assuage our profound fear of annihilation, rooted in our earliest condition of infantile dependence. Vengeance soothes our fear of annihilation by restoring to us an illusory feeling of magical omnipotence.

INFANTILE HEROES

In his analysis of the hero, Nietzsche draws a similar link between the infantile inability to endure the loss of an imagined condition of omnipotence and the pathology of revenge. In making this case, Nietzsche brings in to sharper focus his concern with the dangers that narcissistically driven vengeance pose for personal and social relations. In some respects, Nietzsche follows the Stoic argument that anger and vengeance are symptomatic of a failure to properly treat and cure the painful affects that spring from mortal losses and sufferings. But Nietzsche establishes his therapeutic analysis of the psychology of revenge, a therapy that partly works by satirising and lampooning the infantile stratagems of the hero, on a more sophisticated psychology, one which lays the groundwork for later psychoanalytic theories of narcissism and its discontents.

Nietzsche's first step towards formulating his own philosophical therapy is to identify and analyse the pathological stratagems for dealing with incompleteness and vulnerability. It is because the pain arising from their dependence on uncontrollable goods proves intolerable, he argues, that human beings summon to their aid various means of alleviation. Revenge, he maintains, is prominent among these consolations. He distinguishes between taking revenge, which he describes as an "intense attack of fever," and the desire to take revenge without the strength and courage to carry it out, which he claims "means carrying around with us a chronic suffering, a poisoning of the body and the soul."[15] According to Nietzsche, neither the morality of intention nor that of utility are able to expose and analyse the psychological roots of revenge. "Both estimations," Nietzsche roundly asserts, "are short-sighted."[16]

At first blush, it may seem that Nietzsche is therefore insinuating that it is better to immediately discharge vengeful affects rather than allow them to grow into a chronic ailment, but, as we shall shortly see, he seriously questions this position because it is premised on a crude understanding of psycho-dynamic processes. Nietzsche's much more subtle psychology shows that vengeful discharge often only serves to exacerbate the original distemper. Moreover, the notion that Nietzsche elevates a simple revenge morality over subterranean *ressentiment* is sharply at odds with the fact that he identifies both as products of one and the same fever or disease.[17] His aim is not to defend the absurd position that one form of a disease is better than another, but to understand the pathological root that lies at the source of vengeance in all its various manifestations. In other words, both moral perspectives are shortsighted in the sense that in their haste to establish a fixed point of judgement they neglect to investigate how this fever might be cured. Fixed moral judgements are of little use to the "new physicians of the soul" who attempt to understand revenge as a disease that requires medical treatment.[18] Nietzsche criticises such moral perspectives because they merely judge such phenomena rather than understand its psycho-genesis, mutations and possible transformations. It is this latter task that Nietzsche tackles by means of psychological observation. He addresses both the taking of revenge and subterranean *ressentiment* as symptoms of a diseased soul for which the philosophical therapist seeks a cure. Nietzsche's difficulty on this score, a point we will examine further, lies in distinguishing between successful and unsuccessful *therapeia*.

Nietzsche, then, seeks to understand vengeance as a symptom of wounded narcissism, and in the first instance he chooses to illuminate this connection by examining the pre-Platonic hero. *Pace* Charles Taylor and other critics, Nietzsche does *not* see the pre-Platonic hero as emblematic of a transgressive splendour against which we can measure and condemn the banality and pusillanimity of modern humanism.[19] On the contrary, he conceives heroic "destinies" as the hapless, human, all too human misadventures that befall those who, lacking the wit to find other ways of soothing their wounded narcissism, bring disaster upon themselves and others. Nietzsche satirises rather than lionises the epic heroes, lampooning Ajax's mad vengefulness (or *envy*, as he later describes it) and his choice of suicide as a means of assuaging his wounded vanity.[20] In his discussion of Sophocles' Ajax, Nietzsche makes the following observation:

> [T]he tragic element in the lives of great men frequently lies not in their conflict with their time and the baseness of their fellow human beings, but instead in their incapacity to defer their action for a year or two; they cannot wait.[21]

One does well in this context to recall Epictetus' deflationary jibe at tragic heroism: "Look how tragedy comes about: when chance events befall fools."[22] It is in this vein that Nietzsche sees Ajax not as a tragic hero, but as a tragicomic fool. Like Simon Critchley in his recent analysis of comedy and tragedy, Nietzsche is satirically critical of, rather than "overawed" by, the "monstrous magnitude of the tragic hero."[23] Nietzsche treats the "great" Ajax as a victim of incontinence; Ajax simply cannot wait.

Taking his lead from Sophocles' dramatisation, Nietzsche in *Human, All Too Human* (61) lampoons Ajax's enactment of the heroic ethos. For Nietzsche, Ajax's decision to fall on his own sword in order to salvage his honour is not a resolute act of freedom in the face of fate, but merely a risible, childish failure to contain his passions. He underlines this point by focussing our attention on a seemingly minor implication of the speech the oracle Calchas makes shortly before Ajax commits suicide. According to Calchas' prophecy, Ajax would no longer have deemed suicide necessary if he had simply allowed his violent self-pity to "cool off for one more day."[24] (We should recall that for Nietzsche "the single goal that governs" the free spirit is "to *know* at all times" which "will make him cool and will calm all the savagery in his disposition").[25]

Ajax, then, lacks the wit to soothe and overcome the suffering he experiences as a result of his double humiliation: his defeat at the hands of the wily Odysseus in their dispute over Achilles' armour and the shameful outcome of his attempt to exact revenge—the mad slaughter of the sheep he hallucinates as his enemies. As Nietzsche sees it, Ajax is not sufficiently sharp-witted to outfox "the fearful insinuations of his wounded vanity by saying to himself: who in my situation has not taken a sheep for a hero? Is this then something so dreadful? On the contrary, it is something typically human: Ajax might have spoken some such words to comfort himself."[26] Instead, his passion takes on a life of its own, a transformation Nietzsche registers by making this passion an active, grammatical subject ("Passion does not want to wait"), and he is swept away by a wave of self-pity: "Aias! Aias! How fit a name to weep with! Who could have known/How well those syllables would spell my story?/Aias, Aias! Over and over again/ I cry alas! How am I fallen!"[27] Ajax loses himself to passion, just as his name dissolves into the sound of lamentation. He succumbs to the acoustics of loss.[28] By exaggerating the extent of his losses, Ajax exacerbates his wounded vanity to the point that he can neither staunch the flow of self-pity and self-lamentation, nor endure it for a single day. Overwhelmed by a torrent of self-pity, Ajax seeks solace in the most radical anaesthetic: death.

In lightly mocking Ajax's incontinence, Nietzsche suggests that even though it is universally human (*allgemein Menschliche*, as Nietzsche stresses) to suffer from wounded vanity, and to respond to it by splitting the world into sheep and heroes, Ajax's exaggerated self-pity betrays an infantile refusal to delay gratification, to wait and reflect, that profoundly damages his object relations. For in attempting to maintain his self-image as omnipotent, Ajax cannot tolerate the deprivations the world and others inflict on his mortal, human self, and instead splits himself and his objects into debased and idealised parts, sheep and heroes. Ajax not only splits his world in this fashion, he also expels these parts of himself into others. His mad delusion simply literalises the mechanism of projection. It also makes manifest the confusion that projective identification creates between the intrapsychic and intersubjective world: Ajax is at war not with real others, but with the objects into which he has projected his own anxieties. The tragic element in Ajax's life, as Nietzsche puts it, lies not in any fateful conflict with his time or the baseness of his fellow human beings, but in himself and his incapacity to defer his action. Like the infantile narcissist, Ajax seeks to immediately assuage the trauma of losing his sovereignty through vengefully annihilating the gods and heroes that he imagines laughing at his impotence, and that he obsessively conjures up as he meditates suicide.[29] However, because these sources lie within him, he is "destined" to constantly mistake sheep for jeering heroes and gods, and he can therefore never achieve what he seeks: the definitive restoration of pure sovereignty. In his vain pursuit of complete sovereignty, therefore, he must ultimately turn on himself and by destroying himself quell his narcissistic rage and suffering once and for all.

The implication of Nietzsche's satirical gloss is that by splitting and projecting himself in order to protect his sense of self-perfection, Ajax generates a violent and endless cycle of vengeance that can be brought to a halt only with his own death or suicide. ("The blade so often steeped in Trojan blood will now stream with its master's own, *that none may conquer Ajax save himself!*")[30] The heroic ethos thus generates an either/or: either the constant need to project parts of the self onto others and take vengeance on them for the sake of restoring the phantasy of omnipotence, or when this mechanism finally, and inevitably, fails to alleviate the feeling of narcissistic loss, to annihilate oneself.

Nietzsche thus conceives revenge, in whatever guise it appears, as a feverish sickness of the soul that demands therapeutic analysis. His medical description of revenge carries more than just the overtones of Hellenism's therapeutic conception of philosophy. It is a lexical index of the degree to which Nietzsche brings to bear a medical or therapeutic gaze on psychological phenomena. His therapeutic gaze identifies revenge as a pathology whose roots lie in the mortal creature's anxious awareness of its own insecurity and the precariousness of its most cherished projects and hopes. Unable to bear the painful defeat of their longing for omnipotence, he suggests, human beings resort to stratagems for re-establishing for themselves the image or phantasy of their own self-sufficiency and impermeability:

> *Discharging ill humour*—Any person who fails at something prefers to attribute this failure to the ill will of someone else, rather than to chance. His stimulated sensibility is relieved by thinking of a person and not a thing as the reason for his failure; for we can revenge ourselves on people, but we have to choke down the injuries of chance. Therefore, when a prince [or sovereign—*Fürsten*] has failed at something, his circle tends to designate some individual as the ostensible cause and to sacrifice that person in the interest of all courtiers; for otherwise, the ill humour of the prince would be vented on all of them, since he cannot take revenge on the goddess of fate herself.[31]

Nietzsche's tone here carries something of Suetonius' deadpan humour, and in composing this aphorism Nietzsche may well have recalled one of this Roman chronicler's most dryly entertaining anecdotes about Nero. We can see a monstrously bloated expression of the narcissistic pathology that Nietzsche sets about deflating in the following report from Suetonius:

> Nero was no less cruel to strangers than to members of his family. A comet, popularly supposed to herald the death of some person of outstanding importance, appeared several nights running. His astrologer Babillus observed that monarchs usually avoided portents of this kind by executing their most prominent subjects and thus directing the wrath of heaven elsewhere; so Nero resolved on a wholesale massacre of the nobility.[32]

On the theoretical plane, Nietzsche implies that projection is a means of defending against and warding off the pain we experience in glimpsing the radical limits on our sovereignty. In effect, he constructs this aphorism as a comic satire of infantile narcissism. Nietzsche treats the vain project of sovereignty as material fit only for comedy. As we shall see later in the chapter, he also conceives comic self-acknowledgement of one's finitude and powerlessness as integral to the therapeutic treatment of wounded narcissism.

In the aphorism noted (*Human, All Too Human*, 370) Nietzsche argues that the failure to comically acknowledge the limits of one's own sovereignty has troubling repercussions. The childish way the ego uses illusions to reclaim its feeling of narcissistic omnipotence may be risible, but the consequences are no joking matter. We can see this in Nietzsche's analysis of the sovereign's clownish attempts to regain his majesty. Because the princely or sovereign ego wants to sustain its omnipotence, he observes, the accidents of fate arouse its intense ill humour and aggression. Hence the sovereign seeks to eject or repel all the painful stimuli that register the limits of his power to command and regulate his dominion, but he cannot achieve this aim by accepting the superior power of chance. For if he acknowledges the goddess of fate as a higher power, he merely reminds himself of his own impotence and his powerlessness to prevent further loss and suffering. "His Majesty the Baby," as Freud might say, cannot abide fate's *lèse-majesté*.[33] The prince therefore needs his courtiers to act as nursemaids and find ways to appease the humiliation his narcissistic grandiosity has suffered. His courtiers must reinstate the illusion of his omnipotence lest this humiliation vent itself in indiscriminate acts of infantile rage; his majesty the baby must be consoled. Their task is to insure that the baby remains sufficiently "illusioned," or confirmed in its experience of omnipotence, to borrow from Winnicott.[34]

Nietzsche identifies strategies of projection as the means that facilitate this consolation. The sovereign's courtiers project his ill humour into another, and construct this other as the external cause of his inner suffering. Through this projection they enable the sovereign to discharge his irritation with himself over his own impotence by victimising another, and they thereby also spare him the difficult task of confronting his sovereignty as a mere illusion. Nietzsche brilliantly captures the very essence of projection as a means of unburdening oneself of painful affects:

> There are not a few who understand the unclean art of self-duping by means of which every unjust act they perform is re-minted into an injustice done to them by others and the exceptional right of self-defence reserved to what they themselves have done: the purpose being to greatly reduce their own burden.[35]

If we understand Nietzsche's aphorism in this way as a satire of infantile narcissism, it becomes apparent that he underscores another point: that the sovereign ego is the dupe of its own courtiers or "undersouls."[36] While the sovereign takes himself to be the master of his kingdom, Nietzsche's analysis suggests that he is in fact deluded by his undersouls into believing that his omnipotence remains inviolable. They dupe him for the sake of protecting the commonwealth from his indiscriminate wrath. For these undersouls the sovereign is merely the channel through which they flush out the poisons of the body politic. The ego's majesty is thus doubly compromised: the forces of the underworld and the goddess of fate govern it. Nietzsche's parable, one might say, construes the sovereign as a point of intersection between the unconscious and necessity. On Nietzsche's interpretation, therefore, if the ego fails to acknowledge unconquerable necessity and seeks instead to sustain the illusion of its omnipotence, it becomes little more than a sewer for the soul's toxic affects:

> *Cloaca of the soul.*—The soul too has to have its definite cloaca into which it allows its sewage to flow out: what can serve as these includes people, relationships, classes, or the Fatherland or the world or finally—for the truly fastidious (I mean our dear modern "pessimists")—God.[37]

Only by ejecting from itself all of the bitter affects that spring from the painful and unavoidable violation of its omnipotence does the ego establish a fragile simulacrum of sovereignty. It projects these affects into another and soothes the soul's wounded narcissism by taking revenge against its scapegoats. Revenge is thus a feverish attack of infantile narcissism.

For Nietzsche, then, the narcissistic wound, or "wounded vanity" as he calls it, gives rise to various forms of pathological vengeance.[38] Rather than accepting that losses are inevitable, that the project of sovereignty is beyond human capacities, the subject attempts to assuage its sufferings and restore its sovereignty through revenge. The pathology of revenge consists in imagining a persecutor against whom the subject can then discharge its painful feelings of being persecuted and violated. Seen in light of the subject's inescapable submission to the greater power of fate, however, such revenge can only establish a dreamlike illusion of omnipotence. Nietzsche recognises that without coming to terms with the goddess of fate, without finding another way to master or temper its own drive to omnipotence, the subject finds itself ensnared in a cycle of vengeance; faced with constant defeat by the mercurial powers of chance, it must constantly pacify its wounded vanity by creating new scapegoats whose sacrifice serve as momentary alleviations. As Nietzsche makes clear in his analysis of Ajax and his comic satire of the duped sovereign, the "real" other who is the target of his vengeance is a shadowy projection through whose sacrifice he restores a phantasy of omnipotence.

COMEDIES OF THE SOUL

Applause.—In applause there is always a kind of noise—even when we applaud ourselves.[39]

In the theatre of the self, as Nietzsche imagines it here, the applause of self-congratulation we summon up for our triumphant performances is always based on a "degree of unclarity" regarding ourselves.[40] In congratulating ourselves as victors or heroes we deceive ourselves about ourselves by failing to hear the nonsense, the lack of discrimination, the sheer stupidity in the applause with which we flatter ourselves. Remarking upon the fact that "choices" of vocation are often made without sufficient self-knowledge, Nietzsche observes:

> The problem is largely that of making good, of correcting as far as possible what was bungled at the beginning. Many will recognise that their later life shows a sense of purpose which sprang from fundamental incompatibility: it makes living hard. But at the end of life one has gotten used to it—then he can deceive himself about his life and applaud his own stupidity: *bene navigavi naufragium feci* [When I suffer shipwreck I have navigated well]. And he may even sing a hymn of praise to "providence."[41]

As we have seen, Nietzsche satirises the hero's vanity, suggesting that he does everything in his power to conceal from himself his own haplessness, not only when he suffers misfortune, but perhaps even more so, as he quips, when he is victorious:

> *The denial of chance.*—No victor believes in chance.[42]

Strangely, Nietzsche's comic tickling of human vainglory is entirely lost on almost of all of his critics.[43] Even Nehamas, who makes a point of exploring Nietzsche's multifarious styles, remains largely oblivious to his penchant for humorously deprecating vanity and its masks and self-deceptions;

Staten, who, perhaps more than any other interpreter, attempts to listen carefully to the *tonality* of Nietzsche's texts remains deaf to his sardonic wit and self-parody.[44] Nor should it be thought that Nietzsche's comic turns are merely literary devices of no particular philosophical consequence. Rather, Nietzsche uses black humour as an antidepressant that enables us to laugh at ourselves rather than raging against ourselves and others.

However, not only does Nietzsche *employ* comedy, he also analyses it, and in doing so reveals it as a strategy that human beings use to defend themselves and assuage their narcissistic sufferings. We can distinguish, then, between Nietzsche's *use* of jokes to demonstrate and participate in their tonic, antidepressant effects, on the one side, and his *analysis* of several types of comedy that human beings use in their struggle to assuage their suffering: manic laughter as release, *Schadenfreude* as pleasurable ridicule, and self-humouring as soothing consolation. The objective of Nietzsche's analysis of these types of comedy is to reveal how we use them to counter, conceal or compensate for our human, all too human haplessness and ineptitude. In pursuing this analysis, Nietzsche develops what we might call a comic acknowledgement of the childish methods we employ to sustain our narcissistic phantasy of grandiosity and omnipotence. His theorisation of these clownish ruses and self-deceptions brings with it a sorrowful smile that acknowledges the suffering that drives human beings to employ desperately funny measures.

MANIC LAUGHTER

In *The Birth of Tragedy*, Nietzsche observes in passing that comedy is a therapeutic art that affords us the opportunity of discharging or releasing painful affects of fear and terror. "*Comedy*" he writes "is the artistic discharge [*Entladung*] of the nausea of absurdity."[45] He sees the art of comedy as soothing the painful affects generated by a "chaotic world" that mocks our sovereignty.[46] If a "piercing gaze" into this chaos triggers a nausea with existence, comedy saves us from this illness by discharging our pain through manic laughter.[47] Nietzsche's clarifies this rudimentary observation about comic catharsis in *Human, All Too Human*. Wherever there is laughter, he observes, there is non-sense. According to Nietzsche, manic laughter is a symptom of the relief that ensues from a temporary liberation from the painful constraints of necessity:

> The overturning of experience into its opposite, of the purposive into the purposeless, of the necessary into the arbitrary, but in such a way that this event causes no harm . . . delights us, for it momentarily liberates us from the constraints of the necessary, the purposive and that which corresponds to our

experience, which we usually see as our inexorable masters; we play and laugh when the expected (which usually makes us fearful and tense) discharges itself harmlessly. It is the pleasure of the slave at the Saturnalia.[48]

Like the slave temporarily freed from bondage during the Saturnalia, he suggests, our laughter is merely symptomatic of a temporary release from the fear and suffering that dominates our experience. We explode with manic laughter, Nietzsche observes, when we unexpectedly find ourselves free from the tyranny of pain or when an unexpected stroke of good fortune delivers us from constant suffering.[49] It is for this reason that we can barely distinguish it from the tearful sobs of relief that follow in the wake of a release from intolerable suffering. Pain remains the ground bass of such laughter:

> *Upside down world of tears.*—The manifold discomforts imposed upon men by the claims of higher culture at last distort nature so far that they usually bear themselves stiffly and stoically and have only tears for the rare attacks of good fortune so that many indeed, are constrained to weep merely because they have ceased to feel pain—only when they are fortunate do their hearts beat again.[50]

MELANCHOLIC HUMOUR: CRUEL JOKES

> *Laughter.*—Laughter means *schadenfroh* but with a good conscience.[51]

As Lampert notes, many of Nietzsche's jokes seem wounding and cutting, but his sharp wit is not in the service of *Schadenfreude*. In fact, Nietzsche's psychological acuity illuminates how *Schadenfreude*, the malicious laughter at another's downfall, is something that we can turn back on ourselves in the form of self-ridicule and self-mockery. And just as *Schadenfreude* is a comic antidepressant that works its magic cure through the illusion that we are elevated above our neighbour, self-ridicule performs precisely the same function in the intrapsychic space.

In order to theorise this melancholic discomfort, Nietzsche introduces concepts that Freud later systematised in his psychic topography, namely the conceptual distinction of opposed psychical agencies: the superego and the ego. It is this self-splitting, Nietzsche shows, that makes it possible for human beings to adopt the stance of *Schadenfreude* toward themselves and cruelly laugh at their own misery. Etymologically, of course, melancholia literally means black bile, which is to say, assuming its identity as one of the four humours, black humour.[52]

Now, black humour, as Nietzsche sees it, also shares the same *psychological* structure as melancholic self-abasement, but experienced from the position of the superego rather than the hapless ego. That is to say, in self-ridicule we establish an imaginary identification with the superego and through this identification we are able enjoy its mortification of the ego. Punning on the Nietzsche epigraph, self-ridicule, we might say, means laughing *with* a good conscience. By identifying with the *Über-Ich*, Nietzsche shows, we restore our illusion of sovereignty; it is a perverse means of re-claiming our omnipotence through self-abasement. It follows that this kind of black humour becomes more pleasurable, and its paroxysms of laughter more intense, the greater the degree to which the ego is mortified and abased. Nietzsche sees this antidepressant, self-ridicule at work in the plea-sures of the ascetic:

> There is a defiance of oneself of which many forms of asceticism are among those most sublimated expressions. For certain men feel so great a need to ex-ercise their strength and lust for power that in default of other objects or be-cause their efforts in other directions have always miscarried, they at last hit upon the idea of tyrannising over certain parts of their own nature, over, as it were, segments and stages of themselves . . . they behave like high-spirited rid-ers who like their steed best only when it has grown savage, is covered with sweat and is tamed. . . . This division of oneself, this mockery of one's own na-ture, *spernere se sperni* . . . is actually a very high degree of vanity . . . man takes a real delight in oppressing himself with excessive claims and afterwards idol-ising this tyrannically demanding something in his soul.[53]

On this point, Simon Critchley provides an illuminating preliminary un-derstanding of the psychological structure and purpose of melancholic hu-mour. Drawing on Freud's Nietzschean-inspired conception of self-splitting, he claims that this splitting not only produces the self-laceration of depres-sion (melancholia) and the self-forgetfulness of elation (mania), but a dark, sardonic, wicked humour. Black humour, as he explains, has the same structure as melancholic depression, "but it is an antidepressant that works by *the ego* finding itself ridiculous."[54]

However, there is a slip in Critchley's analysis, and it is one that leads him astray: for it is not the ego finding itself ridiculous, but the superego ridi-culing the weakness of the ego. If Nietzsche is right, this ridiculing by the superego does not, as Critchley claims, "recall us to the modesty and limit-edness of the human condition."[55] On the contrary, through idolising this cruel superego the ego surreptitiously restores to itself a degree of vanity. Freud himself is unambiguous on this point: he stresses that in melancholic self-abjection, which can take the form of cruelly laughing at oneself, the yield of enjoyment derives from satisfying the sadistic, annihilating im-pulse. When we take delight in lacerating ourselves, so he believes, we re-peat our original infantile reaction to our discovery of our powerlessness before the object world. In this case, however, as Nietzsche already demon-strates in his analysis of the ascetic, the sadism that relates to the object is turned back upon the ego. Importantly, then, for Nietzsche and Freud what we discover in the phenomenon of melancholia is the ego as object (or, better still, as abject object) rather than as a subject. Freud explains the abjection of the ego thus:

> The self-tormenting in melancholia, *which is without a doubt enjoyable*, signifies . . . a satisfaction of trends of sadism and hate which relate to an object, and which have been turned around on the subject's own self. . . . The analysis of melancholia . . . shows . . . that the ego can kill itself only if . . . it can treat itself as an object—if it is able to direct against itself the hostility which relates to an object and which represents to objects in the external world.[56]

Taken to its logical extreme, the *Spiel* of melancholia generates *"fort!"* but no *"da!"* It follows that Critchley is wrong to treat the pleasures of masochistic identification with the superego as if it were a tempering of our narcissistic grandiosity and a source of self-cognition. Nietzsche's and Freud's point, by contrast, is that this masochistic identification is a means of compensation for the ego's lack of power, a compensation that perversely takes the form of participating in its own abasement. In other words, *contra* Critchley, this mocking self-abasement is the means by which we *restore*, not temper, our vanity.[57] As Freud is at pains to demonstrate, the melancholic's ill temper proceeds from a "constellation of revolt" which passes "over into the crushed state of melancholia."[58] In a characteristically pithy jest, Nietzsche sums up the covert self-inflation of the melancholic: "Whoever despises himself still respects himself as one who despises."[59] Nietzsche's analysis of the vain striving to restore omnipotence through the desperate measure of identifying with the inner tyrant, the cruel superego and its mocking laughter, succeeds in revealing how we use self-ridicule as a counterweight to the feeling or experience of haplessness and impotence. According to Nietzsche, the melancholic "entertains" and gives himself pleasure, not enlightenment, through self-ridicule.[60]

> Those paradoxical phenomena, like the sudden chill in the behaviour of an emotional person, or the humour of the melancholic . . . appear in people who harbour a powerful centrifugal force and experience sudden satiety and sudden nausea. Their satisfactions are so quick and so strong that they are followed by weariness and aversion and flight into the opposite taste. In this opposite, the cramp of feeling is resolved by sudden chill, in another by laughter.[61]

Here Nietzsche analyses melancholic humour as a flight from the feeling of nausea and weariness that ensues from a massive expenditure of force, or an "orgy" of feeling.[62] What Nietzsche depicts as a *Schleuderkraft* is analogous to the superego: it is an instrument that is generated by and which also discharges psychical tensions, and in the case of the melancholic it does so by abasing the ego. But like any other orgy, according to Nietzsche, the melancholic's orgy of self-violation simply generates another pathology: nausea or weariness. Melancholic humour is thus a sick laughter, or the laughter of sickness, an orgiastic, impatient yielding to the opposite impulse in a desperate attempt to escape self-revulsion.

HUMORING OURSELVES

Yet, as Nietzsche recognised, self-ridicule does not exhaust our comic potential. We can see in Nietzsche's work the same distinction between cruel joking and humour that Freud draws in his paper "On Humour." This humour has quite a different psychological structure to the sadistic ridiculing that merely inverts the melancholic split. We can briefly unpack the psychology of humour by examining Freud's discussion. According to Freud, we soothe and console ourselves for our powerlessness in the face of the traumas of the external world by denying or wishing away its impact on us; this, he believes, is what it means to humour ourselves. He illustrates this with an example of gallows humour: "A criminal who was being led out to the gallows on a Monday remarked: 'Well, the week's beginning nicely.'"[63]

Freud maintains that such humour has something of "grandeur and elevation" which, as he writes,

> clearly lies in the triumph of narcissism, the victorious assertion of the ego's invulnerability. The ego refuses to be distressed by the provocations of reality, to let itself to be compelled to suffer. It insists that it cannot be affected by the traumas of the external world.[64]

Freud distinguishes between the cruel joke in which we ridicule *ourselves* and this species of humour in which we make light of the threats, dangers and harshness of *reality*, and in doing so he conjures up something of the tranquil, untraumatised spirit of Stoicism. In the former we take pleasure in diminishing the ego, but in the latter we preserve and protect the ego by deflecting reality. Freud, in short, sees humour as a triumph of narcissism over the painful threats of reality. Nietzsche also pokes fun at the way we retain our good humour through denying the power of reality over us, instead using such occasions as means of gaining pleasure:

> We laugh at him who steps out of his room at the moment when the sun steps out of its room, and then says "I *will* that the sun shall rise"; and at him who cannot stop a wheel, and says: "I *will* that it shall roll"; and at him who is thrown down in wrestling and says: "Here I lie but I *will* lie here!" But, all laughter aside are we ourselves ever acting any differently whenever we employ the expression: "I *will*"?[65]

Nietzsche evokes laughter here in order to disclose the comical way in which we triumphantly proclaim our mastery of reality in the face of our palpable impotence. Indeed, Nietzsche treats this risible reversal of the active and passive poles that, as we have seen, he analyses in his satire of infantile narcissism, as a blunder universally committed by human beings:

> *To reassure the sceptic.*—"I have no idea how I am *acting*! I have no idea how I *ought to act*!"—you are right, but be sure of this: *you will be acted upon*! at every moment! Mankind has at all ages confused the active and the passive: it is their everlasting grammatical blunder.[66]

Because such humorous self-deceit runs counter to an unmediated appraisal of reality, Freud describes it as "rebellious" rather than "resigned," a "triumph of the ego but also of the pleasure principle, which is able here to assert itself against the unkindness of the real circumstances."[67] Explaining this achievement in terms of his psychodynamic theory, Freud suggests that such self-humouring consolation is made possible by the superego, which cocoons the ego from the traumas of reality:

> in bringing about the humorous attitude, the superego is *actually repudiating reality and serving an illusion* . . . It means: "Look! Here is the world which seems so dangerous! It is nothing but a game for children—just worth making a jest about!"[68]

At first glance this explanation appears to generate a conundrum for Freud, since, needless to say, the superego is normally not such an amiable figure. In order to solve this conundrum Freud adds a comic twist to the tale of his account of our capacity to humour ourselves:

> If it is really the superego which, in humour, speaks such kindly words of comfort to the intimidated ego, this will teach us that we have still a great deal to learn about the nature of the superego . . . if the superego tries, by means of humour, to console the ego and to protect it from suffering, this does not contradict its origin in the parental agency.[69]

In this closing remark of his paper on humour, Freud gives the clue to dissolving the mystery of how the superego can both mock the ego through lacerating jokes, and console it through humorously cocooning it from those external realities that severely limit its narcissistic wishes. It is seldom noted that when Freud introduces his famous jest about the narcissist as "His Majesty the Baby" he is actually referring to the *parents' attitude toward their child*, not to the child himself. In fact, Freud derives his notion of primary narcissism *not* from direct observation of children, but by inferring this condition from the parents' affectionate attitude toward their children.

On the basis of the sheer intensity of parental affection, he asserts, we can infer nothing other than that it is a reproduction of their own narcissism, which they have long since abandoned. Parents, Freud maintains, invest their abandoned narcissism in their children. He describes this narcissistic investment in the following way:

> The child shall have a better time than his parents; he shall not be subject to the necessities which they have recognised as paramount in life. Illness, death, renunciation of enjoyment, restrictions of his own will shall not touch him; the laws of nature and of society shall be abrogated in his favour; he shall once more really be the centre and core of creation—"His Majesty the Baby," as we once fancied ourselves. . . . Parental love, which is so moving and at bottom so childish, is nothing but the parents' narcissism born again, which, transformed into object love, unmistakably reveals its former nature.[70]

Freud's argument, in other words, is that humour saves narcissism by warding off the harshness of reality, and it does so by drawing on that aspect of the superego that is formed on the basis of the parents' narcissistic investment in the child's ego and their desire, as he puts it, "to protect it from suffering." For Freud, humour is the ego's narcissistic rebellion against reality that it funds with the resources of its parents' narcissistic investments. In humour, then, the superego treats the ego as doting parents treat their child; it spoils and mollycoddles the ego, pretending that it can suspend the harsh laws of necessity in favour of "His Majesty the Baby."

So Critchley is right when he jokes that the superego is our amigo, but we must conclude that he is wrong to think that this superego simply replaces or, as he puts it, "takes the place of the ego ideal," the repository of our narcissistic dreams.[71] On the contrary, as Freud shows, the superego that humours the ego with its words of consolation is built upon the parents' narcissism and is thus a continuation of their desire to ward off the unkindness of reality. Indeed, Critchley's claim that we can dispense with the ego ideal, the heir to our phantasies of plenitude, is strikingly at odds with the foundations of precisely the Nietzschean and Freudian metapsychology that he deploys for the sake of theorising comedy and humour. At the core of Freud's theory of narcissism, we might recall, is the claim that we *never* forgo the desire to take pleasure in ourselves or for the oceanic feeling, and that "the development of the ego consists in a departure from primary narcissism and gives rise to vigorous attempts to recover that state."[72] (In casting aside the ego ideal Critchley seems to be the unwitting victim of his own self-humouring: he deceives himself that he can majestically dispatch the ego ideal with the mere stroke of a pen).

We must, therefore, restate the significance of Freud's remarks on self-humouring: it is true that he unexpectedly finds a positive place for the superego, *but* only for a superego onto which our own lost ideal has been projected, and onto which presumably parents also project their narcissism. The real insight of Freud's analysis of humour is that it implies that the cruel superego, the agency formed through the infant's introversion of its own wounded vengefulness, is modified and tempered through the integration or incorporation of the residues of the feeling of plenitude that precedes this wounding.

In other words, Freud broaches the idea that the turning back on ourselves that begins with the formation of an *Über-Ich* agency can only take a healthy form when this agency is informed by and draws upon the resources, images and phantasies of our primary narcissism. Humour, we might say, is made possible by an *Über-Ich* in which our phantasies of plenitude have tempered the vengefulness that is ignited and stoked by our loss of plenitude. Humour is a healthy resuscitation of the residues of our narcissism that prevents the superego from becoming, as Freud puts it, "a pure culture of the death instinct."[73] In the art of humouring ourselves, then, Freud discovers a positive place and function for our narcissism, as indeed he must insofar as he believes that we can only ever modulate and transform, never *abandon* our narcissistic wishes. "To be their own ideal once more, as they were in childhood," he asserts without qualification, "this is what people strive to attain as their own happiness."[74]

By "elevating us above misfortune" humour "save[s] our narcissism from disaster," as Ricoeur puts it, but it does so, Freud believes, in a way that he accords a certain dignity that is lacking in mere jokes, which he criticises for giving us a pleasure that derives from satisfying our appetite for aggression, either against others or ourselves.[75] Freud stresses humour's ability to protect the ego from being buffeted by reality as the key to understanding its positive therapeutic effects on the ego's capacity to bear the ultimate sign of its impotence, or "the most touchy point in the narcissistic system," its mortality.[76]

In this regard, Freud implies that self-humouring saves us from defeat in a manner that makes the ego more amenable to Stoic composure and moderation in the face of an intractable reality. Like the Stoics, Freud argues that the value of humouring oneself lies in the fact that it enables the ego to economise on its expenditure of affects. "There is no doubt," he avers, "that the essence of humour is that one spares oneself the affects to which the situation would naturally give rise."[77] In the case of gallows humour, for example, the ego spares itself the affects of anger, fear, horror or despair; an achievement made possible when the ego airily dismisses the traumas of reality with a jest.[78] The ego's jesting dismissal of the otherwise traumatic reality of its impending death, he maintains, prevents the arousal of anger or vengeance, indeed it transforms the provocations of reality into occasions for it to gain pleasure. For Freud, as Kohut correctly states, "humour" is "a *transformation of narcissism*" which enables us "to tolerate the recognition of [our] finiteness in principle and even of [our] impending death."[79]

It is the Stoics who develop and illustrate the connection between self-humouring and self-composure that Freud merely hints at in his exploration of humour. Seneca, for example, in a letter recounting his growing awareness of his own senescence and imminent death, gives a comical rendition of the Stoic dogma that to fear death is irrational.[80] He does so by recalling how a certain Pacuvius made light of his own death by gathering his admirers together each night to perform with him his own funeral celebrations. Pacuvius uses this comic ritual, we might say, to enable himself to confront his finitude without being terrorised by it:[81]

> Pacuvius . . . was in the habit of conducting a memorial ceremony for himself with wine and funeral feasting of the kind we are familiar with, and then being carried on a bier from the dinner table to his bed, while a chanting to music went on of the words "He has lived, he has lived" in Greek, amid the applause of the young libertines present. Never a day passed but he celebrated his own funeral. What he did from discreditable motives we should do from honourable ones, saying in all joyfulness and cheerfulness as we retire to our beds: "I have lived; I completed now the course/That fortune long ago allotted to me."[82]

Strangely, or at least so it must seem to those who follow Hegel in deprecating Stoicism as an art of "solitary mortification," Seneca suggests that Pacuvius' comically self-mocking defiance of the pathos of finitude should inform the Stoics' own acknowledgement of mortality.[83] Seneca comes close here to embracing what we might call a comic antiheroic paradigm that, as Michael Janover puts it, "acknowledges that to face finitude is to flee it, and that only in laughter and comedy can we touch on the real but ungraspable matter of our mortality without trumping or troping it in clichés or metaphysics."[84]

What Freud adds to this Stoic perspective is a psychodynamic account of the genesis of such humour. As we have seen, for Freud the ego can only manage this humorous feat of "grandeur and elevation" by drawing on the resources of the friendly superego, the psychical repository of the parents' narcissistic investment in it, which enables the ego to dismiss a threatening reality as nothing more than a game for children.[85] Freud explains this achievement as one in which "the subject suddenly hypercathects his [friendly] superego and then, proceeding from it, alters the reactions of the ego," which, without this protection from its superego, would normally react with fear, anger, vengefulness.[86] In other words, Freud attributes a positive function to the amicable superego's comic method of sustaining the ego. It serves a positive function, he maintains, insofar as it soothes or diminishes the ego's bitterness at discovering its own impotence before reality, thereby enabling it to economise in its production and expenditure of ill-humoured affects and to derive a certain mild pleasure from the misfortunes it confronts. If, then, we can overcome the fear of impending death by putting ourselves, through humour, on a higher plane, we can do so only by drawing upon our amicable superego, the psychical vestiges of our parents' narcissistic love. Paul Ricoeur nicely sums up the essential point that Freud drives at in his analysis of humour:

> humour . . . enables us to endure the harshness of life, and, suspended between illusion and reality, helps us to *love our fate*.[87]

Indeed, according to Freud, in the face of the fear of death the ego can only sustain itself by being loved by the amicable superego; this transformation of narcissism, in other words, is necessary for the very survival of the ego:

> The fear of death . . . only admits of one explanation: that the ego gives itself up because it feels hated and persecuted by the superego instead of loved. *To the ego*, therefore, *living means the same as being loved*—being loved by the superego, which here is the representative of the id.[88]

For Freud, therefore, we cannot survive without humour.

COMIC SELF-ACKNOWLEDGEMENT: SORROWFUL SMILES

Of course, it is Nietzsche in his writings who suggests *amor fati* (love of fate) as the mark of higher beings. Yet, in this recommendation is a jesting irony in that for Nietzsche such beings are those who have come to treat the vain project of sovereignty as material fit for comic satire. In this respect, Sartre is correct to contrast Bataille's manic, heroic laughter, which is meant to express a grandly tragic affirmation of fate, with what Sartre aptly describes as Nietzsche's "lighter laughter."[89] "[Bataille's] is the heroic laughter," as Critchley puts it, "that rails in the face of the firing squad 'Go ahead shoot me, I don't care.'"[90] "Laughter blesses," as Bataille remarks, "where God curses."[91] According to Sartre, Nietzsche's laughter is lighter than Bataille's, which, he writes, "is bitter and strained. . . . He tells us that he laughs, he doesn't make us laugh."[92]

If Nietzsche makes us laugh, however, it is, as we have seen, because his analyses disclose the clownish ruses and stratagems through which we attempt to reclaim the illusion of power or worth so that we can attain or sustain a sense of dignity. Nietzsche analyses show how the subject attempts to create for itself the illusion of its potency through infantile strategies of vengeance or mocking self-laceration. By contrast with Bataille's heroic laughter, which expresses a denial of our haplessness, Nietzsche's lighter laughter derives from exactly the opposite achievement. That is to say, Nietzsche utilises his analyses of the comic means we use to deny our haplessness and impotence to elicit from us a smile of self-acknowledgement at

our reliance on these childish stratagems. Nietzsche's satire yields what
Critchley calls a "weaker laughter," which "insists that life is not something
to be affirmed ecstatically, but acknowledged comically" and which "arises
out of a palpable sense of inability, impotence and inauthenticity."[93] It not
only evokes a smile at Ajax's bloated dreams of infantile omnipotence, it
also exposes the minor key versions of this malady. Nietzsche jests, for example, that we have even discovered how to transform our deepest abjection into a mark of distinction:

> *Tried and tested advice.*—For those who need consolation no means of consolation
> is so effective as the assertion that in their case no consolation is possible: it im-
> plies so great a degree of distinction that they at once hold up their heads again.[94]

The culmination of Nietzsche's analysis is not, then, as is often thought,
the heroic laughter of total affirmation, but a smiling, antiheroic acknowledgement of the ruses we use to conceal or flee from our finitude and powerlessness. In this regard, Nietzsche goes further than Freud who, as we have
seen, tentatively suggests that beyond cruel joking there is a healthy form of
self-humouring that enables the ego to bear its vulnerability to the realm of
necessity. Nietzsche utilises comic means and *analyses of comic means*—manic
laughter, cruel jokes, and humouring ourselves—as ways of laying bare the
range of stratagems we deploy to conceal our weakness. It is in Nietzsche's
middle works that we discover what Critchley describes as a humour that
"recalls us to the modesty and limitedness of the human condition, a limitedness that calls not for tragic-heroic affirmation but comic acknowledgement, not Promethean authenticity but a laughable inauthenticity."[95]

Nietzsche brings this comic self-acknowledgement to the foreground in
meditating on the classical themes of tragedy. Reflecting on the notion of
the knowledge or wisdom acquired through suffering, Nietzsche subverts
the idea that it leads to Promethean authenticity or grandiose affirmation.
The wisdom of suffering, he implies, lies not in tragic affirmation, but in the
opportunity it gives us of exposing the ruses we deploy to fend it off, and
the subject who emerges from it is not a grandiose, imperious hero, but one
capable of an ironic acknowledgement of its desperate fabrication of illusions. One who suffers, Nietzsche writes,

> takes pleasure in conjuring up his contempt as though out of the deepest Hell
> and thus subjecting his soul to the bitterest pain. . . . With dreadful clearsight-
> edness as to the nature of his being, he cries to himself: "for once be your own
> accuser and executioner, for once take your suffering as the punishment in-
> flicted by yourself upon yourself! Enjoy your superiority as judge; more, enjoy
> your wilful pleasure, your tyrannical arbitrariness! Raise yourself above your
> life as above your suffering." . . . Our pride towers up as never before: it dis-
> covers incomparable stimulus in opposing such a tyrant as pain is. . . . In this

condition one defends oneself desperately against all pessimism, that it may not appear to be a consequence of our condition and humiliate us in defeat. . . . We experience downright convulsions of arrogance.⁹⁶

We can see here already Nietzsche building a critique of the sadistic pleasures of tyrannising oneself, and of heroic affirmation as a pathological and desperate effort, a critique that leads him to a bittersweet smiling at ourselves and at the pathological measures we use to soothe our wounded vanity:

> And then there comes the first glimmering of relief, of convalescence—and almost the first effect is that we fend off the dominance of this arrogance: we call ourselves vain and foolish to have felt it—as though we had experienced something out of the ordinary. . . . "Away, away with this pride!" we cry, "it was only one more sickness and convulsion!" We gaze again at man and nature—now with a more desiring eye; we recall with a *sorrowful smile* that we now *know something*—we look on as if transformed, gentle and still wearied. In this condition one cannot hear music without weeping.⁹⁷

The wisdom of suffering, Nietzsche implies, lies not in tragic-heroic affirmation, but in comic antiheroic acknowledgement.

NOTES

1. HAH1, 637.
2. Simon Critchley, *Ethics, Politics, Subjectivity*, op. cit., 235.
3. On the contemporary debate in psychoanalysis and social theory about the paradoxical nature of the primal psychical situation as both monadic and symbiotic, or a "dual unity" to use Mahler's formulation, see Margaret Mahler et al., *The Psychological Birth of the Human Infant: Symbiosis and Individuation*, 1975, Basic Books, New York, 55; and Joel Whitebook, "Mutual Recognition and the Work of the Negative," op. cit.
4. CD, 4.
5. Sigmund Freud, "On Negation," in *On Metapsychology: The Theory of Psychoanalysis*, translated by James Strachey, 1991, Penguin Books, London, 439; see also IV, 133–34.
6. CD, 4.
7. Sigmund Freud, "Schreber," in *Case Histories II*, translated by James Strachey, 1990, Penguin Books, London, 204.
8. BPP, 301.
9. Sigmund Freud, "The Unconscious," in *On Metapsychology: The Theory of Psychoanalysis*, translated by James Strachey, 1991, Penguin Books, London, 187.
10. IV, 134–35.
11. CD, 4.
12. CD, 5; see also BPP, 301.
13. Henry Staten rightly claims the idea of vengeance illustrated by the *fort-da* game "stands at the centre of [Nietzsche's] world explication." However, *contra*

Staten, this chapter argues that far from being complicit in the vengeful strategies of reclaiming the illusion of narcissistic omnipotence, Nietzsche's notion of the work of the self on itself entails acknowledging the immaturity of this project of omnipotence.

14. BPP, 286–87. In this passage I follow Freud in using the masculine pronoun.

15. HAH1, 60.

16. HAH1, 60.

17. Martha Nussbaum qualifies this point thus: "In certain ways Nietzsche prefers this simple revenge morality to a morality based on the idea that the human being is, as such, worthless and disgusting. But he is quick to point out, as does Seneca, that the interest in taking revenge is a product of weakness and lack of power—of that excessive dependence on others and on the goods of the world that is the mark of the weak, and not of the strong and self sufficient, human being or society"; Martha C. Nussbaum, "Pity and Mercy," op. cit., 155.

18. D, 52.

19. Charles Taylor, "The Immanent Counter-Enlightenment," op. cit., 386–400, 396 and 400, fn. 15.

20. GS, 135.

21. HAH1, 61; Nietzsche echoes Seneca's therapy for anger: "The greatest remedy for anger is delay: beg anger to grant this at first, not in order that it may pardon the offence, but that it may form a right judgement about it: if it delays, it will come to an end. Do not attempt to quell it at once, for its first impulses are fierce; by plucking away its parts we shall remove the whole"; Seneca, De Ira, 104.

22. Epictetus, quoted in Martha C. Nussbaum, Upheavals of Thought, op. cit., 358.

23. Simon Critchley, Ethics, Politics and Subjectivity, op. cit., 230.

24. HAH1, 61. Nietzsche alludes to the scene where a messenger reports that the oracle Calchas has advised Ajax's half-brother Teucer not to let him out of his view for the whole day: "For on this day, no other, he was doomed/To meet Athena's wrath"; Sophocles, Ajax, in Electra and Other Plays, translated by E. F. Watling, 1980, Penguin, Harmondsworth, UK, ll. 758–59, emphasis added.

25. HAH1, 56.

26. HAH1, 61.

27. Ajax, ll. 460–65.

28. In mounting his most serious charge against the tragedians, that is, that they corrupt the souls of even the best characters, Plato specifically stresses that it is the acoustics of grief that awakens and nourishes the greediest and most unruly lower parts of the soul. "When we hear Homer or one of the tragic poets representing the sufferings of a hero and making him bewail them at length, perhaps with all the sounds and signs of tragic grief, you know how even the best of us enjoy it and let ourselves be carried away by our feelings; and we are full of praises for the merits of the poet who can most powerfully affect us in this way." In D, 157, Nietzsche explicitly repeats Plato in order to challenge what he calls a modern cult of natural sounds that encourages expressions of pain, tears, complaints, reproaches, and gestures of rage and humiliation. In this Platonic moment, Nietzsche interprets this cult as symptomatic of a lack of composure in the modern soul, and a lack of desire for such composure; see Plato, The Republic, bk 10, 605d–e, emphasis added; and D, 157.

29. *Ajax*, ll. 372, 389, 459.

30. Ovid, *Metamorphoses*, translated by Mary Innes, 1968, Penguin Books, London, bk XIII, 295, emphasis added.

31. HAH1, 370. Interestingly, Nietzsche chooses the figure of the sovereign or prince to discuss narcissism and vengeance rather than the "slave," which is what one is led to expect by those who confine their interpretation of Nietzsche to a few passages from the first book of GM and the unpublished notes Elisabeth Nietzsche gathered together under the title of "The Will to Power." For Nietzsche vengeance is evidently a psychological phenomenon that potentially afflicts all human beings *qua* humans, not a pathology that belongs to a "physiological type." Even the most cursory glance at the critique of narcissistic omnipotence that he undertakes here is sufficient to indicate the patent absurdity of the often repeated claim that the "Masters" or blond beasts of GM represent Nietzsche's conception of a healthy, cured soul; on this point see Martha Nussbaum, "Pity and Mercy," op. cit., 166, fn. 44.

32. Suetonius, *Twelve Caesars*, translated by Robert Graves, 1957, Penguin, Harmondsworth, UK, 36. The choice of the deadpan Suetonius to illustrate Nietzsche's point is not an idle one, for reasons that we shall consider below.

33. ON, 85.

34. Donald W. Winnicott, "Transitional Objects and Transitional Experience," in *Playing and Reality*, 1971, Penguin Books, London, 11–17.

35. HAH2, 52.

36. BGE, 19. Nietzsche's account of the dynamics of the internal world draws extensively on Plato's political metaphor of the psyche. Nietzsche often recycles Plato's conception of the psyche-as-polis as a means of thinking about the structure and dynamics of the intrapsychic domain. For a brilliant and detailed analysis of these links between Plato and Nietzsche, see Graham Parkes, *Composing the Soul*, op. cit., 320, 346–62, esp. 355–59; see also Leslie Paul Thiele, "Nietzsche's Politics," *Interpretation* 17, no. 2, Winter 1989–1990, 275–90.

37. WS, 46.

38. HAH1, 61. Here Nietzsche uses the phrase *verletzen Eitelkeit* in the context of his observations about Ajax's madness.

39. GS, 201. Nietzsche's idea of applauding ourselves as we applaud actors on the stage is in line with his notion that we stage ourselves for ourselves. In HAH1, 624, for example, Nietzsche claims that in relation to their "higher self" human beings "are often actors of themselves" insofar as they "later imitate over and over the self of their best moments." We need only think of any aging satanic rock star to understand Nietzsche's point.

40. This phrase is borrowed from HAH1, 164, where Nietzsche describes the "unclarity with regards to oneself and that semi-insanity super-added to it" that is necessary to believe in oneself as a genius. Nietzsche devotes this aphorism to mocking Wagner's and Napoleon's insanely vain belief in themselves as *übermenschliches*.

41. Nietzsche, "We Philologists," quoted in William Arrowsmith, "Nietzsche on Classics and Classicists," op. cit., 14.

42. GS, 258.

43. For recent treatments of Nietzsche's use of comedy and satire, see Kathleen Higgins, *Comic Relief*, 2000, Oxford University Press, New York; the essays by Kathleen Higgins, Laurence Lampert, and John Lippitt in John Lippitt (ed.), *Nietzsche's Future*,

1999, MacMillan Press, London. In his discussion of *Ecce Homo*, Daniel Conway argues that Nietzsche engages in an ironic, self-parodying critique of heroic idolatry; Daniel Conway, "Nietzsche's *Doppelgänger*: Affirmation and Resentment in *Ecce Homo*," in Keith Ansell-Pearson and Howard Caygill (eds.), *The Fate of the New Nietzsche*, 1993, Avebury Press, Aldershot, UK, 55–78. In the same volume, see also Keith Ansell-Pearson, "Toward the Comedy of Existence: On Nietzsche's New Justice," 265–81.

44. Alexander Nehamas, *Nietzsche*, op. cit., 18–21; and Henry Staten, *Nietzsche's Voice*, op. cit., 5. Even though Staten often misses the comic, ironic and sometimes almost jocular tone of some of Nietzsche's aphorisms, arguably his broader point about the significance of tone has some validity: "Tone is just as much a property of the written text as are grammar and figuration . . . and it is in the tone of a voice/text that the libidinal forces motivating utterance are most clearly revealed"; 5.

45. BT, 7.

46. BT, 7.

47. BT, 7.

48. HAH1, 213; see also 160. During the Roman Saturnalia, which began on December 17, the state sanctioned and funded a period of unrestricted license and festivities in which slaves were given temporary freedom to do as they liked. Commenting on the Saturnalia, Seneca derides the hollowness of this unrestricted license. "Remaining dry and sober," he writes, "takes a good more strength and will when everyone about one is puking drunk"; L, 18. For Seneca, that we seek to dull our pain through the manic dissoluteness of the festival merely reflects the extent to which in ordinary life we have yet to conquer the pain caused by necessity. It is precisely this manic laughter that Stoics must resist if they are to conquer pain and necessity, rather than merely seeking release from it through the illusion of its temporary cessation. Seneca fears that rather than fortifying us against misfortune, Saturnalian laughter addicts us to finding relief in escapism and that in doing so it sows the seeds of vengefulness and depression. It is in this context that Seneca famously introduces his analogy between the Stoic work on the self and military maneuvers undertaken in peacetime; L, 18.

49. Freud explains manic laughter or exultation in exactly the same manner. Such manic states, he argues, depend on certain economic conditions: "What has happened here is that, as a result of some influence, a large expenditure of psychical energy, long maintained or habitually occurring, has at last become unnecessary, so that it is available for . . . discharge—when for instance some poor wretch, by winning some large sums of money, is suddenly relieved from chronic worry about his daily bread, or when a long and arduous struggle is finally crowned with success."; MM, 263.

50. HAH2, 217; HAH2, 99.

51. GS, 200.

52. See Raymond Klibansky, Erwin Panofsky and Friz Saxl, *Saturn and Melancholy: Studies in the History of Natural Philosophy, Religion, Art*, 1964, Basic Books, New York.

53. HAH1, 137.

54. Simon Critchley, *On Humour*, 2002, Routledge, London and New York, 101, emphasis added.

55. Ibid., 102.

56. MM, 260–61, emphasis added.

57. A measure of the extent to which Critchley has gone astray on this point is his use of Groucho Marx's black humour as an illustration of the positive function of the superego in supplying us with the antidepressant of humour. In such humour, he argues, "the superego does not lacerate the ego, *but speaks to it words of consolation.* This is a positive superego that liberates and elevates by allowing the ego to find itself ridiculous"; 103, emphasis added. As we shall see, however, for Freud humour works its antidepressant magic not by ridiculing the ego but by allowing it to tame a threatening reality by treating it as a matter of jest, a mere child's game that cannot touch it. Moreover, although there can be no doubt that Groucho's humour is an antidepressant, it seems somewhat odd to claim, as Critchley does, that his black humour achieves this end by *consoling the ego in the manner of a comforting parent,* for parents hardly console by enabling their child to laugh at its own abjection. It seems far more plausible to suggest that Groucho's humour is an antidepressant tonic because it discharges the superego's cruelty through *abasing* the ego, not *comforting* it. It is instructive to compare Critchley's claim with E. L. Doctorow's reflections on his childhood reception of Groucho's comedy: "Groucho we acknowledged was the wit. . . . But there were moments when we felt menaced by Groucho, as if there were some darkness in him, or some inadvertent revelation of the *sadistic lineaments of adulthood* that was perhaps premonitory of our own darkness of spirit as when we laughed guiltily at his ritual abasement of the statuesque, maternal Margaret Dumont"; see, E. L. Doctorow, "Introduction," in Harpo Marx (with Rowland Barber), *Harpo Speaks . . . about New York,* 2000, The Little Bookroom, New York, 8–9, emphasis added.

58. MM, 257.

59. BGE, 78; Gilles Deleuze echoes Nietzsche's point in his penetrating account of the masochist's relation to the law as essentially humourous and rebellious: "The masochistic ego is only apparently crushed by the superego. What insolence, what humour, what irrepressible defiance and ultimate triumph lie hidden behind an ego that claims to be so weak"; Gilles Deleuze, "Coldness and Cruelty," in *Masochism,* 1991, Zone Books, New York, 124.

60. HAH1, 141.

61. GS, 49.

62. GS, 49.

63. OH, 427.

64. OH, 429.

65. D, 124.

66. D, 120. Nietzsche constantly draws on our grammatical blunders as a rich source of insight into the economy of the soul. These blunders are to Nietzsche what parapraxes are to Freud: that is, symptoms from which we can interpret the dynamics within the household of the soul.

67. OH, 429.

68. OH, 432–33, emphasis added.

69. OH, 433.

70. ON, 85.

71. Simon Critchley, *On Humour,* op. cit., 105, emphasis added.

72. ON, 95.

73. EI, 394.

74. ON, 95.

75. Paul Ricoeur, *Freud and Philosophy*, op. cit., 334. However, to qualify Ricoeur, it does not save our narcissism *per se*. Rather, to state Freud's point more precisely: in humour, he suggests, the positive or healthy superego, one in which the residues of our narcissism have been integrated, softens the blows of a reality for the ego; without this humouring the ego would experience its finitude and impotence as profoundly traumatic. The amicable superego thereby enables it to come to terms with its finitude and impotence without the violent denials of vengefulness or its inversion, self-mortification. In other words, Freud establishes a connection between self-humour and self-composure that the Stoics also acknowledge and affirm.

76. ON, 85.

77. OH, 428.

78. OH, 428.

79. Heinz Kohut, "Forms and Transformations of Narcissism," op. cit., 120, emphasis added.

80. This Stoic humour is lost on Hegel and those who uncritically adopt his account of their place in the history of philosophy. Hegel interprets Stoicism as a distinctly *humourless* "flight from actuality" that passes over into a "broken gibber of negation." According to Hegel, Stoicism and the other Hellenistic philosophies, Epicureanism and Scepticism, "knew nothing but the negativity of all that assumed to be real, and was the counsel of despair to a world which no longer possessed anything stable"; see Georg Wilhelm Friedrich Hegel, *Phenomenology of Mind*, translated by J. B. Baillie, 1949, George Allen & Unwin, London, 502, 503; and *The History of Philosophy*, op. cit., 329. For Hegel the "gibber of negation" refers to Pyrrho's radical scepticism, which, he argues, is the inevitable dénouement of the Stoic flight from actuality.

81. I borrow this phrasing from Terry Eagleton, *Sweet Violence: The Idea of the Tragic*, 2003, Blackwell, Oxford, 73.

82. L, 12. For our purposes, C. D. N. Costa's translation is more intriguing: "What he did through *bad conscience* (*mala conscientia*) let us do from a *good* (*bona*) *one.*" Costa notes that the familiar memorial ceremony Seneca refers to here is the Parentalia, a Roman festival in honour of the family dead conducted on February 13–21; the closing line is from Dido's speech in Virgil's *Aeneid*, IV, l. 653. Geoffrey Sumi provides a fascinating and thorough analysis of the theatrical, carnivalesque quality of aristocratic Roman funerals, and the use of humour in this ritual of mourning, a practice the Romans mediated through the performance of an actor (or funerary mime) who sometimes mocked and parodied the deceased. Suetonius describes this theatricality and humour in his account of Vespasian's funeral, reporting that as part of the ritual the Emperor's mime parodied and poked fun at his well-known penchant for frugality; see Geoffrey S. Sumi, "Impersonating the Dead: Mimes at Roman Funerals," *American Journal of Philology* 123, 2002, 559–85.

83. Charles Taylor, *Multiculturalism: Examining the Politics of Recognition*, edited and introduced by Amy Gutman, 1994, Princeton University Press, Princeton, N.J., 50.

84. Michael Janover, "Mythic Form and Political Reflection in Athenian Tragedy," *Parallax* 9, no. 4, 2003, 41–51, 48.

85. OH, 428.

86. Freud's explanation implies that this "hypercathecting" is undertaken by a psychical agency that is neither the ego nor the superego. It remains unclear what, if any, theoretical status Freud attributes to this "subject" that hypercathects the superego. On the theoretical level, he is forced into this clumsy locution because with his discovery of narcissism he also discovers that the ego is not an agent in charge of the drives, but an *object* of the drives. If the ego is an object, or abject object, then the notion that it is the source of intrapsychic agency is displaced, and we begin to open onto the idea that there the psyche does not harbour any one directing agency, but is a series of dynamic relations without a fixed centre.

87. Paul Ricoeur, *Freud and Philosophy*, op. cit., 335, emphasis added.

88. EI, 400.

89. Jean-Paul Sartre, quoted in Sylvère Lotringer, "Furiously Nietzschean," in Georges Bataille, *On Nietzsche*, translated by Bruce Boone, 1992, Paragon House, New York, XIV.

90. Simon Critchley, *On Humour*, op. cit., 105.

91. Georges Bataille, *On Nietzsche*, translated by Bruce Boone, 1992, Paragon House, New York, 59.

92. Sylvère Lotringer, "Furiously Nietzschean," op. cit., XIV.

93. Simon Critchley, *On Humour*, op. cit., 106.

94. D, 380.

95. Simon Critchley, *On Humour*, op. cit., 102.

96. D, 114.

97. D, 114.

6

The Irony of Pity

Pity.—In the gilded sheath of pity there is sometimes stuck the dagger of envy.

Human, All Too Human 2, 377

The preceding chapters have shown that in the middle works Nietzsche elaborates a philosophical therapy that addresses those pathologies arising from the ego's attempts to console itself for the loss of its narcissistic plenitude. We have seen that Nietzsche analyses Schopenhauer's asceticism as symptomatic of a desire to return to the imaginary state of absolutely self-sufficient narcissism from which, if he and Freud are correct, every human creature is untimely ripped. The narcissistic imperative takes on an even darker tone in Nietzsche's dissection of revenge. He claims that narcissism is not only the driving force of nirvanic withdrawal, but also of the majestic rage against others that ensues from the incipient ego's painful discovery of its dependence and vulnerability. Revenge discharges these painful affects by restoring to the ego a phantasm of its omnipotence. This chapter examines Nietzsche's critique of *pitié/Mitleid*, and demonstrates that he treats this as another pathology of narcissism. Boldly stated, he argues that as a psychological transaction *Mitleid* satisfies the ego's desire to assuage its loss of narcissistic plenitude.

This chapter explores Nietzsche's case against Rousseau and Schopenhauer, whom he takes as the primary proponents of the ethics of *Mitleid*. According to Nietzsche, the type of *pitié/Mitleid* they expound is symptomatic of the narcissistic malaise.[1] In making this case, he dramatically reverses their perspective, arguing that *Mitleid* should not be understood as an affective bond with the other, not as a sign of living *for* others, but as a veiled means of restoring self-affection at the other's expense. To show this he analyses the *moral psychology* that underpins the precepts of the ethics of pity. If Nietzsche's psychological analysis is correct, then *Mitleid* is not antithetical to revenge against others, but closely linked to one of its subtle shadings and masks, which he calls envy. This chapter argues that his psychological critique is correct in its claim that the kind of pity identified by Rousseau and Schopenhauer is a disguised aspect of envy, and that this envy is fuelled by the ego's desire to assuage or soothe its narcissistic wound.

While Rousseau and Schopenhauer claim that *Mitleid* is the *only* source of ethical concern for others, Nietzsche argues that their psychology of *Mitleid* uncritically accepts a paranoid-schizoid splitting of the object world, to borrow Melanie Klein's terminology, into the enviable and pitiable. He claims that because these forms of pity are generated by a paranoid-schizoid psychological constellation they are better charac- terised as what we might call hateship rather than friendship. In this re- spect, Nietzsche sees in the psychology of the pitier an immature or in- fantile attempt to resolve the narcissistic malaise. His concern is with theorising a mature transformation of narcissism that does not entail this damaging splitting and projection.

This chapter reconstructs and elaborates three steps in his critical analy- sis of the psychological configuration that engenders the type of pity that Rousseau and Schopenhauer advocate: (1) his claim that pity is deeply complicit in envy and its projective identifications, (2) that it ultimately tends toward a diminution of others, and (3) that the twinning of pity and envy in the construction of the object world blocks the individual's ability to live well with others. In other words, this chapter suggests that Nietzsche builds a strong case for reversing their position: he shows that far from overcoming our "colossal egoism," as Schopenhauer calls it, pity is a species of pathological narcissism that damages the individual's ca- pacity for composing balanced relations with others. Nietzsche especially underscores the point that a morality built on these psychological foun- dations prevents individuals from developing a subtle, penetrating and therapeutically efficacious understanding of another's intrapsychic world and experiences.

THE GILDED SHEATH OF PITY:
ROUSSEAU AND SCHOPENHAUER

In criticising the ethics of pity, Nietzsche specifically targets the conceptual- isation of this pathos or affect that lies at the heart of both Rousseau's and

Schopenhauer's ethical philosophy. In prosecuting his case against their ethics he brings to bear his method of psychological suspicion, claiming that it can help explore and fathom pity's intrapsychic significance in a way that sheds new light on both Rousseau's moral pedagogy of *pitié* and Schopenhauer's metaphysically based ethics of *Mitleid*. His core thesis is that *pitié/Mitleid*, as they conceive it, merely crystallises the structure of affects and defences characteristic of a psyche ensnared by a primitive means of soothing the narcissistic wound.[2] Contextualised this way, Nietzsche argues, *Mitleid* should be treated first and foremost as a pathological stratagem through which the psyche seeks narcissistic gratification. His analysis might stand as an illustration of his broader claim that moral philosophy should not be based on or give credence to belief in conceptual oppositions. For he turns common sense inside out and claims that *pitié/Mitleid*, which Schopenhauer identifies as action devoid of "all egoistic motivations," has its roots in envy.[3] It is his psychological dissections that place Nietzsche several steps ahead of not only Rousseau and Schopenhauer, but also those critics who invoke this tradition of pity against Nietzsche without carefully examining, as he does, its theoretical and psychological presuppositions.[4] We can orient ourselves to Nietzsche's critique of this type of pity by briefly examining Rousseau and Schopenhauer's very similar treatments of the origins and worth of pity.[5]

In Book IV of *Émile*, Rousseau argues that *pitié* should be the first and most important emotion cultivated in future citizens. It ought to be cultivated, he claims, because it is the sharing of suffering that reconciles human beings to their fellow creatures:

> Man's weakness makes him sociable. Our common sufferings draw our hearts to our fellow creatures; we should have no duties to mankind if we were not men. Every affection is a sign of insufficiency; if each of us had no need of the others, we should hardly think of associating with them. So our frail happiness has its roots in our weakness. A really happy man is a hermit; God only enjoys absolute happiness; but which of us has any idea of what that means? . . . I do not understand how one who has need of nothing could love anything.[6]

According to Rousseau, the social bond is forged through an acknowledgement of a shared condition of insufficiency, and it is for this reason that teachers should educate individuals to recognise that "all are liable to the sorrows of life, its disappointments, its ills, its needs, its sufferings of every kind; and all are condemned at length to die."[7] Rousseau's moral pedagogy pivots on the notion that beneficent citizenship derives from educating future citizens to understand that they are equally vulnerable to the sorrows and misfortunes that cast others down. From the notion that attachments are premised on insufficiency, weakness or lack, Rousseau attempts to draw a less than obvious corollary:

[It] follows that we are drawn towards our fellow creatures *less by our feelings for their joys than for their sorrows*; for in them we discern more plainly a nature like our own, and a pledge of their affection for us. If our common need creates a bond of interest our common suffering creates a bond of affection.[8]

Rousseau identifies two reasons for the belief that citizens can form bonds of affection with others *only* by cultivating a feeling for their pain and neediness. In the first place, he argues that granting equal value to others depends on recognising ourselves in them, and that such recognition is anchored in seeing that they share similar experiences of sorrow or insufficiency. Sorrow or vulnerability constitutes the foundation of sociability, understood as the extension of the concern we have for ourselves to others, because it forms the single point of mutual recognition. We only see ourselves in others when they suffer. Martha Nussbaum nicely sums up this specifically psychological (rather than logical) claim integral to the ethics of pity:

The claim . . . is that one will not respond with the pain of pity, when looking at the suffering of another, unless one judges that the possibilities displayed there are also possibilities for oneself. . . . The point seems to be that the pain of another will be an object of my concern only if I acknowledge some sort of community between myself and the other—to the extent that I am able, in imagination, to see that suffering as a possibility for me and to understand, on the basis of my own experience, what its meaning might be for the person who has it.[9]

Secondly, Rousseau claims that recognising the other's neediness and insecurity reassures individuals that their desire for a community between themselves and others is not at risk of being unilateral or nonreciprocal. Our fellow creatures' suffering, as Rousseau notes, "[is] a *pledge* of affection for us." It is their suffering that holds others in bondage to us. Rousseau maintains that sorrow must be the *exclusive* force of sociability, therefore, not simply because it is a *shared* condition, for one might after all point to many other things that human beings have in common, but because it allays the fear that others can remain indifferent or unconcerned about us should they so choose. To put it in slightly different terms, Rousseau treats *pitié* as the only possible social cement because by imagining others as needy and suffering, *pitié* allays the fear of their independence and the threat that it carries that they may abandon us to a condition of loveless solitude. Like those needless and carefree Epicurean gods who are "indifferent to our merits and immune from our anger," happy individuals, so Rousseau fears, must remain divinely unconcerned about other mortals.[10] Such deities can have no sympathy for suffering mortals. Rousseau's moral psychology thus splits the object world into two radically exclusive categories: happily self-sufficient individuals modeled on the carefree Epicurean gods, and needy human creatures bound to one another through nothing other than their shared suffering.

However, according to Rousseau, if these godlike individuals are divinely indifferent to the travails of other mortals, these mortals are certainly not indifferent to the pleasures of the godlike. Rousseau slides from the contention that "we" suffering mortals "are drawn *less* toward our fellow creatures by our feeling for their joys than for their sorrows" to an acknowledgement that such *pitié* constructs a social world shot through with envy:

> *The sight of the happy arouses in others envy rather than love*, we are ready to accuse him of usurping a right which is not his, *of seeking happiness for himself alone*, and our *selfishness* suffers an additional pang in the thought that this man has no need of us.[11]

A similar entanglement of pity and envy bedevils Schopenhauer's attempt to give pity a metaphysical basis. The fundamental theoretical problem confronting Schopenhauer's ethics is how non-egoistic actions can arise from a monadic, predatory ego, or, as Nietzsche puts it, how living for others can derive from egoism. Schopenhauer's "solution" to this problem is unashamedly metaphysical. In *On the Basis of Morality*, Schopenhauer claims that only an insight into the metaphysical unity of all things can explain the origins of pity. He argues that pity follows in the wake of a pure, mystical vision of the shared identity of all human beings as transient phenomena of the one will to life.

It is in view of the "colossal" and "boundless egoism" that forms humanity's innermost core as the phenomenon of an insatiable will to life, an egoism which unchecked generates the *bellum omnium contra omnes*, that Schopenhauer sets himself the task of explaining how the immorality of egoism is overcome in acts of pity.[12] "In the eyes of the egotist," Schopenhauer says, "there is a wide gulf, a mighty difference, between the ego . . . and the non-ego embracing the rest of the world."[13] And this ego standpoint, he adds, has empirical validity: "according to experience, the *difference* between my own person and another's appears to be absolute. The difference in space that separates me from him, separates me also from his weal and woe."[14] Given his presupposition that *Mitleid* is purely disinterested, Schopenhauer's monadic conception of the ego leaves him with the difficult task of explaining how it is possible to transcend the ego's self-interested standpoint. "How," Schopenhauer asks, "is it possible for another's weal and woe to move my will immediately, that is to say, in exactly the same way in which it is usually moved only by my own weal and woe?"[15] This problem is especially acute because he holds that egotistical self-interest is our "chief and fundamental incentive."[16] Egoism, as he describes it, is "boundless":

> Everything opposing the strivings of egoism excites wrath, anger and hatred, and he will attempt to destroy it as his enemy. If possible, he wants to enjoy everything; but as that is impossible, he wants at least to control everything. "Everything for me and nothing for others" is his motto. Egoism is colossal; it towers above the world; for if every individual were given the choice between his own destruction and the rest of the world, I need not say how the decision would go in the vast majority of cases. Accordingly, everyone makes himself the center of the world, and refers everything to himself.[17]

Schopenhauer claims that *Mitleid* is a purely disinterested regard for the well being of others that arises from a direct participation in their *los und leiden*. He argues that the "merging" of egos, which he believes makes *Mitleid* possible, can only be explained metaphysically. It is, he exclaims, "astonishing . . . the great mystery of ethics; it is the primary and original phenomenon of ethics, the boundary mark beyond which only metaphysical speculation can venture to step."[18] For he acknowledges that from an empirical standpoint the difference that egotists perceive between themselves and others is justified.[19] His fundamental metaphysical premise is that all phenomena are manifestations of one and the same essence; plurality and difference therefore belong only to the world of appearances. Schopenhauer explains the ethical consequences of his metaphysical monism thus:

> if plurality and separateness belong only to the phenomenon, and if it is one and the same essence that manifests itself in all living things, then that conception that abolishes the differences between ego and non-ego is not erroneous . . . compassion [*Mitleid*] is the proper expression of that view. Accordingly, it would be the metaphysical basis of ethics and consists in *one* individual's again recognising in *another* his own self, his own true inner nature.[20]

Those who pity, in short, recognise and love their own true inner nature in all others; the partition that normally separates them from others dissolves through this "mystical" act of recognition. Pity, in short, is the practical manifestation of the metaphysical unity of all things.

Schopenhauer believes only this *metaphysical* explanation can show us how we surmount our colossal egoism. Pity he insists does not arise from *imagining* ourselves in the position of the suffering, and believing we are suffering *their* pains in *our* person. Rather, Schopenhauer believes that pitiers experience the other's suffering in just the same way as they experience their own, but in the other person: "*he* is the sufferer not *we*; and it is precisely in *his* person, not in ours, that we feel the suffering, to our grief and sorrow. We suffer *with* him and hence *in* him; we feel his pain as *his*, and do not imagine that it is ours."[21] Pity he claims does not stem from merely *imagining* the other's suffering as our own, but actually experiencing "*his*" suffering "*in* him." This is what Schopenhauer means when he describes the pitier as *participating* in the other's suffering *as such*.

Such immediate participation in the other's suffering is possible, he claims, because the separation between individuals is an illusion—ontologically we are all expressions of one and the same metaphysical will to life. He argues that *Mitleid* involves "the immediate *participation*, independent of all ulterior considerations, primarily in the suffering of another, and thus in the prevention or elimination of it. . . . As soon as compassion is aroused, the weal and woe of another are nearest to my heart *in exactly the same way* . . . as otherwise only my own are. Hence the difference between him and me is now no longer absolute."[22] Schopenhauer's suggestion is that just as our own suffering moves us to seek alleviation, so when we experience the other's misery "in him" this experience provides us with exactly the same kind of incentive to alleviate "his" suffering.

Now if Schopenhauer is correct about the ontological identity of all individuals then it should also be possible for one person to participate directly in another's *pleasures* or *joys*. Yet he does not consistently maintain his metaphysical conviction that there is no ontological gap between human beings. In fact, he qualifies this claim to such an extent that he undermines the metaphysical foundations he uses to support the ethics of pity. For he ultimately claims that it is *only* the suffering of others and *not* their joy that motivates the moral agent. According to Schopenhauer, while other people's distress inspires disinterested action their joy never spurs the same kind of non-egoistic response.[23] This restriction is incompatible with his claim that good persons make no distinction between their own and another's interests and recognise in every creature an "I once more."[24]

Schopenhauer, in other words, unwittingly undermines his metaphysical conviction that pity is the practical expression of the unity of all things. For he claims that far from directly participating in the other's feelings, the *Mitleidigen* "feel no sympathy" for the lucky person—"on the contrary, as such he remains a stranger to our hearts."[25] "The expressions of that pure, disinterested, objective participation in the lot and conditions of another," he claims, "are reserved for him who in any way suffers."[26] The other's good fortune *as such* "may easily excite envy, which, if he should once fall from the heights of fortune, threatens to turn into *Schadenfreude*."[27] According to Schopenhauer, the reverse side of pity is envy of the other's good fortune. Thus in elaborating his notion of pity he gradually unravels his own metaphysical doctrine: while his claim that given the metaphysical unity of all creatures sharing joy is at least in principle possible, he begins with the view that the *Mitleidigen* are merely apathetic toward the other's joy, before finally suggesting that far from being indifferent, they are envious of this joy and cannot have any regard for others until misfortune strikes.

This is the same conceptual shift we witnessed in Rousseau's analysis of pity. It constitutes a dramatic shift in Schopenhauer's perspective; from the initial claim that the only condition for pity is a mysteriously immediate participation in the other's feelings, he now maintains that pity only flows when one's envy is appeased by the sight of the lucky person's fall from grace:

> For as soon as the lucky man falls, there occurs a great transformation in the hearts of others, which for our consideration is instructive. . . . Envy is reconciled and has disappeared with its own cause; *Mitleid* takes its place and gives birth to loving-kindness. Those who were envious of and hostile to the man of fortune have often become, after his downfall, his considerate, consoling, and helpful *friends*. . . . For misfortune is the condition of compassion, and this is the source of philanthropy.[28]

We can see here how Schopenhauer's account of the genesis of pity departs *radically* from his metaphysical claim that pitiers recognise their own inner nature in others and act toward them without any egotistical motive, for he now suggests that this "recognition" is contingent upon others *not* enjoying good fortune lest they stir up envy. Putting the matter somewhat too facetiously perhaps, for Schopenhauer there is "one and the same essence that manifests itself in all living things," and this is the basis upon which it is possible for us to participate in the condition of all creatures. However, apparently this essence does not manifest itself in the happy person, for it is certain that the pitier does not participate in fortunate individuals' happiness in exactly the same manner as they do.[29] Schopenhauerian pitiers are obviously not sharing the feeling of pleasure *in* the happy other, but responding to the displeasure they experience *in themselves* at the sight of the other's state of gratification. The relationships that pitiers forge are profoundly self-interested: on the one side, their pitying response springs from their own painful feelings of deprivation, which leads them to deny, negate or spoil others' pleasure in themselves. On the other, pitiers cleave to the sorrowful and misfortunate because the sight of another's suffering brings them relief from the feelings of deprivation and impotence that fuel envy. Schopenhauer's philanthropic souls suffer less from themselves when they see the other suffer; hence their sense of well-being depends on others' weakness and emasculation. For Schopenhauer the exercise of friendship is therefore contingent upon the diminution or weakening of others; where others continue to enjoy good fortune, they remain estranged objects of envy.

We can see in both Rousseau's and Schopenhauer's moral psychology many of the hallmarks of what Klein describes as the paranoid-schizoid position. A brief elaboration of Klein will help to illuminate the genesis of pity and envy as related aspects of a primitive defence mechanism for dealing with narcissistic loss. As we shall see shortly, Nietzsche's analysis brings to the foreground precisely these dimensions of Rousseau and Schopenhauer's concept of the ethical subject.

Turning to Klein first, she identifies the paranoid-schizoid position as the incipient ego's primitive response to the anxiety that its rage over the loss of its perfection (or the demise of primary narcissism) might also lead it to destroy the good object on which it depends for its material and psychic survival. Indeed this rage, or persecutory anxiety as Klein calls it, seems so potent and threatening that the good object must be rendered sublime and perfect in order to protect it from its own rage. In order to crystallise these intrapsychic processes, Klein formulates the concept of the paranoid-schizoid position: the idea that the ego splits its object world into idealised and debased objects (schizoid splitting) and projects them into the other (paranoia).

According to Klein, the presence of envy is symptomatic of an abnormally strong paranoid-schizoid tendency. Envy arises, she asserts, because we harbour a phantasy of a condition of inexhaustible plenitude or self-sufficiency. This phantasy is disturbed by the painful discovery of our dependence on others and the limits this places on our narcissistic dream of perfection and omnipotence. Following Freud's lead, she holds that we attempt to maintain and nurture this phantasy and that the ego, at least in part, is constituted and develops as a mechanism for warding off the anxiety generated by this loss and restoring the phantasy of plenitude. In this context, Klein conceives idealisation as a projective mechanism that protects this divine image of the self by putting it into the other. She believes that the paranoid-schizoid position serves the ego as a necessary initial stage in fending off and dispersing anxiety. However, individuals who remain fixed in this position, she asserts, establish all the intrapsychic conditions for badly damaged object relations characterised by, among other things, envious spoiling and the consequent inability to accept the other as a separate and independent agent.

While her account of pathological object relations is too elaborate to unpack in detail here, it is possible to discern in her analysis the following account of the relationship between narcissism, idealisation and envy. In order to protect the phantasy of our ideal condition, she argues, we project into our objects the plenitude or omnipotence that we desire for ourselves. In other words, through the mechanism of idealisation the object is endowed with all the qualities of self-sufficiency or plenitude that the ego wants for itself but cannot attain. This idealisation, however, can only be a

transitional solution to the demise of our primary narcissism. For the discovery of the idealised object's independence engenders in the primitive
ego the fear of being abandoned by it and shame over its own needy dependence. According to Klein, this early emotional matrix generates either
a compulsive attempt to control the object or, when it can no longer be controlled, to spoil and destroy it. However, if in its narcissistic rage over the independence of the other and shame over its dependence on it, the ego enviously spoils and destroys the other, it also thereby prevents itself from
assimilating or reintrojecting the good that it has put into the other.

This is precisely the psychological constellation Nietzsche illuminates in
Rousseau and Schopenhauer's account of the moral subject. Both Rousseau
and Schopenhauer's moral psychology remains fixed in the paranoid-
schizoid position and its damaging object-relations. That is to say, their psychology uncritically accepts the primitive mechanism of assuaging narcissistic loss through enviously destroying or spoiling the joy of others, on the
one side, and taking pleasure in their suffering, on the other.[30] Unlike Nietzsche, then, neither Rousseau nor Schopenhauer attempt to theorise the
psychological transformations and modulations of narcissism.

Nietzsche argues that rather than seeking to overcome envy, Rousseau and
Schopenhauer's ethics of pity constructs social relations oriented around the
need to assuage the feeling of self-lack. He claims that the envious subject
soothes itself through *Schadenfreude*. It follows, therefore, that if pity also as-
suages envy it must be closely related to *Schadenfreude*. According to Nietzsche, *Schadenfreude* results from the projection of an envy-fuelled wish for
the other's downfall beyond the social realm into the realm of chance:

> *Schadenfreude* originates in the fact that in certain respects of which he is well
> aware, everyone feels unwell, is oppressed by care or envy or sorrow: the harm
> that befalls another makes him our *equal*, it appeases our envy. . . . The dispo-
> sition bent on equality thus extends its demands to the domain of happiness
> and chance as well: *Schadenfreude* is the commonest expression of the victory
> and restoration of equality within the higher world order too.[31]

Nietzsche comically draws the links between pitying others and taking
delight in their sorrow in the following aphorism:

> What is "elevating" in our neighbour's misfortune.—He has experienced a misfor-
> tune, and now the "compassionate" [*Mitleidigen*] come along and depict his
> misfortune for him in detail—at length they go away content and elevated:
> they have gloated over the unfortunate man's distress and over their own and
> passed a pleasant afternoon.[32]

To reiterate the conclusion of the previous chapter, Nietzsche's therapy for
our narcissistic wound is the comical deflation of our human, all too human

vices. Strangely, as if in clairvoyant agreement with Nietzsche's criticism, in defending pity Schopenhauer himself links it to the gloating of *Schaden-freude*. As we have seen, on the metaphysical plane, Schopenhauer claims that our concern for others springs from a mysterious, direct participation in their feelings. Yet his psychological analysis in fact shows that the emergence of pity turns on the devaluation or diminution of others. Schopenhauer might baulk at the notion that those who take pity on others enjoy their suffering, but even as he attempts to shuffle aside this affect, he nevertheless maintains that without the malicious wishes of *Schadenfreude* coming to pass, pity is impossible. Pity flows, according to Schopenhauer, only when one's envy is appeased by the sight of the lucky person's fall from grace. Bluntly stated, Schopenhauer's own point is that love of others (*Menschliebe*) pivots on their misery. We can see this in his thesis that the appeasement of our envy at the other's joy is the primary condition of pity:

> A man will not obtain demonstrations of genuine philanthropy from others as long as he is well off in every respect. . . . For the lucky man as such we feel no sympathy; on the contrary, as such he remains a stranger to our hearts. . . . Indeed, if he has many advantages over others he may easily excite envy, which if he should once fall from the heights of fortune, threatens to turn into malicious joy. . . . For as soon as the lucky man falls, there occurs a great transformation in the hearts of others, which for our consideration is instructive. . . . Envy is reconciled and has disappeared with its own cause; compassion takes its place and gives birth to loving-kindness. Those who were envious of and hostile to the man of fortune have often become, after his downfall, his considerate, consoling, and helpful friends. . . . For misfortune is the condition of compassion, and this is the source of philanthropy.[33]

Schopenhauer reveals here that the pitying person's disposition is not a product of a direct participation in the other's condition and it does not therefore require any metaphysical explanation. Rather, our pity for others emerges from the easing of our envy over their happiness. This kind of pity, therefore, demands no understanding of the other's suffering at all, let alone the merging of identities that Schopenhauer presupposes in his metaphysical explanation of pity. On Schopenhauer's own analysis, pity is not a mysterious merging of identities, but a psychological metamorphosis anchored in the dissolution of the pain of envy, or, to state this point in positive terms, the return of a feeling of self-plenitude in the acknowledgement of the other's lack. We do not grow "tenderer" toward the other because we feel *his* suffering in *him*, as Schopenhauer puts it, but because in his state of deprivation he no longer causes *us* suffering. In Schopenhauer's example, as pitiers our relationship to the other undergoes a change when we no longer see or imagine the other as enviable, not because we miraculously enter into and are motivated by the other's suffering. Chastising the psychological naïveté of Schopenhauer's metaphysical account of pity, Nietzsche confirms this point in his claim that the *Leid*, which we attend to in the act of pity, is not the other's *Leid* but our own feeling of self-lack. Paradoxically, therefore, for Nietzsche, Schopenhauerian *Mitleid* is not *Mit-Leid*, or suffering *with*:

> That pity [*Mitleiden*], on the other hand, is the *same kind of thing* as the suffering [*mit dem Leiden*] at the sight of which it arises, or that it possesses an especially subtle, penetrating understanding of suffering, are propositions contradicted by experience, and he who glorifies pity precisely on account of these two qualities *lacks* adequate *experience* in this very realm of the moral.[34]

Nietzsche argues that because Schopenhauer fails to understand how his notion of pity is anchored in the desire to restore one's self-affection, he also fails to see that it subverts the very regard for others, or "the realm of the moral," that he unwisely attempts to base on the structure of the emotion as he understands it.

Of course, the corollary of Schopenhauer's position is that while the visible signs of envy may disappear with the misfortune of others, the paranoid-schizoid position which fuels envy remains even more firmly entrenched. For rather than curing envy, this kind of pity merely serves to satisfy the envious need for others to be diminished so that one can feel whole and complete. While by this means pitiers pleasurably assuage their narcissistic wound, it is, as Nietzsche underscores, a damaging and enervating means of doing so because it creates an addiction to finding pleasure in themselves through enviously spoiling the other. According to Nietzsche, the tonic effect of envy is outweighed by its harmful effects not only on the envied but also the envier. The psychological consequence of this addiction to envy is *melancholia*: that is to say, not only do we attack and spoil the other's joy, but inevitably this spoiling constructs a world in which we feel that our own joy may similarly become the object of attack. If Schopenhauer's analysis of the moral psychology of pity is correct, then the others' return to joy must make them strangers to our hearts, excite our envy and with this envy must also come the return of the menace of *Schadenfreude*. Nietzsche makes just this point regarding the disjointed rejoicing of pity:

> The compassionate Christian.—The reverse side of Christian compassion for the suffering of one's neighbour is a profound suspicion of all the joy of one's neighbour, of his joy in all that he wants to do and can.[35]

In other words, within the framework of Schopenhauer's ethics of pity we can regard others as of equal worth only so long as they suffer equally. Suffering thus bridges the gulf between egos, but *not*, as we have seen, because as pitiers we mysteriously enter into or participate in the condition of others, but because their demise brings them down to our level and thus appeases the envy we feel at the sight of their self-sufficient happiness.[36] The sight of others' suffering, in short, makes their independence more palatable to us because in this debased state they no longer arouse in us painful feelings of deprivation or the anxiety that we may be abandoned. To recall Rousseau on this latter point, the *suffering* of others is a pledge of their affection for us. As Schopenhauer's analysis implies, taking pleasure in the other's suffering is a tonic for restoring damaged narcissistic self-affection. It is for this reason, Nietzsche believes, that when persistent feelings of envy threaten to attenuate our self-affection we pursue social or intersubjective means for reviving the pleasant feeling of *Schadenfreude*.

In other words, when we enviously spoil others we surreptitiously restore to ourselves our narcissistic self-affection. Our envy does so by enabling us to construct ourselves as those who, by comparison with the spoilt object, are exempt from suffering, need and loss. Through envy we aim to make the other abject or pitiable so that we no longer feel or experience our own abjection. The damage we inflict through envy reduces the other to the needy, insufficient, pitiable condition that we ourselves experience. It thereby soothes our painful feeling that in the face of a phantasised self-sufficient other we are superfluous or unloved. The imaginative work of envy reaches a successful resolution when it enables us to achieve a reversal of roles and our formerly abject self can feel itself as whole and complete in comparison with the now diminished other:

> Sometimes we love the rich man in the midst of misfortunes; but so long as he prospers he has no real friend, except the man who is not deceived by appearances, who pities rather than envies him in spite of his prosperity.[37]

In Rousseau's framework, pity is the use to which envy puts the imagination. To clarify, it is the means through which Rousseau believes that wounded narcissists can reverse the positions of lack/plenitude: by pitying others we transform ourselves into those who, like the Epicurean gods, are divinely free of anxiety and exempt from suffering and pain. In this respect the conception of the moral subject that lies at the heart of his ethics of pity exemplifies the paranoid schizoid defences of pathological narcissism. It is apparent, to begin with, that his moral subjects have not relinquished or tempered their phantasy of narcissistic plenitude insofar as they harbour the "*regret*" that they do not occupy the privileged position of the needless Epicurean gods. Indeed, it is partly because they bitterly measure their own loss against this phantasy of divine tranquillity, that they brim with painful envy at the sight of others' joy. (In accusing the other "*of seeking happiness for himself alone*" they repeat what Klein describes as the basic complaint of infantile envy: the accusation that its first object "has an unlimited flow of milk" which "it keeps for its own gratification." For Klein this image of a wholly self-gratifying object is the ego's projection of its own most desired state).[38]

Rousseau then begins not with a subject who seeks mutual recognition, but one who suffers deeply from the loss of narcissistic self-sufficiency. The only way he conceives of this subject becoming sociable is to give full rein to its primordial envy to spoil others so that it does not suffer from its own sense of self-lack or narcissistic wound. Envy's conjuring trick is to restore self-affection through diminishing others. This is how Rousseau arrives at the perverse position of affirming a moral psychology in which we experience the other's joy as a source of bitterness and the other's suffering as a source of sweet pleasure. Pity is a disjointed rejoicing.[39] The other's suffering is sweet because it restores to us our narcissistic self-affection.

> Pity is sweet, because, when we put ourselves in the place of the one who suffers, we are aware, nevertheless of the pleasure of not suffering like him. Envy is bitter, because the sight of a happy man, far from putting the envious in his place, inspires him with regret that he is not there. The one seems to exempt us from the pain he suffers, the other seems to deprive us of the good things he enjoys.[40]

It is for this reason that Nietzsche claims that overcoming the feeling of self-lack and restoring the vanity of self-affection is the motivating force of the kind of pity Rousseau and Schopenhauer identify as the source of all our moral actions. Couched in psychoanalytic terms, our feelings of self-lack are a reignition of infantile rage over our asymmetrical dependence upon an idealised, self-sufficient other. Pity serves to soothe this envious rage by overturning the asymmetry that the needy, dependent child fears may lead to its abandonment. These psychoanalytic insights are implicit in Nietzsche's treatment of Rousseau and Schopenhauer. It is because Nietzsche sees how their notion of pity is shaped by this psychological matrix that he argues that it is both self-serving *and* damaging to the other. On the plane of phantasy, he suggests, as pitiers we imagine the others on whom we depend as self-sufficient and we play the game of pity in order to redress this asymmetry. We do so by attempting to make ourselves appear as enviable and self-sufficient individuals on whose beneficence others must depend. In the psychological transaction of pity, as Nietzsche sees it, we aim to spoil others by making their suffering the occasion for undermining their independence and asserting our own. As Nietzsche explains in the following aphorism:

> If we love, honour, admire someone and then afterwards discover that he is suffering . . . our feeling of love, reverence and admiration changes in an essential respect: it grows *tenderer*; that is to say, the gulf between us and him seems to be bridged, an approximation to identity seems to occur. Only now do we conceive it possible that we might give back to him, while he previously dwelt in our imagination as being elevated above our gratitude. This capacity to give back produces in us great joy and exaltation . . . we have the *en*joyment of active

gratitude—which, in short, is benevolent revenge. If he wants and takes nothing whatever from us, we go away chilled and saddened, almost offended. . . . From all of this it follows that, even in the most favorable cases, there is something degrading in suffering and something elevating and productive of superiority in pitying—which separates these two sensations from one another to all eternity.[41]

As Nietzsche analyses it here, as pitiers our giving is motivated by the desire to usurp the position of imagined omnipotence, rather than by the other's desire for our pity. (It is this insight that informs Zarathustra's caution that pity should always be a conjecture—"May your compassion be a divining: that you might first know whether your friend wants compassion.")[42] For Nietzsche the fact that as pitiers we are driven by our desire to restore our self-affection is disclosed by our feeling of offence if the other does not appreciate our "gift" of *Mitleid*:

> *Refusing gratitude.*—One may well refuse a request, but one may never refuse gratitude (or what comes to the same thing, receive it coldly or conventionally). To do so is very wounding—and why?[43]

Through gift-giving inspired by such pity, Nietzsche implies, we try to exact from the other the kind of acknowledgement that can aid us in our attempt to restore our phantasy of plenitude. As a sign of their subordination to us, the gratitude of others can serve to bolster our fragile illusion of omnipotence. In this context, therefore, if others refuse our gift of pitying concern they are, as it were, refusing to grant us the right to feel or imagine ourselves as elevated above them. In this regard, the gift of *Mitleid* is really a gift we attempt to bestow *on ourselves at the other's expense.*

PARADISE LOST

Nietzsche also briefly extends his critical analysis of pity to encompass the form it takes in post-Enlightenment sociological discourse and social practices. The scope of his critique thus expands beyond treating pity as a psychological malaise to examining it as a sociological phenomenon. In *Daybreak*, for example, he analyses the manner in which post-Enlightenment thinkers like Auguste Comte weave the concept of *pitié* and its cognates into the fabric of a political and sociological discourse which is committed to a triumphant belief in progress. Nietzsche's analysis of this Enlightenment discourse suggests that its dream of limitless progress masks a social project that he characterises in terms that recall De Tocqueville's anxiety about the dangers of modern commercially based societies: that is, the danger that market-driven atomisation and deindividuation can easily engender a form of communitarian tyranny.[44] In this context, Nietzsche maintains, the notion of *Mitleid* and its cognates such as sympathy and philanthropy have become little more than bywords for a communitarianism that drives toward the complete adaptation of the individual to the whole. Nietzsche defends the practice of self-cultivation against the theoretical limits and practical dangers of this nightmare communitarianism. However, as we shall see, if Nietzsche objects to market-driven communitarianism in the name of self-cultivation, he does so because he thinks that unlike the modern practices that go by the name of "pity," self-cultivation can enrich the relationship between self and other.

In *Daybreak* (132) Nietzsche claims that *Mitleid*, which, he observes, was once merely a subsidiary or minor Christian norm, has been transformed and valorised in a post-Enlightenment political and sociological discourse that seeks to legitimate what he calls "the moral undercurrent of our age."[45] Nietzsche explains this moral undercurrent as the "weakening and abolition of *the individual*" for the sake of enhancing communitarian integration.[46] According to Nietzsche, a cult of philanthropy was the "secret spur" of all "free thinkers from Voltaire up to Auguste Comte."[47] The teachings of the "sympathetic affects" and "pity" were then given the widest currency by Schopenhauer, J. S. Mill, and, by implication at least, Rousseau and flourished in the socialist doctrines that placed themselves on the common grounds of these teachings.[48] Here Nietzsche clearly rides roughshod over the significant philosophical and theoretical differences between the program of the Enlightenment *philosophes*—nineteenth-century liberalism and socialism. However, if Nietzsche thus conflates a number of very different discourses, his conceptualisation of the social phenomenon he objects to remains much more sharply focussed. In theorising the cult of philanthropy, he accentuates what he sees as the tight connection between the modern form of communal integration and a lamentable process of deindividuation:

> Today it seems to do everyone good when they hear that society is on the way to *adapting* the individual to general requirements, and *that the happiness and at the same time the sacrifice of the individual* lies in feeling himself to be a useful member and instrument of the whole . . . there is . . . a wonderful and fair-sounding unanimity in the demand that the ego has to deny itself until, in the form of the adaptation to the whole, it again acquires its firmly set circle of rights and duties—until it has become something quite novel and different. What is wanted . . . is nothing less than the fundamental remoulding, indeed weakening and abolition of the *individual*: one never tires of enumerating and indicting all that is evil and inimical, prodigal, costly, extravagant in the form individual existence has assumed hitherto, one hopes to manage more cheaply, more safely, more equitably, more uniformly if there exists only *large bodies and their members*.[49]

Nietzsche's analysis of this post-Enlightenment transformation and valorisation of *Mitleid* is significant for our purposes because it reveals the notion of subjectivity and intersubjectivity which underpins his lament over a communitarianism that, as he sees it, *entirely* enfolds the individual into the collective. Nietzsche suggests that the concepts of pity, sympathy, or *vivre pour autrui* have become little more than the ideological stalking horses for the "moral fashion of a commercial society"; a moral fashion, that is to say, that transforms individuals into industrious, calculable instruments of social labour.[50] He argues that what unites the modern mantras of "pity," "impersonal action," "self-sacrifice," "adaptation" and the "blessing of work" is the fact that they share one covert idea: the fear of individuality. "In the glorification of 'work,'" as he writes, "I see the same covert idea as in the praise of useful impersonal actions: that of fear of everything individual."[51] (The scare quotes around "work" are Nietzsche's; he evidently means to imply that the worship of instrumental, material labour, or "hard industriousness" should not be confused with what he considers the more valuable work, the work on the self.)[52]

In this context, then, his critique of pity highlights his resistance to philosophical and sociological perspectives whose conception of human beings is exhausted by the image of *homo faber* and *homo economicus*.[53] Nietzsche challenges the legitimacy of social relations that construct individuals as nothing more than disciplined instruments of labour and uniform members of an integrated collectivity. Such perspectives, he implies, are symptomatic of an anxious desire to cordon ourselves off from the intrapsychic domain. The "blessing of work," he jokes, "is the best policeman . . . it keeps everyone in bounds and can mightily hinder the development of reason, covetousness, desire for independence."[54] Instrumental labour, we might say, is our psychological *cordon sanitaire*.

Of course, Nietzsche concedes, this policing of the self through the discipline of work also has its benefits insofar as the regular satisfaction of small, instrumental problems gives one a sense of "security." However, this is not merely material security, but a security from the temptations of "reflection, brooding and dreaming," and such security, as Nietzsche puts it "is now worshipped as the supreme divinity."[55] In *Daybreak* he defines the post-Enlightenment age as one in which the metaphysical and theological dream of salvation has been displaced by the worship of a divinity that protects one from the risks (and possible gains) of confronting and working on one's own psychical reality. According to Nietzsche, the idol of security that modern commercial society worships is a divinity it has erected in order to save us the trouble of working on and cultivating ourselves.

Nietzsche maintains that by seeking to secure ourselves from the travails of self-cultivation we also create for ourselves strict limits on how we can engage with others. In this regard, his critique of modern communitarianism and its "fear of everything individual" is not a rejection of engaging with others, but of the kind of turning to others and the treatment of their suffering that is integral to a culture in which individuals flee from the intrapsychic realm of "reflections, brooding and dreaming." Because this culture treats our personal engagement with ourselves as a troublesome obstacle that should be overcome, or so he claims, "helping" others can only take the form of ensuring that they too learn to police themselves with instrumental labour and find their happiness in the blessings of self-oblivion. In this context, helping others, to use Nietzsche's metaphors, must mean helping them transform themselves into "small, soft, round, unending" granules of "sand," or, translating these metaphors, into interchangeable, undifferentiated atoms that can be smoothly adapted to meet the imperatives of a commercially driven collectivity. Nietzsche argues that in a commercial culture that deifies security, the practices of "pity," "help," or "sympathy" can only ever be either "superficial" or "tyrannical."[56] These practices must become superficial to the extent that commercial culture compels individuals to flee from the "labyrinth" of the soul, and "tyrannical" to the extent that its market imperatives ultimately exclude nonutilitarian self-cultivation and unprofitable, unassimilable forms of alterity.[57]

Nietzsche claims then that it is a flight from the labyrinth of a complex, differentiated self that underpins modern commercial culture and its transformation of the relations between self and other. In opposition to the desert of undifferentiated atoms this culture creates, Nietzsche conjures up the image of an oasis. It is not, however, an image depicting either the lost glories of Homeric agonism or the splendid isolation of the great individual. Rather, in a passage largely overlooked in the Nietzsche literature, he depicts the self's engagement with others through an overdetermined allusion to the complex thread of Old Testament, classical, Christian and medieval romance images of the paradise garden:[58]

> The question itself remains unanswered whether one is of *more use* to another by immediately leaping to his side and helping him—which can only be superficial where it does not become a tyrannical seizing and transforming—or by *creating* something out of oneself that the other can behold with pleasure: a beautiful, restful, self-enclosed garden perhaps, with high walls against the storms and the dust of the roadway but also a hospitable gate.[59]

Nietzsche's image of the "self-enclosed garden" is one that draws on the long history of Western iconography and ideas of paradise as a *topos* rather than "an abstract state imagined in terms of . . . metaphysical ecstasy."[60] Etymologically, the notion of paradise originally derives from the Persian word, *paradeiza*, for walled garden, or a circular walled enclosure that came to be applied to royal parks. As a recurrent dream in Western literature and iconography, this figure of the enclosed paradise garden has become, as Robert Hughes observes, "saturated in nostalgia: this is the innocence our ancestors lost for us, at the close of a period over whose vanishing we had no control."[61]

From the accent he places on its beauty and restfulness, Nietzsche seems especially drawn to the classical conception of the paradise garden as an "epigram of order," albeit, as the abode of Venus, an orderly *topos* of pleasure.[62] Nietzsche's taste for the classical idea of paradise also becomes apparent in his subtle inversion of Christianity's allegorical interpretation of the garden, which added to the image of the *hortus conclusus* the *porta clausa*, or locked gate. In his metaphor of the self as a garden of paradise Nietzsche replaces this locked gate with the hospitable gate. Nietzsche's alternative to the desert of pity is thus the cultivation of oneself as a paradise garden that is open to the other. To cultivate oneself, as he understands it, is to create oneself as a paradise garden for the other. By contrast, Nietzsche implies, by exercising the kind of pity which precludes us from taking pleasure in the other's joy, and which "helps" by transforming the other into an undifferentiated nonentity, we create a *porta clausa*. Ironically, then, it is through the exercise of pity that we lock ourselves and others out of paradise.

NOTES

1. In this, as in so many other respects, Freud follows Nietzsche. In his case study of the Wolfman, for example, he refers to "the narcissistic origin of compassion [*Mitleid*]," which, he adds, "is confirmed by the word itself"; Sigmund Freud, "From the History of an Infantile Neurosis," in *Case Histories II*, op. cit., 327. John Rajchman also correctly notes that Freud discovers "a sadistic gratification in pity or compassion for the suffering of others"; John Rajchman, *Truth and Eros: Foucault, Lacan and the Question of Ethics*, 1991, Routledge, New York, 59.

2. David Cartwright paints in broad brushstrokes Nietzsche's attack on Schopenhauer for the extraordinary lack of psychological acumen in his *a posteriori* descriptions of pity; see David E. Cartwright, "Kant, Schopenhauer, and Nietzsche on the Morality of Pity," *Journal of the History of Ideas* XLV, January–March, no. 1, 1984, 83–98, 94–96.

3. OBM §15, 140.

4. For an example of the casual use of Rousseau's idea of pity to polemicise against Nietzsche, see, for example, Frederick Appel, *Nietzsche contra Democracy*, 1999, Cornell University Press, Ithaca, N.Y., 156.

5. Schopenhauer self-consciously defends pity against Seneca's, Spinoza's and Kant's moral condemnation of this passion (in *De Clementia, Ethics* and *The Critique of Practical Reason*, respectively) by drawing on Rousseau's authority. Indeed, Schopenhauer inserts large slabs of quotation from the *Discourse on the Origins of Inequality* and *Émile* in an ultimately unsuccessful effort to bolster his argument in the eyes of the judges of the Royal Danish Society for Scientific Study to whom he submitted the essay for competition. However, it should be noted that Schopenhauer also explicitly departs from Rousseau by explaining the possibility of pity *metaphysically*, and in doing so he rejects Rousseau's belief that the flourishing and expansion of the (supposedly) natural sentiment of pity can be explicated in purely psychological terms as the cultivation of the *imagination*.

6. Jean-Jacques Rousseau, *Émile*, op. cit., 182.

7. Ibid., 183.

8. Ibid., 182, emphasis added.

9. Martha C. Nussbaum, "Pity and Mercy," op. cit., 142. Nussbaum acknowledges that this point is controversial because, among other things, it implies that pity may be partial or restricted in its scope. It is partly because pity rests on the imagination that it is open to the so-called "partiality" objection that targets the limits and lack of durability of this emotion rather than its *intrinsic* value. In her later examination of the philosophical debates on compassion Nussbaum attempts to allay the concern about pity's potential narrowness or unevenness that we find evinced by thinkers like Adam Smith and Kant. She does so by arguing that this emotion can be educated and the horizon of concern thereby extended and refined; see Martha Nussbaum, *Upheavals of Thought*, op. cit., 386–92.

10. See Lucretius, *On the Nature of the Universe*, op. cit., 79.

11. Jean-Jacques Rousseau, *Émile*, op. cit., 182, emphasis added.

12. OBM §14, 131–38.

13. OBM §22, 205.

14. OBM §22, 205.

15. OBM §16, 143.

16. OBM §14, 131.

17. OBM §14, 132.

18. OBM §16, 144. Schopenhauer devotes section OBM §22 to this metaphysical speculation.

19. OBM §22, 205.

20. OBM §21, 209.

21. OBM §16, 147. I borrow slightly from David Cartwright's formulation of Schopenhauer's point; see David E. Cartwright, "The Last Temptation of Zarathustra," *The Journal of the History of Philosophy* 31, no. 1, January 1993, 49–65, 54.

22. OBM §16, 144, emphasis added.

23. OBM §16, 146.

24. OBM §21, 212.

25. OBM §19, 174.

26. OBM §19, 174.

27. OBM §19, 174.

28. OBM §19, 174.

29. OBM §21, 209.

30. It is this paranoid-schizoid psychology that partly explains the cruelty of pity, which, as Hannah Arendt argues in her critique of Rousseau and Robespierre, "taken as the spring of virtue, has proved to possess a greater capacity for cruelty than cruelty itself"; see Hannah Arendt, *On Revolution*, 1973, Penguin Books, Harmondsworth, UK, 89.

31. WS, 27.

32. D, 224.

33. OBM §19, 174.

34. D, 133.

35. D, 80.

36. D, 138.

37. Jean-Jacques Rousseau, *Émile*, op. cit., 184.
38. Melanie Klein, *Envy and Gratitude*, op. cit., 183.
39. I borrow this felicitous phrase from Jacques Derrida's brief discussion of the tension between *Mitleid* and *Mitfreude*, see Jacques Derrida, *Politics of Friendship*, op. cit., 54.
40. Jean-Jacques Rousseau, *Émile*, op. cit., 182.
41. D, 138.
42. TSZ 1, "On the Friend."
43. D, 235.
44. For a brief discussion of the similarities between Tocqueville's and Nietzsche's critique of the banality of liberal individualism and its abandonment of self-cultivation, see Keith Ansell-Pearson, *An Introduction to Nietzsche as Political Thinker: The Perfect Nihilist*, 1994, Cambridge University Press, Cambridge, 6–7.
45. D, 132.
46. D, 132.
47. D, 132.
48. D, 132.
49. D, 132.
50. D, 173.
51. D, 173.
52. D, 173.
53. Nancy Love fleshes out Nietzsche's critique of *homo economicus* and illuminates some aspects of it by comparing it with critical theory's perspective on instrumental reason, see Nancy S. Love, *Marx, Nietzsche and Modernity*, 1986, Columbia University Press, New York; and Nancy S. Love, "Epistemology and Exchange: Marx, Nietzsche, and Critical Theory," *New German Critique*, 1987, no. 41, Spring–Summer, 71–94.
54. D, 173.
55. D, 173.
56. D, 174.
57. D, 174; Nietzsche uses the metaphor of the "labyrinth of the soul" in D, 169.
58. D, 174. Graham Parkes briefly touches on this aphorism, and notes that Nietzsche adopts a much more defensive tone in a later note from 1885 in which he imagines his work as a garden through which others can stroll at their leisure and break off bits and pieces to take home as souvenirs. Elliot Jurist also paraphrases the close of D, 174; see Graham Parkes, *Composing the Soul*, op. cit., 168, 419, fn. 20; and Elliot Jurist, *Beyond Hegel and Nietzsche*, op. cit., 249. As well as drawing on a rich history of classical, Christian and romance images in this allusion to the paradise garden and its hospitable gate (*gastfreundliche Pforte*), Nietzsche may also have been making a personal allusion to the walled city of *Pforta*, his boarding school built on the grounds of a twelfth-century Cistercian monastery, which contained its own garden, and which, according to David Krell, became for him a second *Vaterhaus*; see both Krell's text and Donald Bates's photographs in David Farrell Krell and Donald L. Bates, *The Good European: Nietzsche's Work Sites in Word and Images*, op. cit., 21–35.
59. D, 174.
60. The following discussion borrows from the second chapter ("A Garden Enclosed") of Robert Hughes's magnificent study of the iconography of Heaven and

Hell; see Robert Hughes, *Heaven and Hell in Western Art,* 1968, Weidenfeld and Nicholson, London.

    61. Ibid., 48.

    62. Ibid., 47, 51; Robert Hughes points out that the classical idea of the garden as a panerotic landscape containing the walled bower of Venus derives from the elaborate descriptions of Claudian.

7

The Tonic of Friendship

> What I again and again needed most for my cure and self-restoration, however, was the belief that I was *not* thus isolated in *seeing* as I did—an enchanted surmising of relatedness and identity in eye and desires, a reposing in a trust of friendship.
>
> *Human, All Too Human* 1, Preface

This chapter explores Nietzsche's argument that living well with others turns on the work the self undertakes to modify and transform the psychology of pity and envy. It suggests that on the plane of sociability Nietzsche identifies friendship as the counterpoint to this damaged intersubjectivity. The chapter investigates Nietzsche's understanding of both the psychological preconditions and the practice of friendship. On the first score, he argues that a work of self-analysis is necessary to open up a psychological space that moves beyond paranoid-schizoid splitting and projection. In formulating his conception of the self's work on itself he looks back to Stoic *askēsis*, or, as he calls it, the Stoic education in bearing separation, solitude and loss. Nietzsche refurbishes and renovates the Stoic tradition of caring for the self with the aid of a more penetrating understanding of psychodynamics that, in an unsystematic fashion, prefigures much of the psychoanalytic conceptual terrain.

Second, he argues that the work of friendship contains therapeutic and transformative possibilities that are closed off by the damaging social relations engendered by primitive narcissism. For Nietzsche, friendship is both a medium and a test of healthy self-love. It is a *medium* insofar as friendship provides a progressive rather than regressive solution to the problem of narcissism. The aim of Nietzschean friendship is to enable subjects to work with each other on modifying and transforming their primitive narcissism and to achieve a mature form of self-love. In contrast with Rousseauian self-love, this positive self-love does not depend on annihilating or diminishing others, and it respects the differences and distance between selves. Nietzsche conceives friendship as a *test* of healthy individuality because taking joy in the friend's joy (*Mitfreude*) is a sign that one has tempered that form of pathological narcissism that consists in assuaging the fear of solitude and loss through enviously spoiling the other's happiness. Because Stoic-Nietzschean subjects acknowledge their own finitude and separateness they can build up their own psychological resources or inner wealth, as the Stoics call it, as well as their friends'. Because they have tempered the envy that drives pathological projective identifications they do not experience the other's "wealth" as something gained or accumulated at their expense.

Similarly, Nietzschean friends do not treat the other's suffering as a source of their own veiled pleasure or secret contempt, whereas Rousseauian "friends" experience it as the *only* thing that makes the other pleasurable to them. For Rousseauian pitiers the other's suffering sugarcoats the bitter pill that they otherwise choke on, *viz.*, the other's separateness and independence. For Nietzschean friends, by contrast, because they can feel *Mitfreude* they can also experience the other's suffering as a bitter loss that should be repaired. This brings us to a final point: Nietzsche's critique of pity is commonly thought to exclude all regard for the other's suffering, a claim his critics often bolster with the ad hominem charge that Nietzsche cordoned himself off from others from fear of personal contamination. However, if we examine his discourse on friendship it becomes apparent that Nietzsche rejects Rousseauian/Schopenhauerian pity in the name of a dispassionate compassion. Being a good friend, as Nietzsche sees it, entails not just *Mitfreude*, but also a dispassionate, analytic and *active* compassion towards the suffering friend.[1] Whereas Rousseauian pitiers only echo the sorrow of others, an echoing which according to Nietzsche merely inflames their feeling of self-lack, the Nietzschean friend can both dispassionately and acutely analyse their suffering and reflect back their "shining image." Nietzschean compassion, as Bernhard Reginster convincingly argues, is not a response to the friend's suffering *as such*, but to the suffering that causes precious capabilities to be squandered, or that halts someone at something less than he/she might have become.[2] If missed opportunities are the object of Nietzschean compassion, its aim is to enable others to realise their own greatness or, in the terms I have been using here, their higher self. It responds *actively* to these lost opportunities of greatness by creating and projecting an image of the friend's "higher self."

THE ETHICS OF SELF-DIGESTION

Measure of Wisdom.—Growth in wisdom can be measured precisely by decline in bile.[3]

Nietzschean friendship turns not simply on respecting the other's solitude and distance, but on the practice of solitude understood as an analytic work on the self aimed at containing and consuming, rather than warding off or projecting, painful affects of loss.[4] Nietzsche did not conceive solitude as a negative condition of stasis, a simple fending away of others, or, in psychoanalytic terms, as the ego's withdrawal of libidinal cathexis from objects to itself. Rather, Nietzsche conceives the work of solitude as similar in kind and purpose to the philosophical retirement or *secessus* that the Stoics praise for its tonic effect on the self's capacity to engage humanely with others.[5]

Unhappily, Nietzsche's reflections on the philosophical and psychological significance of solitude have for the most part received either scant or superficial treatment. His invocation of the virtue of solitude in the art of living has been misconstrued as a hysterical defence of an autarkic individualism that tends towards either an indifference or an unabashed contempt for others. We can see this problem in Henry Staten's otherwise incisive study, which attempts to trace in Nietzsche's texts the signs and sounds of what he calls a "libidinal economy."[6] Nietzsche's libidinal economy, he argues, oscillates wildly between two extremes: an expansive, unbounded receptivity to others and a violent contraction of the self that makes it impervious to others. Staten locates *Human, All Too Human* and *Daybreak* as poised at the outer limit of the latter point of Nietzsche's psychological pendulum:

> Now whereas in the period of *The Birth of Tragedy* Nietzsche, under the influence of Schopenhauer, had glorified an expansive, even cosmic, receptivity to the being of others and Promethean self-expenditure on their behalf, in *Human All Too Human* and *Daybreak* he begins his reinterpretation of morals by a critique of that receptivity and self-expenditure called pity [*Mitleid*] which Schopenhauer had treated as the root of all moral feeling. Nietzsche now praises as "the highest gratification of the feeling of power" [*Daybreak*, 18] a form of affect that he describes as the most egoistic or self-affirmative as possible. This upward revaluation of cruelty . . . manifests a contraction of Nietzsche's being, an attempt to pull back together and reinforce the boundaries of the self that had spread itself too thin in the earlier glorification of Dionysian martyrdom. . . . As Nietzsche recoils from the expansiveness of the Dionysian his pity becomes nausea, fear of contamination and violation of his being by the touch of the same masses of humanity whose suffering he feels so deeply; and he seeks to fortify himself by an affirmation of ascendant life that tends to become a celebration of isolation, cruelty, and appropriativeness.[7]

As we saw in the previous chapter, Nietzsche begins his reinterpretation of morality with a critique of Rousseauian/Schopenhauerian pity. However, the inferences Staten draws from this insight not only misconstrue the textual sources he uses, but more importantly they are fundamentally discordant with the central project of the middle works: the reconstruction of the Hellenistic therapies of the soul.

Addressing the textual issue first, Staten's quotation from *Daybreak* (18) as evidence that in the middle works Nietzsche sings the praises of cruelty is profoundly misleading. While we cannot do full justice to this aphorism here, suffice it to say that it is in order to *describe* the character of human culture in the era of the morality of custom (*Sittlichkeit*) that Nietzsche invokes the notion of cruelty as a refreshment. According to Nietzsche, during the long era of *Sittlichkeit* the spectacle of cruelty gradually becomes introverted: what began as a means of compensating communal creatures for the punishing constraints imposed on them by *Sittlichkeit* was eventually transformed into cruel self-chastisement and self-sacrifice.[8] Because the communal gods of this culture are refreshed by the spectacle of cruelty, Nietzsche speculates:

> [T]here creeps into the world the idea that . . . self-chosen torture is meaningful and valuable . . . the people told themselves: it may well be that the gods frown upon us when we are fortunate and smile upon us when we suffer— though they certainly do not feel pity! . . . they smile because they are amused and put into good humour by our suffering: for to practice cruelty is to enjoy the highest gratification of the feeling of power. . . . Thus the concept of the "most moral man" of the community came to include the virtue of the most frequent suffering, of privation, of the hard life, of cruel chastisement—not to repeat it again and again, as a means of discipline, of self-control, of satisfying the desire for individual happiness—but as a virtue which will put the community in good odour with the evil gods and which steams up to them like a perpetual propitiatory sacrifice on the altar.[9]

In the remainder of the aphorism, Nietzsche claims that *Sittlichkeit* installs these evil gods in the intrapsychic world of every member of the community. In the intrapsychic world the morality of custom becomes figured through the phantasy of envious gods who take pleasure in our suffering. As a result, we suffer spasms of anxiety whenever we depart from the customary ideal of unthinking submission, suffering and privation. We counter this painful psychical contraction by offering this divinity the pleasing spectacle of our own self-sacrifice as "a substitute pleasure in case he might be provoked by the neglect of and opposition to established usages and by the new goals these paths led to."[10] According to Nietzsche, then, *Sittlichkeit* establishes within the soul a powerful taboo that stifles the ego's attempt to engage in critical, reflexive thought regarding the value of traditional laws and customs:

Every smallest step in the field of free thought, of a life shaped personally, has always had to be fought for with the spiritual and bodily tortures. . . . Nothing has been purchased more dearly than that little bit of human reason and feeling of freedom that now constitutes our pride.[11]

Nietzsche's point bears on the issue of the psychological travails required to challenge and subvert its cruel imperatives. In the first place, he uses the analysis of *Sittlichkeit* to suggest that the ego forges its tiny scrap of reason only by bearing the spasms of anxiety and fear it feels in departing from collective norms and by offering up its own suffering as a propitiatory sacrifice to the cruelly envious gods who find pleasure and refreshment in its suffering. Secondly, Nietzsche suggests that the painful trial of purchasing that modicum of reason which enables one to evaluate the morality of *Sittlichkeit* and thus to live "a life shaped personally," which in a preceding aphorism he identifies with the figure of Socrates, is one each of us must still undertake:[12]

Those tremendous eras of *Sittlichkeit* which precede "world history" as the *actual and decisive eras of history which determined the character of mankind*: the eras in which suffering counted as a virtue, cruelty counted as a virtue, dissembling counted as a virtue, revenge counted as a virtue. . . . Do you think all this has altered and that mankind must therefore have changed its character! O observers of mankind, learn better to observe yourselves![13]

Far from indicating that Nietzsche "upwardly revalues" cruelty or its introversion, then, *Daybreak* (18) demonstrates his concern with the psychological task required to overcome the compulsive force of *Sittlichkeit*. Indeed, to return to the previous chapter's discussion, this aphorism makes it clear that one of the reasons Nietzsche challenges Schopenhauer's ethics of pity is *not* because he fears it as a form of expansive receptivity to others, but because he sees it as a subterranean continuation of the cruelty of *Sittlichkeit*. For Schopenhauer's pitiers fall into a species of atavism, a reversion to the cruel demands imposed by those *Sittlichkeit* gods who frown upon our happiness (*Glück*) and who are put into good humour by our suffering (*Leidens*). Like the evil gods Nietzsche identifies here, the envy of Schopenhauer's pitiers, as he himself acknowledges, is only propitiated or appeased by the other's suffering. It is only through their suffering, as we saw in the previous chapter, that individuals can put themselves in good odour with the *Mitleidigen*.

So in the middle works Nietzsche attacks Rousseau and Schopenhauer's notion of pity not because he sees it as an expansive receptivity to others, a mistaken interpretation that Staten uncritically adopts, but because he exposes it as a subterranean continuation of the *Sittlichkeit* imperative that individuals offer up their suffering as a propitiatory sacrifice. Nietzsche's point then is that the fear of communal disapprobation and the need to placate its cruel gods places a taboo on the ego's capacity to engage in independent thought. Here we see the first glimmer of the reason Nietzsche calls for an education in solitude. It is not, as Staten suggests, because Nietzsche thinks that Schopenhauer's community of *Mitleid* threatens to dissolve the boundaries of the autarkic self and immerse it in the collective *pathos* of shared suffering; on the contrary, he argues that this kind of *Mitleid* constitutes a profound contempt for receptivity to others. In *Daybreak* (18) and elsewhere Nietzsche upwardly values solitude (not cruelty!) because he claims that the ability to bear solitude is one means through which individuals forge that scrap of reason that enables them to assess the archaic, cruel and primitive aspects of *Sittlichkeit* and its "internal" representative, the pangs of conscience. Nietzsche's point then is that the shift from immature conformity, and its xenophobic cruelty, to the real maturity of reason must proceed through bearing the fear that one will suffer the wrath of the envious gods of the community. Nietzsche plays out this thesis by implying a distinction between an archaic conscience and its mature form:

> *The argument of growing solitude.*—The reproaches of conscience are weak even in the most conscientious people [*Gewissenhaftesten*] compared to the feeling: "this or that is against morals [*Sitte*] of your society." A cold look or a sneer on the face of those among whom and for whom one has been educated is feared even by the strongest. What is it that they are really afraid of? Growing solitude! This is the argument that rebuts even the best arguments for a person or cause.[14]

In other words, Nietzsche argues that for those who do not *strengthen* the reproaches of a mature conscience, their archaic *Sittlichkeit* conscience threatens to become lawless (or anarchic) in its indifference to reason and in its paranoid fear of those who move beyond the narrow, irrational boundaries of *Sittlichkeit* or the customary parameters of thought and feeling. Nietzsche counsels "growing solitude," then, precisely because it is the price one must pay in order to resist the irrationality and xenophobia of an immature superego, to borrow from Freud's Nietzschean-inspired lexicon. Indeed, in criticising the archaic features of the superego, Freud follows Nietzsche point for point in the suggestion that *Gewissenhaftigkeit* is a premorality that threatens to become an antimorality. Paul Ricoeur sums this point up brilliantly:

> Freud's contribution here consists in his discovery of a fundamental structure of ethical life, namely a first stratum of morality that has the function both of preparing the way for autonomy and of retarding it, blocking it off at an archaic stage. The inner tyrant plays the role of premorality and antimorality.[15]

To return to Nietzsche, then, he claims that solitude has a positive aspect insofar as it enables the ego to forge a scrap of rationality and with this the capacity to tolerate the separateness and strangeness of others. It is those who fail to bear solitude and separation who simply replicate the cruel hostility of the *Sitte* and its requirement that the community be composed of interchangeable, nonindividuated atoms. In the above aphorism, the most conscientious individuals only tolerate others as long as they comfortingly reinforce the familiar world of customs. Because they fear being separated from this safe haven they cannot tolerate the other *qua* individual. The other's growing solitude painfully reminds them of the dangers of aloneness. They surmount this separation anxiety by sneeringly reasserting the *Sitte* against the other. Excommunicating the other is a way of dealing with the anxiety generated by the threat of isolation. According to Nietzsche, the most conscientious individuals exorcise the fear of their own separateness and the sense that they too are at risk of isolation, ostracism and, at the limit, annihilation, by excommunicating the individual who arouses this fear.

We can illuminate and deepen Nietzsche's account of the irrationality of *Gewissenhaftigkeit*, or the immature form of conscience, by examining the manner in which this archaic mode of conscience makes constant use of what Klein calls the mechanism of projective identification. As we have seen, for Klein the immature ego, or the ego that reverts to the paranoid-schizoid position, wards off anxiety by projecting parts of itself into another. In projective identification the ego symbolically projects these parts, as well as the emotions associated with them, into another who is then regarded as a container of that part of the self. Some theorists, like Thomas Odgen, go further than Klein by treating projective identification not only as intrapsychic but also as an intersubjective or relational encounter:

> feeling-states corresponding to unconscious fantasies of one person (the projector) are engendered in and processed by another person (the recipient). . . .
> In association with this unconscious projective fantasy there is an interpersonal interaction by means of which the recipient is pressured to think, feel, and behave in a manner congruent with . . . a specific, disowned aspect of the projector.[16]

In the case Nietzsche presents, the *Gewissenhaftesten* project their own unintegrated parts into the other and, through their cold sneer, attempt to pressure the recipient of their projection into assuming and processing their own fear of separation or abandonment. Nietzsche believes this form of projective identification, in which we seek through projection to compel another to digest our own anxieties, is a common pathology:

> He who has . . . been sorely slandered may console himself with the reflection: slanders are other people's illnesses that have broken out on your body; they demonstrate that a society is a (moral) body, so that you can undertake a cure on *yourself* that will be of benefit to others.[17]

On the other hand, so Nietzsche implies, when we bear our solitude we have no need to exorcise our fear either by demanding that others supply us with comforting reflections or, where they "fail" to give us this reassurance, coldly casting them out and projecting into them our own affects. Donald Winnicott gives shape to Nietzsche's point in what he calls his "long overdue" discussion of "the *positive* aspects of the capacity to be alone."[18] It is this capacity, he asserts, that "is the only satisfactory basis for making relationships."[19] This is the case, Winnicott claims, because being alone with oneself, and learning how to solace oneself in the absence of the other and the other's constant solicitude, is essential to being able to accede to the other's separateness.

Nietzsche self-consciously draws on a similar conception of the relationship between solitude and connectedness as a central point in the therapeutic tradition that stretches back to Hellenism and Stoicism. Nietzsche makes the Stoic conception of the endurance of solitude an integral aspect of his notion of self-cultivation:

> I have seen the light as to the most universal deficiency in our kind of cultivation and education: no one learns, no one strives after, no one teaches—*the endurance of solitude.*[20]

For Seneca and Epictetus an education in solitude is integral to overcoming the narcissistic and impossible demand that one exercise a monopoly over others. Through this education Stoics aim at cultivating an inward relation of the self to itself, analogous to friendship, that enables them to remain composed in the face of their separateness, rather than allowing this separateness to generate anger and resentment. By contrast, non-Stoics, according to Epictetus,

> do not understand how a man passes his life when he is alone, because they set out from a certain natural principle, from the natural desire of community and mutual love and from the pleasures of conversation among men. *But none the less* a man ought to be prepared in a manner for this also, to be able to be sufficient for himself and to be his own companion . . . *so we ought to be able to talk with ourselves, not to feel the want of others also*, not to be unprovided with the means of passing our time; to observe the divine administration, and the relation of ourselves to everything else.[21]

For Nietzsche solitude is not a contraction of oneself from others or a means of blocking one's receptivity to the other. It is rather a way of processing the anger and fear generated by the unyielding communal demand that one yield one's individuality to the tyranny of the collective conscience:

> When I am among the many I live as the many do, and I do not think as I really think; after a time it always seems as though they want to banish me from

myself and rob me of my soul—and I grow angry with everybody and fear everybody. I then require the desert, so as to grow good again.[22]

In order to conceptualise the work the self undertakes on itself in solitude Nietzsche turns to one of his favorite Stoic metaphoric tropes: the idea of self-digestion.[23] The return to the desert of solitude (and solitude *is* a desert for Nietzsche) is always for the sake of consuming one's own affects. In Nietzsche's terms, solitude involves the work of digesting one's bitter affects rather than forcing others to digest those parts of oneself that one wishes to disavow or flee, or those parts of oneself, which, as it were, one cannot stomach:

> "I am not fond of myself," someone said in explanation of his love of society. "Society's stomach is stronger than mine, it can digest me."[24]

To follow Nietzsche's metaphor here, the work of solitude requires digesting one's harsh, unpleasant affects, the bitterest of which, we might recall, Rousseau identifies with envy, rather than making others digest this bitterness. Significantly, Graham Parkes notes that in the early 1880s Nietzsche strove to understand and appreciate solitude as a practice which counters the impulse to project one's affects into or onto others and which thereby compels one to work on, and refine, the art of living's gastronomic equivalent: the art of self-digestion. Parkes quotes from Nietzsche's early 1881 *Nachlass* as evidence that in the middle period Nietzsche appreciates solitude because it makes it possible to withdraw (or redirect) projections: "Advantage of solitude: we discharge our total nature—even its bad moods—*toward our primary objective* and not onto other things and people. Thus we live it *through!*"[25] Nietzsche's analysis suggests that this solitary or *intra*-psychic discharge proceeds by creating internal objects that can then become the targets for one's affects and moods.

In other words, Nietzsche conceives the work of solitude as a conscious, artful use of the dreamwork to exhaust, satisfy or temper bitter affects rather than putting them into others, after the manner of the paranoid-schizoid defences. Nietzsche not only claims that this kind of solitude enables one to discharge one's bitter affects and moods, but he also comes to see in its play of projections a comic therapy that dampens our narcissistic grandiosity. If Nietzsche is right, such projective dreamscapes enable us to learn to laugh at rather than lacerate our narcissistic wounds. It is through comic self-acknowledgement that we deflate the narcissistic tendency to magnify to tragic proportions the pain of losing our illusion of majesty. Nietzsche illustrates this comic self-acknowledgement by projecting his own pain as a shamelessly importunate dog that constantly demands and cleverly secures his undivided attention:

> *My dog.*—I have given a name to my pain and call it "dog." It is just as faithful, just as obtrusive and shameless, just as clever as any other dog—and I can

scold it and vent my bad mood on it, as others do with their dogs, servants and wives.[26]

That Nietzsche elects to place this aphorism in the fourth book of *The Gay Science* is significant: it suggests that he did not intend the willing of the eternal recurrence of the same to depend on the absurd inflation of oneself into the author of these events, but on the comic deflation of the tragic *pathos* we give to our personal sufferings. We must, in short, understand Nietzsche's doctrine of eternal recurrence in the context of his Hellenistic-*cum*-psychoanalytic notion of domesticating our pain. The claim then that Nietzsche's reflections on solitude are a sign of an apotheosis of a sinister "modern subjectivism," or that he celebrates an "ego bloated and triumphant in empty solitude and infantile dreams of omnipotence" entirely misses the point of the therapeutic purpose and value he ascribes to solitude as a work of the self on itself.[27] In other words, Nietzsche does not conceive solitude as a negative condition of stasis, a simple fending away of others, or in psychoanalytic terms, as the ego's withdrawal of libidinal charges from objects to itself. Rather, Nietzsche conceives the work of solitude as similar in kind and purpose to the philosophical retirement or *secessus* that the Stoics praise for its tonic effect on the self's capacity to engage with others.

> *Society as enjoyment.*—If a man deliberately renounces others and keeps himself in solitude, he can thereby make of the society of men, enjoyed rarely, a rare delicacy [*Leckerbissen*].[28]

Nietzsche certainly does not treat living with others as a Lucullan feast, but he clearly suggests that one of the purposes of enduring *Einsamkeit* is the manner in which it restores to us the ability to take pleasure in and with others. Indeed, he maintains that the work of self-digestion is merely one of the unpleasant labours we must undertake for the sake of another, much rarer and precious end: to enjoy the sweet taste of others. He implies that it is impossible to enjoy these pleasurable relations without making self-digestion the labour of necessity through which one sustains oneself:

> *Ground of ill humour.*—He who prefers the beautiful in life to the useful will, like a child who prefers sweets to bread, certainly end by ruining his digestion and will look out on the world very ill-humouredly.[29]

Nietzsche suggests here that it is childlike or infantile to wish to enjoy oneself with others without undertaking the labour of digesting or integrating, to use Kleinian parlance, those painful affects that we wish to disavow or flee by projecting them into others. It is these projections, he maintains, through which we cast a pall over others and thereby darken the

world for ourselves.[30] Nietzsche recognises that the vain attempt to flee ourselves through projective identification dims the eye and destroys our conviviality. He counsels that we turn our gaze back on ourselves and begin to
identify our projections and acknowledge and integrate those parts of ourselves that we have sought to disavow. Indeed, in this regard Nietzsche's
analysis of the self leads to a therapeutic perspective that is akin to Klein's
notion of depressive integration. As Klein observes in her discussion of the
process of integration:

> [Integration] means facing one's destructive impulses and hated parts of the
> self. . . . With integration and a growing sense of reality omnipotence is bound
> to be lessened, and this again contributes to the pain of integration. . . . Inte-
> gration also means losing some of the idealisation—both of the object and of
> a part of the self.[31]

Nietzsche stresses that acknowledging and comically deprecating our narcissistic demand for a world of immediate gratification (the child's prefer-
ence for sweets only) is fundamental not just to self-cultivation, but to our
ability to look good-humouredly on others:

> Through knowing ourselves as a moving sphere of moods and opinions, and
> thus learning to *despise* ourselves a little, we restore our proper equilibrium
> with others [*Gleichgewicht*]. It is true we have good reason to think little of each
> of our acquaintances, even the greatest of them; but equally good reason to di-
> rect this feeling back onto ourselves; and so since we can endure ourself, let us
> also endure other people; perhaps there will come a more joyful hour when we
> exclaim: "Friends there are no friends!" thus said the dying sage; "Foes, there
> are no foes!" say I, the living fool.[32]

If then we reframe Nietzsche's idea of solitude in terms of his renovation
of the tradition of philosophical therapy, it becomes apparent that he conceives solitude as a work on the self that entails acknowledging and integrating the painful affects that arise from our subjection to finitude, loss
and separateness. Far from celebrating isolation for its own sake, Nietzsche
identifies the capacity to endure the desert of solitude as the only possible
basis for establishing healthy relationships between ego and alter. It is a
therapy concerned with how a subject that emerges from the condition of
narcissistic plenitude can preserve its "isolation without having to be insu-
lated."[33] For Nietzsche the practice of self-digestion entails analysing the
way in which one consoles oneself for the loss of the infantile position of
pure pleasure by projecting painful affects into others and compelling them
to process or consume these affects. As we have seen here and in the earlier
chapter on revenge, one of the keys to this therapy for Nietzsche is learning
how to wed comedy to tragedy.[34]

MITFREUDE: THE TEST OF FRIENDSHIP

Without envy.—He is utterly without envy, but there is no merit in that, for he
wants to conquer a country that nobody has possessed and scarcely anyone has
ever seen.[35]

As we saw in the previous chapter, Nietzsche repudiates Rousseau and
Schopenhauer's attempt to make *pitié/Mitleid* the foundation of ethics, but
this rejection only reveals one half of Nietzsche's critique, for he balances it
with an emphatic declaration of the moral worth of *Mitfreude*. Rousseau
and Schopenhauer explicitly declare that *pitié* or *Mitleid* undermines the
possibility of sharing in another's joy. Ida Overbeck recalls that during the
composition of what later became the second volume of *Human, All Too
Human: Assorted Opinions and Maxims*:

> A bad chapter of Schopenhauer affected Nietzsche especially strongly, the idea
> that man is not constituted to share joy, and can be interested in another per-
> son's misfortune or well-being only temporarily by the detour of former par-
> ticipation in misfortune; that well-being on the contrary, is suited to arouse
> envy; wherefore he concluded also from other premises, that hardship is the
> positive condition of the human race, and that only pity can be the real well-
> spring of morality.[36]

As we can surmise from our earlier discussion, the bad chapter that evidently incurred Nietzsche's ire appears in *On the Basis of Morality* where, in
the course of defending the claim that morality is exclusively based on
Mitleid, Schopenhauer invokes the first ethical maxim of *Émile*: "It is not in
human nature to put ourselves in the place of those who are happier than
ourselves, but only in the place of those who can claim our pity."[37] As we
have seen, in order to defend *pitié/Mitleid* as the basis of human concord,
both Rousseau and Schopenhauer find it necessary to reject the possibility of
shared joy. Their moral perspective takes it as axiomatic that *pitié/Mitleid* is
the only possible basis of mutual association, and that joy can be nothing
more than a source of acrimonious, bitter division. It is not surprising then
that Nietzsche invariably asserts the possibility and worth of *Mitfreude* by implicitly challenging this perspective: "I want to teach . . . what is understood
by so few today, least of all by those preachers of pity: *Mitfreude*!"[38] In rais-
ing the spectre of *Mitfreude* Nietzsche tacitly throws into disarray the psychological and normative presuppositions of this morality of *pitié/Mitleid*.

By asserting the value of *Mitfreude*, Nietzsche completes his critique of
pitié/Mitleid and its psychological underpinnings. If *Mitfreude* is possible, indeed exemplary, as Nietzsche insists, it follows that Rousseau and Schopenhauer's moral psychology and its conception of *humanitas* must be deeply
flawed. According to Nietzsche, their denial of *Mitfreude* is symptomatic of a

pathological narcissism that has a basilisk eye for the other's enjoyment. As we have seen, in Rousseau and Schopenhauer's moral psychology envy has as its reverse side pleasure in another's misfortune, and it is this envy that forms the basis of their ethics of pity. Their moral psychology, he argues, conceives taking pity on another as a means for satisfying an infantile narcissism that is enraged by the sight of another's joy, and wishes to destroy it. It is pathological narcissism, whose unmistakable symptom is its refusal to accept the other as a "vessel of goodness," that stands in the path of friendship, whose symbol is *Mitfreude*.[39] According to Nietzsche, this narcissism infiltrates their conception of the dynamics between self and other in a manner that undermines friendship. It is in his reflections on friendship, therefore, that Nietzsche addresses the problem of surpassing the infantile narcissism he discovers at the root of Rousseau and Schopenhauer's moral vision.

Nietzsche, then, attempts to understand not only how self-love might be restored in such a way that we do *not* take pleasure in ourselves through the other's suffering, but also how we overcome our envy to the point that we can take joy in the other's joy (*Mitfreude*). With Rousseau and Schopenhauer in his sights, Nietzsche makes the following claim:

> *Mitfreude.*—The serpent that stings us means to hurt us and rejoices as it does so; the lowest animal can imagine the *pain* of others. But to imagine the joy of others and to rejoice at it is the highest privilege of the highest animals, and among them it is accessible only to the choicest exemplars—thus a rare *humanum*: so that there have been philosophers who have denied the existence of joying with [*Mitfreude*].[40]

Nietzsche's introduction of *Mitfreude*—whose prefix makes it clear that he is affirming a mode of being with others—is an aspect of his psychology almost entirely neglected by his critics and defenders alike. Yet it is through the symbol of *Mitfreude* that he chooses to articulate his understanding of the rare and exemplary *humanum* (singular) who embodies *humanitas*—the qualities proper to being human. Without comprehending *Mitfreude*, therefore, we cannot complete our understanding of his moral psychology and its therapeutic dimensions. This declaration of *Mitfreude* takes us to the heart of his attempt to recover self-love from its pathological manifestations. On the rhetorical level, Nietzsche shapes this aphorism's main trope—the "ascending" orders of the human creature—so that the transition between the animal and the human coincides with *Mitfreude*; the "highest animal" shades into the properly human exactly at the point of the birth of *Mitfreude*. Hence Nietzsche defines the exemplary human being, the human *qua* human, in terms of the capacity to be with others in a particular way, which he calls *Mitfreude*. The crescendo of superlatives that establishes the lofty status of *Mitfreude* (the highest of the highest of the highest) places the pinnacle of *humanitas* almost beyond reach, but by the same stroke transforms it into a condition whose value more than justifies the struggle to attain such a rarified height.[41] In other words, Nietzsche aims not only to define the human *qua* human in terms of the capacity to participate in the other's joy, he also wants to present *Mitfreude* in a way that reveals it as exemplary—that is, as a model worthy of imitation.

In order to unravel the significance of *Mitfreude* in Nietzsche's psychology we need to briefly explore his criticism of the manner in which Kant conceptualises this affect. In *The Doctrine of Virtue*, Kant pairs *Mitleid* and *Mitfreude* as analogous to contagious diseases to which the human sensibility is equally susceptible. Both can be called "communicable" he writes "like a susceptibility to heat or to contagious diseases [*ansteckende Krankenheit*]."[42] However Kant's alignment of *Mitleid/Mitfreude* misses the important subtlety that Nietzsche introduces into the analysis of these affects. Nietzsche contends that to bring them together under the rubric of contagion, as Kant does, obscures the differences between these two forms of communicability. Kant, he implies, does not provide a sufficiently refined analysis of these passions and the way they shape the dynamics between self and other. It is Kant's failure to explore these complexities that Nietzsche appears to highlight when he points to the possibility that *Mitleid* and *Mitfreude* may have very different psychological presuppositions:

> The Joyless.—A single joyless person is enough to create constant discouragement and cloudy skies for a whole household. . . . *Happiness is not nearly so contagious a disease [ansteckende Krankheit]. Why?*[43]

Contra Kant, Nietzsche claims that we are *not* as susceptible to taking joy in the joy of others as we are to reacting to their sorrows. In fact, Nietzsche's analysis of joy, happiness and good fortune (*Freude/Glück*) exposes the fragility of the assumption Kant smuggles into his account of the emotions through the metaphor of contagious communication. For this metaphor allows him to assume that human beings are naturally susceptible to experiencing pleasure at another's state of happiness, and that like a disease "it spreads by natural means among men living near one another."[44] By contrast, Nietzsche argues that the sharing of joy or happiness demands the therapeutic treatment of our infantile narcissism and its pathologies. Unlike *Mitleid*, which, as his analysis of Rousseau and Schopenhauer shows, indulges and soothes our narcissism, *Mitfreude* is the very opposite of a contagion that spreads by means of mere proximity.

Nietzsche, then, extols the value of *Mitfreude*, yet he also considers it an extremely difficult affective task or accomplishment. As we saw in the previous chapter, Nietzsche argues that the envy that lies at the source of pity makes imagining the joy of others and rejoicing at it a rare human achievement. We can briefly restate Nietzsche's point in terms of the psychoanalytic account of narcissism that we have used to illuminate his analysis of the psychology of revenge and pity. According to Freud, the narcissistic desire for plenitude and omnipotence is not a stage that the ego can surpass once and for all; it is, on the contrary, the ideal that constantly haunts the ego. While the subject must forgo the condition of primary narcissism, the nostalgia for this undifferentiated condition of plenitude continues to shape its self-relation and its relations to others. Later pathologies of narcissism have their roots in the ego's initial, primitive rage at discovering that it cannot command the object world by an act of will, but is dependent upon others who are independent of it. Freud claims that in the earliest stages of its differentiation the ego reacts to the discovery of the basic structural asymmetry of its object relations by vengefully seeking (in phantasy) to consign to the realm of nonbeing those whose independence and self-sufficiency threatens its autarky. When the ego is in the thrall of this narcissistic rage it sees the other's independence and self-enjoyment as a bitter reminder of its own lost majesty. Only the phantasised destruction of the external object's independence can restore to the subject its narcissistic plenitude. As we have seen, this is the upshot of Freud's famous analysis of the *fort-da* game: the primitive ego's first substitutive compensation for the loss of its narcissistic perfection and self-sufficiency is the pleasure of phantasised revenge against those on whom it is asymmetrically dependent.[45]

According to Freud and Klein, the vicissitudes of this primitive desire to spoil others and to deprive them of their pleasure shapes not just the earliest object relations, but also later personal and social relations. Freud accounts for the emergence of the herd "instinct" and its demand for strict equality as one of the derivatives of this narcissistically fuelled envy. In *Group Psychology*, Freud plays this thesis out through his narrative of sibling rivalry and its resolution. Confronted with the impossibility of realising the narcissistic desire to brush aside his/her siblings in the competition for parental love, "the elder child," Freud writes,

> is forced into identifying himself with the other children. So there grows up in the troop of children a communal or group feeling. . . . The first demand made by this reaction-formation is for justice, *for equal treatment for all. . . . If one cannot be favourite oneself, at all events no one else shall be the favourite.*[46]

Freud extrapolates from his narrative the idea that the social feeling is a reaction formation of that primitive envy which emerges from the painful loss of narcissistic omnipotence. Sibling love and neighbourly love are both products of narcissistic resentment; or more precisely, neighbourly love carries this family feud into the social realm:

> What appears in society in the shape of *Gemeingeist, esprit des corps,* "group spirit," does not belie its derivation from what was originally envy. No one

must want to put himself forward, everyone one must want the same and have the same. Social justice means that we deny ourselves many things so that others have to do without them as well. . . . This demand for equality is the root of social conscience and the sense of duty. . . . Thus social feeling is based upon the reversal of what was a hostile feeling into a positively toned tie in the nature of an identification.[47]

As his allusion to the Kantian notion of duty implies, Freud intends his derivation of the sense of justice and equality from envy to account not only for the substantive principle of equal distribution of goods, but also for the formal principle of universalisability. Children assent to the notion of universal rules for the sake of ensuring that their rivals will be similarly discomfited by identical limitations on their narcissism. Freud's explanation of the herd instinct shows that it is precisely because the social feeling is a transmutation of envy that the joy of others cannot be contagious like their sorrow. Since on this interpretation the social tie is derived from the envious desire for mutual deprivation and suffering, the other's joy counts as a fundamental breach of a compact which is meant to assuage the individual's narcissistically driven envy through an equal distribution of suffering and privation. It is impossible not to notice that Freud's analysis of the herd instinct echoes Zarathustra's pillory of the last man's herd mentality minus (but not for that reason necessarily opposed to) his hyperbolic coda: "Everyone wants the same thing, everyone is the same: whoever feels differently goes voluntarily into the madhouse."[48]

While Freud's analysis of the origins of the herd instinct reiterates Nietzsche's account, the latter goes further in the direction of investigating how the work of self-cultivation might also prepare a new foundation for social intercourse.[49] By definition, *Mitfreude* rules out the narcissistic desire to recoup oneself through the sweet taste of the other's suffering. The healthy form of self-love that Nietzsche conceives as the aim of the work of the self must be distinguished from the restoration of self-affection that proceeds through magnifying the feeling of one's injuries and losses in order to enhance the compensatory pleasures derived from exacting vengeance on others.[50] The serpent in Nietzsche's garden, to recall *Human, All Too Human*, volume 2, 62, tempts one to soothe the painful experiences of self-loss by rejoicing in the other's misfortune, and it is this lure that the rare *humanum* resists. And, as both Nietzsche and Freud suggest, it is the inability to bear one's own suffering, and to reconcile oneself to the other's independence, a discovery that generates the imaginary revenge against the world and its envious offshoots, that makes it possible for the sight of the other's sorrow to yield pleasure. In order to rejoice in the other's joy, on the other hand, one must have surmounted the rage ignited by the dissolution of primary narcissism and stoked by the sight of the other's enjoyment. In Freudian terms, the failure to properly work through the inevitable dissolution of primary narcissism must stand as the one of the main obstacles to *Mitfreude*.

Seen in this context, it becomes clear that *Mitfreude* is the perfect measure of the extent to which individuals have overcome malignant forms of narcissism, and conversely, the denial of *Mitfreude* is a sign of a failure to overcome the narcissistic malaise and its splenetic envy. Only by bearing the narcissistic loss occasioned by the discovery of the other's independence, whose reverse side is the recognition of one's solitude and separation, is it possible to overcome the temptation to take "imaginary" revenge on others. Nietzsche describes the chasm between our pathological narcissism and our higher humanity in the following terms:

> *Backward and anticipatory people.*—The disagreeable character of someone who is full of mistrust, feels *envy* at every success of competitors or neighbours, and becomes violent and enraged toward divergent opinions shows that he belongs to an earlier stage of culture and is therefore a relic: for the way in which he interacts with people was proper and suitable for the circumstances of an age when might made right; he is a *backward* human being. A different character, one that has a rich capacity to share in the joys of others, wins friends everywhere, feels affection for all that is growing and becoming, *shares the pleasure of others* in all their honours and successes, and claims no privilege of being alone in recognising the truth, but is instead filled with modest mistrust—that is an anticipatory person striving toward a higher human culture. The disagreeable stems from a time when the rough foundations of human intercourse still had to be constructed, the other one lives on its highest floor, as far as possible from the wild animal that, locked up in the cellars beneath the foundations of culture, rages and howls.[51]

In *Human, All Too Human* Nietzsche frames his critique of the "social feeling" in terms of the affective accomplishment of *Mitfreude*, identified here not only as an achievement for the rare *humanum*, but as the foundation of a higher human culture. Since Nietzsche defines higher humanity in terms of this capacity for intersubjectivity, the practice of self-cultivation and its completion in the condition of self-love should not be identified with a regression to primary narcissism, which simply *precludes* the recognition of others *qua* subjects, nor can it be thought of as continuous with the ego's primitive defences against the loss of narcissism. Nietzsche shows how such defences treat the existence of other subjects as an intolerable violation of the ego's illusory sovereignty, a violation which the primitive narcissist revenges by attempting to annihilate the other as an independent subject or through the stratagem of an equal apportioning of deprivation.

Mitfreude, and the self-cultivation which Nietzsche links with it, is antithetical to primary narcissism and its pathological derivatives since it entails both recognising others as independent agents entitled to make claims, and it pursues the goal of enabling them to reveal themselves in their perfection. Whereas the narcissist is driven by the fear of being outshone by others, Nietzsche's "higher" subjects enjoy their capacity to illuminate, and behold their radiance without envy. The strategies of narcissistic defensiveness, on the other hand, deliver only a debased form of "equality" between subjects:

> *Two sorts of equality.*—The passion for equality can express itself by someone either wanting to pull everyone else down to his level (by disparaging them, keeping secrets from them, or tripping them up) or wanting to pull himself up along with everyone else (by giving them recognition, helping them, taking pleasure in their success).[52]

As the allusion to *Mitfreude* in the last clause of this aphorism indicates, Nietzsche aligns the second notion of "equality" with the anticipated higher human culture. In this higher culture the other's good is not treated as a source of one's own deprivation, and relationships are therefore not structured as zero-sum games. Nietzsche envisages a form of reciprocity that depends not on levelling equality—the levelling of qualitative differences through the quantitative reduction of the exchange principle—but on a mutual commitment to individual elevation. It is a reciprocity, however, that can only be realised if each individual overcomes the feeling of lack and impotence aroused by the sight of another's plenitude or "success," and with it the pathological envy whose summit is the "revolting feeling . . . which argues: because there is *something* I cannot have, the whole world shall have *nothing*! the world shall *be* nothing!"[53]

By contrast, the "backward person" Nietzsche discusses in *Human, All Too Human* (614), remains captive to narcissistic rage. Like Freud's primary narcissist, Nietzsche's backward person tries to maintain a pure pleasure ego by projecting all of the internal sources of "unpleasure" into the world and attempting to deny others whatever pleasures it cannot secure for itself. Nietzsche identifies three symptoms of our narcissistic refusal to come to grips with the dissolution of our sovereignty: mistrust of others, a violent, paradoxical assertion of Godlike omniscience—a paradox that we exorcise through the annihilation of the other's truth-claims—and an envy so overpowering that we indiscriminately target both neighbours and competitors. Far from treating the Calliclean ethic of "might makes right" as his future horizon, Nietzsche considers it a residue of the primitive stages of the individual and humanity.[54] Nietzsche describes the primordial stages of human subjectivity—on the ontogenetic and phylogenetic levels—in terms of narcissistic defences against the loss of sovereignty and the acknowledgement of others' agency and independent identity. In the early stages of culture any divergence from the ego's divine decrees is met with violent repudiation or the imaginary gratification of its need for omnipotence. The "rough foundations of human intercourse," as Nietzsche puts it, can only be built where the ego relinquishes its claim to being the sole possessor and author of the "truth" and sovereign over the world's goods and honours. If this illusion of majesty is threatened, the backward person enviously attacks others, or what amounts to the same thing, short circuits the possibility of envy through levelling—if I cannot be favorite, no one else shall be!

By contrast, properly human intercourse turns on our capacity to participate joyfully with others in a world in which we do not control or monopolise all the sources of the good. Far from claiming that primary narcissism is unsurpassable, Nietzsche thus implies that the child must go through a *Bildungsprozess* that decentres its infantile omnipotence and locates it in a social world, or more precisely a process that enables it to relate to others as a *friend relates to friends*. Like Freud, too, Nietzsche makes it clear that this decentring process requires a painful and *incessant* struggle. While his psychic topography imprisons the "wild animal"—a figure embodying all the elements of narcissistic rage—beneath the foundations of civilization, Nietzsche harbors no illusion that it ever ceases to howl.

Pace the critics of Nietzsche's alleged celebration of narcissism, then, the "higher" individuals he sketches in the middle works do not aim to permanently rend themselves from the weave of the social fabric, or to become impervious to every form of feeling with others. On the contrary, if Nietzsche's analysis of pathological narcissism suggests anything it is that an incapacity to share in the other's joy is symptomatic of the rage and resentment conjured up by the loss of narcissistic plenitude. Nietzsche claims that it can be treated only through the difficult, ongoing work of the self on itself. Because *Mitfreude* is the measure or test of having overcome infantile narcissism, Nietzsche takes friendship as the model for the highest floor of human intercourse:

> *Friend.*—Shared joy [*Mitfreude*] not shared suffering [*Mitleid*], is what makes the friend.[55]

THE PLAY OF FRIENDSHIP

In his *Consolation* to his mother Helvia, Seneca recalls Brutus' reflections after visiting his friend Marcellus in exile on Mytilene:

> I seemed rather to be going into exile myself when I had to return without him, than to be leaving him in exile.[56]

Brutus observes here that not even his return to Rome could compensate him for the sense of exile he experiences in departing from his friend Marcellus. To be without this friend, Brutus laments, makes even his homeland seem like a place of exile, a place where he neither understands nor recognises himself or others. For Seneca, Brutus' words have a double significance:

on the one hand, they suggest to him that the Stoic can and should attain a degree of self-sufficient felicity that not even exile from his homeland can disrupt, and that he can do so by creating a world for himself. On the other, Seneca also acknowledges that to lose such a friend, a friend who has a world to bestow, is to be exiled from oneself. While this acknowledgement of the value of friendship creates something of an impasse in Stoic philosophy, its significance for our purposes lies in its illumination of Nietzsche's notion of friendship that echoes the Stoic tradition. Nietzsche follows Stoicism in conceiving the basis of friendship not in need, utility or dependence; it is a relationship that is something quite foreign to calculations of profit or loss. In his discourse contrasting Christian notions of neighbourliness love and friendship, Zarathustra expresses the point thus:

> I teach to you the friend, in whom the world stands complete, a vessel of goodness—the creating friend, who always has a complete world to bestow.[57]

As with Brutus, Nietzsche implies that if we lose the creative friend we are exiled from the world the friend bestows upon us, a world Brutus values above Rome and citizenship.

We can begin to unpack Nietzsche's notion of the creative friend by examining what is at stake in his claim that *Mitfreude*, not *Mitleid* makes the friend. Many of the reasons for Nietzsche's negative claim have already been explicated: relationships forged on the basis of pity, at least as Rousseau and Schopenhauer understand them, are little more than means of assuaging one's feeling of self-lack through diminishing the other. The imperative of equality, as we have seen, is fuelled by the narcissistic demand that because "I cannot be favourite, no one else shall be." To the extent that such relations of pity are oriented around the principle of equal apportioning of suffering, they necessarily exclude the stronger notion of friendship that Nietzsche discovers in classical and Stoic thought, whose heart lies not in companionship or pity, but in mutual self-creation.[58] Indeed, according to Nietzsche, because of its emphasis on a crude notion of equality Schopenhauer's *Mitleid* is not entitled to be considered a form of being with others or intersubjectivity since the aim of *Mitleid* is to ensure that the gaps or differences between selves are cast into oblivion. *Mitleid* cannot make the friend, therefore, because it entails the annihilation of others *qua* other, in their separateness, but also more particularly in their capacity to enjoy themselves.

Nietzsche's analysis of Rousseau and Schopenhauer thus belies the claim that mutual recognition or understanding plays any part in their ethics of pity. *Mitleid* is not a matter of seeking to be understood or acknowledged by the other and vice versa, but a question of enviously spoiling those whose joy arouses the feeling of self-lack and assuaging this painful feeling by taking sweet pleasure in their downfall. In other words, because Schopenhauer's pitiers cannot tolerate their own narcissistic loss, which, as we have seen Freud represents in terms of the tension between the ego and the ego ideal, they strive to diminish others. This kind of *Mitleid* is therefore antithetical to relationships that aim to temper, transform or modulate narcissistic loss; indeed, quite the reverse—it functions to exacerbate this loss. "We can," Nietzsche claims, "neither aid nor comfort [other mortals] if we want to be the echo of their lamentation."[59]

If we recall the myth of Narcissus that Nietzsche alludes to here we can glean what he is driving at in his critique of pity. In Robert Graves's rendition, Narcissus is enthralled by his beautiful mirror image, but suffers from his inability to possess this beautiful self; he can see but not possess or consume his own beauty. The gap between his ego and ego ideal appears unbridgeable. Narcissus chooses to take his life rather than suffer the torments of this impossible, insatiable desire to possess the perfect beauty he sees in the mirror image. Taking pity on the dying Narcissus, the nymph Echo, whose love he has spurned, repeats his lamentations. But this echoing of his lamentation does not save Narcissus from his torment.[60] If we wish to aid others in their struggle to heal their narcissistic wound, Nietzsche implies, merely echoing their suffering is no remedy.

However, it would be wrong to infer on this basis that Nietzsche's notion of friendship excludes all regard for the other's suffering. His claim that friendship is *made* by *Mitfreude* does not preclude a role for *Mitleid* in friendship. In fact, because Nietzsche builds his conception of intersubjectivity on the basis of friendship he transfigures rather than abandons or rejects *Mitleid*. It should be noted in this context that the German language does not possess a wide range of terms for distinguishing different kinds of regard for the other's suffering; as Nietzsche observes, "'*Mitleid*': how coarsely does language assault with its one word so polyphonous a being!"[61] Despite the fact that in this case a dead, petrified word lies in his way, as he puts it elsewhere, Nietzsche sets about drawing a distinction between the Rousseauian/Schopenhauerian concept of *pitié/Mitleid* and another kind of sharing of suffering that he associates with friendship.[62] We can see roughly hewn traces of this transfigured idea of *Mitleid* in a note from his 1880 *Nachlass*:

> Fellow-feeling [*Mitgefühl*] is increased if joyful feelings predominate; it is decreased if there's more pain than joy incurred. Constantly beholding suffering undermines the constancy/stability of compassion, but one will be all the more sensitive or susceptible to foreign pain/suffering the more one has *Mitfreude*. Such are the most compassionate people, who because they have inner joy, also have all the contradictory woes [or the contradictory woes them!]; unhappy and warlike people are severe or hard.[63]

Nietzsche explores the notion here that the sharing of joy which makes friendship also breathes life into our capacity for sharing other kinds of affects as well, including participating in another's suffering. Logically, if *Mitfreude* makes friendship, and it is this sharing that refines our sensitivity to foreign *Leid*, then friends must also be the most compassionate people (*die mitleidigsten Menschen*). Nietzsche's counterpoint to friendship is that form of sociability exemplified in Rousseau and Schopenhauer's demand that we should only attend to the other's suffering. Nietzsche claims here that by attending to the other's joy we refine our sensitivity to their suffering, whereas by attending to their suffering alone we merely blunt this sensitivity.

However, as we have seen, Nietzsche's argument against Schopenhauer and Rousseau cuts deeper than this: his psychological analysis suggests that their conception of *Mitleid* has envy as its reverse side. He argues that because their moral subjects do not preserve or cultivate a sense of inner joy they can only espy the other's joy as something to be enviously spoiled. It is this analysis that underpins Zarathustra's claim in his critical discourse on the flaws of *Mitleid*:

> Verily, I may have done this and that for sufferers: but better things it seemed I always did when I learned to enjoy myself better. Ever since there have been human beings, they have enjoyed themselves too little: that alone, my brothers, is our original sin! And if we learn to enjoy ourselves better, so do we best unlearn our hurting of others and our planning hurts for them.[64]

In fact, Schopenhauer and Rousseau's moral subjects find themselves in a cycle of self-deprivation, which turns them against the other as a source of joy or as a bestower of a complete world. In this regard, we might recall, Schopenhauer claims that for the *"glücklich Mensch* as such *we* feel no sympathy; on the contrary he remains a stranger to our hearts . . . and easily excites our envy."[65] By contrast with Stoics, who feel exiled when they have to *depart from* the happy or fortunate person, Schopenhauerian pitiers feel that they are in exile, estranged from both themselves and the other, when they are *with* the happy person; they return from exile only when they banish the other from the state of happiness or joy. But the household to which pitiers then return is without joy (*freudlos*)—their envy neither bridges the gap between themselves and their ideal, nor do they allow or encourage the other to bridge this gap. By thus intensifying their own experience of self-lack, pitiers both estrange themselves from the joyful (*freudige*) and intensify their own envy, thus closing the vicious circle of self-deprivation that hardens and arms them against the other's joy; *Unglücks- und Kriegsmenschen*, as Nietzsche says, become hard. Zarathustra's parody of the genesis narrative in the above passage implies a similar point: we cast ourselves and others out of the garden of paradise when we commit the original sin of being tempted to take sweet pleasure in the other's suffering because we take too little pleasure in ourselves.

In *Human, All Too Human* (46), Nietzsche clarifies his notion of the *Mitleid* between friends or the nonenvious *Mitleid* that he alludes to in the *Nachlass* note. Once again Nietzsche puns on the word *Mitleid*, but this time rather than simply claiming that the *Mitleid* is not *mit-dem-Leid*, he makes the bolder claim that in friendship the *Mitleid* is stronger than the *Leid*. That is to say, according to Nietzsche, "we find it more painful, for example, when one of our friends makes himself guilty of something shameful than when we do so ourselves."[66] Nietzsche's subtlety here points to the nature of traffic between friends: we are more affected by our friends' experiences than they are themselves, but, as Nietzsche implies, the reverse is also true, our friends are more affected by our experiences than we are ourselves. As Graham Little aptly remarks *apropos* this traffic, "[p]resumably in the best friendship the roles of container and contained are readily swapped."[67] This active compassion is possible, Nietzsche claims, because as friends we believe in the "purity of his character more than he does" and therefore "our love for him is stronger than his own love for himself."[68]

In other words, for Nietzsche compassionate friendship is marked off from Rousseauian *pitié* insofar as for friends pitying is *not* sweet because it does *not* exempt them from their friend's suffering; on the contrary, they in fact feel this suffering more strongly than their friend and vice versa. And they do so, according to Nietzsche, because they identify with, partly create and also cultivate, their friend's purity of character, or ideal self, rather than, as is the case in Rousseau and Schopenhauer's moral subject, feeling estranged from it and desiring to enviously spoil it. Nietzsche casts this point in cognitive terms: We *believe* in "the purity of his character more than he does" because in friendship we partly create each other's characters in the process of projection. In Nietzschean friendship, then, we project into friends and they project into us this ideal self in order to stabilise, consolidate or contain that which we cannot contain for ourselves.

Nietzsche illustrates this friendship in parodying the platitude "a friend in need is a friend indeed." Here we see the positive *Mitleid*, which is not, as Rousseau's *pitié* is, driven by the desire to discern in the other's need or suffering "a nature plainly like our own, and a pledge of [his] affection for us." Rather, because Nietzschean friendship is driven by the desire to see friends cultivate their higher selves it can countenance the notion that we can bear them leaving us for the sake of finding another who can enrich them in a way that we cannot:

Friends in need.—Sometimes we notice that one of our friends belongs more to another than he does to us, and that his delicacy is troubled by and his selfishness [*Selbstsucht*] inadequate to this decision: we then have to make things easier for him and estrange him from us.—This is likewise necessary when we adopt a way of thinking which would be ruinous to him: our love for him has to drive us, through an injustice which we take upon ourself, to create for him a good conscience in renouncing us.[69]

Nietzsche uses this parodic tableau to illustrate his point that our love for our friends can be greater than their love for themselves. Being a good friend, he implies, requires us to align ourselves with the other's ideal self even if that means creating a good conscience for them in renouncing us. If, as Critchley jokes in his essay on humour, the *Über-Ich* can be our ego's *amigo*, then as friends we become for others their amigo's amigo.[70] Indeed, as Nietzschean friends we are *better* friends to our friends' ideal selves than they are, for their delicacy restrains their *Selbstsucht*. In some cases, then, in order to be a good Nietzschean friend to others we may have to collaborate with their ideal selves even at the expense of their attachment to us. It is with this in mind that Nietzsche claims that one measure of friendship lies in whether as friends we maintain others in good humour with themselves when they leave us. In such friendships we are not oriented towards maintaining possession of others, or governed by the need to secure a "pledge of their affection," but toward ensuring that they become their own friends. Indeed, in Nietzschean friendship our friends should be able to depart from us not simply undamaged, but enriched in their relationship to their higher selves (amigos):

> *In parting.*—It is not how one soul approaches another but in how it distances itself from it that I recognise their affinity and relatedness.[71]

Nietzsche's parody deliberately contrasts this kind of friendship with the Rousseauian and Schopenhauerian notion of pitying. In their framework, as we have seen, we estrange the other from ourselves in order to assuage our feeling of envy, and we treat the other's independence as a sign of contempt for us. In Nietzsche's framework, by contrast, it is possible to estrange others from ourselves for *their* sake, so that they can leave us with a good conscience; the need we respond to in them is not their need for us, but their need for themselves. This is possible, according to Nietzsche, because such friendships are formed on the basis of the desire to cultivate the other's ideal self (or "beauty," as Seneca puts it) rather than on the basis of our fear of separation or abandonment.

Nietzsche illuminates what he means by the higher self and the place it has in friendship in the following discussion of our traffic with this higher self:

> *Traffic with one's higher self.*—Everyone has his good days when he discovers his higher self and true humanity demands that everyone be evaluated only in light of this condition and not in that of his workaday unfreedom or

servitude. . . . But men themselves traffic in various ways with this higher self of theirs . . . many live in awe and abasement before their ideal and would like to deny it . . . it possesses a spectral freedom to come or to stay as it wishes, on this account it is called a gift of the gods, whereas in reality it is everything else that is a gift of the gods [of chance], this however is man himself.[72]

We can see then that Nietzschean friends practise this true humanity by evaluating others in light of their ideal or higher self. Nietzsche implies that we love our friends more than they love themselves insofar as we love in them that spectral ideal that they fear or wish to deny because the happiness it promises also places heavy demands on them. On the first point, Nietzsche identifies the paradox of such self-other relationships: that is, that we are more our friends' friend than they are themselves, and in this sense they therefore exist outside themselves or in the relationship between us. Through such reciprocal projections we become part of them, their amigo's amigo, and they become part of us.

Freud explains the ways we traffic with the higher self in his analysis of the consequences that follow when we are compelled to displace our childish perfection onto the ego ideal:

A man who has exchanged his narcissism for homage to a high ego ideal has not on that account necessarily succeeded in sublimating his libidinal instincts. It is true that the ego ideal demands such sublimation but it cannot enforce it . . . the formation of an ideal heightens the demands of the ego and is the most powerful factor favoring repression; sublimation is a way out, a way those demands can be met without involving repression.[73]

According to Nietzsche, we contain and preserve this higher self or ego ideal for our friends, and because it has more reality for us, we suffer more than they suffer when they feel diminished; or as he puts it, the "unegoistic" in us is affected more strongly than the unegoistic in them. Nietzsche uses the term "unegoistic" in this context as an abbreviated, simplified form of expression intended to capture the sense in which we project onto or into our friends this ideal self. We *believe* in it more than they do themselves insofar as we impart to this spectral creature more reality than it has for them, so to speak. Once again Zarathustra's discourse illuminates Nietzsche's point:

Higher than love of the nearest is love of the farthest and what is to come; higher yet than love of the human is for me love of . . . spectres. This spectre that runs ahead of you . . . is more beautiful than you: why do you not give him your flesh and bones? But you are afraid and run to your neighbour.[74]

In Zarathustra's terms, the friend gives flesh and bones to the other's phantom. In this sense, then, for Nietzsche friendship means both playing host to, but also creating for others their higher self. It entails giving this spectral trace of their lost perfection (which runs along *behind* them, in the past that accompanies the present) a reality and presence that it lacks for them. Nietzsche argues that the facility for projecting oneself onto or into others can thus breathe life into the intersubjective realm. As we have seen, the term projective identification is normally used to explain how selves split themselves into unmixed good and bad parts, and project their hostile, aggressive affects into others so that they can then be controlled or punished. But there is another side to projection.[75] If Nietzsche is right, the creative use of projection plays an essential role in the fabrication of the interpersonal, relational sphere that he calls friendship.[76] In friendship one projects into the other one's own "highest self," or in psychoanalytic parlance, one's ego ideal, the repository of one's lost perfection.

While Nietzsche asserts that we necessarily make others "satellite[s] of our own system," he also differentiates between better and worse ways of imagining and incorporating the other into the self:[77]

> *Seeing one's light shine.*—In the dark states of distress, sickness or debt we are glad when we see others still shining and they perceive in us the bright disk of the moon. In this indirect way we participate in our own capacity to illuminate.[78]

Nietzsche suggests here that it is possible to make others shine for us or grow dark depending on our ability to cut the knot between our self-suffering and the existence of others as independent solar systems. Where our feeling of self-loss is no longer exacerbated by the pain of seeing others shine, where our gaze is not seared by staring directly into their sun-like radiance, we can be gladdened by the radiance of others rather than consumed with the desire to take revenge against them for our own losses and failures. As we have seen, according to Nietzsche, when we are captured by our envious I/eye we take a dim view of happy people, we do not see or imagine their joy as *they* experience it, nor rejoice or revel in their good fortune. Rather our evil I/eye of envy perceives this joy as the source of our deprivation and we unconsciously project into the *glücklich Mensch* our own vengeful, malicious affects and phantasies. True envy, as Lacan puts it, "makes the subject pale before the image of a completeness closed in upon itself."[79] Envy is thus a malady of vision, or more precisely, a pathology that affects the way we "see" the other:

> *Why forbearance?*—You suffer, and demand that we should be forbearing towards you when as a result of your suffering you do wrong to things and men! But what does our forbearance matter! You, however, ought to be *more cautious* for your own sake! What a fine way of compensating for your suffering it is to go on and *destroy your own judgement!* Your revenge rebounds on you yourself when you defame something: it is your *own* eye you dim, not that of another: you accustom yourself to *seeing distortedly!*[80]

But if Nietzsche censures the envious, vengeful gaze which falsifies and looks askance at the other, he must presume a better way of seeing, an undimmed eye, against which it can be measured and condemned.

In the aphorism entitled "Seeing one's light shine" Nietzsche explores vision's reciprocal, intersubjective, communicative potential, and its relationship to the subject's self-love, as an alternative to the scopic regime of envy.[81] He differentiates between this envy in which the "shining" of others is too painful for us to bear without us wanting to darken and diminish this image through projective identifications, and a regime in which our gaze has adjusted to the shining of others and we no longer need to blind ourselves to their brilliance. In *Human, All Too Human* (2, 61), Nietzsche metaphorically identifies the suffering self with the "bright disk of the moon," that is to say, with the moon's refractions of sunlight. Nietzsche's trope implies a symbolic identification of the other who "continues to shine" with sunlight, and the recovery of those in a state of distress with the rising of their own sun. *Even in states of distress*, then, we can bear the other's sun-like radiance without "paling" before the image of this effulgence. If the other can *still* shine (*noch leuchten*) for us when we suffer, Nietzsche implies, this is a sign that our vision remains undimmed and we do not darken the other through envious projections.

Nietzsche thus envisages subjects who can directly perceive in the other a "sun-like" object which illuminates for itself and others its own particular world of beautiful forms. Nietzsche's concern, then, is with how we can attain a gaze that is not seared by looking at the brightest light of others. Nietzsche's conception of friendship therefore turns on what might be called the formation of heliotropic subjects: subjects who can turn to each other as sources of illumination. For the friend who continues to shine also sees in us, even in our darkened state of distress, a medium which reflects the light of our temporarily eclipsed sun. Thus the Nietzschean friend sees our suffering as the dark background against which the light of our nascent, luminous selves can become visible.[82] What captures and captivates the friend's I/eye in this instance is the shimmering of our joyful self, a shimmering which Nietzsche implies is at least partially a projection or illusion. But in this case the projection provides us with resources to overcome our dark state of distress: in seeing our light shine in the other's gaze we participate indirectly in our own luminosity.[83] We see reflected in the other's eye our own capacity to "illuminate"—or, in other words, to create a world for the other. In this way Nietzsche acknowledges that how the other sees us (and how we see the other seeing ourselves) can transform our experience of distress, indeed can enable us to endure and perhaps recover from our malaise. Reflecting back our "bright disk" to us is the friend's means of seducing us into loving our most distant, eclipsed self.

From a Nietzschean perspective, one of the reasons we love our friends is that we project into them our best qualities as if they were safer with them, so that friends come to stand for our highest self or alter ego.[84] But whereas in narcissistic idealisation we merely seek another who we would like to be, a compensatory substitute for what we can or dare not be, in friendship the recipient of our projection, the one in whom our ego ideal finds safe haven, also reciprocates by containing and projecting into the future the alter ego we wish to recover for ourselves. ("I teach you the friend and his overfull heart. But one must know how to be a sponge if one would be loved by hearts that are overfull.")[85] What the friend echoes is not our lamentation over our lack and insufficiency, but our distant (imagined) memory of lost perfection and its anticipated return. If in the problem of finding a progressive solution to our narcissistic desire for the lost feeling of plenitude "everything turns on how that attempt is pursued," as Joel Whitebook puts it, then for Nietzsche the answer lies in such friendship in which we can be ourselves, or *more* than ourselves, with and through others and they can be *more* than themselves with and through us. Nietzschean friendship turns the loss of narcissistic plenitude into a progressive motor of self-development. Because the friend provides a safe haven for our ego ideal and projects it into the future, we experience the tension between the ego ideal and the actual ego as a source of expectation and promise rather than a painful lack that we can assuage through one or another kind of revenge.

To be sure, Nietzsche is acutely aware that to be a friend we must undertake the prior (or parallel) Stoic work on the self through which we digest our bitter affects of loss. For it is this work, especially its comic tempering of our narcissistic grandiosity, which domesticates those pains that make us ill-humoured with ourselves and others. Without this Stoic work on the self, he claims, we take revenge on life or on others. But by the same token, because when we have stoically composed ourselves we can behold the other's joy without the envious desire to spoil it, we can also hold in place the other's higher self. In doing so, Nietzschean friends participate in an imaginative space in which they can mutually create worlds for one another.

NOTES

1. I borrow the phrase "active compassion" from Joan Stambaugh. She observes that linguistically Nietzsche could not draw a distinction between pity and compassion because the German term *Mitleid* covers both concepts. She develops a different, though not necessarily incompatible thesis, to the one this chapter defends. On the basis of Nietzsche's critique of what she calls "ontological revenge," she argues, it is possible to construct a positive notion of an "ontological compassion" that is

borne of the affirmation of the eternal recurrence; see Joan Stambaugh, *The Other Nietzsche*, 1994, SUNY, Albany, 41–57.

2. Bernard Reginster, *The Affirmation of Life: Nietzsche on Overcoming Nihilism*, 2006, Harvard University Press, Cambridge, Mass., 187.

3. WS, 348.

4. Jacques Derrida rightly observes that Nietzsche incorporates solitude and distance into the art of friendship. However, because Derrida treats the notion of friendship as an infinitely malleable rhetorical trope he empties it of all content. That is to say, under his ministrations it becomes a relationship lacking any conceivable content, or in his words, an "X without X, a community of those without community"; see Jacques Derrida, *Politics of Friendship*, op. cit., 42. Arguably, Donald Winnicott develops a much more plausible account of the relationship between solitude and connectedness, and of the paradoxical idea of "sharing solitude," an account which remains grounded in a psychological theory that acknowledges the problems and possibilities of narcissistic plenitude. See his two essays "The Capacity to be Alone," 29–36, at 31; and "Communicating and Not Communicating Leading to a Study of Certain Opposites," 179–92, op. cit. For a more detailed treatment of Derrida's "elusive work" on friendship, see Geoffrey Bennington, *Interrupting Derrida*, 2000, Routledge, London, 110–27, 111; and Simon Critchley, *Ethics, Politics, Subjectvity*, op. cit., ch. 6.

5. See, for example, L VIII.

6. Henry Staten, *Nietzsche's Voice*, op. cit., 5.

7. Ibid., 102–3.

8. Theodor W. Adorno and Max Horkheimer develop this Nietzschean idea of the introversion of sacrifice in the classical theoretical text of the first generation of the Frankfurt school, see Theodor W. Adorno and Max Horkheimer, *Dialectic Of Enlightenment*, op. cit.

9. D, 18.

10. D, 18.

11. D, 18.

12. D, 8. Werner Dannhauser analyses Nietzsche's shifting, ambivalent relationship to Socrates and the Socratic philosophical tradition in what has become the standard reference book in the field; Werner Dannhauser, *Nietzsche's View of Socrates*, 1974, Cornell University Press, New York.

13. D, 18.

14. GS, 50; Nietzsche gives this aphorism an undeniable autobiographical resonance by illustrating the irrational power custom exercises over our conscience with the example of our fear of receiving contempt from those "among whom and for whom" we have been educated—that is, our fellow students and our teachers. It echoes the trauma he experienced a decade earlier over the controversy surrounding BT, especially his shock over Ritschl's silence and the attacks of Wilamowitz. William Calder and Laurence Lampert agree that Zarathustra's parable "On Scholars" is probably his last public reference to the controversy with Wilamowitz over the scholarly merits of BT; see M. S. Silk and J. P. Stern, *Nietzsche on Tragedy*, op. cit., 90–107, esp. 91–93; William Musgrave Calder III, "The Wilamowitz-Nietzsche Struggle," op. cit., 251; and Laurence Lampert, *Nietzsche's Teaching*, op. cit., 331, fn. 54; and TSZ II, 16.

15. Paul Ricoeur, *Freud and Philosophy*, op. cit., 449.
16. Thomas Odgen, quoted in C. Fred Alford, *The Psychoanalytic Theory of Greek Tragedy*, 1992, Yale University Press, New Haven, Conn., 14.
17. WS, 264.
18. Donald W. Winnicott, "The Capacity to be Alone," in *The Maturational Process and the Facilitating Environment*, op. cit., 29. In the same essay, Winnicott claims that the "capacity to be alone is nearly synonymous with emotional maturity"; 31.
19. Donald Winnicott quoted in Martha Nussbaum, *Upheavals of Thought*, op. cit., 208, fn. 84.
20. D, 443.
21. Epictetus, *Discourses*, bk 3, ch. 13, 365, in *The Stoic and Epicurean Philosophers*, 1940, translated by P. E. Matheson, edited by Whitney J. Oates, Random House, New York.
22. D, 491.
23. On the Stoic metaphors of digestion and self-digestion, see, for example, L II.
24. WS, 235.
25. Nietzsche quoted in Graham Parkes, *Composing the Soul*, op. cit., 375–76. However, Parkes also observes that in some notes from later in 1881 Nietzsche evinces a more ambivalent attitude towards solitude, or more precisely, a concern about *too much* solitude, rather than solitude per se.
26. GS, 312.
27. Leslie Paul Thiele, "Twilight of Modernity: Nietzsche, Heidegger, and Politics," *Political Theory* 22, no. 3, August 1994, 469–90, 479; and Simon Critchley, *On Humour*, op. cit., 105.
28. HAH2, 333. Nietzsche is clearly tongue-in-cheek here: he plays on the notion that monastic renunciation (*Entsagung*) from intercourse (*Verkehr*) can serve as a means of intensifying the most sensuous of pleasures, a transformation which he captures through a playful shift from the high, spiritual discourse of the ascetic sublime to the "low," vulgar gastronomic register of *Leckerbissen*.
29. HAH2, 364.
30. See D, 214.
31. Melanie Klein, "On the Sense of Loneliness," in *Envy and Gratitude*, op. cit., 304.
32. HAH1, 376.
33. Donald W. Winnicott, "Communicating and Not Communicating Leading to a Study of Certain Opposites," in *The Maturational Process and the Facilitating Environment*, op. cit., 187.
34. I borrow this last phrase from Bernd Magnus, "Asceticism and Eternal Recurrence: A Bridge Too Far," *The Southern Journal of Philosophy* XXXVII, Supplement, 1999, 35–52.
35. GS, 238.
36. Ida Overbeck, "*Erinnerungen,*" *Conversations with Nietzsche*, op. cit., 110.
37. See OBM §16, 146 where Schopenhauer quotes Jean-Jacques Rousseau, *Émile*, op. cit., 184.
38. GS, 338.
39. TSZ I, "On Love of One's Neighbour."
40. HAH2, 62.

41. In *Ecce Homo*, Nietzsche observes that the purpose of his "art of style" is "to communicate a state, an inner tension of *pathos* through signs, including the tempo of the signs"; see EH, "Why I Write Such Excellent Books," 4.

42. Immanuel Kant, *The Doctrine of Virtue*, translated by Mary J. Gregor, 1964, Harper and Row, New York, §34.

43. GS, 239, emphasis added.

44. Immanuel Kant, *The Metaphysical Principles of Virtue*, op. cit., §34.

45. Cf Victor Wolfenstein, *Inside/Outside Nietzsche*, op. cit., 45–55.

46. GP, 66, emphasis added. "Hatred of favour," as La Rochefoucauld wryly observes, "is nothing but love of favour. Resentment at not enjoying it finds consolation in the balm of contempt for those who do, and we withhold our respect since we cannot deprive them of what commands that of everybody else"; see La Rochefoucauld, *Maxims*, op. cit., no. 55.

47. GP, 67. For an analysis of John Rawls's attempt to save his principle of justice from Freud's derivation of the principles of universalisability and equality from envy, see John Forrester, *Dispatches from the Freud Wars: Psychoanalysis and Its Passions*, 1997, Harvard University Press, Cambridge, Mass., ch. 1.

48. TSZ, "Zarathustra's Prologue," 5.

49. On this point see, Jeffrey B. Abramson, *Liberation and Its Limits: The Moral and Political Thought of Freud*, 1984, Beacon Press, Boston, 125–29. As Graham Little shows, Freud never conceived the bond of friendship as anything other than a continuation of the Oedipal family drama. "Freud experienced and understood friendship," he writes, "not as an opening onto a spiritual world, a world without rivalry and rebellion . . . but a continuation of his own Just So world in which men struggle with one each other or are coerced into a tepid brotherhood in *lèse majesté* or self-defence. It can only be a truce, an uncertain sociability based on limited expectations and the acceptance of ambivalent feelings"; see Graham Little, *Friendship: Being Ourselves with Others*, 1993, The Text Publishing Company, Melbourne, 46.

50. HAH1, 62.

51. HAH1, 614.

52. HAH1, 300.

53. D, 304.

54. On the association between Callicles and Nietzsche, see, for example, Alexander Koyre, *Discovering Plato*, translated by Leonora Rosenfield, 1945, Columbia University Press, New York, 61.

55. HAH1, 499.

56. *Helvia*, 332.

57. TSZ I, "On Love of One's Neighbour."

58. Graham Little, *Friendship*, op. cit., 15.

59. D, 144.

60. See Robert Graves, *The Greek Myths*, vols. 1 and 2, 1955, Penguin, Harmondsworth, UK, 85a–e.

61. D, 133. *Mitleid* is the standard German translation of the Greek, Latin and French terms (respectively) *eleos/oiktos*, *misericordia* and *pitié*. Schopenhauer's and Nietzsche's English translators render *Mitleid* interchangeably as pity, compassion or sympathy. David Cartwright argues that *compassion* rather than pity is a better translation of Schopenhauer's *Mitleid* because this term lacks the pejorative connotations

of condescension and superiority to the sufferer that the word pity has gradually acquired. However, as the previous chapter demonstrates, the notion of *Mitleid* found in Schopenhauer's moral psychology in fact warrants the use of the term pity rather than compassion. This chapter suggests that the nonpejorative notion of *compassion* is better applied to Nietzsche's understanding of the regard for the other built into his notion of friendship. Importantly in this context, as Martha Nussbaum points out, Nietzsche was aware of the conceptual complexities associated with the various words other languages employ to denote the experience of a painful emotion occasioned by the awareness of another's misfortune. Nietzsche, she observes, comments on German and French texts, sometimes using the German *Mitleid* when he wants to pun on the notion that the pitier's *Leid* is not *mit dem Leid*, sometimes the French word *pitié* when he scoffs at Rousseau and the democratic tradition; see David C. Cartwright, "Schopenhauer's Compassion and Nietzsche's Pity," *Schopenhauer Jahrbuch*, 1988, 357–58; and Martha C. Nussbaum, *Upheavals of Thought*, op. cit., 301–4.

62. D, 47.

63. See *Nietzsche Werke: Kritische Gesamtausgabe*, edited by Giorgio Colli and Mazzino Montinari, 1971, Walter de Gruyter, Berlin, 3 [86], no. 150, *Frühjahr* 1880.

64. TSZ II, "On Those Who Pity."

65. OBM §19, 174.

66. HAH1, 46.

67. Graham Little, *Friendship*, op. cit., 58.

68. HAH1, 46.

69. D, 489.

70. Simon Critchley, *On Humour*, op. cit., 103.

71. HAH2, 251.

72. HAH1, 624.

73. ON, 89.

74. TSZ I, "On Love of One's Neighbour."

75. On this point see, C. Fred Alford, *The Psychoanalytic Theory of Greek Tragedy*, op. cit., 14. "Projective identification," he claims, "is not necessarily bad or pathological, even though it always involves a certain alienation of self, in which part of the self is split off and experienced in others. Projective identification may, for example, represent an attempt to communicate with another by almost literally sharing emotions. . . . Not by its presence but by the degree to which projective identification is associated with fantasies of omnipotent control over the recipient of projection, is key to determining the degree of pathology involved."

76. Graham Parkes identifies the importance Nietzsche assigns to projection in the constitution of our experiences and relationships. "[W]hile Freud retained, in spite of his appreciation of the prevalence of projection and introjection, the traditional realist's suspicion of fantasy, Jung followed Nietzsche in assigning a crucial role to the imagination in the constitution of experience"; see Graham Parkes, "Nietzsche and Jung: Ambivalent Appreciation," in Jacob Golomb, Weaver Santaniello and Ronald Lehrer (eds), *Nietzsche and Depth Psychology*, 1999, SUNY, Albany, 208.

77. D, 118.

78. HAH2, 61.

79. Jacques Lacan, *The Four Fundamental Concepts of Psychoanalysis*, translated by Alan Sheridan, 1977, Penguin, Harmondsworth, UK, 367.

80. D, 214; see also TSZ II, "On Those Who Pity": "And if a friend should do you wrong, then say: 'I forgive you what you did to me; but that you did it to *yourself*— how could I forgive that?' Thus does all great love talk: it overcomes even forgiveness and pitying.'"

81. I borrow the notion of "vision's reciprocal, intersubjective, communicative potential" from Martin Jay, who uses it in his critique of Foucault's antiocularism and its neglect of the mutual glance; see Martin Jay, *Downcast Eyes: The Denigration of Vision in Twentieth-Century Thought*, 1994, University of California Press, Berkeley, 414.

82. See also HAH1, 587: "it requires a more powerful vision and a better will to promote what is becoming and is imperfect than it does to see through it in its imperfections and to disavow it."

83. In defending pity, Martha Nussbaum observes, Aristotle argues that pitying another and respecting them are not mutually incompatible. Aristotle claims that when others are dislodged from their *eudaimonia* this merits pity, but though we may pity them, their nobility of character can still "shine through" in the way they bear misfortune; and this manner of bearing their misfortune, according to Aristotle, is what merits our *respect*. Hence we pity their condition, but respect the manner in which they bear their misfortune. Nussbaum uses Aristotle's point to suggest that Nietzsche is wrong to claim that we cannot respect those we pity or, to put it another way, that a pitied person cannot also win our respect. However, as this aphorism makes clear, Nietzsche's argument is with certain kinds of pity that do preclude respect, not with compassion *per se*. Indeed, he transfigures the notion of pity: that is to say, for Nietzsche we respect sufferers not just because they bear their suffering nobly, but because they have the capacity to bestow a world upon us—or, to use Nietzsche's metaphors, because we see in them the bright disk of the moon. Nussbaum quotes from Aristotle's *Nicomachean Ethics* where, in the context of claiming that bad luck or misfortune can adversely affect our *eudaimonia*, he makes the following observation: "Nevertheless even here, when a man bears patiently a number of heavy disasters, not because he does not feel them but because he has a high and generous nature, his nobility shines through"; see Martha Nussbaum, "Pity and Mercy," op. cit., 158; Aristotle, *The Nicomachean Ethics*, translated by J. A. K. Thomson, 1976, Penguin Books, Harmondsworth, UK, Bk 1, ch. 10.

84. I owe this point to Graham Little, *Friendship*, op, cit., 58.

85. TSZ I, "On Love of One's Neighbour."

Consoling Conclusions

What a funny fellow you are Socrates. The people that you call moderate
are the half-witted.

Callicles, *Gorgias*, 491e

Perhaps it is because Nietzsche engages so profoundly with classical, Hellenistic and Roman philosophies and cultures that we find it easy to conceptualise his thinking in terms of the ancient quarrel between philosophy
and poetry. Framed in this way, it becomes apparent that, whether as his critics or defenders, we almost universally take it for granted that his most significant intervention in this perennial debate is to defend the poets and
sophists against Plato's desire to excommunicate them from the well-
ordered *polis*.[1] In terms of the culture wars, it seems, we feel on safe ground
identifying Nietzsche with the inspired poets and the sophistic, agonistic il-
lusionists. As Martin Jay observes, at least "in certain of his moods" Nietzsche is commonly seen as the key modern philosophical fount of "aestheticism," which Jay defines as a conceptual constellation that affirms
"irrationality, illusion, fantasy, myth, sensual seduction, the imposition of
the will, and inhumane indifference to ethical, religious, or cognitive considerations."[2] But, as Michael Janover acutely cautions, "Nietzsche is never
there where you find him."[3] I have suggested that we must significantly qualify our classification of Nietzsche's place in the history of philosophy and
psychology in light of those other forgotten or barely noticed *Stimmungen*.
He expresses these moods through what one of his fiercest critics uneasily
admits is the undeniably more "pacific tenor" of the middle works.[4] While
it is perhaps true that Nietzsche's philosophy is one more footnote to Plato,

Nietzsche, it must be said, does not merely reprise, by turns, the sophistic, bellicose and foolish voices of Gorgias, Callicles and Ion.[5]

Unfortunately, the philosophy and psychology of Nietzsche's middle works have suffered a peculiar fate. On the one hand, as noted in the introduction, many critics, including his severest contemporary opponents, simply consign this period to oblivion, while his French celebrants barely acknowledge its existence. On the other hand, commentators who do examine Nietzsche's middle works for the most part adopt an unwritten convention, which decrees that we should use them only as sticks with which to chastise him for the allegedly irrational, immoral aestheticism of his earlier and/or later works. There is something distinctly odd in this interpretive strategy. For if, as they speculate, the most mature, intellectually respectable and perhaps fruitful thinking in Nietzsche's corpus can be found in his middle works, then these works, rather than his early or later texts, would seem to warrant our closest critical attention. Perhaps the highly chequered political and cultural influence of his early and late works explains, and to some extent justifies, this narrowing of our focus. Yet, if, as some of his staunchest critics claim, *Daybreak* and *The Gay Science* offer us a "very plausible and attractive Nietzsche," a "realist, rationalist, a merry demystifier," then they establish compelling intellectual grounds for examining this other Nietzsche without themselves pursuing this course.[6]

The oddity of the common interpretive manoeuvre that excludes Nietzsche's middle period from claiming our attention as his most intellectually promising work is perhaps best illustrated in Bruce Detwiler's critique of Nietzsche's antidemocratic, elitist politics. Detwiler treats the middle works as "anomalies" because they fail to accord with his portrait of Nietzsche's politics and personality.[7] He acknowledges, for example, that in these works Nietzsche praises democratic institutions as bulwarks "against physical and spiritual enslavement," as "measures of quarantine against the old plague of tyrannical desires," which can protect "the orchards of culture."[8] It is Nietzsche's "personal ideal" during this period, he asserts, that forms the foundation of this political perspective, that is, his affirmation of "wise moderation" and a "pacific disposition" that holds that it is *"better to perish rather than to make oneself hated and feared."*[9]

Yet, like many Nietzsche critics, having spent the greater part of his energy chastising Nietzsche for his Calliclean immoralism, Detwiler does a double take when he acknowledges this other Nietzsche. When Nietzsche refuses to play the Calliclean role that he has assigned him, Detwiler suggests that this period has a "less interesting (because less original) character."[10] Apparently, the democratic, moderate and temperate Nietzsche is too boring to deserve our critical scrutiny. But is this not a faint echo of Callicles ridiculing Socrates' moderation as half-witted? Does it not, we might wonder, illustrate a strange reversal of roles: when Nietzsche refuses to play the Calliclean role they assign him, Nietzsche's critics transform themselves into Callicles and impatiently reprimand him for serving up mediocre, foolish and all too conventional lessons in moderation. To put the point another way, when Nietzsche becomes Socrates' kin, his critics turn away from him precisely for defending the things which they had hitherto reprimanded him for *failing* to defend: reason, temperance and so on. As Socrates and Nietzsche suspect, when they speak of moderation and measure, the majority "hardly listen" and "confuse them with boredom and mediocrity."[11] In this regard, perhaps, Nietzsche failed to realise that he would have to play a comedy not only to satisfy the admirers of his youthful, fawn-skinned Dionysian self, but to satisfy his critics as well:

> *Comedy.*—We sometimes harvest love and honour for deeds or works which we have long since cast from us like a skin: and then we are easily tempted to play the comedians of our own past and throw our old hide back over our shoulders—and not only out of vanity but also out of goodwill towards our admirers.[12]

In this book I have attempted to listen carefully to the moderate, middle Nietzsche and in doing so extend a new terrain in Nietzsche studies that alters the way he is commonly interpreted and the role he is assigned in the history of philosophy and psychology.[13] It suggests that one of Nietzsche's most important philosophical and psychological contributions lies in the attempt he undertakes in the middle works to bring together the Hellenistic and Stoic image and therapy of self-composure with his acute psychological insight into the complex modulations of narcissism. In other words, Nietzsche attempts to bridge the span between the two Delphic mottoes: "Nothing too Much" and "Know Thyself!"

In this respect, Nietzschean moderation is anything but half-witted or foolish. If such moderation is possible at all, he claims, it is the outcome of a complex elaboration of wit—a work on the self that requires the two powers and meanings of wit: humour and knowledge. Nietzsche describes his own self-examination as a "descent into the ultimate depths" that he is driven to undertake by suffering, by "everything that wounds us."[14] For Nietzsche "Know Thyself!" is the imperative of suffering. He adopts the myths of Orpheus' and Odysseus' descent into the Underworld as allegories of his own downgoing:

> *Leaving in Hades.*—There are many things we must leave in the Hades of half-conscious feelings, and not desire to redeem [*erlösen*] them out of their shadow existence, otherwise they will, as thoughts and words, become our demonic masters and cruelly demand our blood.[15]

Like Orpheus, Nietzsche is compelled to descend into Hades in order to save himself from suffering and grief. If we heed Nietzsche's modification of the myth, however, we can clarify his notion of the link between self-knowledge and moderation. Orpheus descends into the underworld and with the enchantment of his music attempts to win back his love, Eurydice, from the king of the shades; the pain of losing her, he confesses in his song, is too great for him to endure. Orpheus descends as a redeemer of his love, and it is his music that he uses to enchant the shades: "As he sang . . . the bloodless ghosts were in tears: Tantalus made no effort to reach the waters that ever shrank away, Ixion's wheel stood still in wonder, the vultures ceased to gnaw Tityus' liver, and Sisyphus sat idle on the rock. Then for the first time, they say, the Furies were wet with tears, for they were overcome with his singing."[16] According to Herbert Marcuse, Orpheus inaugurates the "Great Refusal" of mortality and loss, whose psychological source he claims lies in our phantasy of primary narcissism, or, in Proustian terms, an "imaginary *temps perdu.*"[17] Orpheus, Marcuse claims, embodies the "aesthetic dimension" which he circumscribes as "the redemption of pleasure, the halt of time, the absorption of death; silence, sleep, night, paradise—the Nirvana principle not as death, but as life."[18]

By contrast, Nietzsche focuses on the failure of the redemptive return of love or life that is narrated in Orpheus' ill-fated journey to the underworld. It is precisely the necessary failure of redemption that he recalls in his suggestion that we must leave many things in the realm of Hades. Orpheus descends into Hades as a redeemer, to win back Eurydice, and in doing so to reclaim a life without the possibility of loss or grief. Nietzsche also descends, but, as he says, not as a redeemer (*Erlöser*) intent on reclaiming an original condition of love without loss, and time without decay. Indeed, if we follow Nietzsche in recasting his psychological argument in terms of this myth, then his claim is that we suffer our worst malaises through our refusal to yield to reality and to endure grief, our desire to follow Orpheus and redeem this imaginary *temps perdu.*

As I have argued throughout this book, according to Nietzsche and Freud, it is our inability to mourn the loss of our majestic plenitude that engenders vengeance and, when it turns back on itself, the violence of melancholia. Or, as Nietzsche expresses the point with the aid of another Greek myth of descent, that of Odysseus, when we attempt to redeem our shades they become demonic masters who cruelly demand our blood. From Homer's narration of Odysseus' descent, we discover that we must feed the shades blood before they are able to find words and thoughts.[19] As Nietzsche see it, the attempt to redeem our primary narcissism, to recapture perfect presence, leads to the melancholic malaise in which we feed on our own grief, an all-consuming grief, as we say, or to the various kinds of vengefulness in which we feast on the sweetness of the other's sorrow, a sweetness sweeter than trickling honey.[20]

By contrast with Marcuse, Nietzsche descends not in order to redeem primary narcissism, but to understand the composition and decomposition of the psyche in its conflict with loss and necessity. When we hope for a resurrection of a phantasy of plenitude, he argues, we can only make the human condition, which he, along with Schopenhauer, construes in terms of the figure of loss, appear as a shadow world. As Nietzsche first learned in taking his leave of Schopenhauer, the melancholic malaise eventually ends in a flight from this world of fleeting appearances and perishing beauties. In what is at once both a reference to his own therapeutic project and to the ailments that it treats, Nietzsche writes: "every metaphysics and physics which knows some finale, some final state of some sort, every predominantly aesthetic or religious craving for some Apart, Beyond, Outside, Above, permits the question whether it was not sickness that inspired the philosopher."[21]

It is in his response to his own sickness that Nietzsche stands at the crossroads of Hellenistic-Stoic therapy and modern depth psychology: in the attempt to achieve Stoic composure and moderation Nietzsche descends so that he can understand the damage and violence we inflict on ourselves and others through our subterranean strategies for denying loss and restoring an illusion of majestic plenitude. We must descend, Nietzsche believes, so that we can mediate. In other words, he holds that we can only moderate or temper narcissism by acknowledging its power and understanding its unconscious pathological stratagems. Nietzsche comprehends this descent as the means of forging the psychical resources of a mature individualism: that is, an ego that can act as a "frontier creature," as Freud aptly describes it, that can mediate and negotiate between narcissistic wishes and the realm of necessity, between the underworld and reality.[22]

As we have seen, this mediation can take the form of the Cynic-Stoic *askēsis* of endurance through which we learn to bear our solitude without *ressentiment*. Nietzsche's therapeutic conception of philosophy can also take the form of that Stoic work on the self that we have called humouring ourselves. Here Nietzsche and after him Freud see that Stoic measure depends on rescuing a vestige of our grand, limitless self, the higher self or ego ideal. Like a good friend, this higher self gives us the light we need to navigate when we are in danger of shipwreck, or, like a good parent, assures us that though we suffer shipwreck we have in fact navigated well. It makes our comedy of errors something we could wish to live again and again. Humouring ourselves is thus one of those subtle transformations of our narcissism that is integral to Nietzsche's Odyssean art of living.

NOTES

1. Eric Havelock's account of this clash between two different philosophies and styles of education remains the *locus classicus* on this issue; see Eric A. Havelock, *Preface to Plato*, 1963, Cambridge, Mass.

2. Martin Jay, "'The Aesthetic Ideology' as Ideology; or, What Does It Mean to Aestheticize Politics," op. cit., 45.

3. Michael Janover, "Review of Paul Patton (ed.), *Nietzsche, Feminism and Political Theory*," in *Political Theory Newsletter* 6, no. 1, 1994, 80–83, 80.

4. Bruce Detwiler, *Nietzsche and the Politics of Aristocratic Radicalism*, 1990, University of Chicago Press, Chicago, 179.

5. J. Peter Euben, *Corrupting Youth: Political Education, Democratic Culture, and Political Theory*, 1997, Princeton University Press, Princeton, N.J., 227–28. It is a common rhetorical strategy in Nietzschean criticism to assign him the role of Callicles' modern avatar; see, for example, Frederick Appel, *Nietzsche contra Democracy*, op. cit., 46, fn. 6. However, as Keith Ansell-Pearson points out in his comments on the *Genealogy of Morals*, contra Callicles, Nietzsche derives the origins of law from strength rather than from weakness or reactivity, and the identification of Nietzsche with Callicles on this issue is therefore "quite superficial"; Keith Ansell-Pearson, *An Introduction to Nietzsche as Political Thinker*, op. cit., 218, fn. 3.

6. André Comte-Sponville "The Brute, the Sophist, and the Aesthete: 'Art in the Service of Illusion,'" op. cit., 30.

7. Bruce Detwiler, *Nietzsche and the Politics of Aristocratic Radicalism*, op. cit., 171. It should be noted that to call the "middle years" anomalous is a tendentious judgement, for between 1876–1882 Nietzsche wrote five sustained works, and by reissuing as one volume *Human, All Too Human: Assorted Opinions and Maxims* and *The Wanderer and His Shadow*, Nietzsche himself oversaw the transformation of HAH, a text which on its own already comprises more aphorisms than any of his other texts, into his biggest literary monument. This compilation covers a great array of topics and, arguably, in greater detail than his later published texts: 1396 numbered notes, plus the poem epilogue of HAH1, the dialogues that bookend WS and the two 1886 Prefaces.

8. Ibid. Detwiler quotes from WS, 289, and WS, 275. "This emphasis," he writes, "is in tension with the spirit of *The Birth of Tragedy*, which is in part a paean to the god of excess, Dionysus, and it is in tension with a prominent strand in the later writings which applauds the untrammeled expression of the will to power on a variety of levels"; 178.

9. Ibid., Detwiler quotes from HAH1, 631; WS, 284.

10. Ibid., 171.

11. HAH2, 230. In this aphorism Nietzsche indirectly chastises Callicles for failing to heed Socrates and for confusing self-mastery and self-control with boredom and mediocrity. For Callicles' attack on Socrates' notion of moderation as nothing more than weakness disguised as virtue and a living death, see Plato, *Gorgias*, 491e–492d.

12. HAH2, 393.

13. See also Ruth Abbey, *Nietzsche's Middle Period*, op. cit.

14. GS, preface, 2.

15. HAH2, 374.

16. Ovid, *Metamorphoses*, op. cit., bk X, 226.

17. Herbert Marcuse, *Eros and Civilization*, op. cit., 139; Herbert Marcuse, *An Essay on Liberation*, 1969, Beacon Press, Boston, 90. "From the myth of Orpheus to the novel of Proust," Marcuse writes, "happiness and freedom have been linked with the

recapture of time"; *Eros and Civilization,* 186. Joshua Landy's canny exploration of Nietzsche and Proust illuminates both their conceptions of the art of living; see his essay "Nietzsche, Proust and The Will-to-Ignorance," *Philosophy and Literature* 26, 2002, 1–23.

    18. Herbert Marcuse, *Eros and Civilization,* op. cit., 135.

    19. Homer, *Odyssey,* bk XI, ll. 35–51.

    20. Homer, *Achilles,* bk XVIII, ll. 107–10.

    21. GS, preface, 2. Commenting on this section of the preface, Keith Ansell-Pearson rightly observes that "Nietzsche knows that *his* philosophy is born of sickness"; Keith Ansell-Pearson, "Toward the *Übermensch*: Reflections on the Year of Nietzsche's *Daybreak*," op. cit., 138.

    22. EI, 398.

Bibliography

Abbey, Ruth, "Beyond Metaphor and Misogyny: Women in Nietzsche's Middle Period," *Journal of the History of Philosophy* 34, no. 2, April 1996, 244–56.

——, *Nietzsche's Middle Period*, 2000, Oxford University Press, London.

——, "Circles, Ladders and Stars: Nietzsche on Friendship," in Preston King and Heather Devere (eds.), *The Challenge to Friendship in Modernity*, 2000, Frank Cass, London, 50–73.

Abbey, Ruth, and Frederick Appel, "Nietzsche and the Will to Politics," *Review of Politics* 60, no. 1, Winter 1998, 83–114.

Abrams, Meyer H., *Naturalism and Supernaturalism: Tradition and Revolution in Romantic Literature*, 1971, W.W. Norton & Co., New York.

Abramson, Jeffrey B., *Liberation and Its Limits: The Moral and Political Thought of Freud*, 1984, Beacon Press, Boston.

Adorno, Theodor, "Wagner, Nietzsche and Hitler," *Kenyon Review*, 1946, IX, no. 1, 155–62.

Adorno, Theodor, and Max Horkheimer, *Dialectic of Enlightenment*, 1979, translated by John Cummings, Verso, London.

Alford, C. Fred, *Narcissism: Socrates, the Frankfurt School, and Psychoanalytic Theory*, 1988, Yale University Press, New Haven, Conn., and London.

——, *The Psychoanalytic Theory of Greek Tragedy*, 1992, Yale University Press, New Haven, Conn.

Anderson, Joel, "The Third Generation of the Frankfurt School," *Intellectual History Newsletter* 22, 2000.

Anderson, Lorin, "Freud, Nietzsche," *Salmagundi*, no. 47–48, Winter-Spring 1980, 3–29.

Anderson, R. Lanier, and Joshua Landy, "Philosophy as Self-Fashioning: Alexander Nehamas's Art of Living," *Diacritics*, 31, 1, Spring 2001, 25–54.

Andreas-Salomé, Lou, "The Dual Orientation of Narcissism," *The Psychoanalytic Quarterly* 31, 1962, 3–30.

——, *Nietzsche*, edited and translated by Siegfried Mandel, 1988, Black Swan Books, Redding Ridge.

Ansell-Pearson, Keith, *Nietzsche Contra Rousseau: A Study of Nietzsche's Moral and Political Thought*, 1991, Cambridge University Press, Cambridge.

——, "Nietzsche on Autonomy and Morality: The Challenge to Political Theory," *Political Studies* 39, 1991, 270–86.

——, "Nietzsche, The Will and Modernity," in Keith Ansell-Pearson (ed.), *Nietzsche and Modern German Thought*, 1991, Routledge, London.

——, "Who Is the *Übermensch*? Time, Truth, and Woman in Nietzsche," *Journal of the History of Ideas* LIII, no. 2, April–June, 1992, 309–31.

——, "Toward the Comedy of Existence: On Nietzsche's New Justice," in Keith Ansell-Pearson and Howard Caygill (ed.), *The Fate of the New Nietzsche*, 1993, Avebury Press, Aldershot, UK, 265–82.

——, "Towards the *Übermensch*: Reflections on the Year of Nietzsche's Daybreak," *Nietzsche-Studien* 23, 1994, 123–45.

——, *An Introduction to Nietzsche as Political Thinker: The Perfect Nihilist*, 1994, Cambridge University Press, Cambridge.

——, "The Significance of Michel Foucault's Reading of Nietzsche: Power, the Subject, and Political Theory," in Peter Sedgwick (ed.), *Nietzsche: A Critical Reader*, 1995, Blackwell, Oxford, 13–30.

Appel, Frederick, *Nietzsche contra Democracy*, 1999, Cornell University Press, Ithaca, N.Y.

Arendt, Hannah, *On Revolution*, 1973, Penguin Books, Harmondsworth, UK.

Assoun, Paul-Laurent, *Freud and Nietzsche*, translated by Richard L. Collier Jr., 2000, Athlone Press, London.

Augustine, *City of God against the Pagans*, translated by Henry Bettenson, 1984, Penguin, Harmondsworth, UK.

Bachelard, Gaston, *The Poetics of Reverie*, translated by Daniel Russell, 1969, Orion Press, New York.

Barnes, Jonathon, "Nietzsche and Diogenes Laertius," *Nietzsche-Studien* 15, 1986, 16–40.

Barth, Karl, "Humanity without the Fellow-Man: Nietzsche's Superman and Christian Morality," translated by G. W. Bromiley, in James C. O'Flaherty, Timothy F. Sellner and Robert M. Helms (eds.), *Studies in Nietzsche and the Judaeo-Christian Tradition*, 1985, University of North Carolina Press, Chapel Hill, 353–74.

Bataille, Georges, *On Nietzsche*, translated by Bruce Boone, 1992, Paragon House, New York.

——, "Friendship," *Parallax* 7, no. 1, 2001, 3–15.

Baudelaire, Charles, "The Painter of Modern Life," in *Baudelaire: Selected Writings on Art and Artists*, translated by P. E. Charvet, 1972, Penguin Books, Harmondsworth, UK.

——, *Intimate Journals*, translated by Christopher Isherwood, 1983, City Lights Books, San Francisco.

Bauemer, M. L., "Nietzsche and the Tradition of the Dionysian," translated by T. F. Sellner, in J. C. O'Flaherty, T. F. Sellner and R. M. Helms (eds.), *Studies in Nietzsche and the Classical Tradition*, 1979, University of North Carolina Press, Chapel Hill.

Behler, Ernst, "Nietzsche's Conception of Irony," in S. Kemal, I. Gaskell, D. M. Conway (eds), *Nietzsche, Philosophy and the Arts*, 1998, Cambridge University Press, Cambridge.

Benjamin, Jessica, *The Bonds of Love: Psychoanalysis, Feminism and the Problem of Domination*, 1990, Virago, London.

Bennington, Geoffrey, *Interrupting Derrida*, 2000, Routledge, London.

Berman, Marshall, *All That Is Solid Melts into Air: The Experience of Modernity*, 1983, Verso, London.

Bernstein, Jay M., "Autonomy and solitude," in Keith Ansell-Pearson (ed), *Nietzsche and Modern German Thought*, 1991, Routledge, London, 192–215.

Bespaloff, Rachel, "Priam and Achilles," in Harold Bloom (ed.), *Homer: Modern Critical Views*, 1986, Chelsea House, New York, 33–38.

Bittner, Rüdiger, "Introduction," in Friedrich Nietzsche, *Writings from the Late Notebooks*, edited by Rüdiger Bittner and translated by Kate Sturge, 2003, Cambridge University Press, Cambridge, esp. ix–xv.

Bloom, Allan, *Love and Friendship*, 1993, Simon & Schuster, New York.

Blumenberg, Hans, *Shipwreck with Spectator: Paradigm of a Metaphor for Existence*, translated by Steven Rendell, 1997, MIT Press, Cambridge, Mass.

Bouchindhomme, Christian, "Foucault, Morality and Criticism," in *Michel Foucault: Philosopher*, translated by Timothy J. Armstrong, 1992, Harvester, New York, 317–27.

Bouwsma, William J., "The Two Faces of Humanism," in Heiko A. Oberman and Thomas A. Brady (eds.), *Itinerarium Italicum: The Profile of the Italian Renaissance in the Mirror of its European Transformations*, 1975, Brill, Leiden, 3–30.

Branham, R. Bracht, and Marie-Coile Goulet-Gaze (eds.), *The Cynics: The Cynic Movement in Antiquity and Its Legacy*, 1996, University of California, Berkeley.

Brint, Michael, *Tragedy and Denial: The Politics of Difference in Western Political Thought*, 1991, Westview Press, Boulder, Colo.

Brown, Norman O., *Life against Death: The Psychoanalytic Meaning of History*, 1970, Sphere Books, London.

Butler, E. M., *The Tyranny of Greece over Germany: A Study of the Influence Exercised by Greek Art and Poetry over the Great German Writers of the Eighteenth, Nineteenth and Twentieth Centuries*, 1935, Cambridge University Press, Cambridge.

Calder, William Musgrave, III, "The Wilamowitz-Nietzsche Struggle: New Documents and a Reappraisal," *Nietzsche-Studien* 12, 1983, 214–54.

Calinescu, Matei, *Five Faces of Modernity*, 1987, Duke University Press, Durham, N.C.

Carroll, David, *Paraesthetics: Foucault, Lyotard and Derrida*, 1987, Methuen, New York.

Cartwright, David E., "Kant, Schopenhauer and Nietzsche on the Morality of Pity," *The Journal of the History of Ideas* XXL/1, January–March 1984, 83–98.

——, "Schopenhauer's Compassion and Nietzsche's Pity," *Schopenhauer Jahrbuch*, 69, 1988, 557–67.

——, "The Last Temptation of Zarathustra," *The Journal of the History of Philosophy* 31/1, January 1993, 49–65.

——, "Schopenhauer's Narrower Sense of Morality," in Christopher Janaway (ed.), *The Cambridge Companion to Schopenhauer*, 1999, Cambridge University Press, Cambridge.

Casey, John, *Pagan Ethics: An Essay in Ethics*, 1990, Oxford University Press, Oxford.

Caygill, Howard, "Affirmation and Eternal Return in the Free-Spirit Trilogy," in Keith Ansell-Pearson (ed.), *Nietzsche and Modern German Thought*, 1991, Routledge, London, 216–40.

Chamberlain, Leslie, *Nietzsche in Turin: The End of the Future*, 1996, Quartet Books, London.

Chapelle, Danielle, *Nietzsche and Psychoanalysis*, 1993, SUNY, Albany.

Chasseguet-Smirgel, Janine, *The Ego Ideal: A Psychoanalytic Essay on the Malady of the Ideal*, translated by Paul Barrows, 1985, Free Association Books, London.

Chytry, Joseph, *The Aesthetic State: A Quest in Modern German Thought*, 1989, University of California Press, Berkeley.

Coles, Romand, "Foucault's Dialogical Artistic Ethos," *Theory, Culture and Society* 8, 1991, 99–120.

——, *Self, Power, Others: Political Theory and Dialogical Ethics*, 1992, Cornell University Press, Ithaca, N.Y.

Conant, James, "Nietzsche's Perfectionism: A Reading of *Schopenhauer as Educator*," in Richard Schacht (ed.), *Nietzsche's Postmoralism: Essays on Nietzsche's Prelude to Philosophy's Future*, 2001, Cambridge University Press, Cambridge, 181–257.

Connolly, William E., "Taylor, Foucault and Otherness," *Political Theory* 13, no. 3, August 1985, 365–76.

——, *Political Theory and Modernity*, 1993, Cornell University Press, Ithaca, N.Y.

——, *The Augustinian Imperative: A Reflection on the Politics of Morality*, 1993, Sage, Newbury Park, Calif.

Conway, Daniel, "Solving the Problem of Socrates: Nietzsche's Zarathustra as Political Irony," *Political Theory* 16 no. 2, May 1988, 257–80.

——, "Thus Spoke Rorty: The Perils of Narrative Self-Creation," *Philosophy and Literature* 15, 1991, 103–10.

——, "Disembodied Perspectives, Nietzsche *contra* Rorty," *Nietzsche-Studien* 21, 1992, 281–89.

——, "Nietzsche's *Doppelgänger*: Affirmation and Resentment in *Ecce Homo*," in Keith Ansell-Pearson and Howard Caygill (eds.), *The Fate of the New Nietzsche*, 1993, Avebury Press, Aldershot, UK, 55–78.

Cooper, David E., "Self and Morality in Schopenhauer and Nietzsche," in Christopher Janaway (ed.), *Willing and Nothingness: Schopenhauer as Nietzsche's Educator*, 1998, Clarendon Press, Oxford.

Cottingham, John, *Philosophy and the Good Life*, 1998, Cambridge University Press, Cambridge.

Critchley, Simon, *Ethics, Politics, Subjectivity*, 1999, Verso, London.

——, *Continental Philosophy*, 2001, Oxford University Press, Oxford.

——, *On Humour*, 2002, Routledge, London and New York.

Dallmayr, Fred, "The Discourse of Modernity: Hegel, Nietzsche, Heidegger (and Habermas)," *Praxis International*, no. 8, January 1989, 377–406.

Dannhauser, Werner, *Nietzsche's View of Socrates*, 1974, Cornell University Press, New York.

Del Caro, Adrian, "Ethical Aesthetic: Schiller and Nietzsche as Critics of the Eighteenth Century," *Germanic Review* 55, vol. LV, 1980, 55–63.

——, *Nietzsche contra Nietzsche: Creativity and the Anti-romantic*, 1989, Louisiana State University Press, Baton Rouge.

Deleuze, Gilles, "Coldness and Cruelty," in *Masochism*, 1991, Zone Books, New York, 15–138.

DeLillo, Don, *Underworld*, 1997, Picador, New York.

Derrida, Jacques, *Politics of Friendship*, translated by George Collins, 1997, Verso, London.

Detwiler, Bruce, *Nietzsche and the Politics of Aristocratic Radicalism*, 1990, University of Chicago Press, Chicago.

Dews, Peter, *Logics of Disintegration: Post-structuralism and the Claims of Critical Theory*, 1987, Verso Books, London.

——, "The Return of the Subject in the Late Foucault," *Radical Philosophy*, no. 51, Spring 1989, 37–41.

——, "Modernity, Self-Consciousness and the Scope of Philosophy: Jürgen Habermas and Dieter Heinrich in Debate," in *The Limits of Disenchantment: Essays on Contemporary European Philosophy*, 1995, Verso, London: New York.

Doctorow, E. L., "Introduction," in Harpo Marx (with Rowland Barber), *Harpo Speaks . . . about New York*, 2000, The Little Bookroom, New York.

Dodds, E. R., *The Greeks and the Irrational*, 1951, University of California Press, Berkeley.

——, "Plato and the Irrational," in *The Ancient Concept of Progress and Other Essays on Literature and Belief*, 1973, Oxford University Press, London, 106–25.

Duckworth, George E., *The Nature of Roman Comedy: A Study in Popular Entertainment*, 1952, Princeton University Press, Princeton, N.J.

Duttman, Alexander Garcia, "'What Is Called Love in All the Languages and Silences of the World': Nietzsche, Genealogy, Contingency," translated by A. Beisswenger and G. Richter, *American Imago* 50, no. 3, 1993, 277–323.

Eagleton, Terry, *The Ideology of the Aesthetic*, 1990, Basil Blackwell, Oxford.

——, *Sweet Violence: The Idea of the Tragic*, 2003, Blackwell, Oxford.

Epictetus, *The Discourses of Epictetus*, translated by P. E. Matheson, in Whitney J. Oates (ed.), *The Stoic and Epicurean Philosophers*, 1940, Random House, New York.

Eribon, Didier, *Michel Foucault*, translated by Betsy Wing, 1991, Harvard University Press, Cambridge.

Euben, J. Peter, *The Tragedy of Political Theory: The Road Not Taken*, 1990, Princeton University Press, Princeton, N.J.

——, *Corrupting Youth: Political Education, Democratic Culture, and Political Theory*, 1997, Princeton University Press, Princeton, N.J.

——, *Platonic Noise*, 2003, Princeton University Press, Princeton, N.J.

Euripides, *The Bacchae and Other Plays*, translated by Philip Vellacott, 1973, Penguin Books, London.

Falzon, Chris, "Foucault's Human Being," *Thesis Eleven*, no. 34, 1993, 1–16.

Ferry, Jean-Luc, *Homo Aestheticus: The Invention of Taste in the Democratic Age*, translated by R. de Loaiza, 1993, University of Chicago Press, Chicago.

Ferry, Jean-Luc, and Alain Renault (eds.), *Why We Are Not Nietzscheans*, translated by R. de Loaiza, 1997, University of Chicago Press, Chicago.

Foucault, Michael, "*Omnes et Simulatum*: Toward a Criticism of 'Political Reason,'" in *The Tanner Lectures on Human Values II*, Sterling McMurrin (ed.), 1981, University of Utah Press, Salt Lake City.

——, "The Order of Discourse," in Michael J. Shapiro (ed.), *Language and Politics*, trans. I. Macleod, 1984, New York University Press, New York.

——, "The Battle for Chastity," in Phillipe Aries and André Béjin (eds.), *Western Sexuality: Practice and Precept on Past and Present Times*, trans. Anthony Forster, 1985, Basil Blackwell, Oxford, 14–25.

Forrester, John, *Dispatches from the Freud Wars: Psychoanalysis and Its Passions*, 1997, Harvard University Press, Cambridge, Mass.

Fraser, Nancy, "Solidarity or Singularity? Richard Rorty between Romanticism and Technocracy," *Praxis International* 8, no. 3, 1988, 257–71.

Freud, Sigmund, "Notes upon a Case of Obsessional Neurosis" (1909), in *Case Histories II*, translated by James Strachey, 1990, Penguin Books, London, 36–128.

———, "Psychoanalytic Notes on an Autobiographical Account of a Case of Paranoia" (1910), in *Case Histories II*, translated by James Strachey, 1990, Penguin Books, London, 138–223.

———, *On the History of the Psychoanalytic Movement* (1914), translated by Joan Riviere, 1967, W. W. Norton & Co., New York.

———, "A Metapsychological Supplement to the Theory of Dreams" (1915), and "The Unconscious," in *On Metapsychology: The Theory of Psychoanalysis*, translated by James Strachey, compiled by Angela Richards, 1991, Penguin Books, 223–44.

———, "On Negation," in *On Metapsychology: The Theory of Psychoanalysis*, trans. James Strachey, 1991, Penguin Books, London.

———, "From the History of an Infantile Neurosis" (1918), and "Schreber," in *Case Histories II*, translated by James Strachey, 1990, Penguin Books, London, 233–366.

Fromm, Erich, "Selfishness and Self-Love," in *Psychiatry: Journal for the Study of Interpersonal Process*, William Alanson Psychiatric Foundation, Washington, vol. 2, 1939, 507–23; reprinted in *The Yearbook of the International Erich Fromm Society*, vol. 5, 1994, LIT-Verlag, Münster, 173–97.

Gadamer, Hans-Georg, "The Drama of Zarathustra," in Michael Gillespie and Tracy B. Strong (eds.), *Nietzsche's New Seas: Explorations in Philosophy, Aesthetics and Politics*, 1988, University of Chicago Press, Chicago, 220–31.

Gay, Peter, *Freud: A Life for Our Time*, 1988, J. M. Dent and Sons, London.

Gillespie, Michael Allen, *Nihilism before Nietzsche*, 1995, University of Chicago Press, 1995.

———, "Nietzsche and the Anthropology of Nihilism," *Nietzsche-Studien* 28, 1999, 141–55.

Gillespie, Michael Allen, and Tracy B. Strong (eds.), *Nietzsche's New Seas: Explorations in Philosophy, Aesthetics and Politics*, 1988, University of Chicago Press, Chicago.

Gilman, Sander L., and David Parent (eds.), *Conversations with Nietzsche: A Life in the Words of His Contemporaries*, translated by David J. Parent, 1987, Oxford University Press, New York.

Gödde, Günter, "Die Antike Therapeutik als Gemeinsamer Bezugpunkt für Nietzsche und Freud," *Nietzsche-Studien*, Bd 32, 2003, 206–25.

Golomb, Jacob, "Freudian Uses and Misuses of Nietzsche," *American Imago* 37, no. 4, Winter 1980, 371–85.

———, *Nietzsche's Enticing Psychology of Power*, 1987, Iowa State University Press, Ames.

——— (ed.), *Nietzsche and Jewish Culture*, 1997, Routledge, London.

Golomb, Jacob, Weaver Santaniello and Ronald Lehrer (eds.), *Nietzsche and Depth Psychology*, 1999, SUNY, Albany.

Grana, Cesar, *Modernity and Its Discontents: French Society and the French Man of Letters in the Nineteenth Century*, 1967, Harper Torchbook, New York.

Graves, Robert, *The Greek Myths*, vols. 1 and 2, 1955, Penguin, Harmondsworth, UK.

Guthrie, W. K. C., *Socrates*, 1971, Cambridge University Press, Cambridge.

Habermas, Jürgen, *The Philosophical Discourses of Modernity: Twelve Letters*, translated by Frederick Lawrence, 1987, MIT Press, Cambridge, Mass.

———, "Individuation through Socialization: On George Herbert Mead's Theory of Subjectivity," in *Postmetaphysical Thinking*, translated by W. M. Hohengarten, 1992, MIT Press, Cambridge, Mass., 149–204.

Hadot, Pierre, "Reflections on the Notion of the 'Cultivation of the Self,'" in *Michel Foucault, Philosopher*, translated by T. J. Armstrong, 1992, Harvester, London, 225–33.

———, *Philosophy as a Way of Life: Spiritual Exercises from Socrates to Foucault*, translated by Michael Chase, 1995, Blackwell, Oxford.

———, *What Is Ancient Philosophy?*, translated by Michael Chase, 2002, Harvard University Press, Cambridge, Mass.

Halperin, David M., *Saint Foucault: Towards a Gay Hagiography*, 1995, Oxford University Press, New York.

Hamacher, Werner, "Disgregation of the Will: Nietzsche on the Individual and Individuality," in Harold Bloom (ed.), *Friedrich Nietzsche*, 1987, Chelsea House, New York.

Handwerk, Gary, "Translator's Afterword," in *Human, All Too Human: A Book for Free Spirits*, vol. 1, 1995, Stanford University Press, Stanford, Calif., 361–79.

Hatab, Lawrence J., *Nietzsche's Life Sentence: Coming to Terms with Eternal Recurrence*, 2005, Routledge, New York.

Havelock, Eric A., *Preface to Plato*, 1963, Harvard University Press, Cambridge, Mass.

Hegel, Georg Wilhelm Friedrich, *The History of Philosophy*, translated by J. Sibree, 1900, George Bell and Sons, London.

———, *Phenomenology of Mind*, translated by J. B. Baillie, 1949, George Allen & Unwin, London.

Heidegger, Martin, "The Word of Nietzsche: 'God Is Dead,'" in *The Question Concerning Technology and Other Essays*, translated with an introduction by W. Lovitt, 1977, Harper and Row, New York, 53–112.

———, "Kant's Doctrine of the Beautiful: Its Misinterpretation by Schopenhauer and Nietzsche," in Peter Sedgwick (ed.), *Nietzsche: A Critical Reader*, 1995, Blackwell, Oxford, 104–110.

Heller, Agnes, *An Ethics of Personality*, 1996, Blackwell, Oxford.

Heller, Erich, "Burckhardt and Nietzsche," in *The Disinherited Mind*, 1961, Penguin Books, Edinburgh, 59–77.

———, *The Artist's Journey to the Interior and Other Essays*, 1968, Vintage Books, New York.

———, "Nietzsche's Terror: Time and the Inarticulate," *Salmagundi*, no. 68–69, Fall 1985–Winter 1986, 78–90.

———, "Introduction," in *Human, All Too Human: A Book for Free Spirits*, translated by R. J. Hollingdale, 1986, Cambridge University Press, Cambridge, vii–xix.

Heller, Peter, *Studies on Nietzsche*, 1980, Bouvier Verlag, Bonn.

———, "Freud in His Relation to Nietzsche," in Jacob Golomb (ed.), *Nietzsche and Jewish Culture*, 1997, Routledge, London and New York, 193–217.

Helm, Robert M., "Plato in the Thought of Nietzsche and Augustine," in James C. O'Flaherty, Timothy F. Sellner, and Robert M. Helm (eds.), *Studies in Nietzsche and the Classical Tradition*, 1979, University of North Carolina Press, Chapel Hill, 16–32.

Higgins, Kathleen M., "Nietzsche on Music," *Journal of the History of Ideas* 47, no. 4, October–December 1986, 663–72.

——, *Nietzsche's Zarathustra*, 1987, Temple University Press, Philadelphia.

——, "Gender in *The Gay Science*," *Philosophy and Literature* 19, no. 2, 1995, 227–47.

——, *Comic Relief*, 2000, Oxford University Press, New York.

Hillis-Miller, J., "Nietzsche in Basel: Writing, Reading," *Journal of Advanced Composition* 13, no. 2, 1993, 311–22.

Hollingdale, R. J., *Nietzsche, the Man and His Philosophy*, 1999, Cambridge University Press, Cambridge.

Homer, *The Odyssey*, translated by E. V. Rieu, 1985, Penguin Books, Harmondsworth, UK.

Honig, Bonnie, *Political Theory and the Displacement of Politics*, 1993, Cornell University Press, Ithaca, N.Y.

Horace, *Odes*, translated by G. Shepherd, 1985, Penguin Books, Harmondsworth, UK.

Hughes, Robert, *Heaven and Hell in Western Art*, 1968, Weidenfeld and Nicholson, London.

Hunter, Ian, "The History of Philosophy and the Persona of the Philosopher," *Modern Intellectual History* 4, 3, 2007, 571–600.

Hutter, Horst, *Shaping the Future: Nietzsche's New Regime of the Soul and Its Ascetic Practices*, 2006, Lexington Books, Lanham, Md.

Irigaray, Luce, *Marine Lover of Friedrich Nietzsche*, translated by Gillian C. Gill, 1991, Columbia University Press, New York.

Janaway, Christopher, *Self and World in Schopenhauer's Philosophy*, 1989, Clarendon Press, Oxford.

——, "Nietzsche, the Self and Schopenhauer," in Keith Ansell-Pearson (ed.), *Nietzsche and Modern German Thought*, 1991, Routledge, London.

—— (ed.), *Willing and Nothingness: Schopenhauer as Nietzsche's Educator*, 1998, Clarendon Press, Oxford.

Janicaud, Dominque, "Rationality, Force and Power," in *Michel Foucault: Philosopher*, translation by Timothy J. Armstrong, 1992, Harvester Wheatsheaf, London, 283–302.

Janover, Michael, "Review of Paul Patton (ed.), *Nietzsche, Feminism and Political Theory*," in *Political Theory Newsletter* 6, no. 1, 1994, 80–83.

——, "The Subject of Foucault," in Clare O'Farrell (ed.), *Foucault: The Legacy*, 1997, Queensland University Press, Queensland, 215–27.

——, "Nostalgias," *Critical Horizons* 1, no. 1, 2000, 113–33.

——, "Mythic Form and Political Reflection in Athenian Tragedy," *Parallax* 9, no. 4, 2003, 41–51.

Jay, Martin, *Marxism and Totality: The Adventures of a Concept from Lukács to Habermas*, 1984, University of California Press, Berkeley.

——, "The Morals of Genealogy: Or Is There a Post-structuralist Ethics?" *The Cambridge Review*, June 1989, 70–74.

——, "Review of Jürgen Habermas," *The Philosophical Discourse of Modernity*, *History and Theory* xxvii, no. 1, 1989, 94–112.

——, "'The Aesthetic Ideology' as Ideology; Or, What Does It Mean to Aestheticize Politics?" *Cultural Critique*, Spring 1992, 42–61.

——, *Downcast Eyes: The Denigration of Vision in Twentieth-Century Thought*, 1994, University of California Press, Berkeley.

——, "Modern and Postmodern Paganism: Peter Gay and Jean-Francois Lyotard," in Martin Jay, *Cultural Semantics: Keywords of Our Times*, 1998, University of Massachusetts Press, Amherst, 181-96.

——, "Diving into the Wreck: Aesthetic Spectatorship at the Fin-de-Siècle," *Critical Horizons* 1, no. 1, February 2000, 93-111.

——, *Songs of Experience: Modern American and European Variations on a Universal Theme*, 2005, University of California Press, Berkeley.

Jurist, Elliot L., *Beyond Hegel and Nietzsche: Philosophy, Culture, and Agency*, 2000, MIT Press, Cambridge, Mass.

Kant, Immanuel, *The Doctrine of Virtue*, translated by Mary J. Gregor, 1964, Harper and Row, New York.

——, *Groundwork of the Metaphysics of Morals*, translated by H. J. Paton, 1964, Harpers Torchbook, New York.

——, *The Critique of Judgement*, translated by Werner S. Pluhar, 1987, Hackett Publishing Company, Indianapolis and Cambridge, Mass.

Kateb, George, *The Inner Ocean: Individualism and Democratic Culture*, 1992, Cornell University Press, Ithaca, N.Y.

Kaufmann, Walter, *Nietzsche: Philosopher, Psychologist, Antichrist*, 1974, Princeton University Press, Princeton, N.J.

Kemal, S., I. Gaskell, D. M. Conway (eds), *Nietzsche, Philosophy and the Arts*, 1998, Cambridge University Press, Cambridge.

Kirk, G. S., *Homer and the Epic*, 1965, Cambridge University Press, Cambridge.

Klein, Melanie, *Envy and Gratitude and Other Works: 1946-1963*, 1990, Virago Press, London.

Klibansky, Raymond, Erwin Panofsky and Fritz Saxl, *Saturn and Melancholy: Studies in the History of Natural Philosophy, Religion, Art*, 1964, Basic Books, New York.

Kohut, Heinz, "On Courage," and "Forms and Transformations of Narcissism," in *Self Psychology and the Humanities: Reflections on a New Psychoanalytic Approach*, 1985, W. W. Norton & Co., New York, 5-50, 97-123.

Koyré, Alexander, *Discovering Plato*, translated by Leonora Rosenfield, 1945, Columbia University Press, New York.

Krell, David Farrell, and Donald L. Bates, *The Good European: Nietzsche's Work Sites in Word and Images*, 1997, University of Chicago Press, Chicago.

Lacan, Jacques, *The Four Fundamental Concepts of Psychoanalysis*, translated by Alan Sheridan, 1977, Penguin, Harmondsworth, UK.

Laertius, Diogenes, *Lives of Eminent Philosophers*, vol. II, translated by R. D. Hicks, 1931, Harvard University Press, Cambridge, Mass.

Lampert, Lawrence, *Nietzsche's Teaching: An Interpretation of Nietzsche's Zarathustra*, 1986, Yale University Press, New Haven, Conn.

——, "Nietzsche's Best Jokes," in J. Lippitt (ed.), *Nietzsche's Future*, 1999, Macmillan Press, London.

Landy, Joshua, "Nietzsche, Proust and the Will-to-Ignorance," *Philosophy and Literature*, vol. 26, 2002, 1-23.

Large, Duncan, "Introduction," in *Twilight of the Idols: Or How to Philosophize with a Hammer*, translated by Duncan Large, 1998, Oxford University Press, Oxford.

Lasch, Christopher, "Introduction," in Janine Chasseguet-Smirgel, *The Ego Ideal: A Psychoanalytic Essay on the Malady of the Ideal*, translated by Paul Barrows, 1985, Free Association Books, London.

Lehrer, Ronald, *Nietzsche's Presence in Freud's Life and Thought: On the Origins of a Psychology of Dynamic Unconscious Mental Functioning*, 1995, SUNY, Albany.

Lingis, Alphonso, "The Imperative to Be Master," *Southwestern Journal of Philosophy* 11, no. 2, 1980, 95–107.

Lippitt, John (ed.), *Nietzsche's Future*, 1999, Macmillan Press, London.

Little, Graham, *Friendship: Being Ourselves with Others*, 1993, The Text Publishing Company, Melbourne.

Lotringer, Sylvère, "Furiously Nietzschean," in Georges Bataille, *On Nietzsche*, translated by Bruce Boone, 1992, Paragon House, New York.

Love, Nancy S., *Marx, Nietzsche and Modernity*, 1986, Columbia University Press, New York.

——, "Epistemology and Exchange: Marx, Nietzsche, and Critical Theory," *New German Critique*, 1987, no. 41, Spring–Summer, 71–94.

Lowith, Karl, *Nietzsche's Philosophy of the Eternal Recurrence of the Same*, translated by J. H. Lomax, Foreword by B. Magnus, 1997, University of California Press, Berkeley.

Lucretius, *On the Nature of the Universe*, translated by R. E. Latham, 1951, Penguin, Harmondsworth, UK.

Magee, Bryan, *The Philosophy of Schopenhauer*, 1983, Clarendon Press, Oxford.

Magnus, Bernd, *Nietzsche's Existential Imperative*, 1978, Indiana University Press, Bloomington.

——, "Nietzsche's Philosophy in 1888: The Will to Power and the *Übermensch*," *The Journal of the History of Philosophy* 24, no. 1, 1986, 79–98.

——, "Asceticism and Eternal Recurrence: A Bridge Too Far," *The Southern Journal of Philosophy* XXXVII, Supplement, 1999, 93–111.

Magnus, Bernd, Stanley Stewart and Jean-Pierre Mileur (eds.), *Nietzsche's Case: Philosophy as/and Literature*, 1993, Routledge, New York.

Mahler, Margaret, et al., *The Psychological Birth of the Human Infant: Symbiosis and Individuation*, 1975, Basic Books, New York.

Mann, Thomas, "Nietzsche's Philosophy in the Light of Recent History," in *Last Essays*, translated by Richard and Clara Winston and Tania and James Stern, 1959, Alfred A. Knopf, New York.

Manning, C. E., *On Seneca's "Ad Marciam,"* 1981, E. J. Brill, Leiden.

Marcuse, Herbert, *Negations: Essays in Critical Theory*, translated by J. J. Shapiro, 1968, Beacon Press, Boston.

——, *An Essay on Liberation*, 1969, Beacon Press, Boston.

——, *Eros and Civilisation: A Philosophical Inquiry into Freud*, 1969, Sphere Books, London.

——, *Five Lectures, Psychoanalysis, Politics and Utopia*, 1970, translated by J. J. Shapiro and Shierry M. Weber, Beacon Press, Boston.

Martin, Nicholas, *Nietzsche and Schiller: Untimely Aesthetics*, 1996, Clarendon Press, Oxford.

McCarthy, Thomas, "The Critique of Pure Reason: Foucault and the Frankfurt School," *Political Theory* 18, no. 3, August 1990, 437–69.

Megill, Allan, *Prophets of Extremity: Nietzsche, Heidegger, Foucault, Derrida*, 1985, University of California Press, Berkeley.

Middleton, Peter, "The Burden of Intersubjectivity: Dialogue as a Communicative Ideal in Postmodern Fiction and Theory," *New Formations*, no. 41, Autumn 2000, 31–56.

Miller, James, *Rousseau: Dreamer of Democracy*, 1984, Yale University Press, New Haven, Conn.

——, "Carnivals of Atrocity," *Political Theory* 18, no. 3, August 1990, 470–91.

——, *The Passion of Michel Foucault*, 1994, Flamingo, London.

Murdoch, Iris, *The Fire and the Sun: Why Plato Banished the Artists*, 1977, Oxford University Press, Oxford.

Murray, Peter Durno, *Nietzsche's Affirmative Morality: A Revaluation Based in the Dionysian World-View*, 1999, W. De Gruyter, Berlin.

Nehamas, Alexander, *Nietzsche: Life as Literature*, 1985, Harvard University Press, Cambridge, Mass.

——, "The Ends of Philosophy: Review of Jürgen Habermas, *The Philosophical Discourse of Modernity*," *New Republic*, May 30, 1988, 32–36.

——, "Nietzsche, Aestheticism and Modernity," in Bernd Magnus and Kathleen M. Higgins (eds.), *The Cambridge Companion to Nietzsche*, 1996, Cambridge University Press, Cambridge.

——, *The Art of Living: Socratic Reflections from Plato to Foucault*, 1998, University of California Press, Berkeley.

——, "Nietzsche and 'Hitler,'" *The Southern Journal of Philosophy* XXXVII, Supplement, 1999, 1–17.

Nichues-Pröbsting, Heinrich, "The Modern Reception of Cynicism," in R. Bracht Branham and Marie-Coile Goulet-Gaze (eds.), *The Cynics*, 1996, University of California Press, Berkeley, 329–65.

Nietzsche, Friedrich, "On the Relationship of Alcibiades' Speech to the Other Speeches, in Plato's *Symposium*," translated by David Scialdone, *Graduate Faculty Philosophy Journal* 15, no. 2, 1991, 3–5.

——, "On Moods," translated by Graham Parkes, *Journal of Nietzsche Studies*, no. 2, 1991, 5–10.

——, "The Birth of Tragic Thought," translated by Ursula Bernis, in *Graduate Faculty Philosophy Journal* 9, no. 2, Fall 1983, 3–15.

——, "On Truth and Lies in a Non-moral Sense," in *Philosophy and Truth: Selections from Nietzsche's Notebooks of the Early 1870s*, translated by Daniel Breazeale, 1979, Humanities Press, Atlantic Highlands, N.J.

Norris, Margot, "Darwin, Nietzsche, Kafka and the Problem of Mimesis," *Modern Language Notes*, vol. 95, 1232–53.

Nussbaum, Martha C. (ed.), *The Poetics of Therapy: Hellenistic Ethics in Its Rhetorical & Literary Context*, Apeiron XXIII, no. 4, 1990.

——, "Transfigurations of Intoxication: Nietzsche, Schopenhauer and Dionysus," *Arion*, 1/2, Spring 1991, 75–111.

——, *The Therapy of Desire: Theory and Practice in Hellenistic Ethics*, 1994, Princeton University Press, Princeton, N.J.

——, "Pity and Mercy: Nietzsche's Stoicism," in Richard Schacht (ed.), *Nietzsche, Genealogy, Morality: Essays on Nietzsche's Genealogy of Morals*, 1994, University of California Press, Berkeley.

——, "The Cult of Personality," *The New Republic*, January 4 and 11, 1999, 32–37.

——, *Upheavals of Thought: The Intelligence of Emotions*, 2001, Cambridge University Press, New York.

O'Leary, Timothy, *Foucault and the Art of Ethics*, 2002, Continuum, London.

Overbeck, Ida, *"Erinnerungen,"* in Sander L. Gilman (ed.), *Conversations with Nietzsche: A Life in the Words of His Contemporaries*, translated by David J. Parent, 1987, Oxford University Press, New York.

Ovid, *Metamorphoses*, translated by Mary Innes, 1968, Penguin, London.

Owen, David, *Nietzsche, Politics and Modernity: A Critique of Liberal Reason*, 1995, Sage, London.

Parkes, Graham, "The Orientation of the Nietzschean Text," in Graham Parkes (ed.), *Nietzsche and Asian Thought*, 1991, University of Chicago Press, Chicago.

———, *Composing the Soul: Reaches of Nietzsche's Psychology*, 1994, University of Chicago Press, Chicago.

———, "Nietzsche and Jung: Ambivalent Appreciation," in Jacob Golomb, Weaver Santaniello and Ronald Lehrer (eds), *Nietzsche and Depth Psychology*, 1999, SUNY, Albany.

———, "Staying Loyal to the Earth: Nietzsche as Ecological Thinker," in John Lippitt (ed.), *Nietzsche's Future*, 1999, Macmillian Press, London, 167–88.

Patton, Paul, "Taylor and Foucault on Power and Freedom," *Political Studies XXXVII*, no. 2, June 1989.

——— (ed.), *Nietzsche, Feminism and Political Theory*, 1993, Allen and Unwin, Sydney.

———, "Foucault's Subject of Power," *Political Theory Newsletter 6*, no. 1, May 1994, 60–71.

Porter, James I., *Nietzsche and the Philology of the Future*, 2000, Stanford University Press, Stanford, Calif.

Rajchman, John, "Habermas's Complaint," *New German Critique*, no. 42, Fall 1988, 163–91.

———, *Truth and Eros: Foucault, Lacan and the Question of Ethics*, 1991, Routledge, New York.

Rampley, Matthew, *Nietzsche, Aesthetics and Modernity*, Cambridge University Press, Cambridge, 2000.

Redner, Harry, *The Ends of Philosophy*, 1986, Croon Helm, Sydney.

Reginster, Bernard, *The Affirmation of Life: Nietzsche on Overcoming Nihilism*, 2006, Harvard University Press, Cambridge, Mass.

Rethy, Robert, "The Tragic Affirmation of the *Birth of Tragedy*," *Nietzsche-Studien 17*, 1988, 1–44.

Reydam-Schils, Gretchen, *The Roman Stoics: Self, Responsibility, and Affection*, 2006, University of Chicago, Chicago.

Ricoeur, Paul, *Freud and Philosophy: An Essay on Interpretation*, translated by Denis Savage, 1970, Yale University Press, New Haven, Conn., and London.

Rist, John M., *Augustine: Ancient Thought Baptised*, 1994, Cambridge University Press, Cambridge, Mass.

Roazen, Paul, "Nietzsche and Freud and the History of Psychoanalysis," in T. Dufresne (ed.), *The Return of the French Freud: Freud, Lacan and Beyond*, 1997, Routledge, New York and London, 11–23.

Robertson, Ritchie, "Primitivism and Psychology: Nietzsche, Freud and Thomas Mann," in Peter Colliers and Judy Davies (eds.), *Modernism and the European Unconscious*, 1990, Polity Press, Cambridge, 79–93.

La Rochefoucauld, *Maxims*, translated by L. W. Tancock, 1959, Penguin Books, Harmondsworth, UK.

Rochlitz, Rainer, "The Aesthetics of Existence: Postconventional Morality and the Theory of Power in Michel Foucault," in *Michel Foucault: Philosopher*, translated by Timothy J. Armstrong, 1992, Harvester, New York.

Rorty, Richard, "Freud and Moral Reflection," in Joseph H. Smith and William Kerrigan (eds.), *Pragmatism's Freud*, 1986, John Hopkins University Press, Baltimore.

———, *Contingency, Irony and Solidarity*, 1989, Cambridge University Press, Cambridge.

———, "Moral Identity and Private Autonomy: The Case of Foucault," in *Essays on Heidegger and Others, Philosophical Papers*, vol. 2, Cambridge University Press, 1991, 193–98.

Rosen, Stanley, *The Mask of Enlightenment: Nietzsche's Zarathustra*, 1995, Cambridge University Press, Cambridge.

Rosenmeyer, Thomas G., *Senecan Drama and Stoic Cosmology*, 1989, University of California Press, Berkeley.

Rousseau, Jean-Jacques, *Émile*, translated by Barbara Foxley, 1974, Dent, London.

Sadler, Ted, *Truth and Redemption: Critique of the Postmodern Nietzsche*, 1995, Athlone Press, London.

Safranski, Rüdiger, *Nietzsche: A Philosophical Biography*, translated by Shelley Frisch, 2003, W. W. Norton & Co., New York.

Sallis, John, *Crossings: Nietzsche and the Space of Tragedy*, 1991, University of Chicago Press, Chicago.

Schaberg, William H., *The Nietzsche Canon: A Publication History and Bibliography*, 1995, University of Chicago Press, Chicago.

Schacht, Richard, "Nietzsche on Human Nature," *History of European Ideas* 11, 1989, 883–92.

———, "Zarathustra/Zarathustra as Educator," in Peter R. Sedgwick (ed.), *Nietzsche: A Critical Reader*, 1995, Basil Blackwell, Oxford.

Schachtel, Ernest, *Metamorphosis: On the Development of Affect, Perception, Attention and Memory*, 1963, Routledge & Kegan Paul, London.

Schenk, Hans Georg, *The Mind of the European Romantics: An Essay in Cultural History*, 1979, Oxford University Press, New York.

Schiller, Friedrich, *On the Aesthetic Education of Man, in a Series of Letters*, translated by Elizabeth Willoughby and L. A. Willoughby, 1967, Clarendon Press, Oxford.

Schrift, Alan D., *Nietzsche's French Legacy: A Genealogy of Poststructuralism*, 1995, Routledge, New York.

Schutte, Ofelia, *Beyond Nihilism: Nietzsche without Masks*, 1984, University of Chicago Press, Chicago.

———, "Willing Backwards: Nietzsche on Time Pain, Joy and Memory," in Jacob Golomb (ed.), *Nietzsche and Depth Psychology*, 1999, SUNY, Albany.

Sedley, David, "The Ethics of Brutus and Cassius," *Journal of Roman Studies* 87, 1997, 41–53.

Sellars, John, *The Art of Living: The Stoics on the Nature and Function of Philosophy*, 2003, Ashgate, Aldershot, UK.

Shapiro, Gary, *Nietzschean Narratives*, 1989, Indiana University Press, Bloomington.

Shaw, Tamsin, *Nietzsche's Political Skepticism*, 2007, Princeton University Press, Princeton, N.J.

Shklar, Judith N., *Men and Citizens: A Study of Rousseau's Social Theory*, 1969, Cambridge University Press, Cambridge.

——, "Self-Sufficient Man: Dominion and Bondage," in John O'Neill (ed.), *Hegel's Dialectic of Desire and Recognition*, 1996, SUNY, Albany, 289–303.

Silk, M. S., and J. P. Stern, *Nietzsche on Tragedy*, 1981, Cambridge University Press, Cambridge.

Small, Robin, "Three Interpretations of Eternal Recurrence," *Dialogue* XXII, 1983, 91–112.

——, "Nietzsche and Time Consciousness," unpublished paper, with author's permission.

Sokel, Walter H., "Freud and the Magic of Kafka's Writing," in J. P. Stern (ed.), *The World of Franz Kafka*, 1980, Holt, Rhinehart and Winston, New York, 145–58.

Soll, Ivan, "Pessimism and the Tragic View of Life: Reconsiderations of Nietzsche's *Birth of Tragedy*," in Robert C. Solomon and Kathleen Higgins (eds.), *Reading Nietzsche*, 1988, Oxford University Press, New York.

——, "Schopenhauer, Nietzsche, and the Redemption of Life through Art," in Christopher Janaway (ed.), *Willing and Nothingness: Schopenhauer as Nietzsche's Educator*, 1998, Clarendon Press, Oxford, 79–115.

Solomon, R., "Nietzsche *ad hominem*: Perspectivism, Personality and Resentment," in B. Magnus and K. Higgins (eds.), *The Cambridge Companion to Nietzsche*, 1996, Cambridge University Press, Cambridge.

Sophocles, *Ajax*, in *Electra and Other Plays*, translated by E. F. Watling, 1980, Penguin, Harmondsworth, UK.

Sprung, Mervyn, "Nietzsche's Trans-European Eye," in Graham Parkes (ed.), *Nietzsche and Asian Thought*, 1991, University of Chicago Press, Chicago, 76–90.

Stambaugh, Joan, *Nietzsche's Thought of the Eternal Return*, 1972, Johns Hopkins University Press, Baltimore.

——, "The Other Nietzsche," in Graham Parkes (ed.), *Nietzsche and Asian Thought*, 1991, University of Chicago Press, Chicago, 20–30.

——, *The Other Nietzsche*, 1994, SUNY, Albany.

Starobinski, Jean, "The Accuser and the Accused," *Daedalus* 117, no. 3, Summer 1988, 345–70.

Staten, Henry, *Nietzsche's Voice*, 1990, Cornell University Press, Ithaca, N.Y.

——, *Eros and Mourning: Homer to Lacan*, 1995, Johns Hopkins University Press, Baltimore.

Stern, Daniel N., *Interpersonal World of the Infant: A View from Psychoanalysis and Developmental Psychology*, 1985, Basic Books, New York.

Strong, Tracy B., *Friedrich Nietzsche and the Politics of Transfiguration*, 1988, University of California Press, Berkeley.

——, "Nietzsche's Political Aesthetics," in Michael Allen Gillespie and Tracy B. Strong (eds.), *Nietzsche's New Seas: Explorations in Philosophy, Aesthetics and Politics*, 1988, University of Chicago Press, Chicago, 153–74.

Suetonius, *Twelve Caesars*, translated by Robert Graves, 1957, Penguin, Harmondsworth, UK.

Sumi, Geoffrey S. "Impersonating the Dead: Mimes at Roman Funerals," *American Journal of Philology* 123, 2000, 559–85.

Taminiaux, J., *Poetics, Speculation, and Judgement: The Shadow of the Work of Art from Kant to Phenomenology*, 1993, SUNY, Albany.

Tancock, L. W., "Introduction," in La Rochefoucauld, *Maxims*, 1959, Penguin Books, Harmondsworth, UK.

Tanner, Michael, *Schopenhauer*, 1999, Routledge, New York.

Taylor, Charles, "Foucault on Freedom and Truth," in D. C. Hoy (ed.), *Foucault: A Critical Reader*, 1986, Basil Blackwell, Oxford, 69–102.

———, "Review of *Logics of Disintegration*," *New Left Review*, July–August, no. 170, 1988, 110–16.

———, *Sources of the Self: The Making of Modern Identity*, 1989, Harvard University Press, Cambridge, Mass.

———, *The Ethics of Authenticity*, 1991, Cambridge University Press, Cambridge, Mass.

———, "Inwardness and the Culture of Modernity," in Axel Honneth et al., *Philosophical Interventions in the Unfinished Project of Modernity*, translated by W. Rehig, 1992, MIT Press, Cambridge, Mass., 88–110.

———, *Multiculturalism: Examining the Politics of Recognition*, edited and introduced by Amy Gutman, 1994, Princeton, Princeton University Press, N.J.

———, "The Dialogical Self," in R. F. Goodman and W. R. Fisher (eds.), *Rethinking Knowledge: Reflections across the Disciplines*, 1995, SUNY Press, Albany.

———, "The Immanent Counter-Enlightenment," in Ronald Beiner and Wayne Norman (eds.), *Canadian Political Philosophy*, 2001, Oxford University Press, Ontario, 386–400.

Taylor, Charles S., "Nietzsche's Schopenhauerianism," *Nietzsche-Studien* 17, 1988, 45–73.

Thacker, Andrew, "Foucault's Aesthetic of Existence," *Radical Philosophy* 63, Spring 1993, 13–21.

Thiele, Leslie Paul, *Friedrich Nietzsche and the Politics of the Soul: A Study of Heroic Individualism*, 1990, Princeton University Press, Princeton, N.J.

———, "The Agony of Politics: The Nietzschean Roots of Foucault's Thought," *American Political Science Review* 84, no. 3, September 1990, 907–25.

———, "Nietzsche's Politics," *Interpretation* 17, no. 2, Winter 1989–1990.

———, "Twilight of Modernity: Nietzsche, Heidegger, and Politics," *Political Theory* 22, no. 3, August 1994.

Urpeth, Jim, "Noble Ascesis: Between Nietzsche and Foucault," *New Nietzsche Studies* 2, no. 3–4, Summer 1998, 65–91.

Veyne, Paul, *Seneca: The Life of a Stoic*, translated by David Sullivan, 2003, Routledge, New York.

Vila, Dana, "Beyond Good and Evil: Arendt, Nietzsche and the Aestheticization of Political Action," *Political Theory* 20, no. 2, May 1992, 274–308.

Walther, Helmut, "Nietzsche as Composer," Lecture at a Seminar of the *Gesellschaft für kritische Philosophie*, October 15–17, 2000, Kottenheide, Germany.

Warren, Mark, "Nietzsche and Political Philosophy," *Political Theory* 13, no. 2, May 1985, 183–212.

———, *Nietzsche and Political Thought*, 1988, MIT Press, Cambridge, Mass.

———, "Political Readings of Nietzsche: Review Essay," *Political Theory* 26, no. 1, February 1998, 90–111.

Watling, E. F., "Introduction," in Sophocles, *Electra and Other Plays*, translated by E. F. Watling, 1980, Penguin, Harmondsworth, UK.

Welsch, Wolfgang, *Undoing Aesthetics*, translated by A. Inkpin, 1997, Sage, London.

White, Alan, *Within Nietzsche's Labyrinth*, 1990, Routledge, New York.

White, R., *Nietzsche and the Problem of Sovereignty*, 1997, University of Illinois Press, Urbana/Chicago.

White, Stephen K., "Foucault's Challenge to Critical Theory," *American Political Science Review* 80, no. 2, June 1986.

——, *Sustaining Affirmation: The Strengths of Weak Ontology in Political Theory*, 2000, Princeton University Press, Princeton, N.J.

Whitebook, Joel, "Reason and Happiness: Some Psychoanalytic Themes in Critical Theory," in R. J. Bernstein (ed.), *Habermas and Modernity*, 1985, MIT Press, Cambridge, Mass., 140–60.

——, *Perversions and Utopia: A Study in Psychoanalysis and Critical Theory*, 1995, MIT Press, Cambridge, Mass.

——, "Freud, Foucault and the Dialogue with Unreason," *Philosophy and Social Criticism* 25, no. 6, 1999, 29–66.

——, "Mutual Recognition and the Work of the Negative," in William Rehg and James Bohman (eds.), *Pluralism and the Pragmatic Turn: The Transformation of Critical Theory, Essays in Honor of James McCarthy*, 2001, MIT Press, Cambridge, Mass., 110–45.

——, "Against Interiority: Foucault's Struggle with Psychoanalysis," in Gary Gutting (ed.), *Cambridge Companion to Foucault*, 2005, Cambridge University Press, New York, 312–49.

Williams, W. D., *Nietzsche and the French*, 1952, Basil Blackwell, Oxford.

Winnicott, Donald, "The Capacity to be Alone" (1958) and "Communicating and Not Communicating Leading to a Study of Certain Opposites" (1963), in *The Maturational Process and the Facilitating Environment*, 1972, Hogarth Press, London, 29–36, 179–92.

——, "Transitional Objects and Transitional Experience," in *Playing and Reality*, 1971, Penguin Books, London.

Wolfenstein, Victor, *Inside/Outside Nietzsche: Psychoanalytic Explorations*, 2000, Cornell University Press, Ithaca, N.Y.

Wolin, Richard, "Foucault's Aesthetic Decisionism," *Telos* 67, Spring 1986, 71–86.

Yack, Bernard, *The Longing For Total Revolution: Philosophical Sources of Discontent From Rousseau to Marx and Nietzsche*, 1986, Princeton University Press, Princeton, N.J.

Young, Julian, *Nietzsche's Philosophy of Art*, 1993, Cambridge University Press, New York.

——, *Willing and Unwilling: A Study in the Philosophy of Arthur Schopenhauer*, 1987, Martinus Nijhoff Publishers, Dordrecht.

Index